Policing Democracy

Policing Democracy

Overcoming Obstacles to Citizen Security in Latin America

Mark Ungar

Woodrow Wilson Center Press
Washington, D.C.

The Johns Hopkins University Press
Baltimore

EDITORIAL OFFICES

Woodrow Wilson Center Press
One Woodrow Wilson Plaza
1300 Pennsylvania Avenue, N.W.
Washington, D.C. 20004-3027
Telephone: 202-691-4029
www.wilsoncenter.org

ORDER FROM

The Johns Hopkins University Press
Hampden Station
P.O. Box 50370
Baltimore, Maryland 21211
Telephone: 1-800-537-5487
www.press.jhu.edu/books/

Library of Congress Cataloging-in-Publication Data

Ungar, Mark.
    Policing democracy : overcoming obstacles to citizen security in Latin America / Mark
Ungar.
      p.   cm.
    Includes bibliographical references and index.
    ISBN 978-0-8018-9802-0 (hardcover : alk. paper)—ISBN 978-0-8018-9858-7 (pbk : alk.
paper)
      1. Crime prevention—Latin America.   2. Internal security—Latin America.
    3. Crime prevention—Latin America—Citizen participation.   4. Police—Latin America.
    5. Violence—Latin America.   6. Violence—Latin America—Prevention.   I. Title.
HV7434.L29U54   2010
363.2'3098—dc22
                                                                          2010045411

Woodrow Wilson International Center for Scholars

The Woodrow Wilson International Center for Scholars is the national, living U.S. memorial honoring President Woodrow Wilson. In providing an essential link between the worlds of ideas and public policy, the Center addresses current and emerging challenges confronting the United States and the world. The Center promotes policy-relevant research and dialogue to increase understanding and enhance the capabilities and knowledge of leaders, citizens, and institutions worldwide. Created by an Act of Congress in 1968, the Center is a nonpartisan institution headquartered in Washington, D.C., and supported by both public and private funds.

Conclusions or opinions expressed in Center publications and programs are those of the authors and speakers and do not necessarily reflect the views of the Center's staff, fellows, trustees, or advisory groups, or any individuals or organizations that provide financial support to the Center.

The Center is the publisher of *The Wilson Quarterly* and home of Woodrow Wilson Center Press and *dialogue* television and radio. For more information about the Center's activities and publications, including the monthly newsletter *Centerpoint,* please visit us on the web at www.wilsoncenter.org.

Contents

Figures, Maps, and Tables

Figures

Maps

Tables

Acronyms and Abbreviations

ADN	Acción Democrática Nacionalista (Nationalist Democratic Action, Bolivia)
AKTUPAC	Consejo Nacional del Aymaras, Kechuas, Tupi-guaranies Unido por Ayllus y Comunidades (National Council of Aymaras, Kechuas, Tupi-guaranies United by Ayllus and Communities, Bolivia)
AMHON	Asociación de Municipios de Honduras (Association of Municipalities of Honduras)
AMIA	Asociación Mutual Israelita Argentina (Argentine Israelite Mutual Association)
ANAPO	Academia Nacional de Policía (National Police Academy, Honduras)
Anapol	Academia Nacional de Policía (National Police Academy, Bolivia)
ASEMSIPH	Asociación de Empresas de Seguridad e Investigación Privada de Honduras (Association of Firms of Security and Private Investigation of Honduras)
BID	business improvement district
BIP	Brigada de Intervención Polivalente (Multipurpose Intervention Brigade, Bolivia)
BPC	Brigada de Prevención Comunitaria (Community Prevention Unit, Argentina)
BSFP	Batallón de Seguridad Física Privada (Battalion of Private Physical Security, Bolivia)

CAEEP	Centro de Altos Estudios en Especialidades Policiales (Center for Advanced Studies in Police Specialties, Argentina)
CCRB	Civilian Complaint Review Board (New York City)
CEINCO	Centro de Información y Comunicación (Center of Information and Communication, Honduras)
CEJA	Centro de Estudios de Justicia de las Américas (Justice Studies Center of the Americas)
CERCA	Control y Evaluación de Respuesta, Calidad y Actitud del Servicio de Policía Local (Control and Evaluation of the Response, Quality, and Attitude of the Local Police Service, Argentina)
CES	Cuerpo Especial de Seguridad (Special Security Force, Honduras)
CGR	Controlaria General de la República (Comptroller General of the Republic, Bolivia)
CICAD	Inter-American Drug Abuse Control Commission
CICPC	Cuerpo de Investigaciones Científicas, Penales y Criminalísticas (Body of Scientific, Penal, and Criminalistic Investigations, Venezuela)
CIEN	Centro de Investigaciones Económicas Nacionales (Center of National Economic Research, Guatemala)
CIJs	Centros Integrados de Justicia (Integrated Justice Centers, Bolivia)
CIOCC	Centro de Información, Orientación y Capacitación Ciudadana (Center for Information, Orientation and Citizen Training, Bolivia)
CIP	Centro de Instrucción Policial (Center for Police Instruction, Honduras); Centro Integrado de Procesos de Trabajos Interinstitucionales (Integrated Center of Interinstitutional Work, Honduras)
CMS	Comunidad Más Segura (Safer Community, Honduras)
COA	Unidad de Control Operativo Aduanero (Customs Control Unit, Bolivia)
COCI	Consejos Operativos de Coordinación Interseccional Zonal (Intersectional Operational and Coordination Councils, Argentina)
CONAMAQ	Consejo Nacional de los Ayllus y Markas del Quollasuyo (National Council of Ayllus and Markas of the Quollasuyo, Bolivia)

CONASIN	Consejo Nacional de Seguridad Interior (National Council of Interior Security, Honduras)
COPP	Código Orgánico Procesal Penal (Organic Penal Process Code, Venezuela)
Covipol	Consejo de Vivienda Policial (Police Housing Council, Bolivia)
CPI	Comando de Persecución Inmediata (Immediate Persecution Command, Argentina)
CPP	Código Procesal Penal (penal process code)
CUAKK-B	Confederación Única de ayllus-comunidades-Capitanías del Kollasuyo-Bolivia (Sole Confederation of ayllus-communities-headquarters of the Kollasuyo, Bolivia)
DAT	desk appearance ticket
DDP	Defensoría Del Pueblo (public advocate/ombudsman, Bolivia)
DEA	U.S. Drug Enforcement Agency
DGEP	Dirección General de Educación Policial (General Office of Police Education, Honduras)
DGIC	Dirección General de Investigación Criminal (General Office of Criminal Investigation, Honduras)
DGSEI	Dirección General de Servicios Especiales de Investigación (General Office of Special Investigative Services, Honduras)
DGSEP	Dirección General de Servicios Especiales Preventivos (General Office of Special Preventive Services, Honduras)
DIC	Dirección de Investigación Criminal (Office of Criminal Investigation, Honduras)
DIE	Dirección de Inteligencia del Ejército (Office of Army Intelligence, Venezuela)
DIGESTYC	Dirección General de Estadísticas y Censos (General Office of Statistics and Census, El Salvador)
DIM	Dirección de Inteligencia Militar (Defense Ministry's Office of Military Intelligence, Venezuela)
Diprove	Dirección de Prevención contra el Robo de Vehículo (Anti-Car Theft Unit, Bolivia)
DISIP	Dirección Sectoral de los Servicios de Inteligencia y Prevención (Office of Intelligence and Prevention Services, Venezuela)
DLCN	Dirección de Lucha Contra el Narcotráfico (Anti-Narcotrafficking Unit, Honduras)

DNI	Dirección Nacional de Investigaciones (National Office of Investigation, Honduras)
DNRP	Dirección Nacional de Responsibilidad Profesional (National Office of Professional Responsibility, Bolivia)
EI	Early Intervention
Esbapol	Escuela Básica Policial (Basic Police School, Bolivia)
ESO	Escuela de Sub-Oficiales (School of Subofficials, Honduras)
ESP	Escuela Superior de Policías (Superior Police School, Bolivia)
ETF	Expeditionary Task Force (Fuerza de Tarea Expedicionaria, Bolivia)
FEAE	Fuerza Especial Antiterrorista de Elite (Special Elite Antiterrorist Force, Bolivia)
FEJUVE	Federation de Juntas Vecinales (Neighborhood Council Federation, Bolivia)
FELCC	Fuerza Especial de Lucha Contra el Crimen (Special Anti-Crime Force, Bolivia)
FELCN	Fuerza Especial de Lucha Contra el Narcotráfico (Special Force in the War against Narco-trafficking, Bolivia)
FGR	Fiscalía General de la República (Attorney General of the Republic, El Salvador)
FJC	Family Justice Center
FONAC	Foro Nacional de Convergencia (National Convergence Forum, Honduras)
FSP	Fuerza de Seguridad Pública (Public Security Force, Honduras)
FUNDAPPAC	Fundación de Apoyo al Parlamento y a la Participación Ciudadana (Foundation to Support the Parliament and Citizen Participation, Bolivia)
GACIP	Grupo de Apoyo Civil a la Policía (Group of Civilian Support for the Police, Bolivia)
GAI	Grupo de Acción Inmediata (Immediate Action Group, Bolivia)
GDP	gross domestic product
GEAS	Grupo Especial Antisecuestros (Special Antikidnapping Group, Honduras)
GES	Grupo Especial de Seguridad (Special Security Group, Bolivia, Argentina)

GN	Guardia Nacional (National Guard, Venezuela)
GNP	gross national product
GTIDE	Grupo de Tarea de Investigación de Delitos Especiales (Group of Special Crimes Investigation, Bolivia)
GTO	grassroots territorial organization
HDI	Human Development Index
IADB	Inter-American Development Bank
ICITAP	International Criminal Investigative Training Assistance Program (United States)
IDIF	Instituto de Investigaciones Forenses (Institute of Forensic Investigations, Bolivia)
IGS	Inspección General de Seguridad (General Inspector of Security, Argentina)
IHNFA	Instituto Hondureño de la Niñez y la Familia (Honduran Institute of Childhood and Family, Honduras)
IIDH	Instituto Interamericano de Derechos Humanos (Inter-American Institute of Human Rights)
ILANUD	Instituto Latinoamericano de las Naciones Unidas para la Prevención del Delito y el Tratamiento del Delincuente (United Nations Latin American Institute for the Prevention of Crime and the Treatment of Offenders)
IML	Instituto de Medicina Legal (Institute of Forensic Medicine, El Salvador)
INDEC	Instituto Nacional de Estadísticas y Censos (National Institute of Statistics and Census, Argentina)
INEC	Instituto Nacional de Estadísticas y Censos de Ecuador (National Institute of Statistics and Census of Ecuador)
INFOP	Instituto Nacional de Formación Profesional (National Vocational Training Institute, Honduras)
INPE	Instituto Nacional Penitenciario (National Penitentiary Institute, Peru)
IPCS	Instituto de Política Criminal y Seguridad (Security and Criminal Policy Institute, Argentina)
ISEP	Instituto Superior de Estudios Policial (Superior Institute of Police Studies, Honduras)
IUSI	Instituto Universitario de Seguridad Integral (University Institute of Integral Security, Argentina)

IUSP	Instituto Universitario de Seguridad Pública (University Institute of Public Security, Argentina)
JTF	Joint Task Force, Bolivia (Fuerza de Tarea Conjunta)
LGAP	Ley General de la Administración Pública (Administrative Law, Honduras)
LOPN	Ley Orgánica de la Policía Nacional (Organic Law of the National Police, Honduras, Bolivia)
LPCS	Ley de Policía y Convivencia Social (Law of Police and Social Coexistence, Honduras)
LPP	Ley de Participación Popular (Law of Popular Participation, Bolivia)
MAS	Movimiento al Socialismo (Movement to Socialism, Bolivia)
MICE	Ministerio de Industria, Comercio y Empleo (Ministry of Industry, Commerce, and Employment, Argentina)
MIR	Movimiento de la Izquierda Revolucionaria (Movement of the Revolutionary Left, Bolivia)
MJSDH	Ministerio de Justicia, Seguridad y Derechos Humanos (Ministry of Justice, Security, and Human Rights, Argentina)
MNR	Movimiento Nacional Revolucionario (National Revolutionary Movement, Bolivia)
MP	Ministerio Público (Public Ministry, Honduras, Bolivia)
Mucopol	Mutual de Cooperativas de la Policía (Cooperative Police Mutual Fund, Bolivia)
Musepol	Mutual del Seguro Policial (Police Insurance Mutual Fund, Bolivia)
NCPP	Nuevo Código de Procedimiento Penal (New Penal Procedure Code, Bolivia)
NGO	nongovernmental organization
NYPD	New York Police Department
OAS	Organization of American States
OCAVI	Observatorio Centroamericano sobre Violencia
OIJ	Organización de Investigación Judicial (Organization of Judicial Investigation, Costa Rica)
ORP	Oficina de Responsabilidad Profesional (Office of Professional Responsibility, Honduras)
PAC	Patrulla de Auxilio y Cooperación Ciudadana (Citizen Support and Aid Patrol, Bolivia)

PAHO	Pan American Health Organization
PFA	Policía Federal Argentina (Federal Police of Argentina)
PM	Policía Metropolitana (Metropolitan Police, Venezuela); Policía Militar (Military Police, Bolivia)
PN	Policía Nacional (National Police, Honduras)
PNC	Policía Nacional Civil (National Civil Police, El Salvador)
POFOMA	Policía Forestal y Medio Ambiente (Environmental Police , Bolivia)
PRM	Programa de Respuesta Múltiple (Multiple Response Program, Argentina)
PTJ	Policía Técnica Judicial (Technical Judicial Police, Bolivia)
RIN	Registro de Identificación Nacional (National Identification Registry, Bolivia)
RUN	Registro Único Nacional (Sole National Registry, Bolivia)
SIEMPRO	Dirección Nacional del Sistema de Información, Monitoreo, Evaluación de Programas Sociales (National Office of the System of Monitoring, Evaluation of Social Programs, Argentina)
TDS	Tribunal Disciplinario Superior (Superior Disciplinary Tribunal, Bolivia)
UAI	Unidad de Asuntos Internos (Internal Affairs Unit, Honduras)
UCC	Unidad de Conciliación Ciudadana (Citizen Conciliation Unit, Bolivia)
UCV	Universidad Central de Venezuela (University of Central Venezuela)
UDRI	Unidad de Reacción Inmediata (Unit of Immediate Reaction, Bolivia)
UIC	Unidad de Investigaciones Complejas (Complex Investigations Unit, Argentina)
UMOPAR	Unidad Móvil de Patrullaje Rural (Mobile Rural Patrol Unit, Bolivia)
UNAH	Universidad Nacional Autónoma de Honduras (National University of Honduras)
UNCJIN	United Nations Crime and Justice Information Network
UNDP	United Nations Development Programme
Unipol	Universidad Policial "Mariscal Antonio José de Sucre" (Marshal Antonio José de Sucre Police University, Bolivia)

UNODC	United Nations Office on Drugs and Crime
UPEG	Unidad de Planeamiento y Evaluación de Gestión (Planning and Management Assessment Unit, Honduras)
UPNFM	Universidad Pedagógica Nacional Francisco Morazán (Francisco Morazán University, Honduras)
USAID	U.S. Agency for International Development
USEDI	Unidad de Protección de Dignatarios (Unit for the Protection of Dignitaries, Bolivia)
USPAC	Unidad de Seguridad para la Asamblea Constituyente (Constitutional Assembly Protection Unit, Bolivia)
UTOP	Unidad Táctica de Operaciones Policiales (Tactical Police Operations Unit, Bolivia)
UTR	Unidad Técnica de Reforma Penal (Technical Unit of Penal Reform, Honduras)

Preface

In 1990 I spent the summer in the *barrios* of Caracas working with La Red de Apoyo por La Justicia y La Paz (Peace and Justice Support Network), a nongovernmental organization that investigates rights abuse. Although it was one year after thousands of people in those hillside shantytowns died in anti-neoliberal riots and two years before an attempted coup by a lieutenant colonel named Hugo Chávez ignited their political fervor, Venezuela's two-party democracy and extensive welfare system still seemed to be a promising model for the rest of the region as it emerged from decades of dictatorship. And yet over the next decade the country was unable to stop itself from unraveling amid escalating disorder. In one case I worked on for the Red, a teenager was killed by a police officer, who himself was later killed in a gun battle. They were part of a cycle of violence that seemed immune to political and economic development.

That cycle was also emerging as the nexus of politics, constitutionalism, and civil rights in Latin America. As the region shed military rule, it had to rely on its wholly unprepared police to deal with the many causes of crime and violence that only intensified along with economic and political uncertainty. A growing number of clashes between citizens and the state, questions before the courts, and the more vexing policy challenges revolved around citizen security. Together they seemed to be throwing democracy itself off balance. As crime levels began to skyrocket in the 1990s, democratic consolidation throughout Latin America began to stall.

In this book I attempt to fit all these pieces together. The ways in which judges balance rights and order, officials try to enlist clunky bureaucracies into nimble violence-reduction efforts, and candidates whip up waves of fear just big enough to ride into office are some of the many political, legal, and societal dynamics of citizen security examined in the following pages. Few other issues, and too few studies, capture the multifaceted and often intangible responses of a society to a problem that is engulfing it. I also try to convey how this big picture moves through time: the reactions of citizens whose neighborhoods descend into violence; the temptations of politicians to stave off long-term change with short-sighted action; the strategies police officers adopt to stop new projects from becoming just one more pressure; and, ultimately, the ways in which the standards and institutions of democracy withstand the impacts of criminal violence.

In order to build an analytical framework that incorporated these continually changing patterns, I used a methodology centered on interviews, observations, policy analysis, and statistics. Interviews with people throughout the region, from ministers to gang members, offered an unparalleled way to observe the human dimension of institutional and political practices. So too were firsthand observations of the criminal justice system, from crime scene investigations to neighborhood meetings, which are described for each of the book's case study countries. A critical analysis of promising approaches, from penal process codes to community policing, helped move the book toward its aim of presenting the full process of reform. Because I have been able to return to Honduras nearly every year since 2003, for example, I have been able to see how different policies, and the areas in which they have been tried, have fared. Finally, statistical analysis connecting crime to political and socioeconomic changes helped bring objectivity to the many claims and expectations that surround every citizen security reform.

Acknowledgments

So many people gave their time and expertise to this book that it often felt like a collective project. In each country, officials at the national, regional, and local levels—from executive agencies to legislative commissions—were accessible and informative. Judges, prosecutors, public defenders, prison wardens, morgue directors, and others in the criminal justice systems allowed me to witness their work firsthand. I am particularly indebted to the many police officers who let me accompany them on patrols and in their investigations. The tough work and multiple dangers they face, especially when trying to bring about change, are vastly underappreciated. I am also grateful to the many citizens who generously gave their time. The experiences and opinions of local activists, longtime neighborhood residents, homeless teens, prison inmates, crime victims, and other people I met embody the spirit and goals of this book. Listed below for each country, with their title at the time of our initial meeting, are just some of the many individuals and organizations who contributed in different ways.

In Honduras I was continually amazed by how well people held up under withering levels of violence and poverty. For my time there, I would especially like to thank Gen. Mario Perdomo and Subcommissioner Carlos Chinchilla, director of the country's community policing program. Carlos sent me to police stations throughout the country forming the basis of the book's Honduras chapter. Other police officials who provided support were Education Subdirector Rodolfo Calix Hollmann, Commissioners Rolando Carcomo Piura and Marcos Arnaldo Herrera, Subcommisioners Renan Galo Meza and Leonel Sauceda, Inspector Daniel Molina, former Internal Affairs Unit chief María Luisa Borjas, and the many agents who took me out on patrol in and around Tegucigalpa, San Pedro Sula, and La Ceiba. Security Ministers Álvaro Romero and Óscar Álvarez as well as former security minister Guatama Fonseca gave me provocative interviews, as did many judicial officials, including childhood prosecutor Eduardo Villanueva, Northern Area prosecutor director Walter Menjívar, Public Defense director Jorge Gutierrez Flefil, and Sindy Fortín of the Supreme Court Documentation Center. Also helpful were Congressman José Rodolfo Zelaya Portillo; Danelia Ferrera, director general of the Attorney General's Office; Mirna Andino, executive secretary of the national Anti-Narcotrafficking Council; Julieta Castellanos, rector of the National Autonomous University; and military officers stationed at bases and checkpoints in the capital city area. I also learned a great deal from the fortitude and perseverance of Honduras's human rights officials and activists: Juan Almendares, director of the Center for the Prevention of Torture; Human Rights Commissioner Ramón Custodio; Northern Area Human Rights Commissioner Victor Parelló; Andrés Pavón, president of the Committee for the Defense of Human Rights; Ernesto Bardales, who works with gang members in San Pedro Sula; and José Gustavo Zelaya, legal director of Casa Alianza. Inmates at El Porvenir Penal Colony, the San Pedro Sula Penal Center, and the Central Penitentiary of the Barrio Inglés in La Ceiba talked to me about the inhumanity of their life behind bars. Finally, for their expertise and guidance, I would like to thank Victor Meza and Leticia Salomón of the Honduras Documentation Center.

Bolivia was also an incredible country in which to work and see how people grapple with violence and political instability amid expansive cultural, economic, and geographic differences. For my time there, I would like to thank Juan Ramón Quintana, a terrific person who is one of the most knowledgeable specialists in the areas of democracy and security and who later served as minister of the presidency. In the government and police, I am grateful to former vice president Luis Ossico Sanjinés; Government Minister Saúl Lara Torrico, former government minister Alfonso Ferrufino, Luis Pedraza of the Government Ministry, and Ximena Prudencio Bilbao and Franz Zilvetti Cisneros of the Office of Citizen Security. From the police force I received help from Judicial Police chief Rolando Fernández; Óscar Molina and Gloria Eyzaguirre of the Police Reform Commission; Maj. Hugo Morales of El Alto; and police academy director Juan Carlos Saa. Even in the midst of their busy schedules, many other police officers and community activists went out of their way to take me on eye-opening walks through La Paz, El Alto, Santa Cruz, and Sucre. Sitting in on their community meetings was a real honor. The *defensoría del pueblo* (ombudsman) is an indispensable engine of reform and rights in Bolivia, and for sharing their time I would like to thank Chief Ana María Romero de Campero and future chief Waldo Albarracín of the Permanent Assembly of Human Rights. In the legal area, the Center for Studies on Justice and Participation was very helpful, as were Prosecutor William Alave, Judge Róger Valverde, inmates and staff at San Pedro Prison, and inmates and staff at the narco-trafficking detention facilities.

Argentina, the book's third main case study, was always a rewarding place to work. Knowledgeable and welcoming people throughout the country taught me a great deal about citizen security, democracy, and how beef and coffee allow early-morning patrols to be scheduled after late-night dinners. For my time there, I would like thank Senator and First Lady Cristina Fernández de Kirchner and Senator Marita Perceval for opening up so many doors, and Justice and Security Minister Gustavo Beliz for giving me an opportunity to work on reform both in Argentina as well as with the Inter-American Development Bank. It was humbling to meet with the country's many experts on citizen security, including Martha Arriola of the Security Ministry in Buenos Aires Province; Mariano Ciafardini, national director of criminal policy; Fernando Simón of the Justice Ministry; and Claudio Suárez, chief of the Federal Capital's security program. Buenos Aires provincial security minister León Arslanián, a pioneer in human rights and police reform who gave me the honor of speaking on his panel at the tenth anniversary commemoration of the path-breaking reform he initiated, is a true inspiration. In Buenos Aires Province, Father Luis Farinello of Quilmes and activists in Morón, Ituzaingo, and Almirante Brown and other cities allowed me to observe their meetings and projects.

In Mendoza, the lack of policy change contrasts with the expertise and dedication of those working on security in that province. I am so appreciative to Professor Patricia Gorri, Senator Alberto Montbrun, activists Marisa Repetto and Mauricio Guzmán, and rights lawyer Pablo Salinas for their wonderful friendships and their tireless push for change. Also contributing were former governor Arturo Lafalla, Senators Carlos Abihaggle and Alfredo Guevara, Gustavo Lucero and Andrés Miranda of the Security Oversight Commission, Judge Daniel Correllio, and Supreme Court justices Aida Kemelmajer de Carlucci and Jorge Nanclares. In La Rioja, police commissioners Luis Gallego and Eduardo Poledri, along with the many young people working in the province's community policing programs, were very open and candid. Above all, with great warmth and enthusiasm, police subcommissioner Óscar Ibáñez gave me so much of his very limited time. In San Luis, I would like to thank Martín Salinas for arranging meetings throughout the province. Sitting down with the student body of that province's police academy was a real highlight.

Officials and activists in other countries also offered valuable support. In Uruguay I was helped by Gabriel Courtoisie, a director of the National Rehabilitation Center; Congressmen Felipe Michelini and Daniel Diaz Maynard; national prison director Enrique Navas; and Gloria Robaina, Juan Faroppa, and Carlos Bastón of the country's innovative Citizen Security Program. In Costa Rica, Commissioner Alberto Li Chan, Community Security Director Manuel Espinosa, and Ombudsman Mario Zamora Cordero all allowed me observe community policing up close. In Colombia, I would like to thank the National Police and the Interior and Justice Ministry for inviting me to address the Third International Symposium on Community Policing in 2009 and for allowing me to observe their operations. Speaking at the Second Inter-American Forum in Lima was another invaluable opportunity to learn from those at the forefront of citizen security reform in Latin America.

Another gratifying part of this project was working with other academics and activists focusing on security reform. For sharing their knowledge and experience—as well as their friendship and humor in our collaborative police reform efforts over the last five years—I would like to thank Desmond Arias, Lucía Dammert, Eric Scheye, Renata Segura, and Niels Uildriks. During two faculty fellowships at the Graduate Center of the City University of New York, discussions with colleagues helped me bring in analysis from other academic fields. I also owe gratitude to the many distinguished scholars who provided insight and advice: John Bailey, Margaret Crahan, Diane Davis, Hugo Frühling, and Anthony Pereira. Francisco Bautista Lara, founder of Nicaragua's National Police, was also a great source of wisdom.

Many organizations provided critical support. I would like to especially thank the Woodrow Wilson Center for International Scholars, which jump-started this book in a setting ideal for connecting scholarship with public policy. During my fellowship there, Joseph Tulchin and Cynthia Arnson of the Latin American Program were very supportive, and Jacqueline Saenz and Miguel Guzmán provided excellent research assistance.

The Inter-American Development Bank and the United Nations have also given me an opportunity to contribute to international policy on secu- rity reform, community policing, and violence prevention. Writing reports and participating in meetings on their behalf have been immeasurably use- ful. The Ford Foundation and Latin American Studies Association funded a project I directed on prison conditions, and the Tinker Foundation and Re- search Foundation of the City University of New York funded a community policing project I co-directed. The graduate students I have had the privi- lege of teaching, at both Brooklyn College and the Graduate Center, also taught me a great deal with their own experiences and views.

For the book's publication, I would like to thank Director Joseph Brin- ley and Managing Editor Yamile Kahn of the Woodrow Wilson Center Press and the editors and staff at the Johns Hopkins University Press for their flaw- less guidance of the book's review and production; the anonymous review- ers of the manuscript; freelance editor Sabra Bissette Ledent for her metic- ulous professional editing; and Kathy Alexander, publicist at the Johns Hopkins University Press.

My wonderful friends and family sustained me with encouragement and laughter through the years of work on this book, and my father, Donald Un- gar, was a reminder of the values he gave me. Most of all, I would like to thank Bob Bomersbach for his extraordinary humanity as a person and his unwavering support as my husband. And I have thousands of hugs for our son, Dylan, who has filled my life with immense joy and pride, not to men- tion ideas for police reform, such as having guns shoot cake instead of bul- lets. Watching him grow up reminds me of all the young people trying to do the same in Latin America's crime-ridden *barrios*.

Policing Democracy

Chapter 1

Introduction

The steps that must be taken toward citizen security in Latin America are clear but steep. Since the region began to democratize in the 1980s, reform of the police and criminal justice systems has always been necessary, but rarely urgent. Even as crime began breaking records and topping opinion polls of citizens' concerns in the 1990s, the response of most governments was ad hoc, piecemeal, and ineffectual. The combination of ever-mounting crime and the failure to halt it—along with the ensuing public panic—created a citizen security crisis in Latin America.

This crisis has exposed the limits of the region's long-established form of law enforcement, which is based on a centralized, standardized, and forceful response to crime. Growing awareness of the weakness of this approach has spurred efforts to replace it with problem-oriented policing, which, by contrast, tries to address the roots of crime through citizen participation, preventive social policies, and institutional accountability. But as it spreads, this new approach has become entangled in a set of mutually reinforcing political, institutional, and societal obstacles. As a result, much of Latin America is stuck between the paradigms of traditional and problem-oriented policing, with past practices coexisting with new laws amid a jumble of policies and political tensions that disperse responsibility and allow everyone to sidestep blame. This book is about what countries are doing, and can do, to break out of this impasse.

Both new and established democracies in every region of the world have initiated major reforms in citizen security over the last twenty years, from more streamlined structures to community policing (Das and Marenin 2000; Kádár 2001). Latin America's many advantages in these efforts, from its highly active civil societies to its mechanisms of regional cooperation,

1

have helped launch security reform throughout the region and put it at the forefront of change in the democratizing world. Such efforts have been driven by record rates of violent crime. With a 41 percent increase in homicides in the 1990s, Latin America became the world's deadliest region (UNICRI 1995; PAHO 2002).[1] Since 2000 its average annual homicide rate has been 27.5 deaths per 100,000 persons, compared with 8.8 for the rest of the world, 5.8 for the United States, and 2.3 for Western and Central Europe (see figure 1.1).[2] A full 42 percent of the world's murders each year now take place in the region (Luz and Pérez 2007), and half of the world's ten most dangerous countries—Brazil, Colombia, El Salvador, Honduras, and Venezuela—are in Latin America. About 140,000 Latin Americans are murdered each year, fifty-four families are robbed every minute (Carrión 2003, 51), and one in three people in the region has been a victim of violence. Most ominous, eighty thousand minors are killed violently each year, and murder is the second leading cause of death for persons in the 15- to 25-year age range. In Costa Rica, by most measures the safest country in Latin America, homicides have risen 30 percent since 2000.[3] As Londoño and Guerrero (1999) document, the percentage of families in the region's countries who were victims of property crime, robbery, or assault ranged from 20 percent to over 50 percent each year in the late 1990s. Not only is there more crime throughout the region, but more of it is violent. In 1990 in Venezuela 16 percent of the crimes against property were violent, but in 2002 that number rose to 46.2 percent. By 2008 that country had one of the world's highest rates of other violent crimes such as kidnappings, armed robberies, and carjackings (Overseas Security Advisory Council 2008).

The costs of crime extend beyond individual victims. Through security outlays, loss of labor, reduced investments, and other expenses—and often not including costs to the criminal justice system—crime was estimated to be eating up almost 15 percent of Latin America's gross domestic product (GDP) by the late 1990s (Ayres 1998).[4] Chile, for example, estimates that just homicide costs it nearly US$9 million a year (Fundación Paz Ciudadana

1. "Mueren unos 80.000 menores al año por violencia en la región," *El Deber,* Santa Cruz, November 17, 2006.

2 Interpol International Crime Statistics, http://www.interpol.int; UNODC (2005).

3 Carlos Mora, "Costa Rica atemorizada por el hampa," *La República,* April 17, 2006.

4 According to World Bank reports, the combination of homicides, accidents, and suicides accounts for 20.5 percent of lost years from death and incapacity among men in Latin America, which is well above the global average of 15.3 percent.

Figure 1.1. Regional Rates of Intentional Homicides, 2004

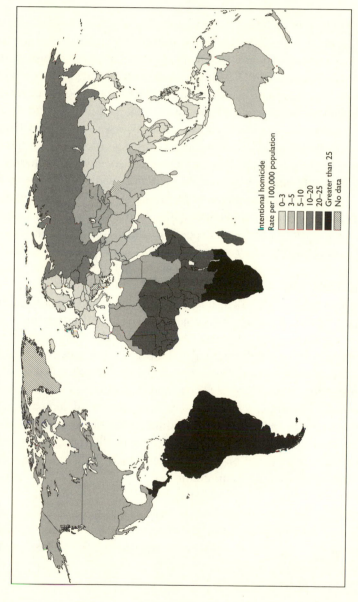

Source: UN Office of Drugs and Crime, http://www.unodc.org/images/data-and-analysis/homicide_rate_map.pdf.

1999).[5] These numbers alone have been sufficient impetus for reforming the agencies, laws, and processes responsible with bringing them down.

Citizen Security Reforms

In Western Europe and the Americas, policing has gone through three main stages. In the first stage, in the 1800s, most of the organized police forces were local, controlled by municipal or regional officials as an instrument of their power (see Lab and Das 2003). In the second stage, with the growth of technology and centralized states in the 1900s, most police came under national control, accompanied by more efficient administration and professional standards. Advances such as the car, two-way radio, and Uniform Crime Reports led to an emphasis on maximizing efficiency through rapid responses. But even as this approach increased society's expectations that the police would help citizens deal with an ever-widening gamut of problems, it reduced police awareness of warning signs and weakened citizen cooperation on crime prevention. Social upheaval in the United States and Europe in the 1960s and 1970s exposed the limits of this standardized approach and opened the way to the third main stage, generally called community policing. This approach put officers back on the streets and gave them more flexibility to address the causes of crime and earn citizens' trust. This approach has also guided, at least formally, many of the police reforms adopted by postcommunist governments in Asia and Eastern and Central Europe (see Kádár 2001; Uildriks 2005).

Twentieth-century authoritarianism held Latin America back from this third stage, because the era's military juntas used the police and courts less to control crime than to subdue society and persecute dissidents. Instead of giving way to community policing, the transition toward democracy in the 1980s civilianized rather than scrapped the professional model. Well into the 1990s police structures continued to be vertically rigid, and crime policy continued to be based on top-down responses. Although police forces were now subject to civil rights controls and oversight by elected officials, police chiefs did not have to adjust their hierarchies, nor did they have to adjust to having their careers tied to demonstrating results. Quantitative measures of efficiency, such as the number of detentions, shut out alternative forms of citizen-based assessment. Steeped in what Goldstein (1990)

---

5 All dollar amounts are U.S. dollars unless otherwise indicated.

calls the "means-over-ends syndrome," policing was rooted in set practices rather than changing conditions—that is, on what the police traditionally did rather than on what they were supposed to accomplish (Eck 2006, 118).

As in the United States in the 1960s, during the 1990s the police in Latin America could not keep up with domestic change. As different social sectors mobilized and education levels rose, people became less tolerant of police forces whose ineffectiveness was more and more obvious. Along with deepening democratic stability and a raft of judicial reforms, the political embarrassment of police missteps, along with the realization that crime policy was almost useless against increasingly complex forms of crime, began opening the way to more preventive law enforcement. An impressive number of reforms resulted, ranging from the superficial to the impossible. But in between was a critical mass of changes that were substantive enough to create a momentum for real change. Although differing among countries, these reforms fall into five general areas described in the sections that follow: (1) agency restructuring, (2) professional support, (3) control mechanisms, (4) legal changes, and (5) community policing. Many initiatives and policies—such as information systems, alternative dispute resolution, neighborhood police modules, and community judges—include and advance several of these changes simultaneously.

Of all these developments, the ones with the most longevity have been those that have incorporated, even minimally, the idea of problem-oriented policing. In general, problem-oriented policing can be defined as the process of grouping criminal acts together to identify and address their causes. It changes the police's response from "one crime at a time" to crime clusters or problems, with prevention rather than number of crimes solved as the central measurable goal (Rosenbaum 1986). This approach requires decentralizing police structures, providing more socioeconomic support, making officers' schedules more flexible, and convincing other state agencies to support and evaluate the police's proactive responses (see Goldstein 1990, chap. 2). With its panoramic perspective, though, problem-oriented policing is legitimately criticized for being too vague to be useful for either analysis or policy. After all, traditional policing also responds to problems, and problem-oriented policing is often used just as a convenient catch-all criticism of it.

But problem-oriented policing is more a process than an application. It approaches an insecurity problem along different lines and then develops responses that, by definition, will vary. For many police agencies this kind of policing has been broken down into a set of specific steps known as

SARA: scanning (determining whether an issue is a problem); analysis (collecting data on the problem to document "its scope, nature, and causes") (Braga 2002, 14); response (analyzing the data to design an appropriate response); and assessment (evaluating that response)—see also Eck and Spelman (1987). By means of this staged and multidimensional diagnosis, problem-oriented policing addresses the causes of crime through actions that can be as concrete as those used in more traditional approaches. The potential and challenges arising from this kind of policing stem from whether it can be tailored to the local, socioeconomic, and criminogenic conditions that any effective policy must address. Beyond aiming for particular goals or more efficiency, problem-oriented policing is about forging a new and more flexible internal disposition geared toward processing problems beyond the traditional triad of patrol, detention, and investigation (see IEPADES 2000). Those problems, though, are not just criminal ones. They also arise from policy, management, and criminal justice. Citizen security reform is thus the process in which the five areas of change discussed in the sections that follow begin to coalesce around crime as well as the weaknesses in the response to it.

As part of the process, citizen security reform should draw on the experiences and results of traditional policing. The current applications of traditional policing, this book agues, have stripped away its strengths in the pursuit of immediate results. Clarity in directives, a focus on high-publicity crimes, strict hierarchies, and other attributes associated with traditional policing are not detrimental in themselves. Trying to get a handle on international drug networks, for example, requires the planning and execution offered by traditional policing. Traditional strategies are also more politically and administratively acceptable, which is no small consideration in the politics of security. But when traditional tactics are subject to immediate or politicized objectives, such as a drug sweep without efforts to understand the appeal of drugs in the target neighborhood, they can be counterproductive. Such ineffectiveness can often be reduced, however, when traditional policing methods are used within a problem-oriented framework. Rather than letting antigang crackdowns and youth social programs run counter to each other because they were developed by different political coalitions, officials can fuse categorizations of youth and incentives for leaving gangs with tough penalties against gang leaders. Such fusion also boosts the political credentials of problem-oriented policing by showing that it is based not on a rejection of traditional policing, but, like the policies it develops, on what works best for particular problems.

1. Agency Restructuring

A main impetus for problem-oriented policing is the realization of how ill-suited traditional police structures are for democratic societies. This awareness has led to agency reorganizations aimed at making the police more accountable, more professional, and more efficient. Most restructuring takes one of three forms. The first is geographic decentralization, in which centralized agencies are broken up into geographically delineated forces. These changes can be partial, in which new provincial and municipal agencies complement national ones, or more thorough, such as the complete replacement of an entire force by local units. The second type of structural reorganization, often accompanying the first, is a functional specialization through the formation of separate investigative and preventive street agencies, at a minimum, along with smaller units. A third form of restructuring is internal. Such change is mostly likely to take the form of reducing the number of ranks or merging the separate hierarchies for officials and sub-officials, which is the principal division within most Latin American police agencies.

2. Professional Support

Expectations of a more professional police force must be backed up by professional support. In Latin America such support comes in many forms. The most significant for the region's chronically and woefully underpaid officers is salary increases. Funds for salaries are limited, however, and so governments try to replace or supplement them with better health care, pensions, and other benefits. Like better salaries, such benefits can boost individual and group morale, which (at least theoretically) should cut down on corruption. Another area of professional support is job security, primarily through firmer and fairer career laws with enforced procedures on promotion and dismissal. Most other forms of support are technical; indeed, police are continually calling for more and better technology and equipment. Crime-mapping software, better forensics equipment, new vehicles, and other material have sweetened reform packages that might have been difficult for police to accept otherwise.

Changes in other areas of criminal justice, while less direct, often involve forms of professional support that benefit the police. Judicial reforms such as decentralization of the Attorney General's Office (Ministerio Público or Public Ministry or MP, also known as the Fiscalía) and quicker processing of detainees can free the police from activities in which they tend to be slow and resentful.

3. Control Mechanisms

Problems in citizen security are so far-flung that oversight must be as wide and adaptive as possible to ensure that the state's security network is more responsible toward both society and itself. To increase legal, fiscal, and public transparency, countries throughout Latin America are introducing or revamping many accountability agencies over the police. These bodies range from broad national ombudsmen (usually called *defensorías del pueblo*) to internal affairs units within the police and disciplinary bodies in each jurisdiction. Other state agencies, such as the Fiscalía, also have oversight and investigative authorities that extend over the police. Even entities lacking official legal powers, such as media outlets and nongovernmental organizations (NGOs), can and do exercise less formal oversight through investigative reports and publicity. The rights of citizens are the main concern of these agencies, particularly NGOs and the *defensorías del pueblo*. However, in an effort to increase transparency and address internal conflicts, additional areas such as finances and officers' work conditions are also often put under their purview.

4. Legal Changes

A host of new laws are empowering or controlling Latin America's police in different ways. Mirroring the dilemma between traditional and problem-oriented policing, these legal changes range from more authority on the street to more limited roles in the postdetention stages of the criminal justice process. The most important and sweeping legal change, discussed far more in the literature on judicial reform than that on police reform, is new penal process codes. In Latin America criminal investigations are notoriously slow and biased—less than 3 percent of homicides lead to a conviction. Thus since the early 1990s fourteen countries have adopted new penal process codes. Although the codes vary, they are all aimed at speeding up trials, clarifying the role of each criminal justice agency, and strengthening due process by replacing glacial and cumbersome written procedures with oral trials, transferring investigative authorities from the police to prosecutors (*fiscales*) in the Attorney General's Office, and creating courts at the investigative and sentencing stages. Many other codes have expanded alternative sentencing and community justice, such as through formation of the popular "judges of the peace." The initial impact of these new codes was impressive. Although the percentage of detainees awaiting trial had been rising in nearly every country in the 1990s, during the first three years the codes were in effect there was an average regional drop of 32.6 percent in the number of unsentenced prisoners (Riego and Duce 2008, 44). However, since this initial period rates have been creeping up again in most countries. But the decrease in unsentenced prisoners in these first few years has been the only significant and sustained reduction of this group in most of Latin America.

As discussed throughout this book, each of the changes fostered by these new codes has had wide repercussions for police work and authority, from detention to trials. The new codes also mark a change in the nature of the law itself. As many scholars have discussed, the law is composed of statutes as well as regulations on how to apply them (see Sarat and Kearns 1995; Nonet and Selznick 2001). Penal codes specify what is illegal, whereas penal process codes are about how to deal with transgressions of them. Generally, penal process codes guide daily application of the law and reflect any disquiet over it. Although rules about what is legal reflect a broad consensus on basic legal tenets that evolve only gradually, rules about their application gauge the constant changes in public opinion and state functioning. Operating as the half of the law that is applied, rules about rules can thus be as important as the rules themselves.

5. Community Policing

Community policing is a preventive approach based on making society the first line of defense against crime and insecurity. It helps citizens step into that role through a range of approaches. The most common are neighborhood watch groups and targeted actions against a specific problem such as a spate of robberies or poor street lighting. Other activities might be joint citizen-police security councils and programs such as youth centers and domestic violence seminars to address crime's causes and help vulnerable sectors. A primary objective of such projects is to bridge geographic, socioeconomic, and other differences among citizens, which aids cooperation among them as well as between them and the police.

Community policing is often buttressed or supplemented by police restructuring designed to facilitate police-citizen interaction, such as by giving more autonomy to neighborhood police chiefs (*comisarios*) or reorganizing the local police into neighborhood divisions that give officers more time and autonomy to work with residents in developing responses to insecurity (see Morash and Ford 2002). The rest of the state also plays a role, particularly by decentralizing social services to the local level and formally incorporating them into crime policy.

This Book's Arguments

Because criminal justice and police structures are slow to change, one of the most appealing features of community policing is that it is less tied to dysfunctional state institutions and their rigid responses. Combined with the other areas of reform, it can help citizen security officials question set practices in ways attuned to political and institutional realities. Oversight, restructuring, and the other changes just described would ideally be substantive and flexible enough to prompt officials to alter or discard practices that no longer work. In the process, these changes would open up different routes to problem-oriented policing by helping balance central control with local autonomy, vertical command with horizontal coordination, and consensus with adjustability.

But this is the core dilemma of citizen security reform: by exposing the biggest vulnerabilities of Latin American states, reform often triggers the states' strongest defenses against change. As in most countries, proposed alterations of long-term practices cause an almost reflexive opposition to them by officials vested in the status quo. Twenty years of democracy in the region has left a long trail of promising overhauls that, as pressures to halt crime heightened institutional resistance and political impatience, were abandoned in favor of short-term actions that only aggravated agency inefficiency and public panic. As officials then try to undo the complications arising from their quick fixes, they lose touch with the causes of crime, the nature of policing, the standards of democracy—and their ability to bring about change. This predicament, the pivot between traditional and problem-oriented policing, is this book's point of departure beyond the existing literature.

That literature, from policy reports to multiauthored books, has established citizen security as a substantive area of academic scholarship. This extensive work, which the following chapters build on, has advanced understanding of the full range of citizen security issues. But it has not yet developed analytical frameworks to explain across different cases why obstacles to reform develop and how they can be overcome. Although each situation is unique, a better delineation of what they have in common will help inform analysis of when external experiences can and cannot apply. In the literature, edited volumes are more parallel than comparative, describing issues alongside each other instead of using them as an opening for deeper insight. By contrast, studies of one problem, time period, or case can miss important connections among issues and patterns through time. In addressing these and other gaps, the challenge for citizen security scholarship can be grouped into three areas that correspond roughly to those this book highlights: institutional relations, daily policing, and the spectrum of reform. Attention to these areas, described in the sections that follow, can widen perspectives on citizen security to take in the full set of motivations behind and the impacts of Latin America's citizen security reform.

Institutional Relations

The first area requiring more focused analysis is institutional relations among those in charge of criminal justice. When zeroing in on a particular citizen security problem, most studies overlook the working relations among the executive branch, legislature, courts, police, accountability agencies, public prosecutor, NGOs, penitentiary system, and others. The observable relations among these agencies are complex enough, and, inconveniently, do not conform to their official roles. Most works on citizen security describe the range of institutional limits to reform (Beliz 2007) or focus on particular ones. Some works study budgets (Ward 2006), but few examine the process of formulating a budget and disbursing public funds. Digging further into formal procedures can help reveal unseen sources of control and the real extent of resource waste and abuse. As the next chapter reveals, the poor and incomplete compilation and analysis of crime statistics are often less a result of disorganization than of manipulation by rival agencies. Similarly, an interinstitutional examination of police corruption can reveal a lot about power and transparency among the many agencies ostensibly in charge of curbing it. And knowing why a security minister keeps only loose track of private security firms or supports a corrupt police chief can demonstrate how democratic standards as well as citizen security policies are compromised.

Institutional relations are also important because of how they respond to outside pressure. Although the network of criminal justice officials and agencies is changing and anything but cohesive, it still often reacts to alterations in the external environment by circling the wagons against change and working to keep itself and its power intact. Just as nondemocratic rules and officials can survive a transition to democracy, so too can they hold out through the move to a new kind of citizen security, when they may then neutralize or directly challenge reform. For example, the continuation of aggressive detention and high incarceration has undermined Latin America's new penal process codes. Getting around such a blockage, as this book discusses, requires a broader approach that accounts for interconnected agencies and practices.

Just as the citizen security crisis goes beyond crime, as supporters of problem-oriented policing argue, its solution must go beyond the expertise and responsibilities of any single agency. But without directive-driven blueprints, such plans are at a strategic disadvantage and may be no match for the clearer but often more abusive methods of traditional policing. Even if a reform is able to recalibrate relations among criminal justice agencies, it has to strike many balances along the way. Reform must control management without stifling innovation and increase citizen participation without triggering police withdrawal. Such goals are difficult to attain, but even reforms that set their sights lower do not necessarily fare better. Because many officials become interested in reform only when an agency's poor functioning draws criticism, the changes they enact usually improve the agency just enough to subdue public criticism but without imposing long-term reform. Initiatives that bring together criminal justice agencies to focus on a specific crime, such as carjacking or kidnapping, produce more impressive results. But such results tend to be inversely proportionate to durability because of the up-front resources needed and the strain of pulling together agencies that normally do not cooperate.

Because of the political, financial, and institutional difficulties of altering so many agencies at once, policymakers in Latin America are often reduced to dealing ploddingly with one agency at a time. Gradually introducing change by sequencing reform projects or concentrating on specific agencies can make sense, especially in the face of resistance, but it often comes at the expense of the larger network of activity associated with citizen security. For example, training the police in new investigative methods has a limited impact without complementary changes in the courts. And increasing the police's detention power may negate community policing programs focused on police-neighborhood relations. Because of the connections within criminal justice, new approaches usually work best if adopted in tandem. For example, one of the main harms to penal process codes is the error-filled crime reports rejected by prosecutors and judges. Those reports are one of the main links between otherwise distinct reforms, such as community policing and penal process codes. As discussed throughout this book, community policing is probably the best way to build the citizen trust that leads to credible evidence and witnesses for trial. But police reports that fall short of standards set by penal process codes are one of the weak links in the chain of institutional relations and actions that make up the criminal justice process. Without a holistic approach toward that larger process, even its stronger elements, such as community policing and penal process codes, are incapacitated.

Beyond specific reforms, more attention to institutional relations would help show how citizen security affects democracy—a subject most studies acknowledge but do not sufficiently explore. Aside from exceptions such as Koonings and Kruijt (2004), most of the literature on citizen security and democracy blocks that path of analysis by taking police resistance and political inflexibility as a given. For example, Sain (2001, 129) characterizes security policy as "permanent political misgovernment," and Amar and Schneider (2003, 12) assert that "punitive policing agenda and hard-line security practices have come to define the role of local government in cities across the Americas." Pointing to abuse as the primary concern and building on the transition literature's view of security forces as an obstacle to democratization, most studies approach citizen security as a problem more of human rights rather than of governance. They often downplay the fluidity of security conditions and the potential for new approaches. Most of the time the police regard such stances as the kind of handpicked criticisms that give them reason to dig in their heels against change. Defensive postures also arise from disorganization, with police heads too unsure about the quality of their own agencies to be open to scrutiny. The obstinacy of the police may stem from what they are hiding, that is, as well as from not being sure what they are hiding. Without understanding these unseen patterns, most studies miss the larger picture of institutional relations, which is beyond the control of any official or set of officials, particularly when they are caught in the growing gulf between law and order on one side and human rights on the other.

Daily Policing

How crime officials act with each other is rooted in how they handle their own jobs. One of the literature's biggest gaps, in fact, is the nature and experience of policing itself. What happens in the course of a day is often the most revealing about what reforms are up against. In addition to (or instead of) stopping crime or obeying orders, a police officer's attention during a shift is often dominated by personnel conflicts, gripes about schedules, and physical exhaustion. In their comparative study of police integrity, Klockars, Ivkovic, and Haberfeld (2004) examine a long list of attitudes and temptations that are part of every officer's shift. Gaines (1993) discusses how stress can motivate officers to be more cautious, but how once it reaches a certain level can "begin to have a debilitating effect." Such individual anxieties, routines, and preoccupations may seem inconsequential for national policies, but they can determine the fate of those policies as well as the fate of their proponents. A passing confrontation with a citizen, a missing fact in a police report, and other small undocumented actions—occurrences that often reflect flagging attention rather than deliberate sabotage—can reverberate through the citizen security machinery.

These factors also exemplify the difficulty in striking a balance between encouraging and controlling the individual discretion at the heart of police work. No matter how clear and restrictive the law, police officers have a range of both formal and informal authority that is wider than that of nearly any other kind of state official. In dealing with the innumerable permutations of citizen security challenges—from poorly lit alleys to murder scenes—police must choose from and combine a broad selection of strategies, tactics, and norms. The resources and reactions that police tap into when doing so are equally broad. Actions such as dispersing street vendors, which local police commonly do in Latin America, are associated with many different legal and societal norms. Kleinig (1996, 24) points out that because police officers are at the front lines of all societal dysfunctions, they "come to see their role punitively, and not simply custodially." Reform efforts and studies of reform must therefore look more closely at how such actions are shaped by training courses, promotion incentives, hierarchical relations, and institutional culture. They also must consider the individual makeup and daily lives of officers to understand what such policies and institutions cannot shape. Corruption, of course, is one practice in which the influences of an officer's routine patrol have far more impact than the rules of the station in which it begins.

The contours of discretion and behavior are often examined in the literature through the perspective of the police "culture." Within any force, how officers act and how they are supposed to act reflect overlapping layers of relationships and perceptions. They include the image of the institution projected by political elites, police connections with different social groups, the divide between management and the street, and relationships among those within each rank. McLaughlin (2007, 3) has closely studied the "cultural construction" of the English police as a valued and iconic part of society, overcoming deep resistance through "considerable attention . . . to image and styling." New York City's Police Department transformed its image over the course of a recent decade from one of corruption and chaos to one of heroism and control. Along with that image are expectations and rules about how officers deal with each other, from their peers to other ranks, and with different sectors, from tourists to public housing residents. Although such standards certainly affect officer actions, often more influential are officers' individual relations and experiences. Reuss-Ianni (1999, 8) describes a general socialization in which officers learn what the job is about and "how to play the game." Peer pressure and the informal and formal powers of higher-ranking colleagues (as chapter 3 discusses in detail) are two of the most important ways to learn that game.

Interviews with police officers throughout Latin America do indeed reveal the elaborate but often unspoken rules by which officers live. Behind the stereotype of the "thin blue line," which refers to police officers' defense of each other and their role in stopping civilized society from becoming ungovernable, is an elaborate set of rules such as: be aggressive but do not step on your colleague's toes; do your part but do not attract attention; never abandon colleagues but "always cover your ass." The challenge of balancing such finely calibrated rules is compounded by the fast-changing conditions and diverse societies in which they are found. One rookie officer in Santa Cruz, Bolivia, for example, said he had the rules down pat but had trouble applying them amid disputes between regional and national commanders and when the names of middle-class drug traffickers protected by the police changed. The more difficult officers find it to follow these rules, the more distant formal image and regulations become.

The combination of discretion and individual mindset also accentuates the unintended consequences of controls over policing. Most reform tries to corral police officers into strictures that the reality of police discretion renders meaningless, or, when combined with excessive bureaucracy, harmful. In response, officers often find it easier and more personally rewarding to avoid rather than abide by the controls over them. Even when they do make an effort to conform their actions to the law, which the majority of police do, they may not find a corresponding regulation. Many officers then use a general edict to detain a potentially violent person whose behavior does not fit into any specific law. The likelihood of abuse is therefore heightened, in turn deepening the divide between challenges to such actions in court and the push by the police for *mano dura* (iron-fisted) laws that give such actions a clear, legal imprimatur. Through the incorporation of daily policing, this book focuses not on what the police are doing wrong—which dominates scholarship and policy—but what the police are doing.

Spectrum of Reform

Most studies of citizen security reform capture only part of its wider political arc. Studies that examine one or two cases, such as those by Hinton (2006) and Eijkman (2007), provide a thorough analysis of the process and politics of security policy. Bailey and Dammert (2006, 15–21) offer a useful summary of the limited short-term results of reform in six cases. But more effort must go into following through on the actors, actions, alliances, sleights, dilemmas, and cut-corners that shape the complete trajectory of reform.

At each stage of the reform process—formulation, implementation, and evaluation—nearly every proposal must traverse a minefield of attacks and delays. The first stage, formulation, requires a coalition able to produce a proposal free of excessive compromises, contradictions, or unrealistic expectations. Just like the "birth defects" of a democratic transition (such as pacts among parties that remove sensitive issues from public contestation), security legislation that neglects certain areas, processes, or questions will later suffer from limitations. Although many works discuss public opinion, for example, few explore how different sectors of society are or are not allowed to add their views to legislative debate. Such debate also often fails to incorporate changing social conditions that foster or legitimize crime, as discussed in Burke's analysis of the "social construction" of crime (Hopkins Burke 2004, 9–13). In particular, proposed bills often target a problem, such as the increasing abuse of a specific drug, that is liable to change. Also overlooked in many analyses of reform's adoption is ideological polarization. Blame for insecurity tends to fall into two categories—socioeconomic conditions such as poverty and youth unemployment on one level and institutional problems such as bureaucracy and corruption on another. Because different kinds of actors tend to gravitate toward one category or the other, this division becomes politicized and reinforced, making it even harder to address both categories.

Weaknesses and poison pills in a policy's formulation continue into the second stage, implementation. Even reforms emerging relatively intact from policymakers can get stuck in the institutions charged with carrying them out. Officials in those agencies either resist those reforms or, in many cases, are unable to implement them. For example, internal affairs offices may find themselves with only a fraction of the financial and political support needed to carry out their work. Both of those potential hazards—lack of support and lack of will—could be reduced through problem-oriented approaches, which tend to include more of the agencies, from school boards to public sanitation works, that deal with the various causes of crime. Such a mutual response could also spread out the political risk of results. Without strong leadership, however, such an approach can succumb to competition and lack of accountability for results.

Evaluation, the third stage, is equally important but almost always the most neglected stage of reform. As chapter 7 describes, this ongoing process is critical to keeping reform on target with its stated aims. Doing so requires open channels from all sectors of society and all ranks of the police, which itself may require some kind of agency restructuring and clearer lines of communications. For example, the police corps in San Diego, California, and Santiago, Chile, were reconfigured into groups responsible for a defined set of city blocks headed by a director with autonomy in agent assignment, resource use, and development of collective solutions. As this book describes, such flexibility can mean the difference between success and failure even in adjacent neighborhoods. But because political capital is often exhausted before evaluation mechanisms are negotiated into a bill, only a fraction of police agencies have managed to initiate such changes. Unless both officers and citizens can express their honest responses to a policy and those responses can be incorporated into its structure, this last but critical stage of reform will enfeeble the overall change.

Getting these three stages on track also depends on the larger timing of democratization. Although most police forces in the region's countries were instruments of authoritarian repression, they were usually spared the purges, restructuring, and downsizing endured by the armed forces during the transition. Understandably reluctant to take on one more fight, as discussed in chapter 2, most elected officials do not meddle with the police as long as crime and abuse remain under control. But such delay has often meant missed opportunities to hitch reform to overall political change. Because problem-oriented policing by definition involves citizens, the path toward it should be part of the realignment of state-society relations during the transition to democracy. But as policing practices settle in and higher crime rates render the public less amenable to new approaches, policymakers are forced to narrow reforms to specific time periods, areas, or units.

And if these reforms fail—a result that such limitations almost ensure—they are unlikely to be attempted again if the chance arises, even if the context and not the policy is at fault.

Together, these three areas—institutional relations, daily policing, and the spectrum of reform—zero in on why citizen security in Latin America is in a crisis. Democracy requires a rule of law that contemporary states are not strong enough to sustain, but problem-oriented policing is a change that can absorb and turn around its weaknesses.

Organization of This Book

This book describes the citizen security crisis in Latin America, the reforms being enacted to address it, and their chances of overcoming a multitude of obstacles. Chapters 2 and 3 lay out the three layers of obstruction to citizen security reform: political, institutional, and societal. Chapter 2 deconstructs these obstacles in detail, showing how they reinforce each other but also leave openings for innovative policy responses. It cites examples from a range of Latin American countries and provides comparative statistics and analysis from them. Presenting a theme that extends throughout this book, chapter 3 looks at these obstacles' roots in and impact on the nature of Latin American democracy. Drawing on historical patterns and contemporary developments, it demonstrates how the citizen security crisis distorts power, physically divides countries, damages civil societies, and makes reform difficult. By detailing such links between security and democracy, chapters 2 and 3 help explain why reform is increasingly pivotal to the legitimacy of democratic regimes as well as to the stability of government itself. The "relationship between personal security and government is tautological," argue Bayley and Shearing (2001, 30). "If people are not provided with protection at some minimum level, government is not considered to exist."

Chapters 4–6 apply this analytical framework to three case studies: Honduras, Bolivia, and Argentina. In the impoverished Central American country of Honduras, the progressive internal security system has been under tremendous strain since its adoption in the late 1990s. In the Andean nation of Bolivia, also poor but far larger and more ethnically diverse, several governments have attempted bold changes to a security system that has become critical to national stability. In contrast to Honduras and Bolivia and most other countries in Latin America, wealthier and more industrialized Argentina has a federal structure in which each province (as in Mexico, Venezuela, and Brazil) has its own police force and citizen security approaches. These three countries were chosen to serve as case studies for several fundamental reasons. First, they demonstrate the range of both obstacles to and opportunities for citizen security reform in three of Latin America's main subregions—Central America, the Andes, and the Southern Cone—and under contrasting societal, economic, and demographic conditions. Second, these countries' different political structures reveal weak points in governance that shape institutional functioning, daily policing, and attempts to improve them. For example, the centralized police of countries such as Bolivia struggle to balance national prerogatives with local demands, while states such as Argentina are characterized by a federal system that is problematic in terms of both citizen equality and state policy. Third, with distinct transitions from authoritarian rule, these countries put on clear display the ways in which up-and-down democratization harms both citizen security and citizen rights. More than most countries, these have undergone changes that have unleashed underlying tensions and revealed the potential in state-society relations. Elected presidents in all three countries have been turfed out of office in the current democratic era, resulting in a volatile mix of instability at the top and the promise of power at the bottom that has given citizens unprecedented forms of access—to both violence and policy organizing—for which they are often ill-prepared. In short, these three countries' stories depict all the faces of the region's citizen security crisis.

Each case study is structured as follows: (1) a description of the history of policing in the country profiled and an overview of national trends in crime and violence, followed by descriptions of the citizen security structure and the main areas of reform; (2) an examination of the obstacles to citizen security reform, outlined in chapter 2, focusing on those most relevant; and (3) a review of the enacted or potential ways, primarily through regional or local initiatives, in which to overcome such obstacles. The case studies also look at the question of democratization and its relationship to citizen security. Although each of these three countries—like the rest of Latin America—began its transition toward democracy in the 1980s, their histories of authoritarianism and patterns of democratization have been very different, thereby affecting citizen security in distinct and path-changing ways.

Chapter 7 applies this theoretical and empirical material to the future. Examining policy from a comparative perspective and in the context of Latin American democratization, it develops recommendations for overcoming obstacles to citizen security reform. It describes strategies from different countries—such as Chile, Colombia, Costa Rica, Uruguay, and

Venezuela—that help overcome the political, institutional, and societal obstructions in areas ranging from national-level education to small pilot programs. As this book portrays, such approaches are often most manageable at the local level, where officials can take advantage of decentralization, the neighborhood connections they have developed, and the failure of traditional policies to enact creative programs. In fact, some of the most notable results have emerged from some of the more violent and neglected areas, which are often the ones most receptive to new kinds of leadership and problem-oriented solutions. By discussing progress in unlikely places, chapter 7 highlights advances that were not expected because of their bleak environments, poor planning, low funding, and other problems. On the flip side, it also discusses programs that failed despite adequate support and funding.

The book's conclusion, chapter 8, brings these recommendations together with the rest of the book's case studies and theoretical frameworks. By outlining the many connections among reform strategies, obstacles, and experiences, it summarizes and steers the book's main points toward future research and policy needs.

Through this approach, this book describes ways in which to understand citizen security reform beyond specific policies, which are often abandoned or supplanted before studies of them are published. Because citizen security reform must outlast specific plans and governments, so should analysis of it. This book's framework also underscores the importance of resisting the demarcation of citizen security policies as either successes or failures. "Success" implies a finality that history does not permit.

Chapter 2

Realms of Change and Obstacles to Citizen Security Reform

Obstacles to citizen security reform appear more quickly than its results. Even the most carefully constructed and broadly supported changes are diluted, undermined, or neglected. Such impediments to change are so potent because they are part of most countries' politics, institutions, laws, and societies.

Indeed, the impediments to citizen security reform spring from the same processes that create it. Politically, governments are often so pressured by panicked societies to deliver short-term results that they discard ministers and policies at a rate often directly proportionate to their inabilities to face down the entrenched agencies with the most to lose from reform but with the greatest ability to block it. These agencies impede change not only through direct resistance but also through their own deficiencies in oversight, investigation, statistics, budgeting, and management. The law, a central counterweight to such trends, often only fuels those trends. Edicts and internal police regulations, unclear and inconsistent provisions, low-quality legal education, and crime policies unattached to criminology are some of the many legal distortions of law enforcement. Meanwhile, society has a hard time breaking through such conditions because of its own economic struggles, anemic organizations, tensions with state officials, and temptations to use destabilizing alternatives.

Different kinds of such obstacles afflict different countries, but they tend to emerge from conditions that are common in Latin America and other regions. Chapters 2 and 3 discuss two levels of such conditions. Chapter 2 examines the surface level of short-term reform, describing eight realms of change and the specific impediments that lie within them to specific proposals. Chapter 3 then delves into the roots of these impediments in the broader and more fixed traits of power, society, and geography in Latin

21

American history and democracy. Together, these chapters show how changes in citizen security, many of them intertwined with deeper patterns of governance, have set the stage for a struggle between the status quo and attempts to alter it.

1. Opinion and Politics

On citizen security more than on most issues, the public and politicians push each other beyond what either intends. Since the mid-1990s, crime has been the first or second biggest concern almost everywhere in Latin America (IUDOP 1998; Consorcio Iberoamericano de Investigaciones de Mercados y Asesoramiento 2010). In some polls crime jumped from fifth place in 2003 to second place in 2005 as citizens' biggest worry,[1] and it is statistically tied with unemployment in the regional Latinobarómetro survey, more than doubling between 2001 and 2007. The survey asked, "What do you consider to be the most important problem in your country?"[2] The public's fear of crime often rises at an even faster clip than the crime rate itself—and sometimes continues to go up even when crime starts to go down. People simply doubt that any decline will last or attribute it to external conditions such as an improving economy rather than to crime policies. The reasonable and often correct consensus is that crime will return to its regular rise and that the government will have no plan for dealing with it when it does. Although crime rates began declining in Buenos Aires after 2003, record increases in the 1990s and highly publicized crimes gave society the impression of uncontrolled criminality that continues to buoy fear. After a series of robberies in 2004, for example, the percentage of city residents fearing crime climbed to 57 percent—a rate similar to that in much more violent cities such as São Paulo in Brazil.[3] Like the panic attacks that people often suffer when fearing the repeat of a trauma, crime has joined inflation and military unrest as an automatic trigger for instability in Argentina.

1. Jorge Sapoznikow, Inter-American Development Bank, "Expertos debaten prevención de violencia juvenil en América Central, Panamá y República Dominicana," press release, October 6, 2006.

2. The Santiago-based Latinobarómetro survey polled 20,212 people in eighteen countries between September 7 and October 8, 2007. The average margin of error was 3 percent.

3. Gabriel Picciano, secretary of administrative management, Ministry of Justice, Security, and Human Rights (Ministerio de Justicia, Seguridad y Derechos Humanos, MJSDH), interview with author, Buenos Aires, May 20, 2004.

Reflecting this fear, polls around the region indicate strong public approval for more police and harsher punishments. One poll in Panama, for example, revealed 80 percent support for an iron fist or *mano dura*.[4] But surveys often present these options without suggesting concrete alternatives such as preventive social programs. In many cases, such as the Panamanian poll, surveys are prompted by growing public rancor, so that complaints about public security system overwhelm ideas for its salvation. When possible solutions are left out, problems seem even more intractable. Broader and more balanced polls, such as Chile's National Survey of Public Safety (Encuesta Nacional de Seguridad Ciudadana), include items such as opinions on specific programs. But most other surveys that go into depth focus instead on questions of personal victimization and "sensation of insecurity." Even when the objective of such polls is to achieve a detailed picture of crime patterns and concerns, such as in the 2008 door-to-door citizen security survey in Santa Fe, Argentina, expectations are raised that people's responses will be reflected in policy.[5]

However, polling is usually drowned out in the media by sensationalism, which ramps up public panic even more directly, often by fixating on a particular crime and judging insecurity by it. For example, the 2008 abduction of a businessman's son in Mexico prompted a national review of crime policy. Such a focus can paint officials into policy and political corners, provoking them to take concerted actions that bring the rate down. As described in chapter 4 on Honduras, for example, many governments react to a spike in kidnappings—a crime with high levels of media exposure—by quickly forming kidnapping units that fail to address long-term causes that prompt kidnappings to rise once attention has moved on. Emboldened reporters enjoying greater press freedoms are able to cover crime scenes more easily and with less interference, exposing the police force's fallibilities. But the police, assuming a defensive posture, rarely provide enough internal training in press and public relations, which only confirms officers' views of this area as tangential to policing and citizens' views of the police as inept. One police officer in Buenos Aires said that when there is a crime in his district, the press tend to report it under headlines blaring "insecurity." He then approaches the journalist on a "not authorized" basis to explain the specifics

4. Betty Brannan Jaén, "Mano dura, una mentalidad medieval," *La Prensa* (Panama City), August 1, 2004.
5. "Realizarán encuestas para armar mapa del delito en Santa Fe," *El Santafesino,* May 25, 2008.

of the case, conducting what is by that time little more than damage control. Moreover, the less public relations training received by officers and the fewer of them working in it, the more likely it is that the information they provide to citizens and policymakers alike will be not be clear and reassuring. Positive programs or developments will go unreported, leaving only the negative ones—of which there is never a lack.

As these cycles accelerate, citizens begin to lose trust in officials who frenetically sacrifice long-term structural change for immediate results. Even without a sense of urgency, most governments lack the political and institutional support to enact long-term plans. Proposals tarred as being soft on crime, or that tackle structural problems head-on, are often dead on arrival. In some cities such as New York and Bogotá, mayors enjoying strong popular momentum for change have initiated a security overhaul based on new models. In most cases, however, the national executive has enough citizen backing to "do something," but not enough institutional backing to "do something" long-term. Despite executive dominance on citizen security policy, many inside and outside of government around the region comment on the lack of executive interest in its details, often rooted in a long-standing but frequently unstated agreement between government and police not to open each other's Pandora's boxes. By the time they do become concerned, problems may be too entrenched to root out. Trapped in these currents of public opinion and political realities, which they help to stir up, most governments paddle through their tenures in office with piecemeal and often contradictory responses.

One of the biggest casualties of such politics is the minister in charge of the police—the interior minister in most Latin American countries. The tenure of any cabinet minister rides on the ups and downs of the issues they oversee, but because of the volatility of citizen security, interior ministers and their staffs cycle in and out of office with especially unsettling frequency. New ministers often discard their predecessors' plans, particularly those that contributed to their predecessors' downfall, to make way for their own. Other ministers avoid change altogether because they anticipate a short spell in office, because they do not want to antagonize the police, or because they want to avoid association with yet more failure.

Such instability is one symptom of the wider political reality in which officials are always thinking about moving to the next position because the current one is perceived to be—and thus continues to be in fact—essentially powerless. In addition to rotating ministers, power declines when presidents eliminate ministries, downsize their staffs, or move police authority among them, such as from Interior to Justice. Such moves often seem designed to head off change rather than to promote it. But even though such decisions can stop a major reform in its tracks, they can also revive a moribund one. For example, Venezuela's Police Reform Commission was created in 2006 by Jesse Chacón, who was one of nine ministers of interior and justice during the first eight years of the government of President Hugo Chávez. The commission conducted extensive national surveys and in-depth studies as a basis for comprehensive change. However, Chávez declined to continue this work after firing Chacón in January 2007, and subsequently proposed sweeping laws that would undermine the commission's detailed recommendations, one of which called for creating an integrated system to coordinate the country's disparate agencies. As crime rose to record levels the following year, Chávez put his authority behind a renewed effort that led to a new Police Service Law and more than seven resolutions to implement unifying national standards.

More dexterous presidents and governors escape from this vice of public pressure and policy impotence by adopting *mano dura* anticrime policies, which are popular, easy to formulate and enact, and the best guarantee for quick results during a limited time in office. Often compared unfavorably and unfairly to their authoritarian predecessors and their abilities to keep order, many elected presidents even affix Cold War–era "national security" language to their policies. Such language opens the door to military involvement in policing and waters down legal oversight of both individual rights and executive action.[6] Executives rarely hesitate to use appointments, special funds, and party patronage to keep legislative and judicial intrusion at bay. Such attitudes support the view of contemporary Latin American regimes as "delegative democracies" in which presidents see themselves as the embodiment of the national will and thus find the "nuisances" of other institutions an "unnecessary impediment to the full authority" that they have been "delegated to exercise" (O'Donnell 1993, 6).

Legislatures do not do enough to check such power. Although they are the primary counterweight to executives, they usually lack the party discipline, budgetary resources, or political heft to counter executive decrees, promote viable policy alternatives, or oversee police practice. Most legislatures are too controlled by the president's party to pass bills that implicitly criticize that party, and even when a different party or no party is in the

---

6. The term *national security* has become so common that many police officials now criticize its use in training.

majority, disorder and a lack of discipline hinder deliberation of feasible policy changes. Hamstrung by such political divides, many legislatures are too afraid to antagonize a powerful police agency or too spooked by public demands to take any meaningful action that might be blamed for any subsequent upticks in crime. Instead, legislators often direct their criticism at the social sectors associated with criminality, often with unrealistic and unconnected proposals bordering on the demagogic. Demands to adopt or reinstate capital punishment are one staple proposal masquerading as decisive action and guaranteed to attract attention.

Both legislatures and courts find it difficult to assert themselves. For one thing, legislatures tend to exercise just a fraction of their oversight power over both civil rights and fiscal matters. In addition to their own reluctance to act, financial and other restrictions curb action by both legislators and judges, raising questions about their authority over the state and the rule of law. Are police roundups justified when the legislature does not provide funds for the investigative training needed to avoid them? What about detentions beyond the time limit set by judges when no judge is available to take the case? Or what about curfews that a government approves but whose excesses it ignores? In a democratic regime, elected officials have the constitutional authority to formulate, regulate, and monitor the rules, funding, structures, and actions of security agencies (see Altamira 1963). In most democracies, the legislature has this "police power," and police agencies are obligated to abide by the laws and decisions that result from it. But the steady erosion of this norm over the course of Latin American history and the failure to reverse it in the current era have blurred the line between the legislature's police power and the power of the police. On a daily basis, in fact, it is often the executive and police officials who decide how those structures, funds, and rules are put into practice. In the process the police themselves often redefine, reinterpret, and reformulate those same laws to the point to which their actions become de facto police power.

Under such conditions would-be reformers face an uphill struggle. Just as in the analysis of the health sector by Kaufman and Nelson (2004, 24–31), they confront "a diverse array of opponents and indifferent groups" in an environment in which "rewards are delayed and uncertain, but political costs of reforms are prompt and clear." Because of public panic, security is an issue particularly prone to such treatment, evident, for example, in the ability of the police and elected officials to boil crime policy down to a choice between *mano dura* and human rights (see Maravall 1999, 157–58).

"While advocates of change must win at all stages of the political process—issue-recognition, decision, and implementation of policy—the defender of existing policy must win at only one stage in the process" (Bachrach and Baratz 1970, 58). As a result, the vast majority of citizen security legislation in Latin America originates in the executive branch and, unless formulated by a new government, strengthens rather than reevaluates existing policy. Such outcomes of executive-legislative relations not only reflect power imbalances, but also increase the uncertainty among citizens (see chapter 3).

Venezuela, where no fewer than ten police reform proposals were under way in 2006, is a good example of both legislative abandonment and general inconsistency in security policy. After the 1958 transition to democracy, two political parties, Democratic Action (Acción Democrática) and the Christian Party (Comité de Organización Política Electoral Independiente), ruled in a pact and rarely enacted the laws needed on police structure, training, and budgets. A lack of oversight also led to widespread abuses, including death squads linked to the police.[7] The election of Chávez in 1998, amid the disintegration of the two parties, promised to break this pattern. Since then, however, the legislature has reflected rather than responded to the politicization of policing and other issues as it has been pulled into the confrontation between the president and the opposition, both of whom are trumpeting abuses by police forces controlled by the other side.[8] After December 2005, when Chávez-allied candidates took full control of the legislature in the wake of elections boycotted by the opposition, constructive criticism of national crime policy all but ceased for several years.

Under some conditions this sorry state of executive-legislative relations can be remedied. One is when a weak president allows the legislature to be more powerful. In the late 1990s, for example, Uruguay passed reforms under the embattled government of Jorge Battle (2000–5), and Venezuela's

7. "Sistema de drogas y reciclaje de químicos eran los funciones del cuerpo para-policial," *El Nacional,* February 13, 1988, D-22. The involvement of the Defense Ministry's Office of Military Intelligence (Dirección de Inteligencia Militar, DIM) and the Technical and Judicial Police (Policia Tecnica y Judicial, PTJ) was suspected.

8. The opposition complains of the repression by police controlled by Chávez allies and by the pro-Chávez Bolivarian Circles (Círculos Bolivarianos), while government allies criticize the Metropolitan Police (Policía Metropolitana, PM) and other opposition-controlled police agencies. One legislator accused the PM of being "criminal and repressive" and accused the police of Chacao and of Baruta of protecting the opposition but killing pro-Chávez activists. William Tarek Saab, member of legislature, Movimiento Quinta República, interview by author, Caracas, February 27, 2003.

legislature enacted a comprehensive penal process code during the waning government of Rafael Caldera (1994–99). In other countries, such as Bolivia under Gonzalo Sánchez de Lozada in the 1990s, stability allowed the passage of sweeping change. The absence of such reform around the region, however, highlights the fact that such cases are exceptions to the rule of inaction.

Push for reform can also come from below—often when the victims of violent crimes that are committed, ignored, or bungled by the police are from the middle or upper classes. Demands to bring the police to heel are particularly vigorous when a highly publicized act of violence or corruption prompts citizens to realize that unchecked excesses—of corruption, violence, or other misdeeds—distract officers from fighting crime. Some of the biggest attempted crime system overhauls in Latin America, such as in Peru and Mexico City, have stemmed from such a widespread belief. In these cases, though, the resulting pressures either dissipated or were channeled into impractical, contradictory, or even *mano dura* proposals. For example, the 200,000-strong march in Buenos Aires in April 2004 after the kidnapping and murder of a middle-class student led to a raft of laws to stiffen criminal punishment. Because many such attempts at reform are made during times of political change, such as in Brazil and Argentina in the early 1990s, support for them often dries up once those temporary political conditions pass. With reform policies rarely outliving the sponsoring governments, the police are emboldened in their claims that the policies would hamper crime fighting or create too much uncertainty, such as the Chilean Carabineros' resistance to structural and personnel changes by a popular democratic regime in the 1990s.

Together, these conditions make it difficult to enact legislation in all five areas of reform described in chapter 1, particularly those, such as control mechanisms and community policing, that require both more funding and oversight. But even when such difficulties stymie change in the short run, they lay the groundwork for it in the long run. Most often they introduce ideas into the public debate that lead to legislation scaled down to fit the limitations. When a security crisis leads to or accompanies an economic collapse or political rupture, the rejection of state elites can open up opportunities for new, more citizen-centered approaches. In fact, in Argentina, Bolivia, Ecuador, and Venezuela the breaking point in the contemporary collapse of constitutional governments was the inability of security forces to handle the citizen unrest that grew out of unmet demands for change.

2. The Law: Criminology and Zero Tolerance

The law, by applying constitutional norms to state action, is supposed to steer and steady such change. Instead, the law is often swept up in it. Criminal laws in Latin America frequently have too much overlap, historical baggage, and inflexible detail to cope with the ever-changing issues of security. As this section discusses, the sheer extent of criminal law and its partiality for zero tolerance policing leave little space for the kinds of citizen participation and transparency that appear contrary to the certainty to which the law strives. Thus throughout Latin America those moving toward problem-oriented policing find it difficult not to succumb to the gravitational pull of this heavy legal structure.

The legal base of Latin American policing comprises penal codes, penal process codes, police codes, *ordenanzas* (ordinances—the part of administrative penal law used primarily to regulate public order); *contravenciones* (misdemeanors—both *ordenanzas* and *contravenciones* are also called *faltas,* and most edicts are a category of *faltas*), *reglamentos* (regulations—these are part of disciplinary penal law and used mostly for internal police matters such as discipline); prohibitions; police orders; *permisos* (permissions—these are the exemptions to regulations); special permits or authorizations; and customary laws made up of unlegislated but long-held practices.[9] Most laws, *ordenanzas,* and *reglamentos* can be replaced or revoked by officials with police power and, in some cases, by the executive agencies that oversee their execution. Although most of these laws are in distinct legal codes covering specific areas, overlap and confusion are common, especially in the areas of policing in which discretion gives judicial interpretation particular weight. Differing views on the use of force, collection of evidence, treatment of at-risk youth, and other key security issues can be and often are supported by different laws, particularly in the absence of judicial clarification. But new national, provincial, and local laws continue to be enacted far more quickly than they are interpreted. The government "changes laws like socks," as one police chief griped, making it hard for him to know which ones apply and how they do.

Commenting on this rush, government and police officials refer to how poorly new laws are adjusted to institutional capacities. For example, ef-

---

9. Many areas of law deal with the police. Disciplinary law delineates police responsibility, administrative law defines sanction authorities and processes, and penal law regulates constitutional order and internal state security.

forts to collect private arms often fail because trust is not built with the targeted community. This problem was evident in 2002, when, in response to a 58 percent increase in firearms killings, Venezuela enacted a disarmament law.[10] The law provided economic incentives to turn in private arms—estimated by the police to number 600,000 in the Federal District alone[11]—but it did not take into account the cooperation needed with community groups to actually collect those weapons. General crime policy is also affected by new laws, such as when court delays slow down detainee processing. For example, the increase in speed that new penal process codes bring to many criminal justice processes is negated by the greater number of arrests that result from wider police power. Because of their ambition, in fact, new penal process codes expose, more than other reforms, the wide gap between the promise of legal change and the reality of legal practice in Latin America. In nearly every country, a combination of inadequate funds, poor training, bureaucratic inertia, and resistance by police agencies resentful of losing investigative power has impeded the application of these codes. Institutional disarray, expected during the initial phase of a democratic transition but continuing in many countries well past it, can thus sideline even the most practical and well-designed legal reform.

The vacuum in criminal justice that results is often filled by zero tolerance policing, a more straightforward approach thought able to cut through the legal thicket. That line of action stems, at least rhetorically, from the "broken windows" theory developed by James Q. Wilson and George L. Kelling in 1982,which asserts that antisocial behavior such as intimidation and harassment, along with the physical deterioration of property, scare off law-abiding citizens and allow crime to take root (Wilson and Kelling 1982). A broken window in a building is a signal that no one cares about the property, encouraging delinquents to gather in front of the building and from there to begin dominating the neighborhood. As residents then minimize their time in the street, the sense of public order slips out of their control even without actual criminal activity. The only effective way to prevent these conditions from setting in, the broken windows theory posits, is by giving the police greater authority to detain people for misdemeanors and antisocial behavior. Proponents of these policies reason that legalized clampdowns on such actions not only prevent potential criminals from being em-

10. "Asesinadas 30 personas en el mes de Octubre," *Últimas Noticias,* November 7, 2002, 20.
11. *El Universal,* April 20, 2002, I-4.

boldened to undertake more serious crime but also reveal illegal arms, suspects wanted for outstanding crimes, and other illegal possessions or activities that would otherwise go unchecked.

In New York City this approach appeared to yield an unprecedented drop in the homicide rate from a high of over thirty per 100,000 residents in 1990 to under ten in 1998, with continuing decreases through 2009.[12] Because such results gave the policy a high level of credence and support early on, it was adopted in the 1990s by police forces throughout the United States. Other countries soon followed, most formally Indonesia, the Netherlands, South Africa, and the United Kingdom. Many other areas adopted different elements of the approach, leading to innumerable permutations and invariably more heated debates. Understanding whether the broken windows theory works in each of these countries requires a connection between theory and tactics under their particular circumstances—that is, what specific approaches do police develop out of the broken windows theory, and how do those approaches serve its goals? In Latin America, the region that probably has adopted its own forms of zero tolerance more extensively than any other, harsh social conditions and weak states make such questions particularly important to understanding the applications and impacts of broken windows theory in new scenarios.

In any country a first connection between theory and tactics is a definition of *disorder*. A study in the Netherlands that set up and observed behaviors such as littering, trespassing, and stealing in six locations is perhaps the only controlled experiment that tested the broken window theory itself (Keizer, Lindenberg, and Steg 2008). In the experiment nearly twice as many people violated clearly posted laws in areas with graffiti and garbage as in the same areas without such contamination. This experiment thus supported the contention that the broken windows theory can best be used to reduce disorder when it defines the types of disorder it is targeting.

In practice, however, disorder is not defined and instead is employed as a general term. Indeed, definitions may be politically sensitive and could box the police into particular approaches while holding them to goals they cannot meet. Many practices associated with broken windows are not well defined, and, as a result, they often provoke controversy. In the United States, for example, the police practices arising from broken windows and zero tolerance include racial profiling, harassment, and deployments "to re-

12. U.S. Federal Bureau of Investigation, Uniform Crime Reports, http://www.fbi .gov/ucr/ucr.htm.

constitute" public spaces for the private gain of local business (McArdle 2001, 4). In Latin America, as this section and the following chapters discuss, the theory has been used to justify roundups, curfews, torture, and extra-judicial killings.

A second and closely related connection between theory and tactics is extent and balance. What are measured and proportionate actions against disorderly behavior, and how far should they go? As discussed in chapter 7, the quality of life enforcement first used in New York City's subways was based on the power to stop people for suspicion of committing a range of minor offenses. Suspects who had identification and no outstanding criminal charges would usually be given a desk appearance ticket (DAT), leading to a fine or community service. Although this approach reduced disorder, its early effectiveness eventually led police to overly depend on it, thereby generating citizen antagonism, police resentment, neglect of larger patterns, and court delays. Early critics also legitimately saw zero tolerance as a form of control and discipline of marginalized people without attention to or rehabilitation of their conditions. However, several elements of that approach continued to be beneficial. One was handgun checks in which a bulge in someone's clothing allowed the police to ask them to empty their pockets, and, if deemed necessary, to subject them to a pat-down. Zero tolerance has even shifted trends in drug use since 1998, when the New York Police Department (NYPD) began to arrest and book individuals for smoking blunts, marijuana in a cigar wrapping (see Johnson, Golub, and Dunlap 2006). Although the use of blunts is a positive trend in the sense that it has replaced heroin and cocaine as the drug of choice among youth, public smoking is considered a public nuisance and a source of disorder. In smaller cities throughout Latin America, many police officers say their biggest problem is drug gangs, which are often groups of pot-smoking youth. But does their detention go hand-in-hand with the use of social services to prevent recurrence? Would driving illicit youth activity behind doors be acceptable? Zero tolerance of such behavior depends on the community definition of disorder and whether the overall impact is beneficial.

A third important connection between theory and tactics is correlation (also see chapter 3). Many of the most comprehensive studies, most notably by the U.S. National Research Council (Skogan and Frydl 2004) and Sampson and Raudenbush (1999), present mixed or inconclusive results for zero tolerance policing. Some reports on New York City show only a tenuous relationship between zero tolerance policy and the drop in petty crimes (Harcourt 1998; Eck and Maguire 2006; Harcourt and Ludwig 2006). Although the broken windows theory surfaced at the onset of the rapid decline in New York City's crime rate, it was in fact only one of the catalysts of the decrease. Sustained economic growth during the decade, the end of the crack epidemic, and demographic changes (particularly a relative decline in teenage residents) were also contributing factors (see Karmen 2000). Zero tolerance was also connected to the broad neoliberal economic approaches adopted by governments after the 1980s, which took forms such as welfare reform, public service privatization, and business improvement districts (BIDs). So zero tolerance was part of these larger socioeconomic and policy trends, which are associated with both decreases in crime as well as negative patterns such as societal exclusion (see Punch 2007) and limited public space, as discussed in the next chapter. But the particular contribution of zero tolerance was to help policy be better attuned to changes in economic and demographic conditions by highlighting the need for social services to address those changes, such as for drug treatment, in ways that address the causes of crime.

Together, these three connections help reveal the differences between traditional and problem-oriented policing, as well as the ways in which they could support each other. In particular, traditional approaches can be employed in the service of a problem orientation by defining the sources of disorder and marshaling state power to reduce them. For example, the hierarchical structure of the police can be effective at coordinating officers' actions, because consistency and clarity are needed to avoid discrepancies in police action. The reactive responses at the core of traditional policing can also work to handle quickly the most urgent security concerns, giving problem-oriented approaches more time to address their deeper sources. On another level, the executive controls associated with traditional policing can best compel involvement by other state agencies. As it incorporates those other actors, the traditional approach can also minimize the politicization of citizen security by keeping intact the authority of officials, while helping them recognize the need for greater institutional and societal involvement.

To hold broken windows policing true to its original intentions—that is, to keep tactics as close as possible to theory—the police and criminal justice system must have certain baseline capacities. For example, because the police come in closer contact than do other state officials with the causes of crime such as drug addiction, all officers must undergo legal training. Coordination with social services, functioning courts to process detainees, and the oversight of government agencies, courts, NGOs, and the media are also required. In other words, in order to work, policies based on the broken windows theory must combine the co-production part of its approach, in which different agencies work together, with the incivilities component, in which antisocial behavior is curtailed. To take one example, handing out summons for chronic drunkenness works only if the courts and social services are able to stop the revolving door of nights spent in jail. In reality, though, co-production is usually outpaced by the focus on incivilities (Taylor 2006, 106–8). In many areas of Latin America and other regions, zero tolerance is often applied with little outside support and few controls, turning it into a *mano dura* approach that is little more than a continuation of police practices from the predemocratic period that provide legal cover for the police to control society's "dangerous" elements. Zero tolerance can thus give the illusion of improvement without necessarily incorporating the structural changes that make it self-sustaining. It reflects a lack of continuity, coordination, and confidence in the criminal justice system.

Although zero tolerance policies are relatively recent, gaining predominance in the 1990s, they have a strong legal basis. Helping to institutionalize and drive this approach are the edicts and other internal regulations that most Latin American police forces have been acquiring since the colonial era. These edicts and regulations empower the police to detain citizens for an expanding range of subjectively defined activities and behaviors, from "vagrancy" to "suspicion of criminal intent." For example, the provision in Chile's 1901 penal code allowing police to make arrests based on physical appearance was not eliminated until 1998. Although the majority of these provisions are public, the citizens most affected by them tend to be the least aware of their rights when detained under the provisions. And though technically legal, most edicts often include exemptions from regular judicial procedures—such as required notification of a judge within a certain time period—and contain vague wording that expands police power beyond the intended limits of constitutional law. Because of the upper hand that edicts and other internal rules give officers, actions and detentions based on them take up a large part of officers' time. In Guatemala, for example, an estimated 80 percent of detentions and arrests are for alleged misdemeanors (Scheye 2005, 2). As police operations become centered on edict detention, statistics are also affected, with the number of such detentions serving as a police force's self-referential measure of success. Thus once in place, a *mano dura* approach starts to legitimize itself as arrests begin to replace conviction and recidivism rates as the barometers of policy success.

In nearly every country in which such regulations have been struck down for being unconstitutional or abusive, governments have tried to reinstate them in new forms or by increasing use of other regulations such as checking a person's identification or police record. For example, Venezuela's 1939 Law of Vagabonds and Crooks allowed the police to detain anyone deemed "suspicious" and was one of the main bases for police detentions until it was finally declared unconstitutional in 1997. It was quickly replaced, however, by stepped-up checks for identification or a criminal record, which usually involved detention in a police station. Edicts have also been substituted or supplemented by newer "social control" laws enacted since the democratic transition. Often introduced as part of zero tolerance policing (in some cases as measures within special police operations), these laws span the range of police functions and increase the unregulated control of the police over citizens even as the temporary conditions or operations end. At other times the repressive laws and measures applied to guerrilla groups are used against criminals, such as in Venezuela in the 1970s and Peru in the 1990s, supported by extra roundup powers and special courts that are allowed to continue.

The main tactics of zero tolerance policing, particularly detention for lacking identification or for "antisocial" behavior, demonstrate how laws can be counterproductive to law enforcement. They distract from a focus on serious crime and the causes of crime, distend judicial backlogs, raise tensions with citizens, and complicate any moves toward problem-oriented policing. Without follow-up or coordination with social services or the courts, such actions do not serve the broken windows purpose of stopping more violent crime. In Costa Rica, for example, nearly fifty thousand misdemeanor violations are reported each year—a figure that drew attention after the Supreme Court prohibited detentions for them.[13] But as many criminal justice officials admit, the real problem is that these detentions involved no civilian assessment or even police reports that could inform crime policy. The region's new penal codes have raised the bar on the evidence necessary for detention, but instead of scaling back their actions to adjust to the new codes, most police officers have only accelerated their arrests of suspects, most of whom are quickly released. Using edicts and other powers to resist the new codes and other reforms, the police then thicken the line being drawn between "public order," associated with a strong state, and "human rights," associated with delinquents. As discussed in chapter 3, human

---

13. Most of these misdemeanors carry a fine, and the ruling was based on the argument that because a fine is a form of debt to the state and because the constitution prohibits incarceration for debts, detentions for misdemeanors are illegal.

rights groups then often find themselves on the defensive over abuses by the police. Though such abuses are among the most extensive form of rights violations in the region, they are skillfully portrayed as a necessary price for crime control. Indeed, one of the five principal problems that Ecuador's police defined is that "Human Rights Organisms have carried out campaigns to discredit the Police Institution, which has affected the morale of its members" (Policía Nacional de Ecuador 2006).

3. Police Career: From Recruitment to Advanced Training

In Latin America the regulations that detail each stage of an officer's job are mocked by the irregularities that most affect it. Such weaknesses complicate agency restructuring, community policing, and any other reform that entails some change in an officer's responsibilities or evaluation. The contradictions between police career laws and practices begin with recruitment, which in most countries falls short on entrance requirements and incorporating a representative cross section of the population. El Salvador's rush to deploy its postwar police allowed many youth gang members into the force (Call 2003b), and in Guatemala's rush to fill its police ranks after the civil war, nearly one-third of its officers did not fulfill the minimum education requirements and nearly half received less than three months of training (Sequén-Monchéz 2003, 148). Many NGOs and reformers point out the short training periods and advocate lengthening them. The average length of training for new recruits in Latin America is six months, which is short but arguably adequate if the expectations and standards of the training are high. Basic training in the New York Police Department's academy is also six months, but recruits must meet stringent standards. One wrong answer on the use-of-arms exam, for example, results in automatic dismissal.

A lack of clarity in expectations also tends to attract applicants for reasons not associated with the professionalism or reality of the job. Many come from police families or seek steady employment, but others, in part because recruiters fail to disavow such ideas, have exaggerated visions of their law enforcement prowess, or, like some cadets in Peru's central police academy, admit their attraction to the unofficial financial benefits.[14] Lim-

14. Escuela de Altos Estudios Policiales, Policía Nacional de Perú (Advanced School of Police Studies, National Police of Peru), interview by author, Lima, June 18, 2001.

ited and uneven training then continues into the force. In the Dominican Republic, where about 80 percent of police personnel did not graduate from the police academy, only 20 percent are promoted based on their official levels of training and preparation (Bobea 2003, 217). Miami, Florida, has also learned that the drawbacks of fast recruitment often outweigh the advantages of recruiting more officers over a short time period (see Dorschner 1993). Without quality control, this approach can produce more slain crime suspects, a declining quality in written police reports, internal conflicts over issues such as promotion, and more administrative demands that draw energy away from daily law enforcement.

Throughout Latin America, academies for both high- and low-ranking officers have gradually responded to their weaknesses. Most have expanded their curricula to incorporate subjects such as human rights and the perspectives of civilian specialists. In addition to collaboration with local universities (discussed in chapter 7), the growth of security studies by private universities has also widened the educational base of the police. In some countries and provinces the focus of reform on the academy has paid off. In Uruguay the Escuela Nacional de Policía (National School of Police) has some of the region's best facilities and extensive curricula, both of which have contributed to the higher morale among officers and citizens' trust of them. This impact has even allowed the academy, according to its director, to expand in a time of financial cutbacks.[15] But in most countries police academies have not fundamentally altered the basic emphasis on physical preparation and formalistic knowledge of laws rather than critical analysis, open discussion, and application to societal realities. In Venezuela the police themselves rate their basic training as poor—particularly on social conditions, firearm use, and human rights.[16] Because the police have depended historically on the military for training and intelligence, the military's "logic of arbitrary repression" (Kruijt and Koonings 1999, 10) and "indiscriminate stigmatization of adversaries" (Koonings 2003) have been ingrained into the preparation of Latin American police officers. As discussed in chapters 4–6, many police academy directors and teachers around the region feel too constrained by expectations to experiment with new approaches. Moreover, the great majority of academy directors seem to be either long-serving vet-

15. Celso Rodríguez, director, Escuela Nacional de Policía, interview by author, Montevideo, August 20, 2003.
16. Inspectors and subinspectors receive up to four years of education, but most Metropolitan Police officers receive only three months.

erans whose embrace of new approaches is limited or outsiders whose ambitious plans dissolve amid internal intransigence. In other words, the first
skirmish between traditional and problem-oriented policing often takes
place in the police academies.

In most countries such educational deficits are being addressed through
programs sponsored by NGOs and universities. But such efforts tend to be
geared toward particular specializations without subsequent coordination
with human resource planning. In fact, as discussed in this book, a perennial problem is that few officers actually work in the areas in which they
were trained. For example, fewer than fifteen of the thousands of police
trained as investigators in Guatemala are actually working as investigators
(Scheye 2005, 2), while in Venezuela just 52 percent of officers carry out
patrols, investigations, or other activities related to citizen security (El
Achkar, forthcoming). This problem extends from the lower-level officers
used as guards and drivers to the higher-level officials who are never able
to use the specialized training they received in areas such as financial or
other white-collar crime. Even in Costa Rica, where the police have more
political and financial support than do those in most other countries, officers complain about the paucity of educational opportunities, about promotion procedures that do not take into account educational background,
and about the courses they do take that lead to a miserly 1.5 percent increase
in salary.[17] Higher-ranking officers often stress the lack of coordination between police academy and higher-education courses, because they are
taught by different institutions and often in different locations. In the middle ranks, officers sent abroad for foreign training are often marginalized
once they return, because the training itself is considered a perk (probably
awarded unfairly, in other officers' eyes) rather than a step toward institutional change. In addition, in response to recent educational improvements,
the better-educated officers are held back in the lower and middle ranks by
superiors suspicious of their new approaches. When imposed from outside,
such educational opportunities are often rejected as patronizing external
criticisms of the country's own police training.

Education can be bolstered through its link to promotion. In nearly every
country certain courses are required for moving up. But in the promotion
process successful completion of those courses is often outweighed by less
objective criteria. Indeed, promotion in most police agencies is not based
on a critical evaluation of positive actions or specific skill development. In-

17. Police officials, interviews by author, San José, Costa Rica, June 18–30, 2006.

stead, it depends almost entirely on the officer's seniority, academy exam score, ranking, and whether he or she has caused any problems. Most forms used for individual promotion are usually one or two pages, with few if any probing questions about the agent's actual police work. Enough officers jump ranks through extraordinary means to elicit vehement complaints among the lower ranks throughout the region. Such favoritism can result in officers being rejected for advancement without cause or assigned to high-crime districts.

All of these educational shortcomings harm policing by limiting officers' abilities to detect the causes of crime, to adapt to changing situations, and to convince their superiors to incorporate new ideas about police work in policy. The scant coordination between the police and social services on problems such as drug abuse also limits the ability of the police to develop and promote such changes—for example, categorizing at-risk youth in different neighborhoods. This dearth of new approaches at the top then depresses incentives for new approaches at the bottom, particularly in the high-crime urban areas where they are most needed. Any positive steps that individual officers do manage to take are then often lost by changes in minister, policy, or chief. Automatic rotation, which officially happens every two years in most countries, makes it particularly difficult for officers to follow the professional track so neatly outlined in police career laws. In some countries or within certain ranks or units, and often unofficially, rotation can be even more frequent. In Guatemala, for example, *comisarios* often rotate within a period of less than one year, which is problematic in such an ethnically diverse country, where it takes time for officers to understand each of the communities they serve.

4. Police Structure: Hierarchy, Decentralization, and Proliferation

Like other state services, security has been decentralized and outsourced throughout Latin America in the current democratic era. This process has spread along three main dimensions: (1) the decentralization of the police force into geographically defined agencies; (2) a functional breakup of the police into units based on functional specializations (such as preventive, investigative, traffic, penitentiary, and special crimes units); and (3) the growth of private security enterprises that have taken on many police services. Most of these changes, particularly the breakup of powerful national police forces, were overdue. The formation of local police forces allows the municipalities to tailor policy to local conditions, in particular, while the functional separation allows a sharper focus on different crimes and the formation of special units allows the police to adopt cool names such as the "Leopards" and the "Cobras." As discussed in the sections that follow, however, the complications created by these changes often overwhelm their advantages.

Geographically Defined Agencies

As Schumpeter (1950), Dahl (1998), Oxhorn, Tulchin, and Selee (2004), and others recognize, decentralization can improve many areas of state service, because governments usually respond better to citizens when they are closer to them—particularly in services with heavy societal contact such as policing (see Ostrom 1975). Decentralization can also bolster democracy by allowing minorities to use the smaller political arenas to press their demands (as indigenous groups in Indonesia and Mexico are doing) or through local initiatives for equitable resource reallocation (such as participatory budgeting in many Latin American municipalities).

Like many broad changes in governance, however, decentralization often lacks adequate policy deliberation, political objectivity, or operational justification. This is particularly true of citizen security, where provincial and local police are created too quickly, often because they are the easiest way in which the government can respond to political pressures from below or break up poorly functioning national forces. In Ecuador, for example, municipal governments began enacting security programs because of the lack of a national plan (Pontón 2005). Municipal guards in Chile and Guatemala, a precursor of local policing, were also created through local initiatives (Frühling 2003). But without careful preparation, provincial and municipal forces repeat and often amplify the poor management, accountability, and policies of their national progenitors. Although crime does not get simpler at the local level, the range of agencies to deal with it is narrower, giving local executives a smaller base of expertise and support.

Decentralization also accentuates executive and legislative imbalances. Compared with their national counterparts, provincial legislatures and municipal councils have less of the political leverage, information, and funding needed to regulate police action. In Costa Rica the local police lack regulatory statutes that clearly demarcate their roles from those of the national police. Above all, decentralization highlights financial differences by making local areas more protective of their own security budgets. Throughout Latin America this situation has engrained differences in policing quality by allowing wealthy areas to bankroll their own vastly superior security agencies.

Even the most carefully delineated decentralization efforts also raise tensions among federal, regional, and local governments. Broadly understood as the transfer of fiscal, administrative, and political power to various subnational levels, decentralization falls into three main approaches: (1) deconcentration, in which administrative offices are physically dispersed but policy control remains at the center (see figure 5.1 in chapter 5 on Bolivia's national police structure); (2) delegation, in which some decision-making authority is transferred to the subnational level; and (3) devolution, in which maximum decision-making authority is handed over to subnational governments. Because security requires national policies, a decentralized security system usually adopts one of the first two approaches, allowing national officials to retain policy and often operational control. In addition, as Willis, Garman, and Haggard (1999) point out, when decentralization is carried out by strong national parties—as in most of Latin America—the federal government retains more control than when decentralization is implemented under multiple parties that leverage regional power. When decentralization comes laden with political conditions—what one officer calls an "all strings attached" relationship—the local autonomy central to success is limited. One form of such continuing central control is the use of the military in policing. As this book discusses, the armed forces are brought into police operations through many routes: special raids (such as against gangs), takeovers of high-crime areas (such as in Buenos Aires Province), the formation of joint military-police units (such as the antidrug units in the Andes), and control over issues such as narco-trafficking. The process of decentralization itself can be destabilizing. Mexico City increased insecurity by creating "gaps in authority and power" that cause greater police abuse and corruption as new and old agencies jockey for power and territory (Davis 2003).

Functional Breakup

A second form of police propagation is a breakup into units based on functional specializations, which is also long overdue. But even the rudimentary separation into preventive agencies (to prevent violations) and judicial agencies (to investigate them) is often plagued by poor coordination, overlapping activities, and spotty oversight. Such problems are amplified when agencies are placed under different ministries. For example, Costa Rica's eleven different police forces belong to five national ministries as well as to the judiciary and municipal governments. But the more agencies chasing after the same problem, the more likely they are to trip over each other in policy and logistics. For example, discord often arises between the more socially focused local drug policy and the more repressive national militarized approaches, while control over international goods often involves clashes among military, border, and customs units. Moreover, the increasingly international scope of crime contrasts with the limited internal jurisdictions of police forces, and the flow across borders of some of the most lethal forms of violence in Latin America—from gang wars to contraband—flourishes amid unsynchronized policing. And yet steps to coordinate or centralize these bodies can foment intrainstitutional conflict, such as that among Italy's three national police forces and between city police and the Interior Ministry police in France. By contrast, in the United States geographic and political separation has resulted in a proliferation of police forces with minimal institutional conflict. But Latin America, with its own particular historical legacies and geographic disparities, has the worst of both worlds: institutionally rigid and politically powerful police at the federal level and more unprofessional and unaccountable agencies at the provincial and municipal levels.

At times, proliferation has been more bureaucratic than functional. As one Bolivian planner remarked, the organizational diagram of his police force began to resemble a Christmas tree with new units hung on them like ornaments. One trendy form of such decentralization is "touristization," in which areas of high visitor traffic get extra deployments or even their own police, such as in Mexico City, Guayaquil, and Caracas. Although such a strategy may make sense by providing extra security in areas of high vulnerability and consumption, it can also perpetuate geographic divisions, as discussed in the next chapter. Creating new units may also be a way to marginalize issues such as human rights or community policing while appearing, for public relations purposes, to prioritize them. And when new units are integrated into daily operations, their growing number slows down decision making and dilutes implementation. Often, old units continue to operate despite having been officially dismantled. Particularly in the areas of internal affairs and antinarcotics, agencies have used their institutional powers to withstand the will of civilian overseers, showing the kind of skillful adaptation to external shocks discussed in chapter 1.

Venezuela demonstrates the downside of decentralization. The country has twenty-four state forces and ninety-nine municipal forces, with 126 police agencies, 105 of which were formed after enactment of the 1989 Decentralization Law (a 363 percent increase between 1990 and 2006).[18] In addition to the Body of Scientific, Penal, and Criminal Investigations (Cuerpo de Investigaciones Científicas, Penales y Criminalísticas, CICPC) and the Office of Intelligence and Prevention Services (Dirección Sectoral de los Servicios de Inteligencia y Prevención, DISIP), military police forces are also involved in policing, including the Defense Ministry's Office of Military Intelligence (Dirección de Inteligencia Militar), the Office of Army Intelligence (Dirección de Inteligencia del Ejército, DIE), and the National Guard (Guardia Nacional, GN). The military police overlap with state and municipal police, often with friction. In 2001, for example, GN personnel were forcibly placed in the stations of the Federal District's Metropolitan Police (Policía Metropolitana, PM),[19] which operates alongside nearly a dozen municipal forces in the Federal District. As in other countries, such Balkanized arrangements place the burden on local governments and cause wide disparities in service. Caracas, which has one of the largest and most varied police networks of any city, has surpassed South Africa's Cape Town as the world's most crime-ridden city; according to the Justice Ministry, it was the scene of an astonishing 152 murders a week in 2008.[20] The wealthy eastern half of the city has ten times more police officers than the poor western half, which has over 70 percent of the city's residents and most of its crime. Over two-thirds of all criminal reports originate in the biggest western municipality, Libertador.[21] Such differences are repeated throughout Latin America. In Medellín, Colombia, the poorer Zone 1 has a homicide

18. Venezuela has an average of 457 officers per 100,000 inhabitants, but in seventeen of twenty-four states the number of officers is below the standard of 350 per 100,000 inhabitants (El Achkar forthcoming).

19. In early 2001 six hundred GN officers were deployed in key parts of the capital, in part to take over many of the areas not being covered by striking local police. Using checkpoints at key intersections—and seizing massive amounts of narcotics and large numbers of vehicles, crime suspects, and weapons—they lowered the crime rate in the first six months of 2001 by 16 percent. "Hubo sólo 5 homicidios en áreas cuidadas por el GN," *El Nacional,* July 18, 2001.

20. Associated Press, "Hundreds Protest Violent Crime in Venezuela," June 21, 2009.

21. "El avance fué muy escaso," *El Universal,* July 23, 2001, 4–1. By investing 33 percent of municipal income in security during the 1990s, the mayor of Baruta municipality was able to reduce its crime rate by nearly a third.

rate of 101 per 100,000 persons, while the rate in the wealthier Zone 5 is just 27 per 100,000 persons (RCMP 2006).

Private Security

Perhaps the biggest form of proliferation in policing has taken place in the private rather than the public sphere. Throughout Latin America private security agencies have grown rapidly in the democratic era. In Venezuela, for example, the number of private security firms has quintupled since the 1990s (Sanjuán 2003, 122). This surge has led, as the next chapter discusses, to a greater number of private officers than public officers in most Latin American cities. This growth clearly represents societal demands to fill the gaps left by poor public police services. But like the expansion of local, functional, and specialized forces, private firms complicate basic policing and coordination. In addition, more than state police forces, they pose a challenge to the nature and legitimacy of the state itself by questioning the government's ability to fulfill one of its most fundamental tasks.

5. Management: From Street Patrols to National Budgets

A complex organization like the police, particularly amid changes such as unit proliferation, must be well managed. But in Latin America police management is weak for a host of reasons. During the first years of the recent democratic transition, most of those reasons were external as sudden democratic expectations and harried decentralization bore down on the police's fossilized hierarchies and inflexibly militarized structures. Growing awareness of these weaknesses since then has led to more deliberate comprehensive steps to improve management, such as more accountable appointments. But failure to synchronize those steps with internal practices—in particular, relations among ranks and the use of human and financial resources—has limited results.

Poor management affects an entire force, but is most evident and damaging in the police station (*comisaría*), the heart of crime fighting. The mid- and low-ranking officers that staff *comisarías* do not have enough autonomy, are punished for mistakes, and are not encouraged to undertake innovation. Together, professional insecurity and arbitrary discipline discourage them from developing ideas, projects, or other forms of problem-oriented policing. In most areas they usually just monitor a single corner without training in proactive crime prevention.[22] Meanwhile, rotation and exhausting work schedules make officials both resentful and reluctant to take on the extra work needed to implement new policies.[23] These built-in disincentives not only shape daily policing but also undercut the structural reorganization that tries to make it better.

Instead of embedded management practices, much of the debate over human resources in Latin America is instead over the scarcity of police. Although countries vary greatly, the regional average is one officer for every three to four hundred persons, leading to calls for more personnel. But this rate is not particularly low (New York and other large cities have about one for every two hundred persons), and increases in numbers unaccompanied by structural reform or citizen trust do not bring more security. In fact, a comparison of large U.S. cities shows no correlation between police numbers and crime rates.[24] Furthermore, low numbers of active officers usually reflect the poor management of resources more than their scarcity. In the United States roughly 60 percent of officers are on patrol, and because most agencies are divided into shifts, only about 15 percent of a force is out at any given time (Bayley 1998, 29). These percentages are similar to those reported by Latin American police. But regionwide the police presence is thinned further by the inordinate amount of time it takes officers to complete forms (calculated as on-duty time) and the use of street officers for special assignments, for traffic patrol, or as guards for officials, buildings, and government installations.[25] So not only does the use of human resources lower the actual police presence below that in official reports, but it also adds to the disgruntlement of officials when they are actually out on patrol. As this book's case studies describe, however, a facade of resistance covers up the real interest in change within the lower ranks. Street officers are far more open to change than their superiors are willing to recognize (or interested in recognizing) because the ineffectiveness of the ad hoc operations that determine their work is so evident to street officers on a daily

22. Commissioner, subcommissioner, and two subcommissioned officers, PFA Comisaría 32, interviews by author, Buenos Aires, May 25, 2004; Mittrany (2008).

23. With their average seventy-hour workweek, most Venezuelan police officers work 40 percent more than other state employees. Rafael Rivero M., "Cuánto y qué gana un policía," *Diario de Caracas,* June 14, 1990, 20.

24. Sewell Chan, "Counting Heads along the Thin Blue Line," *New York Times,* March 26, 2006.

25. In Guatemala such use is blamed for the police force's scarce coverage of national territory (Sequén-Monchéz 2003, 147).

basis. However, the blame for this ineffectiveness and the burden of addressing it fall mainly on their superiors. When they remain unaddressed, such fundamental differences in experience and responsibility then deepen divisions within a police force.

Technology can only go so far in improving policing under such conditions. Mapping and results-based programs such as CompStat (short for Computer or Comparative Statistics) are being introduced in the region to help police respond more quickly and accurately to crime statistics and patterns. New York and other early adopters found that such programs brought police together with prosecutors, probation and parole officers, and other criminal justice officials. At these meetings police chiefs are questioned on crime patterns in their districts, and response strategies are developed by all participants. However, as this book discusses, CompStat and similar programs in many Latin American cities stop at politically uncomfortable questions about how statistics and human resources have been handled. The numbers produced by CompStat are publicized, but not followed up in the service of problem-oriented policing to identify chronic perpetrators, weapon types, and other information that can prevent future assaults rather than simply respond to prior ones. Unless such an information system is hooked into management, it becomes an electronic white elephant.

In 2000 former New York City police chief William J. Bratton developed a plan for the metropolitan police in the Federal District of Venezuela. Centered on model stations, small kiosks, and CompStat, the plan brought murder rates down from 236 between January and June 2000 to 132 for the same period in 2001, with a 30 percent fall in crimes in other areas.[26] But structural weakness ultimately led to the plan's undoing. Police chiefs in many areas had no control over their personnel, who often did not show up, making implementation difficult. A basic level of trust by residents was also lacking, and even the model stations and kiosks did not provide the hoped-for sense of security; indeed, several people were killed right in front of some them.[27] The benefits of such programs come not from their technology, but from channeling updates on the causes of crime up and down the chain of command between policymakers and police stations. But as information is blocked and distorted along these channels, such technology is often adopted as a solution rather than as the instrument it is.

<hr />

26. William J. Bratton and William Andrews. "Driving Out the Crime Wave: The Police Methods that Worked in New York City Can Work in Latin America," *Time,* July 23, 2001.

27. "Roban y matan a taxista frente a módulo policia," *El Universal,* July 4, 2001.

Corruption complicates efforts to tackle such management problems. It is universally cited in the citizen security literature, but its patterns, sources, and connections are understudied. As this book describes, there are three main levels or forms of police corruption. The most common are the innumerable petty acts by individual officers. Among the lower ranks who patrol traffic and the streets, unchecked corruption often supersedes policy and training as the main determinants of their schedules and community relations. A second higher-level form of corruption is that found in police agencies, most often perpetrated by those in charge of fines, issuance of identification cards, customs, or other areas involving goods or fees. As discussed in the following chapters, corrupt agencies affect the functioning of the entire criminal justice system. A third level of corruption is the money in "official" financial transactions that is embezzled in contracts, skimmed from budgets, or sliced out of other "routine" transfers. Such illicitly gained funds allow chiefs to loosen the strings to which the government budget is attached.

Anticorruption efforts to stem these and other harms usually focus on internal accountability. But often overlooked is how the larger political structure has allowed finances to become one of the least transparent but greatest sources of police power. Formally, in nearly every country the legislature and the executive (usually the finance minister) determine and approve the police budget; controllers, ombudsmen, and other units have some accounting oversight. In reality, though, the police propose a budget, and it is either approved or altered by a certain percentage, depending on the overall budget needs and the political power of the police at the time. Very little debate is held over the specific use of different budget items, thereby missing an important opportunity to review police efficacy, management, and internal power relations. As members of the legislatures in several countries acknowledge, scrutiny of police budgets gets lost amid the more urgent or controversial issues that accompany the yearly budget process.

Compounding this neglect is the inattention to the perennially unresolved debates over financial issues such as salaries. Low salaries are the most common explanation for at least the first and second levels of corruption. In most countries the lowest-ranking officers earn $200 a month and the highest-ranking about $750 (El Achkar forthcoming). Thus officers say that the current salaries would have to triple to provide an adequate income. But for several reasons governments are reluctant to raise them. For one thing, they believe (and not unreasonably) that low salaries are more than compensated for by bribery and other sources of funds. However, both scholarship (see Rose-Ackerman 1999) and experience counsel against simple salary increases as a solution. For example, to curb the high levels of corruption between 2004 and 2007, Tijuana, Mexico, raised the salaries of most municipal police officers to a rate higher than that of any of their colleagues around the country, but the increases did not put a dent in organized crime's hold on the officers.

On another level, salaries already make up the bulk of police budgets in nearly every country, and so legislators are even more reluctant to increase them. However, because of mismanagement, salaries rarely provide a stable standard of living. For example, over 70 percent of Nicaragua's police budget goes to salaries (Bautista Lara 2006, 71–73), and yet only in 2002 did it cover basic food costs, which inflation then drove up. At the same time police still lack adequate budgets for basic items such as equipment. The Ecuadorian police estimate that the equipment such as vehicles and munitions currently available is only 25 percent of what is needed and that the general budget is only half of what it should be (Policía Nacional de Ecuador 2003). Thus without more careful accounting, increases in salary are unlikely to provide the expected return in either individual well-being or collective effectiveness.

6. Information

Crime statistics are the starting point for citizen security policy, but throughout Latin America they are uneven, incomplete, and unreliable. As this book discusses, the reasons for such inadequacy include incomplete survey data, dismissal of noncriminal information, and the ways in which police and statistics agencies report, or fail to report, crimes. Often there are great discrepancies in reporting by different agencies, and most processes of collection and compilation are not particularly scientific. In smaller stations, attending officers frequently jot down reports in log books with little room for detail and without standardization. In Venezuela about one-third of all crimes are reported to the disparate offices of the judicial police, which lack a mechanism to consolidate and channel them, or even to include the crime reports received, managed, and retained by state and local agencies.

One of the biggest gaps in Latin American crime statistics is the *cifra negra* (black figure) of crimes not reported at all. In Mexico and Argentina this figure amounts to 70–75 percent of all crimes, between 60 and 80 percent in Venezuela, just over half in Nicaragua, and nearly two-thirds in Colombia, Guatemala, and El Salvador (Bautista Lara 2006, 122).[28] However, these numbers may be as unreliable as crime statistics, because only good victimization surveys elicit citizen openness. Such unreliability is revealed by looking comparatively at the reported numbers. In Costa Rica, for example, police estimate a *cifra negra* of 70 percent, which is among the highest in the region and contrasts with the country's relatively low rate of crime and good relations with society. Therefore, this figure probably reveals both the underestimates in other countries as well as Costa Rica's relatively more honest efforts to report this rate accurately.

The crime-reporting problems are on clear display in table 2.1. Like the *cifra negra,* the more complete and consistent numbers from countries with lower crime rates such as Chile, Costa Rica, and Uruguay reveal better reporting. In Chile numbers vary because some years they include attempted as well as committed crimes. Crime reports in most other countries are characterized by unreliable or unreported statistics for many years since the 1990s. Of the numbers that are reported, there are often improbable jumps or drops from year to year. In Colombia and other countries, such changes are caused by reliance on different sources, with the police reporting lower numbers.

Documentation of particular crimes or criminality in general is only as useful as its reliability. Although crime reporting and tracking are improving, the resulting statistics still provide only the roughest of guides for crime policy. Throughout Latin America the lack of reliable crime statistics bedevils not just the police, but also congresses, ombudsmen, and other agencies trying to monitor and evaluate crime policy. As poor statistics extend into the criminal justice system, the management of victimization, detentions, and trials becomes more difficult.

Of all major crimes, the two reported most reliably are homicide, the most serious crime, and auto theft, reported for insurance purposes. Even though it is a partial and imperfect proxy for crime, homicide is used here to map general statistical reliability across countries—an approach adopted by other studies such as those by Fajnzylber, Lederman, and Loayza (2000) and Camara and Salama (2004). Appendix A lists Latin America's homicide rates for each year between 1995 and 2009. It includes the lowest and high-

---

28. In Venezuela the figure of 80 percent is based on a poll of ten thousand Venezuelans in which only 11 percent of those who said they were crime victims reported the crimes (Sanjuán 2003, 120). The estimate of 60 percent is from the Venezuelan Violence Observatory (Observatorio Venezolano de Violencia 2007).

Table 2.1 National Crime Rates, 1997–2006 (per 100,000 persons)

Country	1997	1998	1999	2000	2001	2002	2003	2004	2005	2006
Argentina	2,275	2,557	2,902	3,054	3,197	3,675	1,550[a]	n.a.	3,115	3,128
Bolivia	1,837	2,535	n.a.	580	436	353	372[a]	380	317	337
Brazil	n.a.	n.a.	n.a.	n.a.	2,978[a]	3,251[a]	3,793[a]	n.a.	n.a.	n.a.
Chile	4,396	10,172	10,767	9,276	1,763[a]	1,941[a]	2,322[a]	2,555[a]	n.a.	n.a.
Colombia	579	550	539	506–1,187[a]	2,141[a]	3,453[a]	2,850[a]	n.a.	n.a.	n.a.
Costa Rica	1,279	1,246	1,289	n.a.	1,076	1,021	1,111	1,185	1,145	1,232
Ecuador	n.a.	n.a.	n.a.	n.a.	n.a.	946[a]	703	752	849	815
El Salvador	n.a.	n.a.	n.a.	n.a.	842	696	1,366[a]	1,453[a]	749	n.a.
Guatemala	n.a.	198	200	240	n.a.	n.a.	434[a]	412[a]	n.a.	n.a.
Honduras	n.a.	30.8[a]	n.a.	n.a.	n.a.	n.a.	n.a.	n.a.	n.a.	n.a.
Mexico	n.a.	1,434	1,439	1,391	1,522	1,504	1,778[a]	1,986[a]	1,426	1,460
Nicaragua	n.a.	n.a.	n.a.	n.a.	n.a.	n.a.	n.a.	n.a.	1,906	2,177
Panama	875[b]	n.a.	n.a.	n.a.	757	716	n.a.	n.a.	1,237	1,391
Paraguay	n.a.	89	110	76	n.a.	n.a.	n.a.	n.a.	245	259
Peru	756	n.a.	n.a.	n.a.	601	604	589	618	n.a.	n.a.
Uruguay	n.a.	2,092	2,048	2,222	3,599	3,987	5,534	5,266	n.a.	n.a.
Venezuela	n.a.	1,032	1,042	976	n.a.	n.a.	n.a.	n.a.	n.a.	n.a.

Source: Unless indicated otherwise in a note, United Nations Survey of Crime Trend and Operations of Criminal Justice Systems, Sixth, Seventh, Eighth, Ninth, and Tenth Waves.

Note: The table includes homicide, assault, kidnapping, rape, robbery, theft, attempted robbery and theft, and drug offenses. "n.a." indicates a lack of reliable data for those years.

[a] CEJA (2006).

[b] Author's estimate based on raw numbers reported.

est reliable estimates provided by national police forces, judiciaries, government statistics agencies, independent observatories, and academic researchers. A quick review of this table reveals two major gaps. The first is the wide gap in numbers in many years; the second is the variations between concurrent years, with statistically improbable oscillations.

Aside from chronic underreporting, these gaps reflect at least four discrepancies that expose the weakness of crime statistics in Latin America. First, numbers reported by international agencies often conflict with each other. For example, the Inter-American Development Bank (IADB) reports a homicide rate of 19.7 per 100,000 persons in 2000 in Brazil, whereas the Pan American Health Organization (PAHO) cites a rate of 29.3. In Honduras, Interpol reported a homicide rate of 154.2 per 100,000 persons in 1998, far above the rates of 40–60 reported in both the prior and following years by PAHO and that country's police.

Second, estimates based on comparing raw figures with national populations, which nongovernmental sources are more likely to do, tend to be higher than those of national statistical bodies, indicating a pattern of official underreporting. In Costa Rica, for example, the press reported a homicide rate of 25.9 in 2001, whereas the state's Organization of Judicial Investigation (Organización de Investigación Judicial, OIJ) said it was only 6.1. For 2004 the OIJ reported a homicide rate of 212, while the press reported 275.

Third, additional discrepancies arise from the categorization of homicides. Most countries report only *homicidio doloso,* intentional homicide, while others include forms of unintentional homicide, such as involuntary manslaughter, or the general category of "violent deaths," which does not specify deaths that are not technically homicides. Some police distinguish between "homicide" and "murder." Murder refers to the equivalent of first-degree homicide, and homicide refers to all other cases. Although both should be included in homicide rates, reporting only "homicide" lowers the final tally. In Venezuela killings of suspects while "resisting arrest" are not included (and it is a significant number, because thirty-nine suspects are killed for every officer death in "confrontations"). Also excluded are killings in prisons (more than one per day) or other violent deaths that go uncategorized.[29] Statistical utility is also diminished when other forms of homicide are not separated out, such as when killings by police or criminal suspects are folded into the final tally—a number that accounts for up to one

29. "Deadly Message," *The Economist,* July 19, 2008, 47.

in five homicides in countries such as the Dominican Republic. The extreme swings and questionable variations in crime reports that result from this methodological sloppiness, such as the Dominican Republic's report of a 100 percent increase in youth crime (Bobea 2003, 194), demonstrate their lack of reliability.

A fourth discrepancy is among criminal justice agencies. In Brazil the homicide rates reported each year by the civil and military police differ almost continually by two hundred homicides (Ribeiro 2007). In El Salvador until 2004 there were consistent gaps of between 20 and 40 per 100,000 persons in the homicide rates reported by the National Civil Police (Policía Nacional Civil, PNC), the Attorney General of the Republic (Fiscalía General de la República, FGR), and the Institute of Forensic Medicine (Instituto de Medicina Legal, IML)—see Pleitez Chávez (2006, 13) and Savenije and Van der Borgh (2004, 157).[30] But in 2005 these three agencies formed the Technical Homicide Board (Mesa Técnica de Homicidios), which, together with outside agencies such as the Observatorio Centroamericano sobre Violencia (OCAVI), has verified and consolidated reports. As a result, differences for 2005 narrowed considerably, from police estimates of 47.7[31] to OCAVI's estimates of 55.0 per 100,000 persons.

Although not all countries adopted such official changes in statistics collection, the narrowing gap in reported numbers does indicate improved coordination and accuracy in general. Studies that examine and document trends over time generally report more consistent numbers. PAHO's estimations of Costa Rican homicides, for example, were in the range of 7.0–8.0 between 1996 and 2005. Statistics also tend to be most reliable in urban areas when collected by groups such as the UN-funded Violence Observatories or by a consortium of agencies (see chapter 7). In Quito, for example, information is compiled by an Interinstitutional Technical Committee composed of the police, prosecutor, National Gender Office, public hospitals, and academic institutions. Overall, the more consistent statistics are from the region's stronger states, such as Argentina, Chile, Costa Rica, and Uruguay, where homicide rates approximate those of North America. But the high-crime countries are in the majority in the region, and thus that is where clarification is most needed.

---

30. In 2004, for example, the police reported 2,768 homicides and the *fiscal* reported 3,897 (OCAVI 2009).
31. Reported in Observatorio de la Violencia (2007).

Table 2.2 Average Annual Gap between Lower and Upper Homicide Rate Estimates, 1995–2009

Country	Average annual gap
Argentina	2.3
Bolivia	7.1
Brazil	3.9
Chile	3.9
Colombia	10.6
Costa Rica	5.6
Dominican Republic	2.1
Ecuador	2.7
El Salvador	24.7
Guatemala	17.5
Honduras	20.0
Mexico	14.2
Nicaragua	2.4
Panama	0.4
Paraguay	1.1
Peru	2.9
Uruguay	2.0
Venezuela	29.4

Source: See appendix A.

Reflecting these discrepancies, table 2.2 uses the numbers detailed in appendix A to provide the average yearly gap in homicide statistics between 1995 and 2009. Such averages, of course, are a very crude reflection of statistical gaps. Many reports do not cite the source or methodology of their numbers, and yet they are repeated in the media and other studies. As one government ministry official in Bolivia said, his ministry tends to accept any reasonable number because it lacks the ability to evaluate them independently. When the gap is particularly high, as it was for many years in Venezuela, the higher numbers easily become ammunition for those proposing crackdowns. So even when a reported rate is almost certainly too high, it can still be wielded politically. In addition, the average gap in many countries is artificially narrowed in years in which only one reliable statistic is reported, and is exaggerated by outlying numbers far larger than in other reports. But, overall, these averages reveal inherent flaws in crime compilation and reporting in Latin America. In many cases, the average gap exceeds the lower estimate of homicides, affirming that crime statistics should be approached with suspicion.

Because of these problems, countries depend less and less on statistics as a basis for policy, depriving it of an important foundation. Even in Costa Rica's relatively well-supported security structure, the lack of a modern system of information prevents the formation of consistent policies.[32] For example, the 2003–7 plan of the Ecuadorian national police reported a 5.79 percent increase in crime reports but a 5.71 percent decrease in detentions without explaining what accounted for the contrary pattern or how to address it (Policía Nacional de Ecuador 2003).[33] Civilian policymakers, who are just as uncertain about how to critically apply crime statistics to policy, if not more so, often selectively use numbers when approving of stronger policing. Ironically, though, giving the police more power after crime rates rise may reduce their incentives to be more effective crime fighters. Furthermore, if a crime statistic as central and basic as the national homicide rate is unreliable, then so are the abilities of reformers to gather their arguments for change, of legislators to know which areas need emphasis, and of officials to measure progress. Without consistently dependable criminal justice numbers, public officials can find it difficult to know why reforms in community policing and oversight reforms are needed, what they need to address, and whether they are reaching their goals.

7. Criminal Justice: From Crime Scenes to Prisons

Much of the information needed by the judiciary is contained in the evidence and testimony of witnesses uncovered during a criminal investigation. Investigation is the most important task carried out by the police because it is the primary way in which they track down criminals, secure convictions, identify patterns of violence, and prevent future offenses. But officers throughout Latin America are inadequately trained in investigation, and so they haphazardly carry out the steps needed to secure evidence and witnesses such as crime scene protection, coordinated forensics, and cooperative relations with the public. To make up for their lack of preparation, funding, and societal trust, police officers resort to blunt and ineffective tactics such as mass roundups *(razzias)* in poor neighborhoods *(barrios)*, witness intimidation, indiscriminate detentions, and armed "confrontations"

32. Carlos Mora, "Costa Rica atemorizada por el hampa," *La Nación,* April 17, 2006.
33. Policía Nacional de Ecuador, *Plan estratégico para el Quinquenio 2003–2007,* Quito.

that end in the suspects' deaths. For example, although Venezuelan law clearly states that the police may take only an "informative" declaration from detainees and that *fiscales* must monitor detainee rights in police stations, in practice the police take many declarations in station basements without observation.[34] Even though such tactics may "resolve" or rustle up enough material for a particular case, each time they sacrifice a bit of future effectiveness.

Coming at the beginning of the investigative process, such tactics also taint the rest of it. Although reform packages are placing a greater emphasis on technical training in criminal investigation, nearly every country still allots far more material and human resources to preventive policing than to investigative policing. In fact, no judicial police budget receives more than 5–10 percent of the total security allocation. A case in point is Venezuela's CICPC, whose budget has barely risen since 1999. Its Homicide Division has just a single ballistic analysis team, and the agency says it needs to triple its ten thousand officials.[35] In the United States about 15 percent of police officers carry out investigations—a low number, but far higher than that in most Latin American countries, which hovers between 2 and 10 percent (Bayley 1998, 71).[36] Not only are the numbers of investigative police low, but they are undermined by competition from the preventive police forces, a lack of forensic and technical support, and chronic judicial delays.

The investigative incapacity of the police is often matched by that of the judiciary—a fact readily used by the police to redirect blame for insecurity and impunity, particularly when the courts manage to fall below the police in public opinion polls. But like the police, criminal justice officials such as judges, prosecutors, and public defenders lack the budget, training, and autonomy to carry out their jobs fairly and efficiently. Meanwhile, their efforts to overcome common institutional constraints or assess important areas such as rehabilitation and alternative sentencing are drowned out by the technical and politicized accusations that ricochet around the criminal justice system. For example, when police grouse about the release of a detainee for "technical" reasons, such "clemency" usually stems less from a judge's

34. Carolina Oliva, liaison with legislature, Office of the Attorney General, interview by author, Caracas, April 6, 1995.

35. Jerssen Mojica, inspector, CICPC, interview by author, Caracas, February 26, 2003.

36. About 2 percent of all Venezuelan police officials work in investigation, and the rest carry out patrols or administrative tasks. Victor Amram Lazes, commissioner, PTJ, interview by author, Caracas, July 2, 1998.

leniency than from other factors such as prison overcrowding or a lack of appropriate treatment programs.

New penal process codes, the cornerstone of criminal justice reform in contemporary Latin America, have the potential to overcome such problems. In many countries the codes have produced impressive results—but primarily at the beginning. In Nicaragua citizen crime reports rose by 4 percent and police detention dropped by 30 percent in the first year after the new code went into effect in 2004. Along with new conditional release laws, Venezuela's new code led to a nearly 40 percent drop in the prison population between mid-1999 and mid-2000. As criminal justice officials took advantage of alternative sentencing to reduce backlogs, similar results were seen in other countries. But as time has passed and crime has continued its relentless rise, the codes have become increasingly exposed politically. In most countries they have become a convenient target and are blamed for fostering crime and impunity by protecting criminals' rights (see Sieder 2004; Rocha Gómez 2007). Grappling with the demands of the new codes, many officials are only too happy to encourage that view. By introducing new procedures, guarantees, and courts—particularly oral trials—these new codes, by definition, mean an upgrade of the entire criminal justice system. But they are not supported by the funds or training needed to change practices and convince officials to come on board. In Ecuador the new code came into force in 2001, but the government did not form any coordinating agency to oversee its implementation or provide the funds needed for the greatly expanded prosecutor. In Guatemala budgetary constraints have limited language interpretation, which the new code requires, while numerous pretrial motions violate the provision that the criminal dossiers (*sumarios*), which are the complete file of relevant information prepared for a trial, be completed "as soon as possible." In the Dominican Republic the *sumario* is limited to sixty days, but it can be and often is extended as many times as deemed necessary. In other countries new codes lack guarantees for offenses that are "minor" but nevertheless involve extended incarceration without access to counsel.

More attention to the implementation of these codes by criminal justice officials, as well as more citizen support for them, would help to solve these problems. For the police, new codes mean stricter controls on evidence collection, detention, questioning, and level of proof. Not only are police officers under greater scrutiny—a perceived affront to their long-standing autonomy—but their investigative authorities have been given to *fiscales,* who, in turn, have had to learn to run criminal investigations. In Venezuela and Bolivia police accuse *fiscales* of continuing to protect defendants' rights, as they did under the old codes, instead of prosecuting them, which is their responsibility under the new code.[37] Judges appointed in new types of courts face a particularly steep learning curve, but many of them (as police and prosecutors are quick to point out) are ill-prepared for their new responsibilities. Venezuela adopted a new penal code in 1998. The Organic Penal Process Code (Código Orgánico Procesal Penal, COPP) goes further than most other new codes. For example, it allows both judges and citizens (*escabinos*) to head most criminal trials.[38] But good design has not forestalled poor implementation. Saying that "we speak different languages," police inspectors accuse prosecutors of lacking both the will and the training to carry out the COPP. And although the *fiscales* have formulated criteria to implement the COPP,[39] delays and abuses continue in both the MP and the police. Many Venezuelan police agents continue to withhold information from judges, use false witnesses, and tamper with evidence,[40] often justifying such actions with their belief that judges free criminals and that public defenders hide incriminating evidence.

But police continue to blame the COPP rather than their own weaknesses —a position enthusiastically taken up by politicians and the media. In the first year after its approval, Venezuela's new code was subject to a barrage of alarming articles. "The COPP makes police action difficult," admonished one headline. "The police do not detain a criminal because of the COPP," screamed another.[41] A year later, the chief of the CICPC said he attributed the rise in crime to "three fundamental factors . . . the economic crisis, the political transition, and the application of the COPP."[42] And a year after that, the interior minister blamed "high rates of social violence . . . in large part on the COPP." The police of Vargas state, which has some of the coun-

---

37. Mojica, interview.

38. Luis Enrique Oberto, president, Comissión Legislativa, interview by author, Caracas, June 29, 1998; IADB (1998, 5–15).

39. Dilia Parra, director, Instituto de Estudios Superiores, Ministerio Público (Institute of Superior Studies of the Attorney General), interview by author, Caracas, February 25, 2003; Omar Jiménez, prosecutor 18, Guarenas, interview by author, Caracas, February 26, 2003.

40. "La Ley Antidroga es una Patente de Corso de Jueces y Policías," *El Nacional,* September 9, 1988, 12; "PTJ: Un cuerpo que vive entre la enfermedad y la depuración," *Diario de Caracas,* June 21, 1989, 18.

41. First headline, *El Universal,* July 3, 1999; second headline, *El Universal,* July 4, 1999.

42. *El Universal,* February 2, 2000, http://buscador.eluniversal.com.

try's most violent *barrios,* complained that most of their detainees were being released because of code protections.[43] It was certainly true that far
more detainees were being released because of the code's provisions, such
as an emphasis on the presumption of innocence, but studies comparing detention and crime rates demonstrated no impact on crime in Venezuela. And
in fact the number of resolved cases jumped considerably, from just over
86,000 in 1999 to nearly 179,000 in 2003 (Chen, Leonte, and Lopez 2008).
Nevertheless, around the region blame is commonly placed on the penal
process codes. One of the five main security problems in Ecuador, according to its police, is the "implementation of the new Penal Process Code,
which permits detainees of police operation to be put in liberty immediately
by the judicial authorities" (Policía Nacional de Ecuador 2006).

Execution of the new codes is further restrained by the limited number of
criminal justice officials. Throughout Latin America public defenders have
far too many cases to provide adequate defense for the great majority of
them. Most criminal justice officials—particularly public defenders themselves—recommend a maximum of 150 cases, especially because most
Latin American countries make an adequate legal defense a constitutional
right and because public defenders represent about 80 percent of detainees
in most countries. By all measures Costa Rica comes closest to that number,
but is still far from reaching it.[44] In most other countries public defenders estimate that they handle over 320 cases at one time—and those in juvenile
justice well over 400. And these caseloads will only grow because the number of penal cases is rising about 25 percent each year.[45] Public defenders
not only take on far too many cases to deal with most of them effectively,
but also are further slowed by a lack of clarity about "obligations and
duties,"[46] are paid less than most other lawyers, often have little job secu-

43. "Asesinadas 30 personas en el mes de Octubre," *Últimas Noticias,* November 7,
2002, 20.
44. In 1979 each Venezuelan defender *(defensor)* handled an average of under seventy cases; by 1995 the average had shot up to over three hundred (Dirección de Planificación, Consejo de la Judicatura, 1994). Rarely can government and private legal aid
centers make up for such inadequacies. Free legal clinics are underfunded, have high
turnover rates, and are concentrated in capital cities.
45. Montserrat Solano C., "Causas asfixian a la defensa pública," *El País, San José
de Costa Rica,* November 17, 2001.
46. María Antioneta Acuñade, president, Asociación de Defensores Públicos de
Venezuela (Public Defenders Association of Venezuela), interview by author, Caracas,
May 22, 1995. The institutional affiliations of public defense agencies vary; they may
be in the judiciary, in the executive, or on their own.

rity, and are subject to little oversight. In El Salvador higher salaries have created a bigger public defender corps, but working conditions remain poor. Argentina hires "adjunct" defenders *(defensores)* who may weaken due process when up against more experienced *fiscales.* In Rio de Janeiro an estimated 60–70 percent of the small-time drug dealers in prison would not be there if they had better lawyers,[47] and in São Paulo State poor public defense means that only a fraction of offenders benefit from the 1998 alternative sentencing law. Countries are beginning to hire more public defenders, restructure their agencies, and give them more autonomy.[48] But they have a long way to go before public defense meets its constitutional obligations.

These deficiencies contribute to a low percentage of crimes investigated and a low percentage of arrests—between 2 and 5 percent—that lead to conviction. As discussed in this and other chapters, if suspects are not identified quickly there is little chance that the crimes will be solved. In El Salvador fewer than one in ten violent crimes are investigated (Programa Centroamericana de la Federación Luterana Mundial 2005).[49] In Mexico less than 5 percent of crimes and 7 percent of homicides lead to a conviction.[50] In Ecuador only twenty of ninety reported homicides in 2003 led to a detention, and an average of sixty persons were arrested for the 750 crimes that occurred each day (Arroba 2003; Pontón 2005, 369). In Venezuela only 36 percent cases of reported crime were closed, and only 2.7 percent ended in a court sentence (Sanjuán 2003). When crimes are broken down by geography and gender, the rates of crime resolution can fall to especially low levels. In Costa Rica 80 percent of rape cases do not go to trial—even though the victims must often describe the attacks on seven different occasions—and the courts hand down convictions in only half of the 20 percent of cases that they do hear.[51] In Guatemala, which has alarming rates of fem-

47. Julita Lemgruber, ex-chief, state prisons, interview by author, Rio de Janeiro, February 3, 2005; Fraser (2001),

48. Argentina's Act 24.946 of 1998 gave *defensores* more organizational autonomy, created a professional career law, and established mobile defenders *(defensores volantes)* to coordinate the many levels of defenders' work. María López Puleio, attorney coordinator, Defensoría General de la Nación, interview by author, Buenos Aires, December 17, 1996.

49. The crimes covered are homicide and robbery.

50. Centro de Investigación para el Desarrollo, "El subsistema de seguridad ciudadana y justicia penal, y la procuración," CIDAC, June 9, 2003, http://www.cidac.org .vnm/pdf/DFUNAMZEPEDA.pdf; "Critical Threat," *The Economist,* June 15, 2002, 36.

51. Carlos Arguedas, "80 percent de denuncias por el delito de violación no llegan a juicio," *La Nación,* July 3, 2005.

inicide, only 5 of the 1,897 killings of women between 2001 and 2005 resulted in a court conviction.[52] In addition, as discussed in other chapters
the rates of homicide solution tend to be lower in rural areas than in urban
areas. Although the average rate of solution in the Ecuadorian city of
Guayaquil is 30 percent, for example, in many rural provinces it is less than
10 percent.

Such judicial ineffectiveness is also weighed down by other problems
discussed in this chapter such as criminal statistics. In Costa Rica the OIJ,
the investigative wing of the police, exposed big gaps in judicial functioning through a criminological study in San José that connected a majority of
incidents to a specific downtown area and a particular group of generally
young offenders. In the process the OIJ discovered that nearly half of those
arrested had been detained previously and that nearly half of the police's
crime reports on these cases had informational inadequacies that led judges
to throw them out. In many cases the authorities neglected to take notice of
the fact that those who were arrested for one crime were wanted in connection with earlier crimes (Programa Estado de la Nación 2004). Costa Rican officials, who estimate that from one-third to one-half of murders are
not solved,[53] respond to such conditions by complaining of poor cooperation between the preventive Public Force and OIJ detectives.

Finally, throughout the region the failures of the criminal justice process
are most evident in its final stage: prison. Because the police rely on edicts
and because of their "abuse of preventive detention," most people are imprisoned for property- or drug-related crimes.[54] In fact, the Inter-American
Drug Abuse Control Commission (CICAD) of the Organization of American States (OAS) estimates that up to 80 percent of detentions are drug-
related.[55] Because suspects are locked up much faster than the courts can
process them, a regional average of about 60 percent of detainees in Latin
America have not been tried at any given time (see table 2.3), and many

---

52. "Impunity Rules," *The Economist,* November 18, 2006, 40–41.

53. The number of unsolved homicides grew from 28 of 184 in 1995 to 78 of 212 in
2004 (or of 275, depending on the source of homicide statistics). Estimates of 37 percent are given by Álvaro Sánchez Córdoba, "Homicidios son más complicados," *Al Día,*
April 12, 2005, 4; and reports of up to 50 percent by Otto Vargas M., *La Nación,* December 28, 2004, 10.

54. Ingeniero Freixas, ombudsman, Argentina's federal prisons, interview by author,
Buenos Aires, November 3, 1994.

55. Inter-American Drug Abuse Control Commission, Organization of American
States, interviews by author, Washington, DC, February 17, 2005.

wait for trial beyond the two-year limit specified in the regional Pact of San José. Prisons are woefully underfunded, from basic needs such as medicine to rehabilitation services and renovation of dilapidated facilities, and thus the region's penitentiary systems have become inhumanely violent and overcrowded. With the exception of Chile and Mexico, in Latin America prison violence is responsible for hundreds of prisoner deaths each year, with mass riots almost an annual occurrence. Indeed, Latin America has been the site of the most deadly incidents of prison violence in the modern era.

Prison officials say on the record that such conditions result from a shortage of money, but off the record they point to a shortage of political will. The two are, however, closely linked: officials do not fund or back up policies considered soft on crime or criminals. Even alternative sentencing, such as community service for nonviolent or first-time offenders, is often passed over by judges who opt for imprisonment. Indeed, up to 70 percent of cases in Western Europe and North America end with alternative sentences, but in some Latin American countries such as Brazil less than 5 percent of cases do. Venezuela's Assistance Centers, which have helped nearly 130,000 persons and kept recidivism below 4 percent, are underfunded and inconsistently applied (Elia de Molina 1992). In most countries many detainees, such as those held for drug violations, are excluded from bail. Meanwhile, lack of personnel and poor resocialization programs prevent the majority of those eligible for release from being freed. In many countries the "principle of opportunity," in which the prosecutor can offer an alternative to incarceration, is also underused. Thus imprisonment—and all the inefficiencies and abuses that ensue—remains the primary end point of the long criminal justice processes described in this book. Like *homo sacer,* a subject under Roman law who committed a crime that put him beyond legal protection (Agamben 1998), imprisoned criminals are both controlled by the state but beyond the law, and they are in facilities whose practices counter their officially rehabilitative aims. The prisons have also become incubators of crime, offering detainees an opportunity to become more integrated into organized networks, many of which operate freely from within prisons. Thus although imprisonment in Latin America may be the ultimate blow of the iron fist, it also belies the claim of that approach to reduce crime.

The judiciary's role extends beyond specific cases. As in most democracies, the courts have "police power" to rule on the constitutionality and application of police laws and actions. On issues ranging from state power to civil rights, a history of executive dominance and police violence makes this role critical. Although nominally nonpolitical, the judiciary is also highly

Table 2.3 Prison Populations in Latin America, by Country and Category

Country	Prison population (year reported)[a]	Per 100,000 persons	Percentage increase since 1992[b]	Over intended capacity (%)	Unsentenced (%)[d]
Argentina[e]	56,313 (2002)	148	134	40 (prov. avg.)	70 (avg.)
Bolivia[f]	7,207 (2005)	76	33 (est.)	62[c]	75
Brazil[g]	330,642 (2004)	183	145	81[c] (state avg.)	45
Chile[h]	36,374 (2004)	212	58	47[c]–50	51
Colombia[i]	68,545 (2004)	152	102	39	43
Costa Rica[j]	7,619 (2004)	19	114	28[c]–67	moderate
Cuba[k]	55,000 (2003)	487	n.a.	~175	moderate
Dominican Republic	13,836 (2004)	157	28	156[c]–215	74
Ecuador	13,045	100	63	40–43	severe
El Salvador[l]	12,117 (2004)	184	113	7[c]–35	75+
Guatemala[m]	8,307 (2003)	69	n.a.	13[c]	62
Honduras[n]	11,236 (2004)	158	97	109[c]	90
Mexico	191,890 (2004)	182	109	33 (state avg.)	varies by state
Nicaragua[o]	5,610 (2004)	100	n.a.	13[c]	17
Panama[p]	10,630 (2003)	354	120	51[c]–212	moderate
Paraguay[q]	4,088 (1999)	75	n.a.	24–26	80–90
Peru[r]	32,129 (2004)	114	85	41[c]	55
Uruguay[s]	7,100 (2003)	209	117	86	65+
Venezuela[t]	21,342 (2003)	83	–32	13[c]–60	70+

Note: "n.a." indicates data are not available.

a For Brazil, Colombia, Dominican Republic, Ecuador, Mexico, and Nicaragua, the original source is the country's national prison association. Most figures are also reported in Penal Reform International, "Newsletter #40," March 1999, http://www.penalreform.org.

b Agence France Presse, March 1, 2000; Penal Reform International, "Newsletter #40," March 1999, http://www.penalreform.org.

c United Nations Centre for International Crime Prevention (Instituto Latinoamericano de las Naciones Unidas para la Prevención del Delito y Tratamiento del Delincuente, ILANUD).

d International Observatory of Prisons (Observatoire international des prisons), http://www.oip.org; and national prison associations.

e In federal countries with separate provincial penitentiary systems the differences among the systems can be wide.

f Government Ministry, General Office of Penitentiary Regulations (Ministerio de Gobierno, Dirección General de Régimen Penitenciario), http://www.bolivia.gov.bo/BOLIVIA/paginas/sitiosestado.

g *The Economist,* February 24, 2001, 37.

h Dammert (2006).

i National Penitentiary and Jail Institute, Colombia.

j Population estimate: Ministry of Justice, Costa Rica.

k International Centre for Prison Studies, World Prison Population List, 6th ed.; Nils Christie, Oslo University.

l Population estimates: International Corrections and Prisons Association.

m Prison Reform International, "Newsletter #53," December 2003.

n Population estimates: International Corrections and Prisons Association.

o Unsentenced: CEJA (2006).

p International Centre for Prison Studies, World Prison Population List, 6th ed.

q Population estimates: ILANUD.

r National Penitentiary Institute (Instituto Nacional Penitenciario, INPE); Reuters, "Peru Admits Jails Packed with Unsentenced Inmates," April 24, 1996. In that article the justice vice minister said the rate of unsentenced inmates was about 90 percent.

s Navas (2005).

t This drop in the prison population stemmed almost entirely from a reformed 1998 penal process code, which freed many detainees. Since then, the population has risen back to average levels. Sources: Penitentiary Security, Office of Information and the Press Department of the Office of Defense and Civil Protection, Ministry of Justice, Venezuela.

susceptible to political pressures, which in much of Latin America extend from judges' nominations to constitutional jurisprudence. The Backroom party deals in the selection of judges (despite the initial selection of candidates by judicial councils), the use of temporary judges vulnerable to professional reprimand and dismissals, and small judicial budgets (between 2 and 5 percent of the total budget in most countries) also keep the courts off balance and the channels of pressure wide. As for citizen security, court officials acknowledge that the direct and indirect pressure to be tough on crime is most evident in judges' tendencies to choose incarceration over alternative sentencing in cases of violent crime.

Such pressure is also seen in how closely courts hew to a wide interpretation of police power. In contrast to unequivocal court action against abusive authoritarian-era laws are the region's rulings on demonstrably unconstitutional *mano dura* laws. In upholding this legislation, judges tap into a long history of jurisprudence. Since its first use in the 1827 U.S. Supreme Court case *Brown v. State of Maryland* as the authority to limit citizen actions for the good of social order, the term *police power* has been interpreted along a spectrum ranging from narrow conceptualizations limited to specific actions to broad conceptualizations with an all-encompassing promotion of the general good.[56] The broad approach has predominated in Latin America's history, and it has been used to legalize actions such as police control of civil society groups. In 1922 Argentina's Supreme Court extended police jurisdiction to the "general good," including economic matters, and in 1950 it said that the power of the police is "justified by the necessity of the defense and strengthening of morality, health, collective fitness, and the community's economic interests."[57] While less overarching, such legal leaning continues on both police actions and the power of police agencies. Ecuador's judiciary has given special police courts the jurisdiction to try police for offenses not committed as part of their duties, giving precedence to the Police Code over the national constitution. In 2001 Venezuela's Supreme Court ruled that the armed forces can be used to help guarantee public order. In addition, although the "delegation" of legislative

56. *Brown v. Maryland,* 12 Wheaton 419 (1827).

57. *Ercolano c/Lanteri de Renshaw* (*Jurisprudencia Argentina,* 1922, 136:170). The broad approach was dominant in the United States until 1877. See *Aron Rabionovich* (*Jurisprudencia Argentina,* 1950, 217:469). By contrast, most Argentine scholars support the narrow interpretation, citing the dissenting opinion in *Renshaw.* See *Anglo c/Gobierno Nacional* (*Jurisprudencia Argentina,* 1934, 171:366) as an example of wide police powers.

powers to the executive is unconstitutional, a "general delegation" of police power to the executive is often allowed in situations such as emergencies or in the absence of needed norms.

In addition to cutting off a critical legal channel, such jurisprudence reveals ambivalence in democracies' relationships with the law. The state carries out the law but is also bound by it, deriving strength from the consistency and predictability that laws engender, but limited by the oversight and accountability they demand. This balance is most tenuous in times of uncertainty or transition, when state agencies often resist changes in policy, personnel, or government. Even in democratic regimes the daily functions of state agencies are often more suited and accustomed to less constitutional but more efficient internal regulations such as on detentions. But because the law is the only legitimate basis of state action in a democracy, state agencies learn to justify or couch their actions with it. For example, joint police-military raids in poor neighborhoods or searches without a warrant are often retroactively legitimized through "emergency" decrees. On policing, the law may sometimes lead not to a reduction in undemocratic practices but a greater aptitude for hiding them. Instead of simply responding to expansions of police power, judiciaries are supposed to restrict them by delineating the range of acceptable actions by state agencies. For state practices in which monitoring is difficult, that means drawing the tightest legal circle possible around officials' discretion. As discussed in other chapters, because officers must make so many decisions in the course of their work without oversight, discretion is an integral part of policing. Similar to "the hole in a doughnut," discretion "does not exist except as an area left open by a surrounding belt of restriction (Dworkin 1977, 31). As Latin America's courts continue to stick to positivist interpretations that justify law as it is written and overlook its normative intentions, with rulings that rarely venture beyond specific cases to the laws and policies behind them, they loosen that belt of restriction and allow other agencies to expand the discretionary center through exceptions such as curfews and military police actions.

8. Police-Society Relations

It is not surprising that most Latin Americans mistrust their police. In all but four of the region's countries at least two-thirds of the population has little or no confidence in the police. In the other four countries, only about half the population expresses trust in the police.[58] "We just don't see the police do anything," said one resident of the Bolivian city of Sucre. "Crime is not as high here, but they seem to use that to excuse their inaction." Such remarks indicate that the public's dim view of the police goes beyond catching criminals. It is also about the exercise of power in daily policing and how it affects police-society relations. Many complaints by citizens are based on what they regard as a lack of respect and degrading words. At times, such attitudes extend to specific violations such as the failure to ask permission before entering private property. More generally, people suspect any reforms to be Trojan horses to give the police even more power. Indeed, worldwide community policing is equated with "community spying" (Brogden and Nijhar 2005, 14). So even when policy improves and such improvement is recognized by society, building citizen trust also requires changes in the innumerable types of contacts that comprise daily policing.

This relationship goes both ways, with citizen distrust and resentment usually reciprocated fully by the police. Feeling that the complexity and danger of their work are not appreciated and the strain on their personal lives is not acknowledged, many officers begin to see civilians as unsympathetic, unaware, and even aggressive. When police chiefs continue or adopt militaristic and siege mentalities (see Skolnick and Fyfe 1993), the rank-and-file officers are even more likely to believe, as do many in Venezuela, that society sees them "as an enemy."[59] Much of daily policing operates through this prism. In explaining violent contacts with civilians, for example, many police claim that they detected "suspicious attitudes" or had experienced some form of aggression. Such reactions often come as a surprise to the involved civilians when brought up in arbitration forums,

58. Latinobarómetro 2003. The results indicate the percentage of valid responses of "little or no trust" to the question "Would you say that you trust the police a lot, a little or not at all?" The countries in which about half of the people trust the police are Chile, 51 percent; Colombia and Costa Rica, 55 percent; and Uruguay, 49 percent. Other country results: Argentina, 77 percent; Brazil, 63 percent; Costa Rica, 55 percent; El Salvador, 64 percent; Guatemala, 78 percent; Honduras, 67 percent; Mexico, 83 percent; Nicaragua, 62 percent; Panama, 63 percent; Paraguay, 76 percent; Peru, 77 percent; and Venezuela, 78 percent. In Peru 53.1 percent of respondents in a 2007 Lima-area poll disapproved of the police (Instituto de Defensa Legal 2007), and less than one-third of respondents in other polls say they have a lot or some confidence in the police (Mendoza, Hugo, and Neild 2007).

59. Valmore Leegos, CICPC detective, interview by author, Caracas, February 26, 2003.

heightening tensions and stereotypes. But ironically most distrust between citizens and police arises from the same two suspicions: protection of criminals and selectivity in responses to insecurity. Both the police and citizens regard each other as collaborating with criminals and only willing to cooperate when it serves their own interests. "Some police are good and help solve problems," said one shopkeeper in the *colonia* of San Miguel in Tegucigalpa, "but overall they do not do anything besides protect their own interests."

Not only are such views more likely for police agencies (many state agencies operate unperturbed by public distrust or even hostility), but they also can severely undercut their work, mainly because the majority of crime suspects and evidence is brought in by the public. Investigators do not locate suspects based on evidence, as commonly believed, but in practice round up suspects in order to gather the evidence needed to prosecute. Thus the need for cooperation from both detainees and the public at large makes it more difficult and more important to move toward problem-oriented policing. Because cooperation is regarded by most people as risky or a form of collusion, police officers are, in turn, less inclined to promote the kind of societal relations that would reduce reliance on abusive information-gathering tactics.

In addition to harming investigation, such conditions deprive community policing programs (the main channel for problem-oriented policing) of the uncensored dialogue and cooperative policy formulation they require. These conditions also weaken the abilities of these programs to avoid being pulled down into local power relations. The Venezuelan city of Maracaibo created hundreds of Neighborhood Security Committees to support the police, but they largely lack the oversight needed to avoid entanglements with that high-crime city's deep social divisions. Like many state-sponsored reforms, citizen-based security initiatives are often hobbled by the citizens themselves. Neighborhood councils and patrols become co-opted by neighborhood commissioners, by drug traffickers, or by program directors who channel funds to their friends. But more common than domineering neighborhood organizations is the lack of them. Most communities are deficient in the cohesion, finances, and experience needed to form durable groups that can consistently identify the causes of insecurity—much less break down the fear, distrust, and violence that characterize their relationships with the police. As economic trends continue filling poor urban areas with newcomers, even established neighborhoods have difficulty maintaining community organizations, in turn limiting the knowledge and information that reach the police.

Conclusion and a Look Ahead

Interactions among the realms of change outlined in this chapter deepen Latin America's citizen security crisis by multiplying the difficulties of reform. For example, a politicized promotion process helps perpetuate bad management, and weak internal affairs units enable police stonewalling. More broadly, societal unrest or political uncertainty can be used by police to drive a wedge between reformers and executive officials giving priority to short-term stability. Even community policing, designed to avoid all of these traps, can become snared in them because of a lack of agency restructuring and training. With no shortage of police, politicians, and journalists ready to pounce on the weakness in any reform, the failure of a specific program can result in repudiation of the entire problem-oriented approach.

Moreover, as discussed in the next chapter, these realms of change are part of the larger picture of contemporary democracy in Latin America and other regions. Patterns of political power, geographic differences, and societal fragmentation have deep roots in history, many of which democratization accentuates. As a result, problematic political, institutional, legal, and societal conditions are not as amenable to change as reformers often anticipate. But by laying out the connections and joint consequences of these obstacles to change, this chapter and the next outline a framework for understanding how to overcome them. On this basis, the case studies and concluding chapters that follow show how the citizen security crisis can be more precisely addressed in both theory and policy.

Chapter 3

Citizen Security and Democracy

Citizen security has become a crisis in Latin America, primarily by feeding off the weaknesses of democracy. Frustration over crime and disorder has led to the biggest public protests since the regional transition to democracy in the 1980s and has helped to trigger the collapse of six constitutional governments since 2000. Presidents were forced out in Argentina, Bolivia (twice), Ecuador, Honduras, and Venezuela (temporarily). One United Nations report on eighteen Latin American countries found that a majority of people would support an authoritarian regime if it solved their country's problems, of which crime is a principal one.[1]

Leading up to and beyond such attitudes and breakdowns, however, is crime's corrosion of everyday life. Amid political and economic uncertainty, when the malleability of institutions and the swings in public opinion are at their highest, insecurity has been both a constant and a constantly changing feature of contemporary Latin America. In particular, as this chapter asserts, it has permeated three core areas of governance in the region: (1) power relations within state and society, (2) geographic differences among regions, and (3) civil society in each country. Citizen security has profoundly changed all three areas, and in ways that complicate democratic governance. A closer look at those areas, which this chapter undertakes, can help explain the persistence of obstacles to reform, even amid Latin America's changing socioeconomic and political conditions.

Most generally, democracy can be defined as a regime that structures and channels citizens' control over their government. The many principles and

1. See United Nations Development Programme, http://www.undp.org/dpa/press release/releases/2004/april/0421prodal.html.

practices cited as integral to a democracy, from universal suffrage to the subordination of the military to civilian control, can be grouped into sets. One set is the balance of power, in which the branches of government —normally, the executive, legislative, and judicial—have clearly delineated powers that are counterweights to each other. A second set of principles constitutes the rule of law in which civil and political rights are upheld, primarily through an independent, functioning judicial system that is accessible to all citizens. Building on the first two sets, the third is a state able to implement policies in response to societal needs throughout its territory. All of the specific goals within these sets are carried out using a range of instruments such as written constitutions, oversight commissions, and electoral rules. Because of their importance, a transition to democracy can thus be regarded as "the process of establishing, strengthening, or extending" these instruments (Garretón Merino 1995).

In practice, however, these instruments are impaired. Constitutions are undermined by decrees, elections by party clientalism, and civil rights by politicized judges. Together, such impairments can stall a transition from authoritarianism to democracy.[2] Recognizing this slow progress, many studies assess a transitioning regime by the degree to which it falls short of standards associated with a stable and consolidated democracy. But instead of examining what characteristics the Latin American democracies have not attained, this book looks at those they have attained. As this chapter argues, three areas of democratic life—power, geography, and civil society—reveal how fragmented these democracies are. The accumulation and use of power, the geographic disparities among regions and sectors, and the interactions and development of civil society all show how the principles of democracy splinter as they open up and expand. The obstacles to citizen security identified in the previous chapter incubate in these three areas, with minimal impact until they accumulate and together push consolidation off course. For example, pockets of disillusionment with law enforcement can erupt into political rallies that shape the public agenda, while informal power relations within the police can block reforms by legislators who are unaware of those power relations. In short, like other politically charged issues, citizen security reveals the fractured forms of democracy into which Latin America has settled over the last two decades.

2. By the liberal use of adjectives such as "imperfect" or "illiberal" the literature has done a better job of describing what these regimes are not instead of what they are. See Armony and Schamis (2005), who argue that the literature has created a false division between "old" and "new" democracies.

Power

Democratization opens up channels of power, but not always in ways that advance or augment democracy. Security forces, charged with the state's physical might, are one of those channels. As Dahl (1998, 149) affirms, "perhaps the most dangerous internal threat to democracy comes from leaders who have access to the major means of physical coercion: the military and the police." One of the achievements of Latin America democracy is reversing or minimizing that long historical tradition by subjecting security agencies to the rule of law rather than the interests of rulers. However, within the complexities of modern society the continuation of that achievement means more than simply subduing the police. It is not just the *level* of these agencies' power that shapes democracy, this book argues, but its *character*. And increasingly that character is one of uncertainty. The manifestations of power that are dangerous to democracy are not just reversions to authoritarianism, but failures to stabilize into coherent forms and predictable practices. In a democracy, above all, the state's power to control citizen security is accumulated and expressed not by force but by accessibility and consistency. It is not about what the state imposes on citizens, but what kind of information and cooperation it receives from them and what kind of service it provides for them. For example, acknowledging in August 2008 that his crime crackdown and planned structural reorganization were not working, Mexican president Felipe Calderón issued a more modest appeal for citizens to participate in crime prevention and report crime more often. Focusing on three relationships of power—those between police and society, those within the state network, and those among officials within each agency—this section discusses why the fragmented and uneven nature of power in democratic Latin America make advances in citizen security unlikely.

Police and Society

Expression of power between actors, as many scholars point out, is a relationship rather than simply a form of control. In a formulation by Bachrach and Baratz (1970, 21–23), A has power over B when B bows to A's wishes, and when A can threaten to invoke sanctions that B regards as deprivations. The police usually have such power, and they make full use of it. But because for many citizens the police are the primary form of state contact for many of their needs, and because the police need citizens to prevent and solve crimes, such exercise of power is tempered by a mutual incentive to cooperate in many types of interactions. Thus the police often hold back on uses of power such as arbitrary arrests, and citizens refrain from legal actions. But these clear lines of engagement, both positive and negative, are being blurred in ways characterized by their lack of predictability. In Latin America the public is increasingly seeing policing as not simply discriminatory or deprivational, as in the past, but also illegitimate and unpredictable. In most places it is anyone's guess whether officers will in fact try to solve a robbery, whether a police presence calms or inflames a domestic dispute, and whether a routine stop will mean a shakedown. Connections between police and organized crime, private security, and local elites make relations even more uncertain with citizens, who see officers as placing the interests of those entities above theirs. As Marenin (1996) stresses, the police maintain not only order, but a particular order that privileges certain groups, and often with an "erosion of the capacity and willingness of state agents themselves to abide by the rule of law" (Koonings and Kruijt 2004, 2). As a result, people usually do what they can to avoid the police, even when they are crime victims or witnesses. In situations in which police behavior is grudgingly accepted as legitimate, people still want to cut it off before it leads into the even more uncertain zone of criminal justice, which can trap crime perpetrators and victims indefinitely. When charges of abuse are involved, the improbability of discipline against the offending officer, as chapter 2 discussed, only adds to the tension and arbitrary nature of police-society relations.

The State Network

Along with police-society relations, some of power's most vital arteries connect the network of agencies that make up the modern state. For these interstate channels to work democratically, each agency must be both accountable to laws and empowered to carry out policies (see Geddes 1994). But powerful entities that do not abide by the rules, as many scholars have discussed, have played outsized roles in the formation and character of the modern nation-state (Hobsbawm 1985; Kennedy 1987; Tilly 2003). The military has been predominant among such "reserve domains of power." In regions like Latin America where most armed threats have been internal rather than external, the police have been predominant as well. In every subregion of Latin America they were central actors in the extended civil wars following independence in the 1800s. As the fast economic growth that began in the late 1800s put a premium on minimizing the social disruption that comes with it, the police became a primary building block of the modern state. As those states became increasingly authoritarian in the 1900s, that role gave police agencies greater political and infrastructural power, freeing them from many of the rules and constraints to which other state agencies were bound. But unlike the military, which was usually purged and restructured during democratic transitions at the end of the 1900s, the police agencies that were also part of the repressive apparatus remained largely untouched by fledgling governments unable to take on yet another challenge. With political and economic uncertainty continuing in most countries —and with the military no longer available to contain it—the police then emerged as their countries' primary security force and guardians of the state's monopoly of legitimate violence. Through their physical power in society, institutional power in the state, and political power in the government, the police have made themselves indispensable on the range of security issues, from neighborhood safety to the mass political upheavals that have threatened governments throughout the region.

Once the underlying strengths, allegiances, and interests of state agencies come into greater focus, so too do the ways in which power is transmitted. A good example is information, which, like the law, is supposed to facilitate free expression and check abuses in a democracy. But just as information is hidden in the free market, it is also hidden in the public arena. On one level the police's de facto control over evidence, witnesses, and other information makes judges, *fiscales,* and public defenders dependent on them. From the technical mastery of advanced weapons to politicians' dirty laundry, information is also used by police officers (as well as by criminal organizations) to shape criminal policy. Such informal controls complicate the accountability mechanisms described in chapter 1, as well as the citizen-police distrust explored in chapter 2. Policing is also affected when the technology to track a certain crime statistic leads officials to emphasize that particular crime over others. By contrast, the lack of information is experienced most acutely by criminal defendants, whose basic right "to receive an explanation of what has been done" (Sklar 1999, 53) is routinely violated as they wait years in inhumanely overcrowded prisons without regular access to a lawyer.

Access to local power figures and civilian criminal justice officials, or foreign agencies, is also a form of power currency among officers. Many police agencies wield their agreements with other governments to gain a political upper hand. Many programs become too closely associated with those officials who guide them through the decision-making mill, which increases the likelihood that the program will end when those officials end their tenure. The United States, regional reform's biggest funder, has shown how aid may also deepen both donor and recipient divisions. During the Cold War,[3] American training of foreign police reflected differences between the civilian-oriented approach of the State Department and the Office of Public Safety in the U.S. Agency for International Development (USAID), on the one hand, and the more militarized approach of the Defense Department and its regional counterparts, on the other. Such tensions were tamped down by Section 660, the 1974 amendment to the Foreign Assistance Act prohibiting assistance to foreign police. But the differing post–Cold War priorities in Latin America among the main U.S. agencies working on security —State Department, Justice Department, Defense Department, and US-AID[4]—have revived these contradictions, such as between offering training on new due process rights and funding new police units that ignore them. Drug trafficking in the Andes and youth gangs in Honduras, as this book discusses, are two issues over which such clashes have occurred, weakening citizen policy in recipient countries.

Such uses of outside power raise larger questions about the nature of democracy and the state. Just as judiciaries under the thumb of an authoritarian elite may gain more independence in dealing with certain issues than those in a transitional democracy trying to maneuver among competing elites, a stable, narco-dominated *fiscalía general* can be more "independent" in dealing with low-level cases. Even in internal state relations "the line between state and society is not the perimeter of an intrinsic entity, which can be thought of as a freestanding object or actor," observes Mitchell (1991, 90). "It is a line drawn internally, *within* the network of institutional mechanisms through which a certain social and political order is maintained" (emphasis in original). When such penetration sets the basic practices of a state agency, it can alter the basic actions and standards of democracy. Thus when organized crime controls a police unit, who is actually providing security? When agencies are more respectful of certain legal stan-

3. Between the late 1960s and early 1990s the presence of the U.S. Drug Enforcement Agency (DEA) abroad expanded from eight cities to over seventy sites; the number of DEA officials rose from 34 to 416 (Nadelmann 1993, 483).

4. In the State Department the main agency is the Bureau for International Narcotics and Law Enforcement Affairs. In the Justice Department reform is conducted mainly through its International Criminal Investigative Training Assistance Program. And in USAID it is conducted through Governance, Conflict Management (GCM) and the Office of Transitional Initiatives (OTI).

dards to avoid attention to their corrupt activities, what happens to the rule of law? States riddled with illegal activities tend to be considered "weak or in crisis" (Van Reenen 2004, 33–34), but in fact such activities may become integrated into what become some of the more stable realms of state functioning. It is not just pieces of state power that are being seized, but the nature of state power itself. The penetration by organized crime of Central America's criminal justice bodies, as well as the other cases discussed in this book, thus complicate the concept of "authoritarian enclaves" (Garretón 2002, 85) and assumptions about the complementary advancement of democracy, state strength, and the rule of law.

State Agencies

A third significant dimension of power is the people employed by state agencies. Like the police, the matrix of units and officials who form large bureaucracies runs on various currents of power. Many of these currents become visible in the realms of change discussed in chapter 2, such as the ongoing competition for promotion among officers or for influence in a newly decentralized police force. To survive and thrive in such environments, officials must draw on different sources of individual power. For the police, four of the most important types of such power are hierarchical, evaluative, innovative, and reputational. Hierarchical power, based on rank and position, begets obedience of an officer's directives and commands. It is usually accompanied by evaluative power, which is the ability to distribute or withhold resources, promotions, raises, and other objects of value. Innovative power allows the bearer to design new programs or policies—and then get them implemented. Closely related is reputational power, which is based on personal qualities such as charisma and respect by colleagues. In many institutions the biggest drag on effectiveness is when innovative power and reputational power do not allow officials to move up the ranks to acquire hierarchical and evaluative power. In a police force the combination of a militarized history, the centrality of seniority, and the distortions affecting "high" organizations with too many ranks makes such movement particularly sticky. Moreover, as in other agencies, power is awarded to and well guarded by police veterans who entered into the system early and assiduously worked their way up. Top-heavy structures crowd out those below, slowing the efforts of mid-ranking officials to develop new programs, transmit information from the street to headquarters, or reward patrol officers' innovation. When officials manage to break through such barriers, automatic rotations can stop the accumulation of knowledge and relationships that help uncover the causes of crime and help turn reputational power into hierarchical power—that is, the management problems described in chapter 2 can often be traced back to the power relations among officers.

These three dimensions of power—state-society, interstate, and intrainstitutional—are evident throughout a democratic regime. They directly and indirectly shape many of its basic practices and standards, including accountability, a key principle discussed in the first two chapters. After a history of authoritarianism, as the scholarship emphasizes, state institutions that abide by the law are a linchpin for nearly every democratic standard. If a democratic regime is consolidated when all the major actors "become habituated to the resolution of conflict within the specific laws, procedures and institutions sanctioned by the new democratic process" (Linz and Stepan 1996, 8), then mechanisms to advance and monitor such habituation are indeed central to democracy. In the many definitions of accountability, two general dimensions are cited as essential to it. The first is explanation, transparency, and answerability—the power to know what is happening and why. The second is judgment and sanction—the ability to punish those who violate laws.[5] Accountability agencies, such as those discussed in chapter 1, have become increasingly able to reach the first goal and, under favorable conditions and cooperative courts, the second one as well. Ombudsmen in the Andean region, for example, have successfully addressed cases involving abuses such as price fixing, violence against army cadets, and discrimination against indigenous persons. But they still struggle to alter the conditions that contributed to such abuses, such as loose regulations over companies, military bodies, and local governments. In many instances, though, accountability agencies can be thrust into the center of political controversies that force governments to strengthen them. For example, the 2010 Gulf of Mexico oil spill led to demands to strengthen the U.S. Interior Department's Minerals Management Service, which oversees oil extraction practices. In such cases, accountability agencies will be allowed to become sufficiently independent and institutionalized to help bring about "horizontal accountability" among state agencies (O'Donnell 2003) or between the state and the private sector.

5. This dual definition is used by Schedler, Diamond, and Plattner (1999), as well as by those favoring narrowing it to the state actors responsible for the law. It is also included in discussions of both horizontal accountability among state agencies (O'Donnell 2003) and the "vertical relationship between citizens and rulers" (see Schmitter 1999, 59; see also Schmitter and Karl 1991).

In most countries, however, accountability is under threat by the widespread belief that it hinders the decision making necessary to overcome persistent economic and political problems. Governments "immobilized by oversight mechanisms," as Mainwaring (2003, 4) explains, may be "perceived as indecisive, ineffective, or inept." Unconstitutional activities, from individual corruption to federal intervention, are tolerated if the public views them as necessary to—or as a reasonable price to pay for—decisive action. With crime now one of the public's biggest concerns, support for crackdowns that may even involve extrajudicial killing is clashing with laws and agencies formed during democratization to hold the police accountable to basic standards. In a poll in Maracaibo, Venezuela's second-largest city, 91 percent of respondents did not "feel secure" with the police, but an astonishing 47 percent favored police killing of delinquents (Gabaldón and Bettiol 1988). Stated differently, outright fear of a state agency does not necessarily mean that citizens want it to be held accountable. Even pro-reform governments such as Chile's have had to be on good terms with public safety agencies, forcing it into a "trade-off between promoting citizens' rights and defending the police from allegations of misbehavior" (Fuentes 2006b, 155–56). So despite the fact that accountability agencies around the region have made important advances in gathering knowledge and administering punishment, they have yet to realize a more substantive third dimension—uprooting the sources of unaccountable action.

Even though the biggest underlying reason for poor accountability is an acceptance of its absence, shifts in public opinion can alter unaccountable exercises of power. Peruzzotti and Smulovitz (2006, 4) emphasize "the growth of alternative forms of political control that rely on citizens' actions and organizations" and that can set accountability mechanisms into gear through social mobilizations, legal claims, and media exposure. However, because of the institutional and political insularity of the police, such strategies are less effective in law enforcement. As Schedler (1999, 25) has observed, "Civil association may represent strong 'factual power,'" but citizen groups "can never match the state's monopoly of legitimate physical violence or its privileged position as the source of law." Weak opposition to get-tough policies in most countries further enhances the government's ability to hide the abuses arising from them. Support for a policy of *mano dura* by a wide cross section of society provides additional cover by neutralizing the argument that it targets a particular class or geographic area. Accountability is certainly compatible with tough action because it can help make the police more efficient, but *mano dura* proponents usually cast them as inherently incompatible, as discussed in chapter 1, thereby neutralizing the contribution of accountability to traditional policing. Such manipulation of the levers of power between state and society and within the state clearly maligns democracy's principle of accountability when it comes to citizen security.

The communities suffering the most from crime are the ones with the least power to work with or challenge the police—that is, they experience the greatest economic pressures, ethnic tensions, residential turnover, and suspicion of both police officers and anyone who cooperates with them. As numerous authors describe (see Holston and Caldeira 1998), the decision by police officers to use force often depends on the citizen's demeanor and perceived power. And the vast majority of these discretionary judgments are not challenged or overseen through accountability mechanisms, demonstrating the difficulty of reversing trends beyond the individual cases that are documented. Legal and constitutional analyses often miss most of what happens beneath the surface of public scandals and indictments, such as detention beyond the legal time limit, forced confessions, and evidence tampering. Such actions are particularly difficult to monitor because they happen on the street and to citizens with little access to the means for challenging them. Similar to the invisible matter that makes up the bulk of the universe, the sum of daily actions gives shape to the state and its power relations with society.

A closer look at ombudsmen (*defensorías del pueblo*), the main accountability agents in contemporary Latin American democracies, will highlight these barriers. Around the region ombudsmen are empowered to investigate abuses by any state agency, most often by directing the complaints to the appropriate channels. The high volume of complaints filed about police abuse is testament to the need for accountability on security. For example, well over half of all grievances to El Salvador's human rights commissioner involved the National Civilian Police (Chinchilla 2003, 215), and in Peru the police received the third highest number of citizen complaints.[6] In 2004 Nicaragua's Office of Internal Affairs received 1,113 reports that led to the investigation of 639 police officials (Programa Centroamericana de la Federación Luterana Mundial 2005). And in the city of São Paulo the police auditor received 16,000 complaints of police abuse in just the first two and a half years of that agency's existence (Miller 2002, 16). Because of their importance to such issues, along with the great strides

6. Defensoría del Pueblo, Peru, http://www.ombudsman.gob.pe/modules.

they have made on many of them, *defensorías* enjoy high levels of citizen support around the region. Most governments also express rhetorical support for them, which is, at least for Costa Rica, considered to be genuine.[7] But most *defensorías* find themselves constricted by pressure from the executive branch, a dependence on state funds, a lack of patronage networks, resistance by the bureaucracies they try to pry open, and a mandate that stretches them too thin. As a result, *defensorías* tend to be most effective against weak governments, such as in Peru in the late 1990s, or responding with popular backing on highly charged issues such as rigged elections or utility price hikes. As Schedler (1999, 23) points out, "an accounting party, if it is to be serious, cannot stand on equal footing with the accountable party. At least in its sphere of competence, it must be even more powerful." Most Latin American accountability agencies lack the resources and autonomy to be on such footing in most areas of state power.

Such limits on ombudsmen have prompted most countries and provinces to establish agencies with the sole purpose of monitoring the police (see table 3.1). Although varying in size and legal reach, almost all of these agencies have the authority to investigate police wrongdoing, publicize abuses, and prod judicial and executive agencies to action. In most countries they have focused primarily on internal management (usually corruption) and civil rights (abuses from arbitrary detention to extrajudicial killing). To minimize politicized interference in such sensitive matters, most internal affairs agencies are bolstered through measures such as legal and financial autonomy and mixed civilian and police staffs.

Internal affairs units in Peru, Argentina, and other countries have made major advances, but the majority have been stalled or rolled back by use of the state's financial, institutional, and political powers. For example, starved of resources and inundated with minor complaints that prevent investigation of serious ones, many units cannot carry out investigations or are forced to allow the police to investigate themselves. Internal affairs units in countries such as Paraguay, Nicaragua, and Panama have not had much control over police abuses. Even Peru's internal affairs structure, one of the most extensive in the region (see Basombrío Iglesias 2006), has been weakened by resistance from the police, overlap with the inspector general, and the revolving door of six interior ministers in the five years after Alberto Fujimori's regime ended in 2000 (Gobierno del Perú 2002). Like their *defen-*

---

7. Mario Zamora Cordero, adviser, La Defensoría de los Habitantes de Costa Rica, interview with author, San José, April 7, 2006.

Table 3.1 Police Accountability Mechanisms in Latin America

Country	Police accountability agencies and procedures
Argentina[a]	Inspección de Seguridad (most provinces)
Bolivia	Dirección Nacional de Responsabilidad Profesional; Tribunal Disciplinario Superior
Brazil[a]	Ouvidoria da Polícia (fourteen states)
Chile	Administrative procedures; military courts
Colombia	*Defensoría del pueblo* (national ombudsman)
Costa Rica	Consejo de Personal
Dominican Republic	Comisión Nacional de Derechos Humanos; Instituto de Dignidad Humana—Policía Nacional
Ecuador	*Defensoría del pueblo*
El Salvador	Dirección General de Inspección—Policía Nacional Civil
Guatemala	Comisión de Derechos Humanos de Guatemala; Inspectoría General—Policía Nacional Civil (IGPNC), consisting of the Oficina de Responsabilidad Profesional (ORP, investigates charges), the Oficina de Derechos Humanos (ODH), and the Régimen Disciplinario (REDIS)
Honduras	Unidad de Asuntos Internos; Consejo Nacional de Seguridad Interior
Mexico[a]	Varies by state; federal-level Consejo Nacional de Seguridad Pública
Nicaragua	Dirección de Asuntos Internos
Panama	Unidad de Asuntos Internos
Paraguay	Unidad de Asuntos Internos
Peru	Police ombudsman; Dirección de Asuntos Internos (Interior Ministry); *defensoría del pueblo* (national human rights ombudsman)
Uruguay	Inspección Nacional de Policía
Venezuela[a]	*Defensoría del pueblo* (national); Dirección del Inspector (local and state)

Source: Author.
[a]In federal countries, differences among provinces or states are wide.

soría counterparts, these internal affairs units are weaker than the institutions they try to hold accountable. As a result, many police are able to use edicts, "social order" statutes, and other regulations to build a legal firewall against them. Internal affairs units are also circumvented, ignored, or second-guessed by the other bodies with which they work in investigating malfeasance. Security officials often act less than expeditiously when sending material on specific cases, and the judges and executive officials who try and sanction charges of police abuse are often more lenient than accountability agencies.

Limits on time, information, and resources on many fronts force internal affairs units to respond to rather than prevent abuse, just as traditional policing does with crime. Such ineffectiveness is evident in administering discipline, a major instrument of state authority often exercised through hierarchical power. In most countries charges against police officers are handled in one of three ways: (1) through internal police procedures, usually by the accused officer's superiors or special courts; (2) through the *defensoría del pueblo* or human rights commission; or (3) through the prosecutor's office (*fiscalía*), either directly or via the police or *defensoría*. Serious cases sent through all three channels may end up in criminal court. But the tendency of the police to close ranks behind accused colleagues slows action by already overwhelmed administrative, *defensoría*, and judicial officials. Venezuela's police officers are rarely convicted of abuse, or they receive sentences far shorter than civilians convicted of the same crime (PROVEA 1996). Of the three hundred specific cases of police abuse documented by rights groups in Venezuela between 2000 and 2005, only thirteen led to formal accusations and two to sentences (La Red de Apoyo 2006, 27).

Because of such conditions, in many countries charges are processed internally. Although it may make administrative sense, this approach can keep much information away from internal affairs units and civilians. For example, Ecuador's tripartite system of tribunals, district courts, and National Court of Police Justice used to try accused officers is officially independent, but its impartiality is open to question because many of its judges are retired police officers. Limited in their controls, many governments opt for purges to try to sweep away all problematic officers in one fell, highly publicized swoop. Not only can such purges create a mass of angry former officials motivated to create trouble, as in Argentina, but they also usually fail to eliminate the uses of power that allow police abuses to survive those personnel changes, such as in Bolivia.

All three of the countries featured in the case studies in this book established police accountability units in the late 1990s. Each of their experiences reveals how, even amid dissimilar politics and similar problems, accountability can rarely venture beyond a regime's political tolerance level. Public pressures for action by the state, amid a lack of confidence in it, justifies officials' self-appointed prerogative to utilize certain agencies unhindered. Amid the institutional changes and mismanagement discussed in chapter 2, such selectivity limits oversight during the life span of state policies, from initial formulation to excesses in implementation. It is only in such fragmented states that repeated actions on specific abuses have just temporary impacts. Accountability agencies may have notched up many victories, but they have yet to win the war. Because of tolerance of abusive policing, accountability agencies find it difficult to attain not only answerability and punishment, but also the more elusive and arguably more important goal of addressing and reversing the causes of abuse.

Geography

Although one of the most important attributes of a regime is whether it "can exercise authority throughout the society" (Weiner and Huntington 1994), the disparity in the quality of basic security provided to different regions within nearly every Latin American country is ever-widening. These differences entrench unequal power relations, exploitative state actions, and societal mistrust. As one of the most overlooked dimensions of criminal justice, geography thus amplifies the obstacles to citizen security reform. To explain how, this section discusses three overlapping layers of geography—decentralized state structure, urbanization, and privatization—and how they shape policing and criminal policy.

Decentralized State Structure

A primary cause of the geographic differences among regions is the unprecedented decentralization of Latin American states. Like many other services, citizen security has been decentralized to the regional and local levels, resulting in a record number of police forces. But decentralization may turn out to be not just more inefficient than centralization, as chapter 2 discusses, but more undemocratic as well. In most countries subnational governments do not necessarily allow more participation, accountability, or rights. Instead, decentralization can breathe life into the local prejudices and political clientalism that were held in check by national standards. Even if such patterns do not metastasize into "decentralized despotisms" (Mamdani 1996), their impacts on daily life can be wide-ranging and deep, as evidenced by the lack of protection for civil liberties in many rural areas of Argentina, Brazil, and Venezuela. Such subnational power has been latent throughout Latin America's history. Because the region's populist and authoritarian regimes stopped or carefully controlled change through the 1900s, local powers were able to survive through the century's otherwise transformative changes such as urbanization, economic modernization, and the formation of mass parties. Many current efforts to rationalize or renegotiate police controls between central and regional governments are now being complicated by these local powers. For example, recalcitrant provinces of federal states such as Argentina are resisting change; Mexico City and other areas are attempting to "impose authority on a police system . . . fragmented and out of control" (Davis 2009); and in Bolivia local powers are posing threats to the integrity of the state itself.

Amid economic inequalities, decentralization can also mean wide differences in the quality of state services, including police, among regions and cities. In every country per capita urban crime rates are far higher than the national average. Ecuador's National Institute of Statistics and Census (Instituto Nacional de Estadísticas y Censos de Ecuador, INEC) reports that the murder rate in the country's cities is about three and a half times the rate in rural areas, for example, and in Bolivia 80 percent of murders occur in its three urban departments. Although Venezuela's national homicide rate was 48 per 100,000 persons in 2007, Caracas's was between 130 and 166.[8] Eager to be relieved of this urban burden, provinces without large metropolises tend to support decentralization. The smaller and more self-sufficient provinces benefit from decentralization, but poor ones usually end up worse off. In Nicaragua, which has one of Latin America's more equitable distributions of income, the high-poverty rural areas representing 16 percent of the population have only four hundred officers, which is one for every 2,188 persons, whereas the rest of the country has one for every 710 persons (Bautista Lara 2006, 114). Moreover, because citizen security depends on agencies beyond the police, the proportionately greater presence of some agencies determines not only the level but the *kind* of protection. For example, a scarcity of public defenders or social services can diminish certain components of citizen security, such as prevention and civil rights, even more than a shortage of police. This dimension of inequality accentuates the state's fragmentation in part by propagating the obstacles to citizen security throughout a country.

Urbanization

Decentralization has an even greater impact within urban areas, where violent crime is concentrated in the neighborhoods least able to afford quality policing but most in need of it. Many scholars in the fields of human ecol-

8. "Deadly Message," *The Economist,* July 19, 2008, 47; Foreign Policy Magazine On Line, "The List: Murder Capitals of the World," http://www.foreignpolicy.com/story/cms.php?story_id=4480.

ogy and social urban geography, postulating "an intimate congruity between the social order and physical space," have documented this relationship between demographics and crime (Georges 1978, 3). For example, Burgess (1925) and Shaw and McKay (1969) found the lack of social organization and community control in inner-city Chicago to be the primary source of crime. The variables explaining crime must be carefully defined, however, because the differences among areas defy any neat generalization connecting social disorder and criminal activity. Just as in the Dutch example cited in chapter 2, several studies of New York City indicate for each precinct "a strong relationship" between crime and behaviors that lead to misdemeanor summonses or detentions (Kelling and Sousa 2001). But legal scholars such as Harcourt and Ludwig (2006) caution against drawing a direct line between social disorder and crime, because more specific factors such as waves of cocaine use or the presence of certain individuals may have been more significant in New York's high-crime areas.

Although some scholars such as Gaitán Daza and Díaz Moreno (1994) have found no correlation in Latin America between violence and specific demographic traits such as city size, the instability of urban life worldwide is one common characteristic thought to aggravate crime. As in other regions, urbanization in Latin America usually accompanies economic growth because expanding cities have the jobs and infrastructure that attract and absorb new residents. But if this economic potential fails to materialize or begins to dissipate, cities will struggle to support swelling populations. Latin America reflects the impacts of this phenomenon more clearly than other regions, with an urbanization rate of 75.3 percent, which is comparable with that of far wealthier North America (77.2 percent) and Europe (74.8 percent) and nearly twice the rates for Africa (37.9 percent) and Asia (36.7 percent).[9] Some studies in Mexico have revealed how heavy indigenous migration to the cities aggravates youth tensions (Rus and Diego 2007). Such urban pressures are also evident in ownership instability; an estimated 65 percent of Latin America's urban properties are considered "extralegal," or lacking valid property rights that would allow their longtime occupants to use them as collateral for loans.[10] Although it is applied more widely in

9. Most urbanization has occurred since 1950, when 41 percent of people lived in cities. By comparison, such change has taken twice as long in North America, where the urbanization rate was 53.8 percent in 1925 (Cerrutti and Bertoncello 2003, 4).

10. According to a study of twelve Latin American countries by the IADB and Peru's Institute of Liberty and Democracy, as quoted in Andrés Oppenheimer, "Latin America's Underground Economy Keeps Booming," *Miami Herald,* October 15, 2006.

high-crime neighborhoods, zero tolerance policing generally does not incorporate either these economic trends or the sociological ones discussed earlier. Limited officer flexibility and discretion, as discussed further in chapter 7, often close one of the few channels for such trends to be brought into policy. For example, a police force that fails to study which properties are targeted by offenders deprives itself of a useful tool for reducing both crime and fear (see St. Jean 2007). Thus geographic distinctions based instead almost entirely on raw crime rates is one reason why zero tolerance is often little more than a *mano dura* (see chapter 2).

Privatization of Security

Meanwhile, middle- and upper-class areas are more equipped to form neighborhood organizations that can break the cycle of distrust with the police. The national inequality discussed in chapter 2, as it widens the gap in the kinds of residences people can afford, has also made middle- and upper-class areas more physically separate. Indeed, an increasing number of those areas are gated and privately guarded. Many of them have grown from or been based on the self-enclosed communities that have long been part of Latin America's demographic development, from colonial-era mansions and "company towns" in the 1800s to recreational "clubs" and closed residential districts in the 1900s (Cabrales Barajas 2002; Borsdorf 2003). Amid the modern era's growth of crime and free markets, security has become a public service from which these areas have increasingly chosen to opt out. Since the 1980s and particularly in the 1990s, the number of private security firms has grown in every region of the world, from 7–9 percent in the industrialized countries to nearly 11 percent in the developing regions (Frigo 2003). Indeed, private security officers now outnumber their public counterparts in cities throughout Latin America, Africa, and Asia. Every Latin American country has experienced such growth,[11] particularly in the number of firms guarding gated communities, which have expanded out of the upper-income areas where they began to the less affluent and different types of residential arrangements such as urban high-rises. In Mex-

11. The growth in private security since the mid-1990s is an estimated 9 percent in Chile and 10 percent in Costa Rica, the region's safest countries (the rate for Costa Rica is based in part on estimated 50 percent growth since 2002). Although this growth began in the 1980s, most Latin American private security firms are less than ten years old. In the Dominican Republic, for example, forty-seven of the ninety-eight firms registered in 2000 were formed since the mid-1990s (see Díaz 2001).

ico City, for example, about 750 gated communities with roughly fifty thousand mostly middle-class housing units were built between 1990 and 2001 (Parnreiter 2002).

The popularity of the private sector, however, contrasts with its transparency. Because of the constant turnover, off-the-books hiring, and high bankruptcy rates resulting from small profit margins and high-interest loans, the information on private security firms is notoriously unreliable, with the basic statistics varying wildly (see table 3.2). The reported number of private security officers in Mexico is up to 140,000 registered officers and an estimated 600,000 unregistered officers.[12] The 2007 estimates for private security officers in Guatemala range from 80,000 to 200,000.[13] In total, about 1.6 million registered private security employees are working in Latin America, and about 2 million more are working informally or illegally.[14]

The effects of private security on both the state and society are far-reaching. Within the state, governments buy into privatization in different forms. For example, the wealthiest of Lima's municipalities contract out to private firms for policing,[15] and the police in most cities say they depend on their private sector colleagues for information. Because many private security agencies are staffed by moonlighting state officers, there is much overlap between the public and private agencies, even when governments do not enter into formal contracts. Laws regulate these enterprises, but, according to estimates by police administrators in most countries, well under half abide by them and so operate essentially unfettered. The lack of oversight in the public police also affects security, with many on-duty state officers prioritizing the businesses and homes they serve off-hours. A bigger danger of such lax regulation is that many employees of the private agencies were dismissed from the force or unable to get in, with obvious implications for both the quality and safety of the services they provide.

12. Lower estimate of 140,000: *The Economist,* January 27, 2007. About 70 percent of private security officers are former state police officers (Uildriks and Tello 2010, 211).

13. Both estimates are a leap from the estimated 15,000 of the 1990s. Lower estimate: Otto Pérez Molina, military general and 2007 presidential candidate, interview by author, New York, June 19, 2007; higher estimate: "Impunity Rules," *The Economist,* November 18, 2006, 41. Today the private security force is more than ten times larger than the 20,000-strong police force.

14. Most Latin America firms began in the late 1990s. Although most have fewer than a hundred employees, an estimated 320 have over a thousand (Frigo 2003). In addition, Latin America's globalized markets allow capture of a large share of the private security sector by multinational firms such as Securitas, Group 4 Securicor, Chubb, and Prosegur.

15. Lima's municipal security chiefs, interviews by author, Lima, June 20, 2001.

Table 3.2 Estimated Size of Latin America's Private Security Sector

Country	Number of firms		Estimated number of employees		State police officials
	Registered	Unregistered	Official	Unofficial	
Argentina	712		75,000–150,000	80,000–200,000	by province
Bolivia	100+[a]		7,000		22,000
Brazil			580,000	1,500,000	by state
Chile	800		45,000		36,000
Colombia	551		190,000		
Costa Rica			20,000		17,000
Dominican Republic	98		20,000–30,000		27,000
Ecuador	200	100			
El Salvador			25,000		20,257
Guatemala			combined: 80,000–200,000	20,000	
Honduras	116	284	20,000	60,000	12,000
Mexico	322	1,400	140,000	600,000	by state
Nicaragua	67		9,329[b]		7,000
Panama					
Paraguay			combined: 45,000	15,000	
Peru				100,000	92,000
Uruguay					21,300
Venezuela	522		75,000		by state

Sources: Argentina: 712 different firms are listed with the federal government, http://www.seguridadprivada.com.ar; Bolivia: García Soruco (2003); Brazil: "Bullet-proof in Alphaville," *The Economist,* August 16, 2001; Chile: Arrivillaga (2003); Colombia: Clawson and Lee (1996, 2000); Costa Rica: Alberto Li Chan, police commissioner, interview by author, San José, June 19, 2006; Dominican Republic: Díaz (2001); Das, Dilip (2005, 248); Atalo Mata, "Nuevo dirección de control de empresas de seguridad privada," *Es Mas,* Noticieros Televisa, October 14, 2004, http://www.esmas.com; Ecuador: Carrión (2003, 75); El Salvador: Vaquerano (2006); Das, Dilip (2005, 265); Luis Laínez, "El crimen afecta el desarrollo de Centroamérica, advierte la ONU," *El Mundo,* May 26, 2007; Guatemala: lower estimate of employees: Otto Pérez Molina, military general specializing in intelligence, architect of Peace Accords, and 2007 presidential candidate, interview by author, New York, June 19, 2007; higher estimate: "Impunity Rules," *The Economist,* November 18, 2006, 41; Honduras: Jorge Nery Chinchilla O., director, Unidad Planeamiento, Evaluación y de Gestión (UPEG), interview by author, Tegucigalpa, June 14, 2005; Mexico: Azaola (2007, 12); Nicaragua: Perry et al. (2007, 242); Paraguay: Harvard University Law School Faculty and Universidad de Colombia del Paraguay (2007); Peru: Dana Ford, "Peru Mining Security Firm Faces Investigation," Reuters, February 2009; Uruguay: Enrique Navas, National Interior Ministry, interview by author, Montevideo, August 24, 2003; Venezuela: Morais de Guerrero (1998).
Note: Empty cells indicate that data were not available.
[a]Only in the three main cities: Cochabamba, Santa Cruz, and La Paz.
[b]2005 estimate.

Criminal Policy

Decentralization, private security, gated communities, and other geographic trends can be said to relieve pressure on the state by sharing and dispersing its security burden. But in most cases they also deflate the momentum for criminal justice and other security reform. Privatization also helps to justify casting the net of zero tolerance more widely over "high-crime" areas and the people associated with crime, disorder, and moral decay. Policy then becomes a channel for discrimination against youth, immigrants, indigenous persons, the dark-skinned, sexual minorities, and other sectors associated with criminality and particular neighborhoods (see Benjamin 1969; Foucault 1995; Galtung 2004). As discussed throughout this book, people from these groups who are also newcomers—increasingly common in the flexible labor markets of the neoliberal era—feel distrusted in both residential and commercial areas. As private guards become increasingly ubiquitous, the exclusion upon which their work is based takes on a legal sheen and societal justification. In this environment, legal interpretations by the police, such as the assertions of one Venezuelan state police chief that police codes restrict certain people from moving "freely in the streets," become unremarkable and unchallenged assertions of police power.[16] As a price for the legitimacy that political consensus brings to the law, constitutional rights are not given to all citizens but are instead portioned out and selectively distributed (see Habermas 1998).

When geographic lines spin out and crisscross society, they divide up not just the law and political jurisdictions, but groups and neighborhoods as well. "Apart from examining legal systems and the practices of social control agencies, explanations of exclusion require an account of barriers, prohibitions and constraints on activities from the point of view of the excluded," points out Sibley (1995, x). In Latin America, where the excluded are a majority confined to a minority of space, such an approach can reveal the hidden nature of citizen security. The exclusivity of consumerist spaces, broad notions of incivility, and long-standing social prejudices all find ready expression in *mano dura* policies. Such patterns then take on a geographic manifestation as both citizens and state officials divide up the areas in which they live and work as a way to make insecurity more manageable. Thus while individuals associated with crime are "free to go elsewhere but allowed to arrive nowhere" (Papastergiadis 2006), so too are law-abiding cit-

16. Amnesty International, "Urgent Action," February 12, 2002; Amnesty International (2000).

izens restricting the physical ranges of their own lives. Such views may be even more common in the uncertain era of globalization. In areas with diminishing economic autonomy, exclusion of criminal suspects, such as those from certain neighborhoods or deported from the United States, helps maintain boundaries in a world that is rapidly shedding them.

Civil Society

Instead of examining such tendencies, studies of civil society in Latin America and other regions reflect on its role as a catalyst of democracy. Most generally, civil society is regarded as an "arena where manifold social movements . . . and civic organizations from all classes" organize to "express themselves and advance their interests" (Stepan 1988, 3–4) or to "question" and "resist" the state (Keane 1988, 27–28). For broad "civic culture" theories, civil society is a "school of virtue" that promotes cooperation, aggregates interests, and equalizes representation of otherwise unequal social sectors (Almond and Verba 1963; Putnam, Leonardi, and Nanetti 1994). Narrower conceptions view civil society as temporary constellations of groups that crystallize around particular demands or mediate between the state and the market. Even from these narrower perspectives in which civil society comes to life only on certain occasions, its contributions to democracy are clear. It has mobilized to bring down repressive regimes, forge new policies, and turn itself into a permanent check on state action. From the formation of neighborhood justice centers to the development of community policing, citizen security has been among the many issues to benefit from these efforts.

The democratization literature, in particular, emphasizes civil society. As Latin America threw off its military regimes in the 1980s, this expansive area of scholarship generally began assessing institutional stability, accountability, and effectiveness. As democracies survived but continued to be weak, scholarship shifted to the contrast between democratic durability and vulnerability. Much of this work focused on citizens, pointing out the limited ways in which democratic regimes do and do not incorporate their individual and collective demands, which is one of their primary functions. For example, Von Mettenheim and Malloy (1998, 11) stress civil society's access to policymaking, and Hagopian and Mainwaring (2005, 8–9) explain how "mass attitudes" and "quality representation" can steer a democracy through rocky periods. Stripping down democracy to the level of individ-

ual citizens, O'Donnell, Cullell, and Iazzetta (2004) return to the importance of human agency to revive democracy's principles by making claims
to them.

Although civil society may be the engine of democratization, it is also
being altered by the process. This section discusses the connected ways in
which civil society directly or indirectly undermines itself and its own security through fear, exclusion, vigilante violence, economic frustration, and
responses to youth. As scholars such as Turner (1983) and Habermas (1989)
point out, certain conditions or catalyzing events can help civil society overcome constraints to its effectiveness. Incidents of police brutality, for example, can galvanize civil society to push for reform. But unlike socioeconomic or other issue areas in which large sectors of civil society find common ground on identity and goals, the fear of crime and divisions over crime
policy often muffle society's voice and blunt the impact of actions such as
protests and local activism. In the process, socioeconomic divisions are reinforced rather than reduced, with zero tolerance leading back to a reflexive resort to physical power. Citizens then easily lose their way in both opinion and
impact on their own security. As a fragmented "sphere of publics" rather than
"the realm of a single public" (Calhoun and McGowan 1997, 250), civil society thus stumbles in the critical space between awareness and action, and,
along with the state, between traditional and problem-oriented policing.[17]
Thus impediments to specific reforms such as community policing emerge in
part out of attributes that are difficult to identify and address through policy.

That said, one of those attributes is fear of violence and crime, which
characterizes daily life in contemporary Latin America and fragments its
societies. Much work, such as the edited volumes by Londoño, Gaviria, and
Guerrero (2000), Morana (2002), and Dammert and Paulsen (2005) on urban violence, explore the impacts of unhealed injustices and the resentments of neoliberal inequality. Going past the "dualistic divide" between
academics and policymakers in their approaches to violence, Moser and
McIlwaine (2004) describe the conditions that allow vigilantism, gangs,
and other manifestations of violence to take root and replicate. Their definition of the causes and attributes of violence has been followed by sociological and anthropological studies of violence that further demonstrate its
extent. For example, Briceño-León (2008) discusses the factors that cause

17. Arendt (1959) describes two actions: to begin (*arkhein*) and to carry through
(*prattein*).

violence, such as the gaps between rich and poor and between educational and employment opportunities, as well as the factors that indirectly facilitate it, such as urban density and political crises. Wilson (1998, 311) concludes that "most of the variations among individuals in criminality can be accounted for by personal traits, family socialization, and (perhaps) school influence." Others distinguish among types of violence. Scheper-Hughes and Bourgois (2004) examine public, private, political, symbolic, and psychic forms of violence, and Buvinic, Morrison, and Shifter (1999) distinguish between goal-centered instrumental violence and "emotional" violence in which the act is "an end in itself."

But it is social exclusion and individual alienation that perhaps best capture what these disparate strands mean for citizen security and citizen action. As violence becomes predictable in the expectation of its likelihood but unpredictable in its time and form, it contracts the physical and social scope of civil association. As a staple of public discourse and the daily media, violence becomes a part of life to which people pare down their schedules and interactions. The perpetual fear of it reconfigures people's relationships with each other, with space, and with the state. In many cases, what Rotker (2002) calls a "citizenship of fear" has led to an internal war with fatality rates associated with traditional war but without its markers of ideology and mobilization. As that war's unwitting combatants, residents learn not to trust "anyone who looks at you for more than a few seconds" and turn to "practical, unpublished maps" with an increasing number of no-go areas (Rotker 2002, 17). Many of those areas are populated by recent migrants from the countryside whose frustration is compounded by the distress of confronting violence worse than that they from which they fled.

The evidence of battle is everywhere. As urban *barrios* blend into each other, residents retreat into homes barricaded with guns, dogs, walls, and window bars. Around the world, as Young (1999, 18) points out, "the most commonplace barriers and by far the most costly are those that we are forced to erect to protect our own houses." Many residents in poor areas even say they must have someone home at all times to prevent a robbery, which further depresses household income as well as attendance at neighborhood meetings. Mirroring internal police relations, citizens who are able to bring order to such areas gain reputation and informal power as they organize gangs, private militias, vigilante groups, parapolice squads, and other forms of organized revenge. Such groupings have always existed in Latin America, but they have now adjusted to and have become part of democracy.[18]

They add to public insecurity, complicate crime fighting, and implicate the state for both its ineffectiveness against and collusion with criminal activity. Many of these groups are formed by police officers, using police uniforms and credentials, and fund themselves by trafficking drugs and contraband vehicles.[19]

Many ordinary citizens regard vigilantism as an expression of their priority of safety over rights and as their own application of the state's *mano dura* policy to achieve that priority. Even when adjusting for documented increases resulting from greater attention to the issue, the number of lynchings and the justifications for them have clearly risen appreciably since the mid-1990s. By most estimates, vigilantism is responsible for the deaths of about six thousand people each year in Latin America.[20] Even in relatively low-crime cities such as San José, one-third of the people expressed support for "social cleansing"; in higher-crime cities nearly three-quarters did so (Londoño and Guerrero 1999). This increase is driven in part by the diversification of vigilante groups, which ranges from spontaneous mobs to "social work" groups to clandestine organizations with police ties. Their targets have also widened. The initial focus on individuals suspected of particular crimes has extended to those from marginalized social sectors to police officers and mayors suspected of corruption. Vigilantism is also fueled by customs from the days before democratization. In countries such as Guatemala and Bolivia the practice is most common in areas where nonstate or semistate entities, such as local militias, were in control of security during the authoritarian era (see Abrahams 1998; Snodgrass Godoy 2006). Vigilantism also reflects fissures, both avoidable and unavoidable, in Latin American law. As discussed in the section in chapter 2 on penal process codes, the law comprises both rules and the rules about the rules. Even if certain rules are accepted, such as against armed aggression, the rules about applying them may not be. The inefficacy of the state, along with the societal mores that are changing more rapidly than the state, often opens up schisms over how to handle violations of the law.

18. Operating in at least seven states and the Federal District, for example, death squads have been responsible for killings hundreds of Venezuelans. "MIJ evalúa a 327 cuerpos de policía del país," *El Globo,* November 25, 2000, 3.

19. For example, one of the very few legal actions against parapolice leaders in Venezuela was paralyzed by the lack of protection for witnesses. "El Defensor no quiere que lo envíen al Rodeo," *Tal Cual,* September 18, 2002.

20. Scott Johnson, "Vigilante Justice," *Newsweek International,* December 20, 2004.

In Venezuela, where homemade brochures in the early 1990s exhorted *barrio* residents to "declare war" against delinquency, reports by newspapers, NGOs, and the police reveal an increase in lynchings from only a handful in 1995—a year when 57 percent of respondents in a national poll favored the practice[21]—to almost one a week since 1997.[22] Even in *barrios* with better physical conditions and community organizations, meetings of "self-defense" groups attract a large attendance, and lynchings have become more open and more brazen, with bodies often left in the middle of the street.[23] The two factions of the Tupamaros in the Caracas *barrio* of 23 de Enero demonstrate how vigilante groups can appropriate law enforcement. The main faction, "Living Hope," was officially organized to engage in social work and received state funds for it through phantom NGOs. But its members gradually became more involved in crime, both for and against. Many of them have been accused of recruiting young men to sell drugs, as well as to kill over a dozen "presumed delinquents" in the name of its anticrime campaign. Residents willing to discuss the Tupamaros seem to either fear or tacitly support them. One young resident approvingly described the group's anticrime tactics. When group members witnessed a robbery, he said, "they tied up the robber, poured gasoline on him, and set fire." They responded similarly to a man "smoking crack in front of children. Twice they advised him to stop. The third time, they went to his house at night, took him to the roof, and threw him off."[24]

As societal antipathy toward constitutional norms segues into active hostility, acceptance of *auto-justicia* grows and acts of tolerance become signs less of trust than of cease-fires. As Brysk (2000), Armony (2004), and Snodgrass Godoy (2006) describe, this is the flip side of civil society, which challenges the positive association between civic engagement and democracy. The "ties and groups through which people connect to one another and get drawn into community and political affairs" may include groups and forms

21. *El Nacional,* March 14, 1995, and *Diario de Caracas,* March 15, 1995, 2. That year the interior minister met with leaders of some "auto defense" groups to seek their cooperation "to better guarantee security." "Escovar Salom se reunirá con empresas de vigilancia y grupos de autodefensa," *Ultimas Noticias,* February 2, 1995.

22. See copies of *Ultimas Noticias* from 1995 to 2000. This newspaper's crime coverage is both detailed and accurate. Also see PROVEA (2002); *El Nacional,* March 12, 1997, D-17; and *El Informador,* June 11, 1998, A-5.

23. Residents of the *barrios* of Catia, La Vega, and Brisas del Paraíso, interviews by author, 1998 and 2003. "Un hombre linchado en Carabobo," *Diario de Caracas,* October 1, 2002, 4–10.

24. Interview by author, Caracas, February 16, 2003.

of organizing that promote violence and intimidation (Skocpol and Fiorina 1999, 2). Determined to stop security from slipping into the uncertainty that characterizes economics and politics, society sacrifices its most vulnerable sectors. As inequalities and tensions multiply, civil society becomes "not an inherently consensual arena" but "a terrain of struggle" over the distribution of and access to resources, entitlements, and, increasingly, rights. As fear of crime spreads further across neighborhoods, times of day, and types of people, it "robs subjects of their capacity to act with or against others. And when large numbers fall under the dark clouds of fear, no sun shines on civil society. . . . Fear eats the soul of democracy" (Keane 2002, 235).

Despite the depth and extent of violence in Latin America—or perhaps because of it—the region's governments have not come to grips with it. Even with better statistics and quantification of the economic costs of crime, officials are slow to develop holistic responses to fit the scope of the problem. Beyond specific crimes, this gap between action and the reality of violence is part of the region's citizen security crisis. Along with its extent, the complexity and local attributes of violence further underscore the need for an approach that accounts for the specific conditions in which violence thrives. Changes over the years in Latin America's poor urban areas, along with conversations with their residents, put all these factors in stark relief. Killing for tennis shoes and cutting off fingers for rings in Caracas, a frantic robbery of relatives' homes for cocaine money in Buenos Aires Province, and knife fights among neighbors in El Alto, Bolivia, all reveal the unnerving and unpredictable nature of violence. It is no wonder that policymakers shy away from hitching their careers to antiviolence policies.

A part of this violent push back against insecurity is a push against rights. Although human rights were a catalyst of the antiauthoritarian movements, they have been slowed and sometimes halted in the democracies experiencing growing opposition to rights for presumed criminals. Human rights language and strategies have even been co-opted, such as when the "right" to security is used to trump other rights and to rally mass protests in countries such as Argentina, Mexico, and Guatemala. Perhaps most revealingly, for most Latin Americans "impunity" no longer concerns unpunished abuses from the authoritarian era but unresolved crimes in the democratic one. In much of Latin America, rights and justice have become increasingly contextual—proper in some cases but not others and for some people but not others. Human rights organizations, whose role against dictatorships earned them lasting influence and respect in contemporary democracy, have broadened their focus to include current police practices (see Fuentes

2006a). But in the process they find themselves cast as defenders of criminals rather than of rights, thereby often inadvertently bolstering police resistance when they take the same kinds of critical stances that worked against the military. Such positioning can also signal to executive officials that they can move against individual liberties. In Venezuela, for example, the Chávez government faced few repercussions for rebuffing the rights organizations pressing it for information on police practices. Amid such forms of "rhetorical coercion," progressive policies and the kinds of citizenship critical to a democratic society are run aground (Krebs and Lobasz 2007, 412). Such practices extend to the daily acts of the criminal justice system. "A situation in which one can vote freely and have one's vote counted fairly, but cannot expect proper treatment from the police or the courts severely curtails the citizenship" at the core of democracy (O'Donnell 1993, 1361).

Socioeconomic conditions also underscore the need to look past the traditional explanations to understand how civil society is fractured by the conditions in which it lives. With one in three Latin Americans living on less than two dollars a day, many of the root causes of crime are certainly socioeconomic. Substandard education, unemployment, and poverty in general have all been correlated with crime (see Gabaldón 2002, 254). Correlation does not mean causation, however, and so proving a direct link requires specifying the variables in any proposed causal relationship. To demonstrate this relationship, statistical studies of economics and crime often play out first through direct statistical connections, usually with time lags to account for changes over time, followed by a deeper look at the explanatory phenomenon behind the numbers. Focusing on the statistical relations, a study by Fajnzylber, Lederman, and Loayza (2000)—probably the most comprehensive look at straightforward links between crime and socioeconomic determinants in Latin America—finds that the per capita gross national product (GNP) changes signs in different regressions (that is, it has both positive and negative correlations) and that education is not statistically significant. Other studies also indicate that households with low levels of education or income do not report significantly higher levels of violence (Bautista Lara 2006, 45). At the macroeconomic level, low-income countries such as Nicaragua, Peru, and Paraguay have relatively low violent crime rates, whereas several higher-income countries such as Brazil, Mexico, and Venezuela have relatively high ones.

In many studies the other socioeconomic condition most consistently and directly linked to crime is inequality. Affirming a 2002 study by Fajnzylber,

Lederman, and Loayza, a report by Di Tella, Galiani, and Schargrodsky (2002, 4) states that "income inequality, measured by the Gini coefficient, has a robust, significant and positive effect on the incidence of violent crimes." This association continued in work throughout the decade such as in a 2008 study by Briceño-León, Villaveces, and Concha-Eastman of the link between inequality and homicide in Latin America. Ever since data on inequality have been collected, Latin America has had one of the world's highest levels. With the richest 10 percent having an income eighty-four times higher than the poorest 10 percent (Kliksberg 2001, 106), the region's overall inequality rate of 49 is much higher than Africa's rate of 44 and East Asia's rate of 32 (Casas, Dacha, and Bambas 2001, 24). All Latin American countries have higher coefficients than the global average of 40, and those of several countries reach as high as 60.[25] The highest-earning 10 percent of Latin Americans receive 48 percent of national income, while the poorest tenth receive just 1.6 percent, compared with 29.1 percent and 2.5 percent, respectively, in rich countries (de Ferranti et al. 2004). Like the gross domestic product, inequality has been largely regarded as having one of the clearest social impacts as years of stagnation increase frustration over deferred promises of change. But growth has picked up significantly in much of the region since the 1990s, leading to higher and more equally distributed GDPs. Inequality, too, has subsided, with particularly significant decreases in Brazil and Mexico, the region's two biggest countries. Even as inequality has been pinpointed as having the strongest correlation with crime, many studies, such as Neumayer (2004), show that link to be spurious or insignificant.

Table 3.3 indicates that even a time-based relationship is not straightforward. It correlates change in the homicide rate with three socioeconomic indicators: inequality, unemployment, and the Human Development Index (HDI), which combines life expectancy, literacy, education, and GDP per capita. Placing these statistics on perpendicular axes provides a picture of regional trends that helps visualize the statistical strength of the relationship between homicide and socioeconomic conditions. Figure 3.1 charts homicide against inequality, and figure 3.2 charts it against the HDI. In figure 3.1 the spread of countries over all four sectors, with only a minority in the right-hand sector reflecting parallel patterns, indicates that a decade of change in the homicide rate does not correlate significantly with the economic vari-

25. See "Gap between Rich and Poor," http://www.infoplease.com/ipa; and IAD (2009).

Table 3.3 Socioeconomic Conditions: Change, 1995–2005

Country	Homicide rate	Ratio of top 20 percent to bottom 20 percent in national income	HDI	Unemployment
Argentina	+0.7	n.a.	+3.3	−5.0
Bolivia	−25.0	+33.7	+5.6	n.a.
Brazil	+1.4	−3.7	+4.7	+5.0
Chile	−1.9	−1.7	+4.8	+2.0
Colombia	−28.4	+5.0	+3.8	+5.5
Costa Rica	+0.5	+2.6	+3.2	+1.2
Dominican Republic	+14.3	+1.8	+5.6	+2.7
Ecuador	+3.6	+8.1	+3.8	n.a.
El Salvador	−12.2	+4.3	+4.3	n.a.
Guatemala	+1.7	−9.7	+6.3	n.a.
Honduras	−2.0	+0.1	+4.7	n.a.
Mexico	+0.6	−3.4	+4.3	−1.0
Nicaragua	+0.5	−4.3	+7.3	−9.8
Panama	−11.0	+9.2	+3.7	−4.0
Paraguay	+ 9.3	−1.4	+1.8	+2.3
Peru	+3.4	+3.6	+3.6	+1.2
Uruguay	−4.9	+1.3	+3.1	+2.0
Venezuela	+1.9	+1.6	+2.2	+2.7

Sources: Homicide rate: see appendix A; ratio: UNDP (1998, 2008); HDI: UNDP (1995–2005); employment: Mednik, Rodríguez, and Ruprah (2008).
Note: Scale is 1–100; "n.a." indicates data are not available.

able most linked to it. Indeed, the single largest group of countries experienced declining homicides amid rising inequality. In figure 3.2, all countries' HDIs increased, but less than half had a corresponding decrease in homicide, which runs counter to the assumption that improved HDI decreases murder rates.

The intuitive but often statistically weak link between socioeconomic factors and crime points to a need to better specify how and when they are connected. Many studies do so by looking at how poverty incites violence (Concha-Eastman 2002; Salama 2008). For example, finding that GDP growth and the Gini coefficient are statistically significant, the 2000 Fajnzylber report asserts that "stagnant economic activity . . . induces heightened criminal activity," and "the fact that this result holds not only for robbery but also for homicide rates may indicate that an important fraction of homicides results from economic motivated crimes that become violent" (p. 246). Other authors describe how inequality has become a sym-

Figure 3.1. Relationship between Changes in Inequality and Homicide Rates, by Country

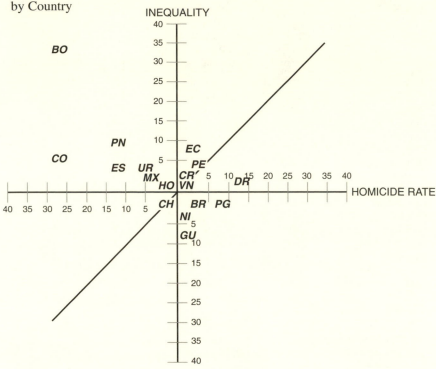

Source: Homicide rate: see appendix A; inequality: UNDP (1998, 2008).
Note: Horizontal axis indicates the change in homicide rate, measured by murders per 100,000 persons between 1995 and 2005. Vertical axis indicates changes in the ratio of the country's top 20 percent in national income to the bottom 20 percent in national income between 1995 and 2005.

bol of societal antagonism toward free trade, an unstable labor market, and the "plundering of the financial sector" (Reygadas 2006, 127) associated with the neoliberal economic policies adopted throughout Latin America since the 1980s. More specifically, Sánchez, Núñez, and Bourguignon (2003) argue that the poverty-crime correlation is strongest when poverty rates increase rapidly—that is, poverty may foment crime when it heightens frustration and dehumanization in ways that overwhelm mores against violence. In weak states with uncertain policies, low expectations of punishment only intensify that pattern. And if changing citizen attitudes toward legal norms explain how economic problems lead to crime, then they also reveal how much civil society itself has changed as well.

Figure 3.2. Relationship between Changes in HDI and Homicide Rates, by Country

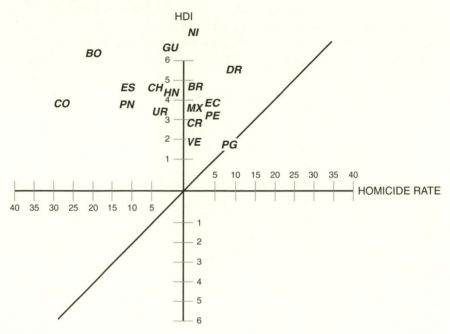

Source: Homicide rate: see appendix A; HDI: UNDP (1995–2005).
Note: Horizontal axis indicates the change in the homicide rate, measured by murders per 100,000 persons between 1995 and 2005. Vertical axis indicates the changes in the national Human Development Index (HDI), which combines measurements of life expectancy, literacy, education, and GDP per capita, between 1995 and 2005.

Like vigilantism and poverty, youth crime also demonstrates the impacts of citizen security on civil society. Violence by and directed toward youth, at rates that far surpass those of any other age sector in Latin America, is arguably the single most serious threat to the region's current and future well-being. Violence—homicide, suicide, and accidents—killed eighty thousand Latin America youth in 2006. About 29 percent of all homicides occur among people 10–19 years of age, and fully 36 percent of annual deaths of young men are homicides (Vanderschueren 2007), with the result that the youth homicide rate is up to three times higher than the national rates. At 36.4 killings per 100,000 persons between 10 and 29 years of age, Latin America's rate far surpasses those of other regions, which range from 0.9 per

100,000 persons in the high-income areas of North America and Europe to 17.6 per 100,000 persons in Africa (WHO 2007). The three countries with the world's highest youth homicide rates are in Latin America: Brazil, Colombia, and Venezuela.[26] Youth unemployment is up to three times the general rate in these and many other countries, and only about half of all Latin Americans finish high school (Kliksberg 2001, 109). Contradictory policies and restricted uses of public space not only contribute to these conditions but also demonstrate how unsettled society is in its response to them.

After the term *juvenile delinquency* was coined in 1815, its legal definition gradually expanded, along with that of police power (see chapter 2). Originally limited to serious crimes, the term soon encompassed a wide range of antisocial or marginal behaviors. As discussed throughout this book, youth crime has also become a central focus of Latin American policy. According to Alladi Venkatesh and Kassimir (2007, 7–8), the current era of democracy then "accelerated two trends" in legal approaches toward youth "clearly in tension if not outright contradiction": first, "a punitive turn in juvenile justice and the treatment of young people in public space," and, second, "an explosion of new legal instruments, discourses, and organization around the rights of children and young people." Restorative justice and rehabilitation are gaining ground in Latin America as applications of the second approach (see chapter 7). But clashes between these two strategies still dominate policy in the region, especially as a greater number of agencies with different views become involved. For example, the Human Rights Commission of San Luis Province in Argentina has brought greater attention to young people's socioeconomic rights, since 70 percent of them are not completing high school, making "juvenile delinquency a predominant" source of insecurity throughout the province.[27] Many of the resulting policy clashes center on basic legal questions such as minors' legal responsibility. The United Nations Standard Minimum Rules for the Administration of Juvenile Justice, commonly known as the Beijing Rules, state that legal re-

26. In Venezuela 54 percent of murder victims are under 25 years of age, and homicide is the primary cause of death of poor young people (Sanjuán 2003, 122). In Brazil youth homicides reached 51.7 per 100,000 youth, a rate that is a hundred times greater than that of most countries (UN-Habitat 2004). In the Dominican Republic nearly half of killings are of people between the ages of 20 and 29; 93 percent of El Salvador's homicide victims are 15–17 years old.

27. Joaquín Sorocco, government minister, interview by author, San Luis, August 8, 2002.

sponsibility "should not be fixed at an age that is too early, taking into consideration the circumstances that accompany emotional and intellectual maturity." The consensus of experts is that the earliest such age is 15, which is reflected in the laws of most countries. In most of Latin America, juvenile law covers youth between 16 and 18 years of age. They are held responsible for their acts, but in a separate legal category as "minor offenders." And yet because of the increasing number of arrests in nearly every country of persons between the ages of 14 and 18—for example, the chief of the Chilean Carabineros reports that in Chile arrests in this age range rose fivefold between 1986 and 2003 (Blanco and Bernales forthcoming)—there has been growing pressure to stiffen the penalties against this group and to lower the minimum age for legal responsibility to 14. Problems such as poor education, family violence, and the geographic patterns discussed earlier are quickly overshadowed in such debates.

Meanwhile, these debates feed into broader policy conflicts between crackdowns and prevention. El Salvador, for example, seems unable to move past its contradictory *super mano dura* crackdowns and its *mano amigo* social programs and court reforms.[28] In Nicaragua, many strong social programs from the 1980s continue to provide generous support for youth, but in 1999 the country enacted the Integrated Development Plan for the Prevention of Juvenile Violence "to clamp down on visible youth crime and thereby restore a sense of security among the urban populace," and the police systematically arrested suspected gang members without judicial warrants (MacClure and Sotelo 2003, 681). Despite socioeconomic conditions similar to those in its gang-infested neighbors to the north, Nicaragua has kept gang memberships low—and both approaches are credited for that result. Even when minors enjoy relatively strong rights protection, regular police actions toward youth in most countries are far more selective and discretionary than they are for other social sectors. Laws that are less clear and more flexible, such as dispersing crowds after a concert, tend to affect youth disproportionately. For example, the most serious confrontations in Argentina since democratization have involved police and youth between 15 and 18 years of age, and police profiling in the United States excessively affects African American youth. In short, to maintain control and respond to community demands, police divide society into groups that they *serve,* such as elderly people, and those that they *control,* such as youth.

28. On judicial reform, see Call (2003a). For an analysis of the exclusion of youth from legal protection and social services, see Savenije and Van der Borgh (2004).

That tendency toward control is most apparent in the use of public space. In contrast to adults, who are withdrawing more and more into private or guarded areas, most Latin American youth depend heavily on public space, because many of them are crowded out of their homes and because their identity, self-esteem, and status are built on how they act socially. In the midst of socioeconomic instability, however, these processes of socialization are warped. Generally, the higher levels of vulnerability, the hostility to authority, and the resentment at having adult responsibilities all amplify youth problems in Latin America. When these traits are combined with the consumption of drugs, music, and clothes, the rest of society regards adolescent socialization as unfit for public space. In polls, residents typically identify groups of youth in the street as the neighborhood's biggest "problem," whether or not they do anything illegal. Such responses help legitimize even extreme responses, such as killing teenagers in Honduras's basketball courts. Thus for local police officers striving to fulfill a community's sense of order, control of youth is almost always a priority. But the skills they need to provide and sustain that order, such as identifying causes of crime and developing responses to them, are the very ones most lacking in their education. Instead, youth policy is painted in broad strokes. Loitering, loud voices, and myriad forms of misconduct—such as "deviance" or "lack of adaptation," in the words of some police officers interviewed for this book—become characteristics used to mark youth delinquents and serve as a legally backed rationale for detention. Ironically, many young people report that the public focus on such behavior often increases its appeal by giving it an "outsider" or "rebel" association. Such valorization of antisocial status, in turn, deepens society's perceptions of youth not as individuals but as the instigators of local problems and of jarring cultural changes.

Such perceptions allow even greater problems to fester. One of those problems is youth gangs. Although most officials consider them to be the biggest threat to citizen security in Latin America, in most countries research and policy on gangs are marked by stale information and discordant approaches. Reflecting the dominance of traditional over problem-oriented policing, this clash begins with the policy premise that gangs must be controlled rather than understood. Often missing is the recognition that understanding is the first step toward control. In most countries gangs can be identified and understood through many characteristics: level of establishment (from initial perceptions as a distinct group to physical control of a neighborhood); links (to institutions such as schools); cultural touchstones (from music groups to fascist ideology); various benefits (recognition, protection, solidarity) and costs (danger, alienation, conflict, discrimination by the community); goals (from local dominance to international drug trafficking); and actions taken to realize them (from intimidation to armed violence). Failure to document these traits, along with differences among police officials in the definition of a gang, can result in either exaggeration or underestimation, usually leading to greater police discretion without greater effectiveness. Just as many city police in the United States have focused on isolating pit bulls rather than on how owners train them, police officers tend to profile youth who fit certain descriptions rather than the circumstances that cause that behavior. Also lacking are studies and consistency across time, geographic areas, and government jurisdictions. Clashes between different fields are common as well. Sociological studies that advocate improving the status of youth, for example, often collide with criminologists' emphasis on first combating violence. The resulting paralysis then allows policy to be hijacked by immediate political needs—a tourism campaign, for example, can turn a group of kids into a gang. Meanwhile, undercurrents are often undetected. In particular, the failure to understand socialization allows the gangs in Central America to create the culture, organization, and language that lay a foundation for growth by appealing to children and meeting their needs for structure, identity, and protection.

Although youth are already the primary targets of policing, societal demands for security around youth are among the tensest and most immediate. They sharpen the dilemma of choosing between traditional and problem-oriented policing, with efforts to address poverty and education clashing with clamors for crackdowns. Across social sectors, families want to protect their own kids while also demanding actions against others. Youth, who are the objectives of policy rather than contributors to it, are reluctant to go to the police even when they are victims—and they are more often victims than victimizers. As a result, most contact between youth and police is characterized by conflict and distrust. Although the continuation of such clashes exposes the drawbacks of traditional policing, amid public pressures for action they also can justify its continuation. Even when such encounters are mediated in public meetings that allow students to describe in detail their complaints about the hostility of residents and businesses, as well as the lack of public space and after-school jobs, the lack of follow-up only adds to their frustration.

Acting on this fragmented template, the civil society that instituted modern democracy in Latin America is not the same one that is trying to maintain it. Fear, exclusion, vigilante violence, economic frustration, and responses to youth may all help keep insecurity at bay in the short term, but they may make it worse in the long run, in part by weakening the capacities of the society that resorts to such approaches.

Conclusion

Because they add to the obstacles outlined in chapter 2, the patterns in power, geography, and civil society just described also affect democratic principles. The supposed trade-off between security and civil rights facilitates special operations, "social control" laws, and other repressive actions that remove criminals from the street but put a squeeze on the rule of law and other democratic standards. The neoliberal globalization of the last twenty years has limited what government can provide just as more questions emerge about whether democracy has lived up to its expectations. Democratization is not a tide that lifts all boats—in Latin America and other regions, agencies and organizations differ widely in their power and their acceptance of constitutional norms. Furthermore, the less police officials have to listen to elected leaders, the weaker is the legitimacy of those officials and the state's monopoly on legitimate violence. When such conditions lead to a public questioning of democracy or the overthrow of democratic regimes, then the threat that a security crisis poses to democracy is evident.

Chapter 4

Honduras

Reina Grazzo's rounds as a police officer in the outskirts of La Ceiba, a tumbledown city of 100,000 on Honduras's Caribbean coast, are unusual. Instead of following the usual fixed schedule, she attends sporting events, wakes, and other family or community events taking place on—but more often off—her shift. The knowledge she gathers in the process has proven invaluable. For example, because more people have come forward with names, the police have been able to limit gang shootouts in residential blocks. According to Grazzo,

> We try to develop a diagnosis of problems, to base our work on it. When we first started in 2003, people were shutting their doors and going to sleep at six in the evening because of the sheer terror outside. So we got community leaders together, and formed a Citizen Security Committee. We put the same officers in the same areas so people would get to know them. We set up centers for youth. . . . People then started coming to us, and we even got requests from other communities. So while things are not perfect now, people are no longer going to bed before sunset.[1]

Grazzo's approach demonstrates how problem-oriented policing can boost traditional law enforcement, but it also raises residents' expectations of help with their innumerable social and economic problems. As in other Latin American countries, in Honduras the move toward problem-oriented policing runs the risk of putting more demands on a divided and often cor-

1. Reina Grazzo, Policía Nacional, Comunidad Más Segura, interview by author, La Ceiba, February 25, 2004.

105

rupt police force still struggling to find traction in a very inhospitable terrain. Nothing exemplifies that challenge more starkly than the fact that, according to official numbers, Honduras's crime rate climbed to the highest in the world in 2009, which was more than double the average rate in Latin America. This chapter examines citizen security in Honduras's democratic era through the beginning of the Porfirio Lobo presidency in 2010. Specifically, it looks at how the political, institutional, legal, and societal conditions discussed in chapter 2 have not just slowed the move to problem-oriented policing, but also have been wielded deliberately to block it.

In Honduras a new era in citizen security dawned in the late 1990s as the country adopted one of Latin America's most comprehensive security overhauls. The establishment of an entirely new civilian police force in 1998 and a new penal process code (*código procesal penal,* CPP) in 1999, followed by other changes such as a national community policing program that began in 2002, contrasts with most other countries' gradual changes. But the reversal of reform has been nearly as rapid. The country's subsequent crackdown on crime, which repudiated and nearly dismantled the entire reform, has been one of the region's most resolute applications of a *mano dura* approach. As a result, more than in other countries the tension between traditional and problem-oriented policing is on full display in Honduras. Past practices clash with new laws, rights groups clash with state officers, and information clashes with itself—all amid pressures impeding the necessary but politically treacherous long-term structural change. Even as they recognize the benefits of problem-oriented policing, officials and the institutions they run remain wedded to the conviction that crime fighting is an exclusive police function based on forceful responses. Thus even though it is not a typical case, Honduras illustrates most clearly both the extensive ambitions and the underlying tensions of Latin American police reform. In an analysis of policing since the authoritarian era, this chapter will discuss how Honduras's efforts to break out of this deadlock demonstrate the risks of both following and not following the path to reform.

History

As in other parts of colonial America, policing under the Spanish depended almost entirely on provincial and municipal officials in the viceroyalty of New Spain, which covered modern-day Mexico and Central America. That tradition continued into the first century of independence. Though limited to local jurisdictions, the power of the police continued to be wide. Law enforcement officers were particularly fixated on stamping out anything unseemly, from vagrancy to indulgence in alcoholic beverages such as *chichi*. "Disorder lunches with abundance, eats with poverty, dines with misery and goes to sleep with death," lyrically warned the *Official Gazette* in 1869.[2] The most cohesive policing agency in the territory that is now Honduras was the Civil Guard of Tegucigalpa, formed in 1876 and based on the 1870 Urban Police Law. This unit focused on sanitation, property protection, and general public order. Like the police today, though, it was criticized for lacking coherent rules and for being too small to carry out its duties. As a result, the government formulated a police law that required each officer to "know all of the residents" in his jurisdiction and be able to recognize each one immediately (Article 37). The day this law went into effect—January 15, 1882 —is considered to be the founding of the National Police (Policía Nacional) of Honduras.

In 1888 a follow-up police law formed an urban unit, a rural unit, and a mineral police unit to protect the country's mines and other industrial sites. Although they were a major advance, these laws did not bring the expected organization and leadership to the police; the central government continued to exercise virtually no control over the police, and so its role was filled by political parties and the armed forces. The 1895 Law of Municipalities, which allowed local governments to set up their own forces, only served to divide the police even more. Such segmentation was addressed in part when an academy to train top officials was established in 1899 and one to train the lower ranks in 1921 (fifteen years after it was first proposed). A new police law was enacted in 1906, with reforms in 1916 and 1920 to expand officials' power to crack down on minor crimes such as soliciting prostitutes and not paying debts.

These and other laws also expanded the police by creating investigation and traffic units, among others. In 1922 Honduras established five National Police districts, and rural units were formed later. However, lack of funding, administration, and political stability prevented this enlargement from providing truly national coverage. Local authorities still held sway over public order, which, over time, led to variant police practices. This perennial division was finally ended by the 1963 military coup in which the Special Security Force (Cuerpo Especial de Seguridad, CES) replaced the weak Civil Guard.[3] The long-standing focus on social scourges such as "vagrancy and child delinquency" was supplanted by larger political aims. Police of-

2. Anales del Archivo Nacional, Fascicle 8, Year IV, August 1970, 23–24.
3. *La Gaceta*, No. 18.149, December 12, 1963.

ficers received tough military training and served in the 1969 war with El Salvador (Inestroza 2002, 329). In 1975 the CES was replaced by the Public Security Force (Fuerza de Seguridad Pública, FSP), which was under the control of the armed forces and the defense secretary. Its structure was far more organized and professional than that of any previous police force, and it had specialized units to deal with areas ranging from investigation to finance. In the decades that followed, the FSP, along with the secret police and the National Office of Investigation (Dirección Nacional de Investigaciones, DNI), were involved in disappearances, extrajudicial executions, drug trafficking, and other crimes. Battalion 316 and other death squad units were particularly active during the 1980s when the United States turned the country into a "USS Honduras" staging area for its proxy war against the leftist Sandinista regime in neighboring Nicaragua. So although Honduras had been ruled by elected governments since 1982 when a new constitution was adopted, regional conflict and military control continued to suppress real constitutional governance.

Citizen Security Overhaul

Democratization in the 1990s finally began to bring change. In 1993 the DNI was eliminated and a Public Ministry (Ministerio Público, MP) was established through the MP Law (Decree 228-93), which also created the Office of Criminal Investigation (Dirección de Investigación Criminal, DIC) "as an organ dependent on the MP, with exclusive responsibility to investigate crimes, discover those responsible and provide . . . all necessary information to exercise penal action." Although the police continued as part of the armed forces, the country's *fiscales* and judges were now in charge of investigation, and after training by the United States, Spain, and Costa Rica they began operating in 1995. The MP also became home to a new narco-trafficking unit (Dirección de Lucha Contra el Narcotráfico, DLCN), which plays a critical role in security policy. Bigger changes soon followed. The constitutional reform of 1996 transferred public security authority out of the armed forces, the Security Secretariat (Secretaría de Seguridad) was created in the executive branch in 1997, and the 1998 Organic Law of the National Police (Ley Orgánica de la Policía Nacional, LOPN—Decree 156-98) officially formed a new civilian police force to replace the FSP, with standards and structures similar to those that peace accords introduced to neighboring countries (see appendix B for a profile of the citizen security structure and the police force). The new National Police were given roles in Honduras's eighteen states in practically every area of law enforcement, including criminal investigation, prison security, and social services such as aid for children.

The police force is headed by the Security Secretariat (figure 4.1). Its chief, the security secretary (formally the Secretario de Estado en el Despacho de Seguridad), as well as other top directors, are named by the president. The secretariat is divided into two broad subsecretariats: Prevention and Investigation. Under the Prevention subsecretariat are three agencies. The first is the General Office of Preventive Police (Dirección General de Policía Nacional Preventiva), usually called the National Police (Policía Nacional, PN) because it is the country's biggest and most visible single police agency, responsible for street policing, detention, transit, and general crime prevention. The second agency, the General Office of Special Preventive Services (Dirección General de Servicios Especiales Preventivos, DGSEP), runs the penitentiary system, administers juvenile detention facilities, and oversees private security. The third Prevention subsecretariat agency is the General Office of Police Education (Dirección General de Educación Policial, DGEP), which is in charge of education, professional development, and the four police academies. The lowest-ranking street officers attend the Center for Police Instruction (Centro de Instrucción Policial, CIP), established in 1982. There they receive a six-month basic training course that covers transit, criminal investigation, special operations, prison control, and tourism. Higher-ranking subofficials go to the School for Subofficials (Escuela de Sub-Oficiales, ESO), founded in 2005, and candidates for *oficial* study at the National Police Academy (Academia Nacional de Policía, ANAPO)[4] for four years, with a specialization in their final year. ANAPO has about 210 students at any one time, and most instructors are civilians. The fourth academy, the Superior Institute of Police Studies (Instituto Superior de Estudios Policial, ISEP), was created in 1996 to provide advanced degrees in police science. It offers courses in areas such as policing strategy, criminal justice, and administration.

The Investigation subsecretariat is divided into two main bodies. The first is the General Office of Criminal Investigation (Dirección General de Investigación Criminal, DGIC), commonly known as the Investigative Police, which investigates most crimes (officially under MP direction). The second is the General Office of Special Investigation Services (Dirección General de

4. Formed in 1976 as the Escuela Nacional de Policía (ENAPO).

Figure 4.1. Citizen Security Structure, Honduras

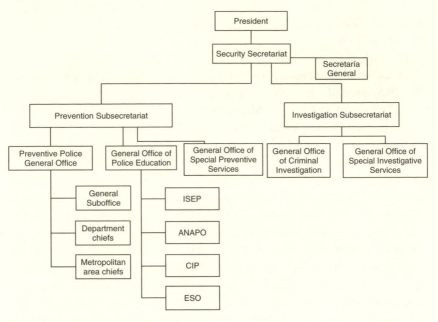

Source: Security Secretariat, Republic of Honduras.

Servicios Especiales de Investigación, DGSEI), which investigates economic crimes such as drug trafficking, money laundering, and contraband. The DG-SEI has had an erratic integration into the security system, primarily because its agents lack the specialized training they need for the complex crimes they are in charge of investigating. Since 2006, however, its officers have caught up by spearheading operations against organized crime networks such as car traffickers. DGSEI also oversees the Migration and Frontier Police (Policía Migratoria y de Frontera), which supports the Population and Migration Office (Dirección General de Población y Política Migratoria). These and other subunits are formed at the discretion of the security minister, potentially complicating the management difficulties outlined in chapter 2 by sidestepping the institutional and nonpartisan checks on agency proliferation.

Within the Security Secretariat are a large number of specialized units, such as the PN's Transit Police, the Feminine Auxiliary Police (Policía Auxiliar Femenina), the Department of Antidrug Analysis and Information (Dirección de Análisis e Información Antidrogas, DAIA), and sections on kidnapping, the family, children, drugs, and gangs. Among the most powerful of these specialized divisions are the Cobras, an elite counterinsurgency squad that, like SWAT (Special Weapons and Tactics) teams in the United States, is used for special operations such as antiriot. Before democratization, the Cobras were an antiguerrilla force used against labor unions and activists. Since then, they have been used to quell prison uprisings, coordinate antigang activities, disperse illegal land occupations, and bolster security in high-crime zones. Their headquarters, whose entrance features an oversized mural of their namesake, has also become a center for critical discussion of criminal policy.

Since 2006, in the years that the government has provided an official count, police officers in Honduras numbered between eight thousand (according to judicial officials) and ten thousand (according to police officials).[5] This discrepancy reflects the fact that the police include part-time and administrative officials. The ratio of police to citizens is about one to every 715 persons by the higher estimate or one to every 895 by the lower estimate.

Accountability was built into the country's new citizen security structure. In 1998 the Honduran legislature, the National Congress, proposed creating a Police Inspector (Inspectoría de la Policía) and a National Police Council (Consejo Nacional de Policía) made up of executive, justice, and NGO officials. Although neither agency was actually formed at that time, the LOPN established two major accountability agencies. The first was the National Council of Interior Security (Consejo Nacional de Seguridad Interior, CONASIN), whose formal responsibilities include formulating security policy, coordinating state agencies, advising the president, receiving complaints about officials, and, most generally, "supervis[ing] police activities." Composed of a wide range of groups, from local NGOs to state agencies such as the Human Rights Commission and the Association of Municipalities (Asociación de Municipios de Honduras, AMHON), CONASIN was conceived to be the primary channel for civil society's input on citizen security. The second accountability agency established by the LOPN was the Internal Affairs Unit (Unidad de Asuntos Internos, UAI), designed to be the primary internal affairs office and empowered to investigate wrongdoing by any police agent and to detain officers if necessary. Other accountability checks operate in the security bureaucracy. Within the police, the Preventive Police (Policía Preventiva) and the DGIC each have an Office of Professional Responsibility (Oficina de Responsabilidad Profesional, ORP)

---

5. This number had increased steadily since 2002, when the police had 6,663 officers, as well as 567 administrative, technical, and service personnel (Rivera 2002, 6).

that conducts internal reviews of police misconduct. Outside the security structures, a Human Rights Commission conducts investigations of police abuse and criminal policy. The *fiscales* also investigate police abuse.

Crime and Criminal Policy in Honduras

Since it was formed, the Honduran police force has had to deal with frequent changes in security ministers and criminal policies that have swung between iron-fist crackdowns and community policing. When Elizabeth Chiuz Sierra became security secretary in 1998, she halted the depuration (cleansing) of police then being carried out by the Transition Board. But when Gautama Fonseca was named security secretary in 2000, he renewed the depuration, attempted to rein in the increasingly out-of-control Citizen Security Committees, tried to improve prison conditions, and attacked corruption and organized crime. He often went around Congress, which helped to limit political obstruction but ultimately hurt his chances at altering institutional practice. President Ricardo Maduro (2002–6) had two security secretaries, Col. Juan Ángel Árias in the first year of the administration and Óscar Álvarez for the duration. His successor, Mel Zelaya (2006–9), appointed Álvaro Romero as security secretary, who was then replaced by Jorge Alberto Rodas Gamero in January 2008. Police general Mario Perdomo became vice minister.

As in other countries, these changes at the top have made it hard for policymakers to get a grip on one of Latin America's worst crime levels. El Salvador and Honduras have had the highest homicide rates in Latin America since 1995.[6] In Central America alone a crime is committed every ninety seconds. Robbery and kidnapping are the most common serious crimes in the region overall, whereas homicide is the most common in Honduras.[7] Emblematic of the concentration of violence in Latin American cities, 86 percent of all Honduran homicides are urban, making Tegucigalpa and San Pedro Sula, the country's two biggest cities, among Latin America's most dangerous (Observatorio de Violencia 2010). Top officials, however, sometimes refer to a "false perception" of rising criminality, and in any case pre-

6. In 1998 the rates were homicides, 154.2; assaults, 44.10; robberies and violent thefts, 5.12; and rapes, 1.17. Interpol, "International Crime Reports," Lyon, France, 1998.

7. María Siu, "Delincuencia atemoriza a Centroamericanos," *La República,* San José de Costa Rica, October 21, 2002.

fer to discuss progress on particular crimes rather than overall trends. In 2003, for example, the government reported declines in homicides, kidnappings, and assaults.[8] Although some sources document a decline in homicides between 2002 and 2004 (see appendix A), others show an increase in 2003 (see table 4.1). And the comprehensive tracking of statistics after 2004 by the Violence Observatory (Observatorio de Violencia), discussed later in this chapter, verify that homicides and other violent crimes have been on a relentlessly upward trajectory.

Since 2005, in fact, Honduras's crime rate has been among the highest in Latin America. Accompanying this increase has been, more anecdotally, the quick resort to violence during the commission of many crimes. As economic strains have grown alongside the influx of consumer goods into the country, even murders over cheap electronics have become common. More demand by a growing pool of perpetrators, as well as the greater resistance exerted by their victims, means that a taxi driver who relies on a cell phone that cost him a month's income will not give it up easily. Killings for these reasons, as in other countries, have increased citizens' fear of crime as well. Particular cases, such as the June 2006 midday shooting of the president's niece (who did not resist the attempted robbery), have seared society, creating deep fears.

Public panic over this growing crime rate, which gave rise to a *mano dura* by Maduro's National Party government, put the security reforms of the 1990s under strain. A businessman whose son was killed by criminals, Maduro was elected president in 2001 on a "zero tolerance" anticrime campaign platform. His initial criminal policy was based on his "Mi Compromiso Contigo" (My Commitment to You), a mixed basket of tough and preventive approaches such as more citizen participation, a purge of the police, and judicial reforms, particularly in juvenile justice. This mix opened the way to "Si Se Puede" (Yes, it can be done), a program made up of a range of rehabilitative and educational programs such as "Despertar" (Awake), a series of educational workshops to help parents, particularly in low-income areas saturated by youth gangs.[9] More lasting was the national community policing program Comunidad Más Segura (Safer Community), which is discussed in detail later in this chapter.

On the tough side, almost immediately upon taking office Maduro increased the size of the police force and flooded the streets with six thousand

8. Óscar Álvarez, security minister, interview by author, Tegucigalpa, July 18, 2003
9. Sandra Castillo, "Familias hondureñas vislumbran nuevos horizontes para sus hijos," January 20, 2004, http://www.casapresidencial.hn/reportajes/200104.php.

Table 4.1 Reported Homicides in Honduras, 1999–2009

	1999	2000	2001	2002	2003	2004	2005	2006	2007	2008	2009
Homicides	2,563	3,176	3,488	3,252– 4,167	6,231	2,155	2,417– 2,760	3,018	3,262	4,473	5,262
Rate per 100,000 persons	42.7	50.8	54.4	49.6– 63.5	89.8	30.7	37.0– 39.6	46.2	49.9	57.9	66.8

Sources: First row: 1999, 2000, 2001, and 2002 (lower number): Department of Strategic Planning (Departamento de Planeamiento Estratégico), Preventive Police. 2002 (higher number) and 2003: Department of Systems Engineering (Departamento de Ingeniería en Sistemas), DCIG, February 2003. 2004, 2005 (lower number), and 2006–9: Observatorio de la Violencia, Universidad Nacional Autónoma de Honduras, *Boletín Anual.* The discrepancy in the 2002 rates is an example of the poor system of criminal statistics. The higher rate for 2005 reflects Security Secretariat reports of an average of 231 violent criminal and noncriminal deaths per month, a number that some NGOs claim just includes criminal deaths. See also "Honduras, país convertido en 'tierra de nadie,'" *El Heraldo,* June 12, 2006, 2–3.

soldiers—an influx that nearly matched the number of police officers. The security budget was pumped up with an extra 200 million lempiras (just over $10 million at an exchange rate of 19.66 lempiras to one U.S. dollar) each to the police and the military. The government used these expanded forces to launch a series of crackdowns, such as the Honduras Segura program of joint police-military patrols in which armed forces were used in policing operations and an aggressive antigang campaign called Libertad Azul (Blue Liberty). This approach was credited for the 2003 crime drop, touted strongly by the government, whereas the Security Secretariat specifically attributed improved security more generally to the army's involvement. Apart from its high costs and risks, however, policing by soldiers is often another way to put off the needed long-term change. In the stream of announcements of new operations and equipment involving the military, in particular, police education and structure were rarely mentioned. This short-term approach also revealed a financial curiosity that has appeared in Bolivia and other countries: political will tends to suddenly produce the funds sought unsuccessfully the rest of the time. In short order, this tide of militarized money swept away much of Maduro's early prevention and treatment legislation.

The police were greatly strengthened by the new laws as well as by the additional personnel and funds. The primary legal instrument of the new approach was the 2002 Law of Police and Social Coexistence (Ley de Policía y Convivencia Social, LPCS—Decree No. 226-2001), which authorizes the police to "control" the people in any given area and to arbitrarily detain "vagabonds"—people who lack an honest means of living or are suspected of not having "licit" purposes in the neighborhood in which they are found. Much of the law's language—such as Article 100's focus on "in suspicious form" and a "state of societal danger"—gives the police wide discretion. But the law does not incorporate forms of mediation or education initiatives to help the police to better use this enhanced authority. Administratively, the LOPN, like any other law, gives overlapping controls to the National Police and the Municipal Police (Policía Municipal).[10] By means of these powers the law has been used as a tool of discrimination. One NGO for Hondurans of African descent says that such laws justify ingrained racism in which police just "assume" that Afro-Honduran men are criminal.[11] AIDS activists claim that the police use the LPCS as a form of zero tolerance against people with HIV despite the protections of the special HIV/AIDS law.[12] Lesbian and gay activists say that it is used to round up "suspected homosexuals" on charges of vagrancy.[13] The LPCS was quickly taken up to drive home the argument, reiterated in daily reporting, that the root of the crime problem is certain people who are irredeemably criminal. The new law makes "a clear differentiation between honest Hondurans and bandits (*bandoleros*)," one newspaper editorialized, "that is, between those who live within the law and those who break it."[14]

Youth and the Maras

Young people are a primary focus of criminal policy, and any lingering questions of how Maduro might balance repression and prevention were answered by his focus on youth gangs, known primarily as *maras* and

10. Use-of-force regulations are found in the penal process code, the Organic Law of the National Police, the Law of Peace and Social Coexistence, and United Nations norms. These laws allow the police to use firearms when nonviolent means have failed, when they are following a judge's orders, or when they need to prevent the imminent or actual commission of crimes—any of which to ensure the capture of a suspect, to overcome someone resisting legitimate police order, to avoid worse public dangers, to defend others from physical or psychological harm, or to maintain or restore public order.

11. Karen Vargas, Organización de Desarrollo Étnico Comunitario (ODECO), interview by author, La Ceiba, February 24, 2004.

12. Manual Soliz, Project Hope, interview by author, San Pedro Sula, February 20, 2004.

13. Activists, Comunidad Gay Sampedra, interviews by author, San Pedro Sula, February 2004; Colectiva Violeta and Ku Kulcan, interviews by author, Tegucigalpa, July 2005.

14. Edmundo Espinal Díaz, "La Policía Nacional de Honduras" (editorial), *Diario Tiempo,* January 16, 2004.

pandillas.[15] Hundreds of neighborhood gangs are active in Honduras, but almost all of them have become part of the MS-13 and 18th Street *maras.* Originating among Central American youth in Los Angeles, MS-13 and 18th Street are often known in Honduras as the "Californian" gangs or super-*clikas.* Together, they have an estimated 100,000 members in thirty-three U.S. states as well as in Mexico and Central America, held together by a tightly run structure with a strict code and a strong sense of identity. The biggest concentration of *mareros* (gang members) is in the three countries in northern Central America—Honduras, El Salvador, and Guatemala. And with its about 30,000 *mareros* or 500 per 100,000 persons (the numbers most officials agree on despite the differences discussed shortly), Honduras has more members of these *maras* than both Guatemala and El Salvador combined; Guatemala has about 14,000 (111 per 100,000 persons) and El Salvador up to 12,000 (153–180 per 100,000 persons).[16] Filling a vacuum left by the government repression that wiped out youth leadership in the 1980s and early 1990s, MS-13 became prominent in Honduras in 1989 and 18th Street about four years later.

The *maras'* role in the country's crime rate is usually exaggerated, however; only about one in five *mareros* is considered criminally violent. The police estimate off the record that only about one in three violent crimes is committed by *maras,* and the percentage of deaths nationally linked to gangs ranges from NGO estimates of 13 percent to official estimates of about 25 percent.[17] But the gangs are heavily involved in a range of serious crimes, from robbery to assault, and the many killings they do carry out use methods—such as decapitation—that would capture maximum media attention. Both MS-13 and 18th Street have also established neighborhood "tax" collection operations, and increasingly are part of international drug trafficking networks. As a result, the gangs receive nearly all the blame for crime in Honduras, and the national media coverage and the political rhetoric are saturated with descriptions of their activities.

15. The distinction between *pandillas* and *maras* is mostly usage—*pandillas* is the legal term used, and *maras* is the term adopted by the gangs themselves as well as the media. The main unstated difference is that *maras* are more organized, violent, powerful, and criminal than *pandillas,* which is often used as an umbrella term.

16. Salama (2008); Cruz (2008); "Guatemala, El Salvador y Honduras quieren impedir delitos desde cárceles," *La Prensa,* August 19, 2008. Of the other Central American countries, Nicaragua has about 81 gang members per 100,000 persons, Costa Rica 62, Panama 43, and Belize 36.

17. Prosecutors, judges, and police, interviews by author, 2003–7.

Enjoying high levels of public approval and the almost unanimous backing of Congress and the judiciary, criminal law has focused nearly exclusively on the gangs.[18] While less sensationalistic, the substantial international press coverage of the *maras* keeps attention trained on youth violence as well.

The centerpiece of the anti-*mara* policy was the August 2003 amendment of Penal Code Article 332, commonly referred to as the Law of Illicit Association or the Ley Anti-Maras (Anti-Maras Law). By casting a wide net of alleged criminality over all types of gang association, this law has probably blocked the path to problem-oriented policing more than any other area of criminal policy. It increased imprisonment of *mara* and *pandilla* leaders from six to up to twelve years (although for many the sentence has been far longer) and imposed hefty fines.[19] Despite its shaky legal basis, Article 332 was approved unanimously by all five political party blocs after a single "debate." It then quickly became a focal point of policing, from routine patrols to joint military raids, and has led to the arrest of up to 1,400 suspected *mareros* each year.[20] But most of those arrests do not lead to convictions. Of the 638 *mareros* that Article 332 netted in its first eighteen months, 37 percent were released for lack of evidence, and of those sent to a judge 22 percent had their cases dismissed (Centro de Documentación de Honduras

18. Most independent Honduran officials and activists believe that the major media outlets are paid by the government for favorable coverage. Editorials in *La Prensa*—"Edad punible," January 26, 2003, and "San Pedro Sula, como en zona de guerra," February 13, 2003—cite polls showing that crime is Hondurans' main concern. And the president had consistently high levels of approval for his security policy.

19. Article 332 "punishes with nine to twelve years imprisonment and a fine of 10,000 to 200,000 lempiras the heads of *pandillas* and other groups whose purpose is to take actions tending to physically attack, damage goods, threaten or extort persons or commit any act that constitutes a crime. The same punishment of imprisonment . . . reduced a third, will apply to the rest of the group members. Chiefs or ringleaders are those who stand out or identify as such and whose decisions influence the spirit and actions of the group." The 1983 code called for imprisoning heads of illicit organizations for between one and three years and focused on "illicit associations," defined as groups whose actions were "contrary to the law, public morality, or whose aim is to commit crimes." In 1997 Article 332 was revised to increase the range of incarceration to three to six years.

20. In 2003, 900 suspects were incarcerated under the law, followed by 1,390 in 2004, 1,334 in 2005, and 1,028 in 2006. There were 202 arrests in the first trimester of 2007. Estimates made by the Centro de Documentación de Honduras. Víctor Meza, executive director, Centro de Documentación de Honduras, interview by author, July 4, 2006. At the height of such detentions, gang members made up over a third of the population of two of the country's main prisons.

2004, 28).[21] These percentages indicate a high level of arrests based on just circumstantial indications of *mara* activity, such as tattoos. In fact, most of those arrested are not tried because of judicial inefficiency and a lack of evidence. According to some rights groups, of all those arrested under Article 332 in 2004, only 3 percent were sentenced, and the rest remained incarcerated in legal limbo.

As a result, Article 332 dumps the *mara* problem into the prisons, where up to two-thirds of prisoners are awaiting trial.[22] In those facilities the *mareros'* capacity for immediate harm is mortgaged for forms of organizing that vastly increase their capacity for harm in the long term. Moreover, *mareros* learn quickly how to get around the law. Many gang members now shun the trademarks of gang membership—particularly tattoos and style of clothes—which in more and more cases is prompting prosecutors and judges to declare that accusations against the gang members lack the higher level of proof that the penal process code requires.[23] This reluctance to prosecute antagonizes both police and executive officials, who blame such judicial obstinacy for reversing the police's hard work. At best, police officers say that the CPP "makes their work difficult,"[24] and at worst they are more inclined to kill suspected *mareros* on the street. The Human Rights Commission estimates that over 80 percent of detainees are beaten, adding that such abuse is not investigated by overwhelmed judges and *fiscales*.[25] Although the internal discipline of the police has improved, adds one com-

21. An Article 332 prosecution proceeds as follows. A suspect is detained after being caught red-handed committing a crime. The police pass the investigation report to the MP, who studies the report to decide whether to go to the *fiscal*, in which case formal action is taken against the detainee. The judge on duty receives the case and assigns the defendant a public defender if he or she has not hired a private attorney. The next stage is the oral hearing in the presence of the *fiscal*, who tells the judge the facts of the incident, the laws violated, and the evidence collected. The judge then decides whether to hold the defendant for judicial detention or preventive detention, the latter only if the *fiscal* requests it.

22. Mario Durón, communications director, Centro de Documentación de Honduras, Tegucigalpa, August 7, 2003, and confirmed by Jaime Banegas, director general, Sistema Penitenciario de Honduras, telephone interview by author, September 8, 2003.

23. In the trial for the December 23, 2004, massacre of Chamelecón in which gang members killed twenty-eight passengers on a bus, the defense's argument that none of the defendants had tattoos was especially criticized. "Coordinador de fiscales defendió a 'La Pantera,'" *Diario La Prensa*, January 7, 2004.

24. Marcos Arnaldo Herrera Rodríguez, police commissioner, interview by author, Tegucigalpa, July 8, 2005.

25. Eduardo Villanueva, childhood prosecutor (*fiscal de la niñez*), interview by author, Tegucigalpa, July 15, 2003.

mission official, many citizens do not file reports on police abuse because they are fairly certain that the accused police officers will learn the identities of their accusers. In the cases this commission official has handled, from "robbery to torture," there "are no witnesses," and when there are, they are weakly protected.[26]

Beyond its focus on *maras,* Article 332 has been used to widen police action in general. As the human rights commissioner unequivocally asserted, the law "practically authorizes the police to act with extraordinary powers that allows them to substitute for the MP and without any real oversight and destroying the presumption of innocence."[27] Because it increases the police's unaccountable power, Article 332 increases the inefficiency of the police as well. Police sweeps, in particular, tend to net the less dangerous and newer *mareros.* For example, less than half of them—45.4 percent in 2005 and 43 percent in 2006—could even be identified as members of a specific *mara.* And the detailed and diverse descriptions of their roles reveal that most of them who did identify with a *mara* were not central to it. Indeed, the descriptions of their roles—as couriers, recruiters, and drug runners—indicate that for the most part they take instead of give orders.[28] Nevertheless, many of them are indicted as leaders, indicating a very elastic interpretation of the clause that defines leaders as those "whose decisions influence the intentions and actions of the group."

Taken as a whole, Article 332 erodes a range of basic rights, from the presumption of innocence to the freedom of association, because it specifies not crimes but the possibility of committing them. In addition, the law expands police discretion by including "pernicious *pandillas,*" which are defined in LPCS Article 90 as "groups of adolescents between 12 and 18 years of age, who meet and act to attack other people or . . . to damage public or private goods or carry out excesses that alter public order." Because it shifts the focus of criminal policy from prevention toward detention, Article 332 also undermines judges by allowing detention without a judicial order. In short, along with other laws Article 332 incapacitates the rule of law because the law to which the police are supposed to be held does not match democratic standards. Such abuses have led to mounting pressure

26. María del Carmen, Northern Area Human Rights Commission, interview by author, La Ceiba, February 24, 2004.
27. Ramón Custodio, human rights commissioner, interview by author, July 4, 2006, and April 7, 2010.
28. Warden, officials, and prisoners in Centro Penal Barrio Inglés, interviews by author, February 24, 2004, and in Centro Penal San Pedro Sula, March 1, 2004.

from organizations such as the UN to modify the law by perhaps reducing its sentencing range. But Congress dismisses such efforts, and it stated in 2007 that any reforms would increase rather than decrease punishment.

Despite the centrality of *maras* in policing, the varying estimates of their numbers are additional indications of media sensationalism, the unstable statistical foundation of Honduras's criminal policy, and the lack of a consistent working definition. An estimated 475 *maras* are operating in Honduras, almost all connected to MS-13 and 18th Street. Also active are many satellite gangs, such as Los Vatos Locos, which are loosely allied with the Californian gangs. Many of these gangs, as well as independent gangs, school gangs, middle-class gangs, and others such as Los Chicos Bandos, are also connected to organized crime. When police officers estimate gang numbers, some include these groups and others do not. As a result, estimates of the number of *mareros* are chronically inconsistent. For example, police estimates of the number of *maras* in Tegucigalpa alone jumped from 45 in 1993 to 175 in 1994, and then down to 109 in 1999 and back up to 134 in 2000 (Andino Mencía 2006).

In 2000 the police's gang unit, Unidad de Prevención de Maras, estimated the number of *mareros* at 31,164, up from 25,940 the year before. Since then, police estimates range between 50,000 and 70,000, and the head of the police's gang division believes there are 36,000 active members and 70,500 sympathizers.[29] Executive officials tend to inflate these numbers, loosely throwing out estimates of between 60,000 and 100,000 members, collaborators, and sympathizers.[30] Not to be outdone, the press has suggested that there are up to 140,000. Often included in this population is the huge number of street children in the cities, estimated to be between 7,500 and 20,000.[31] Most of these children are not part of gangs but are associated with them because of their tendency to commit petty crimes and be addicted to sniffing glue. The police add that about 30,000 children do not see anything wrong with joining a *mara,* and that number may very well be included in many estimates of total gang membership. All these numbers are unsubstantiated by any public or independent study, and they are far above the estimates by religious groups of between 10,000 and 12,000 *mareros,*

29. Renan Galo Meza, director, División de Prevención de Maras, interview by author, June 2006 and November 2007.

30. "La venganza de los marginados," *El Progreso,* March 31, 2005.

31. Lower estimate: Reddy (2002); higher estimate: Casa Alianza director José Manuel Capellín, in "Major Bid to Tackle Gang Culture," *Honduras This Week,* May 13, 2006, 6.

and by most NGOs of between 30,000 and 36,000.[32] On the lowest end of the NGOs' statistical range is an estimate by the San Pedro Sula group Jóvenes Hondureños Adelante–Juntos Avancemos (JHA-JA) of fewer than five thousand active Honduran *mareros.*

No matter what number is used, a large gap exists between gang membership and actual arrests. At least in part because of scarce or mismanaged resources, the police carry out only about a third of all court orders for capture (Centro de Documentación de Honduras 2004, 177). At the height of anti-*mara* operations between August and December 2003, the police netted a total of 1,109 *mareros*—561 of whom were released[33]—and only 105 during the same period the next year. A sign of the dearth of critical analysis in criminal policy is the failure of journalists or opposition politicians to ask why the police can only find one in fifty *mareros* at best. At the same time, there is little doubt that the crackdowns had an impact, a fact that must be acknowledged by the international organizations that criticize Article 332. Because of police repression, many *mareros* have become less active —*calmarse,* as many of them put it—often leaving the cities for the countryside to reduce the chances of being caught. The resulting reduction in the *maras'* actions and concentrations and the ongoing police repression also have made it more difficult for *mareros* to replenish their ranks. An additional disincentive for younger and inexperienced youth to join gangs is the fact that, because of the difficulty encountered in collecting evidence against seasoned *mareros,* the majority of adult detainees are freed but the majority of underage detainees are not. However, even if it can rein in the *maras,* the policy of *mano dura* is no substitute for the rehabilitative programs, functioning juvenile facilities, efficient courts, and methodologically sound criminal policy needed to eradicate rather just suppress *mara* activity. When and if the police let up on their crackdowns, gang activity is likely to increase because the conditions that caused it have not changed.

32. The only exception among NGOs is the Christian Youth Association, which puts the number at 125,000. It claims that 55 percent are between the ages of 15 and 17, and 14.6 percent are between the ages of 12 and 15. Comisionado de Derechos Humanos, "Inicia la discusión del dictamen de ley para rehabilitar," *Boletín Informativo,* No. 1554, August 16, 2001. Police say that about 30,000 children actually do belong to gangs. The Inter-American Institute of Human Rights (Instituto Interamericano de Derechos Humanos, IIDH) estimates that 36,000 children in Honduras belong to gangs, or more than in the rest of Central America combined (IIDH estimates for Guatemala are 14,000, El Salvador 10,500, and just 1,800 for Nicaragua).

33. DGIC Departamento de Estadísticas, February 2004.

This reality points to the need to combine traditional and problem-oriented policing, such as by helping the criminal justice system focus on actual *mara* leaders at one end of the spectrum and at-risk youth at the other. Although some of the rifts between the police and courts were ameliorated by the Interinstitutional Penal Justice Commission set up to improve coordination among criminal justice agencies, legal contradictions allow conflict to continue. Article 332 spells out severe punishments for *pandilla* heads, but LPCS Article 91 mandates that *pandilleros* engaging in threatening or illicit behavior be handed over to a judge who then determines the socioeconomic correctives to be applied. But many police officers do not see a big difference between an 18-year-old *pandillero* and 19-year-old *marero,* who may be treated very differently under the law. Their ongoing comments on juveniles being allowed to go free has fueled demands, as in other countries, to lower the age of criminal culpability. In Honduras most people support lowering the age to 14, even if that means renouncing international treaties that recommend otherwise. However, such proposals ignore the fact that Hondurans between the ages of 12 and 18 can already be tried in juvenile courts, and that those between the ages of 18 and 21 are considered "minor adults." Only 5 percent of all crimes are committed by persons under 18, and just less than 1 percent of those crimes are homicides. But overlooking those facts and implicitly rejecting the concept that children are not legally responsible prevent a serious look at the conditions that cause children to commit crimes in the first place.

Police Structure and Functioning

Such a stiffening of laws and rhetoric, however, has not always been backed by the agencies that enforce them. The LOPN carefully laid out a network of agencies to counterbalance each other and make policy as transparent as possible. In particular, it reserved most security powers not to the Security Secretariat, but to the subsecretaries, CONASIN, and the Direcciones Generales (General Offices). On accountability, primary authority went to the Internal Affairs Unit. But as the politics of policing played out, official and actual power diverged. The Security Secretariat became a powerful political entity able to neutralize CONASIN, the UAI, and other actors. And yet a lack of coordination prevented criminal policy from being implemented efficiently. As discussed in chapter 3, the de facto use of power can alter institutional relations, practices, and authorities without actually changing the law. Although the security secretary gained dominance over outside checks, the subsecretariats and Direcciones Generales heading the Security Secretariat grew increasingly autonomous. In both law and practice, at least until the Police Law was reformed (as discussed below), they have had far more independence than their counterparts in most other Latin American security ministries. Each unit operates "without hierarchal control" (Article 11) under its own administrative structure and budget, which limits the secretary's control. Although the secretary names the subsecretaries, each one is guaranteed a four-year tenure,[34] and their wide powers—such as naming officials and controlling funds—allow them to be "isolated centers of power" over which the Security Secretariat has little official control. Security officials' professional status is determined by the Labor Law (Ley de Trabajo), which is controlled by the labor minister, and so the Security Secretariat has limited control over their careers as well. In another limitation, the country's Administrative Law (Ley General de la Administración Pública, LGAP) prevents the security secretary from changing the secretariat's administrative structure without enacting a new law. Thus from its inception Honduras's new security structure has suffered from a lack of both internal coordination and outside checks.

In fact, the most common and consistent criticism by police and governments officials alike is of a persistently poor coordination rooted in constant competition and proliferation. For example, nine different police agencies are involved in drug trafficking. The DLCN (the Anti-Narco-trafficking Unit) is limited by a high turnover and a stagnant budget, and many officials say off the record that the competition between the antinarcotics units in the DGSEI and DGIC is a major problem. Better coordination usually happens only in a well-planned action such as joint drug operations by border agencies, investigative units, the Cobras, the PN, and the army.[35] However, as in other countries, the Honduran police complain that when such joint operations come up short, the response is to create yet another unit that only complicates the planning and execution of future actions. For example, when a special antikidnapping squad (Organización del Grupo Especial Antisecuestros, GEAS) made up of DGIC and PN officials was formed in 2003, the DGIC ended up withdrawing because it was placed under the PN and the Security Secretariat's DAIA. New units also move the security system further away from the accountability built into the original model.

34. Tenure is set by the Law of the Jurisdiction of Administrative Challenge (to try cases in which the state is a party) (Ley de la Jurisdicción de lo Contencioso-Administrativo). Under the law, the investigative police are an auxiliary to the judiciary and the MP.
35. "Facilitaron armas se enreda lucha antidrogas," *El Heraldo,* April 7, 2003.

Most criminological analysis, for example, is carried out by the DGSEI, units of the DGIC and the PN, and the Center of Information and Communication (Centro de Información y Comunicación, CEINCO). Operating since 1993, first under the police and then under the Security Secretariat, CEINCO provides antidrug operations with intelligence collection, analysis, and operational planning.[36] It also maintains a registry of arrests, operations, and seizures related to illegal trafficking in weapons, ammunition, explosives, and other materials in connection with drug trafficking. Such controls give this unit institutional and political powers beyond those in the laws that established the national security structure, shaping internal power in unintended ways. Even more problematic, as discussed shortly, are CEINCO's connections with criminal activity.

In Honduras as in other countries, poor operational coordination and weak legal checks are most evident in criminal investigation. In fact, the most pronounced and deliberate change in power within the Honduran security system has been the funneling of authority away from the investigative police. That deterioration began with the 1990s reforms. Investigation depends administratively on the DGIC, but technically and juridically on the MP. That distinction meant little between 1995 and 1997 when the DGIC (then the DIC) was under the MP, which had the authority to "direct, orient, and supervise the activities" of the investigative police, but it has meant a lot since then. When the Public Ministry Law began allowing legal actions to be lodged against their personnel, the security forces countered with a "ferocious" campaign (a characterization used by several officials), tacitly supported by politicians, against the MP. Their efforts, along with conflict between the DIC and the PN, succeeded in use of the 1998 LOPN to transfer the DIC over to the executive's Security Secretariat. However, because of counterpressures by the Foro Ciudadano (Civic Forum), a consortium of twenty-five civil society groups, the central office of investigation remained in the MP (Orellana 2004, 9). The Foro pointed out that placing the investigative police within the executive instead of the Public Ministry would go against the trends in other countries, and it warned that that putting the investigative and Preventive Police under the same command might politicize

36. Most of this work is carried out using computers. U.S. counternarcotics assistance to Honduras is directed mainly to the counternarcotics units of the Frontier Police, the Security Secretariat, and the MP. Funds from the Bureau of International Narcotics and Law Enforcement Affairs (known by the acronym INL) also go to the two special investigative narcotics units in the DGSEI and the DGIC, as well as to programs that focus on the prevention of drug use by minors.

public security and continue the country's militarized and centralized model of policing.

In short, with the 1998 reforms the DGIC continued to operate officially under the Fiscalía's direction, but it became dependent hierarchically and administratively on the Security Secretariat. This uneasy compromise resolved the debate over investigative powers at the time, but sowed the seeds for later conflict by splitting up this key authority. In fact, the change in the DGIC's affiliation led to deterioration in the preparation, professionalism, teamwork, and transparency of criminal investigation. The DGIC is empowered to initiate investigation, collect evidence related to a crime, order the closure of a business in which a crime occurred, question witnesses, and participate in raids. But many times these actions are carried out without the knowledge or direction of the *fiscales*. Many police openly admit that they work on many cases without the Fiscalía's knowledge. Such parallel functioning of these two agencies, neither of which is allowed to interfere with the other, has led to collisions over these and other investigatory procedures in which cooperation is paramount.

More damaging have been the direct attacks on the DGIC from within the Security Secretariat. Civilians directed the DGIC until 2001, but then its leadership positions were systematically given to PN officials. Soon after it was established, the Security Secretariat initiated a "process of counter-reform and deterioration of the police . . . characterized by halting the process of depuration of corrupt officers and those involved in rights violations and in death squads." According to one analyst, the security secretary "privileged the Preventive Police and weakened the Investigation Police," which also halted the purge.[37] DGIC personnel grew from the original 300 officials in 1995 to a high of 550 under the MP. That number then fell to fewer than 330 after the DGIC was moved into the Security Secretariat (Centro de Documentación de Honduras 2004, 5). DGIC officials now estimate that they need at least three thousand investigators, which is three times their current count.

The Security Secretariat also created the DAIA in part as an investigative counterweight to the DGIC, even though the law clearly states that only the DGIC carries out criminal investigations. As the department began to usurp the DGIC, and as the security secretary reinforced the PN through other measures, the resources available for DGIC training and funding be-

37. Julieta Castellanos, "El tortuoso camino de la reforma policial," *El Heraldo,* October 8, 2002.

gan to decline. The PN was authorized to carry out functions previously exclusive to the DGIC such as guarding crime scenes and collecting and protecting criminal evidence. It also conducts investigations under certain conditions, such as for crimes whose punishment does not exceed five years in prison or in areas without DGIC "representation" (LOPN Article 43). The latter condition opened a big loophole, because the PN now has a far more extensive national presence than the DGIC. For example, the DGIC says it focuses its efforts in Tegucigalpa, which by law prevents the PN from carrying out investigations in the city. But in fact the DGIC is not present in most high-crime *colonias* (jurisdictions comprised of contiguous neighborhoods, often with up to 100,000 residents). The resulting shifts in interinstitutional power balances have been hastened even more by the droves of senior detectives leaving the DGIC, further damaging its capacity and justifying additional reductions in its authority.

Because of the PN-DGIC overlap and rivalry, both forces often pursue the same cases. Many victims go to both agencies to increase the likelihood that a crime might be solved, which only adds to the confusion and stretches out delays. Moreover, this approach often does not help anyway, because, as most criminal justice and many police officials agree, neither PN nor DGIC officials are able to carry out basic investigations. Although the PN was given more control in this area, its officers had had at most a short investigative course at the Centro de Instrucción Policial that did not include much of the needed technical training. Many investigative officers complain that evidence is often contaminated by PN officers who arrive first at a crime scene or during the investigatory process, and that a lack of follow-up by the forensics or criminology laboratory prevents officers from submitting many cases to the prosecutor. Poor protection of the crime scene is in fact a persistent and highly charged problem, with officers touching, discarding, and otherwise contaminating or failing to register evidence. Indeed, at crime scenes more time is given to accommodating local officials who show up with camera crews than to formulating a hypothesis or noting what bystanders are saying. In one deadly hijacking of a public bus in May 2007, the DGIC even failed to protect the scene itself or to collect shoeprints and bullet shells. Moreover, despite the scores of people at the scene, the judge issued a provisional dismissal of the three suspects in custody because the only witness available refused to identify the suspects. The lack of witness evidence is endemic. In a 2003 nationwide poll, 62 percent of citizens acknowledged that they knew the names of the criminals in their neighborhoods, but were afraid of reporting them because they did not trust the judiciary to convict them (Centro de Documentación de Honduras 2004, 47–49).

Police Management

Within the police there is a chronic lack of personnel, with *comisarías* of just seven or eight officers expected to cover *colonias* having up to 100,000 residents. Although nearly two thousand officers have joined up since 2002, raising the numbers in some areas by 80 percent, the police presence still varies widely within the country, reflecting the kind of geographic disparity discussed in chapter 3. The DGIC has no presence in many areas, and even the National Police does not have a permanent presence in over 50 of the country's 299 municipalities. For example, the high-crime Valle de Sula district of Choloma has had just ten officers and one permanent vehicle for 70,000 residents. At the national level, officials say that the force needs at least 26,000 officers, or over three times the current amount.

One source of such discrepancies and deficiencies is the police budget. Nearly 90 percent of the approximately $35 million annual police budget is dedicated to the PN, and some 80–85 percent of it goes to salaries. This concentration of funds for the Preventive Police and their salaries is typical in Latin America, depriving the judicial and other units of resources. Although most of the budget is earmarked for salaries (as in other countries), most officers are not paid a living wage. Much of the blame is placed on the Office of Human Resources, largely regarded as an instrument of the security minister to distribute funds based on political alliances. Most studies recognize the low salaries and professional dissatisfaction of the police throughout the region, but they usually do not explore the consequences for daily policing. Like their colleagues in other countries, the Honduran police complain of poor resources, professional insecurity, and a lack of health benefits. The average salary of 4,000 lempiras (about $200) per month,[38] which is what even new detectives earn, leaves them not much better off than others in the marginalized areas where most of them live.

Rotation inflicts further damage on officers' living standards and family life. Because it is usually too difficult to move entire families with a change in assignment, many officers are separated from their families for long periods and are forced to live in substandard housing. Indeed, for much of their

38. Villatoro Aguilar, police subcommissioner, interview by author, Tegucigalpa, June 27, 2005; confirmed by others.

careers in the lower ranks, officers may live up to eight hours from their stations. In regions farthest from urban concentrations, such as in the north, groups of up to twenty officers rent a single house together.

Nearly all police officers complain about their unmanageable schedules. Many work from seven in the morning to midnight with just every other weekend free, and others have twenty-four-hour shifts with six hours off and a break of seventy-two hours every fifteen days. They complain of an excess of responsibilities, such as guarding political officials and controlling street demonstrations, and of being pulled into community problems such as land disputes in which many of the people involved regard them as repressors, meddlers, or enforcers of unjust rules. Under these conditions, stress in the police ranks has led to high rates of depression, alcoholism, and drug addiction. Roughly 70 percent of officers who leave the police are forced out because of abandoning their posts and displaying a lack of discipline. Most of this behavior, says a police counselor, can be traced to work-induced mental disorders and personal anxiety.[39] The added stress on those who remain often leads to neglectful actions and mistakes such as evidence contamination. It also undermines their ability to move up. Police promotions are conducted twice a year. After a certain amount of time on the street, lower-level officers are eligible to take a course for promotion to Class 1, 2, or 3 lieutenant. Along with time on the job and general performance, courses at the academies are "the main filters" for promotion.[40] Most officers say (not convincingly) that the promotion process is fair, but then they often point out that the unclear guidelines for promotion allow favoritism to flourish. Many others complain about the absence of scholarships or opportunities for specialized studies.

The poor capacity of the police, along with the growing sophistication of crime, has gradually pulled the military into police operations such as neighborhood sweeps, inundations of gang territories, suppression of prison riots, and antidrug operations in combined military-police units. Although police officials stress the official separation of police and military, with soldiers limited to providing back-up, the relationship between the two is in fact more complicated. Military involvement brings rapid results, but it is harmful in the long term because soldiers' combat training is at odds with

39. Evelyn García R., psychologist, Policía Nacional, interview by author, Tegucigalpa, June 27, 2005.
40. Rodolfo A. Calix Hollmann, subacademic director, Dirección General de Educación Policial, interview by author, Tegucigalpa, July 22, 2003.

the rules and goals of policing a democracy. In 2002 most of the sixty-nine inmate deaths in the El Parvenir Agricultural Penal Colony fire were caused by soldiers (this incident is discussed in more detail later in this chapter).[41] But even without the armed forces, the police are increasingly militarized, donning military uniforms and combat boots, which only fosters intimidation in civilian areas. Their greater discretion does not, however, improve their efficiency. For example, armed with Decree 123-2002, described later in this chapter, the police have carried out several raids in Tegucigalpa, where contamination of the scene—stemming in part from the lack of investigative personnel—led the Fiscalía to free the detainees. Without investigative acumen or citizen trust, such actions often just displace their target. Anti-*mara* sweeps and raids look great on television, but often disperse *mareros* into a wider swath of territory.

Along with such practices, poor resource management has turned much of Honduras into a battle zone. Weak control of police materiel in particular allows more arms to enter the general circulation and adds to the estimated 500,000 illegal weapons that make up about two-thirds of all firearms in the country and are responsible for between 75 percent and 82 percent of killings since at least 2005, when this statistic began to be independently documented.[42] Over 80 percent of youth killings are estimated to have been committed by firearms, 78 percent of which were AK-47 assault rifles (Programa Centroamérica 2006). Killings with Uzis are also common in many Tegucigalpa neighborhoods. Several laws and legal provisions prohibit and control arms possession and use. Only certain officials are allowed to have high-caliber weapons such as the AK-47, which, along with semiautomatic revolvers and pistols (45-gauge and 11.5-gauge), are strictly limited by the 2003 Special Law for the decommission of AK-47 and other Prohibited Arms (Ley Especial para el Decomiso de las Armas AK–47 y Otras no Permitidas). The 2004 Law of Arms Possession and Control (Ley de Tenencia

41. Noring Reyes, warden (director), interview by author, El Porvenir, February 23, 2004.

42. Firearms accounted for 75.9 percent of homicides in 2005, 78.0 percent in 2006, 75.8 percent in 2007, 78.6 percent in 2008, and 81.4 percent in 2009 (Observatorio de la Violencia 2006, 2007, 2008, 2009, 2010). Other groups estimate that arms are responsible for about fourteen hundred injuries each year ("Crecen víctimas por armas de fuego," *Diálogo Centroamericano,* no. 33, September 1998). The UN estimates that about half a million illegal arms are in circulation, and most national sources estimate a total of a million firearms. "Inicia proceso para registrar un millón de armas en el país," *El Heraldo,* December 5, 2002. But the police's Arms Registry Office reports 204,000 registered arms and an estimated 500,000 unregistered ones.

y Control de Armas) punishes possession of "arms of war" (such as the AK-47) with up to six years of imprisonment, and Police Law Article 332 punishes trafficking and possession of AK-47s with ten years of imprisonment and a heavy fine. The 2000 Law of Control of Firearms, Munitions, Explosives and Similar Weapons (Ley de Control de Armas de Fuego, Municiones, Explosivos y Otros Similares) limits the number of arms that can be registered to five per person. Efforts are under way to tighten these laws. Security Secretary Romero wanted to limit firearms ownership to one, and only for the home. But the current law has no requirement of background checks or good conduct, and anyone can buy a sophisticated firearm for upwards of $20 on the street. Control by and within the police is also lax. Investigations always seem to turn up AK-47 parts lying around police stations, and less than half of murder weapons are found and tested. Police are also victims of this uncontrolled arms use; about four officers are killed each month.

Many of these counterproductive practices begin in the police academies. ANAPO has inadequate resources, with only a barely functioning forensics laboratory. Moreover, according to ANAPO's directors and others, limited budgets for training (with just one small computer lab at ANAPO and none at the Centro de Instrucción Policial) and equipment and uniforms (including shoes) contribute to high turnover and desertion. Lack of funds also sidetracks directors' plans to offer more specializations, such as a master's program in investigation.[43] Casa Alianza has a weekly training course for police, but, as one of the instructors points out, so many of them leave the force that it has little impact.[44] CIP's six months of training for cadets focuses on the use of arms, but with little legal or sociological education, and many of its graduates—working as street officers—are functionally illiterate. Many CIP graduates did not finish elementary school and, some officers say, only studied at CIP for four months. As for the center itself, its infrastructure is very poor, and it needs twice its normally allocated budget. Plans to make admissions more selective and to extend the training course to ten months have been delayed under pressure to keep up the numbers. At the upper levels, even the DGIC agents with some university education can-

43. ANAPO staff and Caballero Baca, assistant director, ANAPO, interviews by author, Tegucigalpa, June 16, 2006.
44. Juan Carlos Ávila, Street Team, Casa Alianza, interview by author, Tegucigalpa and Comayaguela, August 2, 2003.

not build on that education through more advanced training in investigation or other specialized fields. Some of these problems were foreseen in the original reform, which tried to bolster police education by widening it. In particular, the LOPN established an Academic Council, which includes representatives of the country's two main universities, National Autonomous University (Universidad Nacional Autónoma de Honduras, UNAH) and Francisco Morazán University (Universidad Pedagógica Nacional Francisco Morazán, UPNFM), but in reality cooperation or integration has been limited.

Unreliable statistics also undermine the police's functioning. Without a national system of crime reporting or an official information network-sharing system between the DGIC and *fiscales* (with each unit logging its own very different numbers), tracking both crimes and cases is a challenge. Even for a statistic as central as homicides, the PN, DCIG, courts, and capital city morgue each report different numbers. Morgue officials say that many of the bodies they receive are not recorded, and that other bodies are not sent to them at all.[45] To resolve these informational discrepancies and absences, in 2005 the UN-sponsored Violence Observatory began collecting and categorizing all incidences and fatalities involving violence. But in its first few years it was physically or electronically restricted from Security Secretariat data. When the Observatory reported rising murder rates in June 2006, the new security minister accused its staff, mostly national and international specialists, of a leftist bias based on their NGO affiliations.[46] He also claimed they did not use the available information, but he acknowledged that such information was not readily available. Even the small percentage of crimes that is reported is not necessarily transmitted accurately, as many people who try to file a complaint or report will confirm. For example, one summer morning in June 2006 a woman in the Tegucigalpa *colonia* of Kennedy tried to report a knife attack the night before. But she was brushed off by several different officers as she went to different stations. The most concrete suggestion she received was to go to headquarters downtown, which her limited time and money did not allow. In addition to adding fuel to public frustration, such practices undercut the criminal justice system.

45. PN and DGIC officials; Sindy Fortín, director, Centro Electrónico de Documentación e Información Judicial, Corte Suprema, Tegucigalpa Morgue, interviews by author, June–July 2005.

46. Álvaro Romero, security minister, interview by author, Tegucigalpa, June 13, 2006.

Criminal Law and Procedure

Diverting attention from such institutional practices is the great deal of misplaced blame on supposedly lax laws, which falls primarily on the penal process code, a favorite target of police and government wrath. Amid a drumbeat of often unchallenged assertions that justify actions such as forced confessions, such blame by the police and government aggravates the perceived conflict between new laws and individual rights. Honduras actually experienced Latin America's biggest drop in unsentenced prisoners after adopting its penal process code, from 156.6 in 1999 to 102.2 in 2005 (Riego and Duce 2008, 44). But the police see that as a weakness of enforcement rather than a hallmark of due process. Like his colleagues in other countries, Óscar Álvarez, Maduro's security secretary, asserted in a 2003 interview that there was a fundamental divide between the larger philosophy of most criminal justice officials, whose leftist ideology leads to a "guaranteeist" prioritization of civil rights provisions, and the rightist *mano dura* approach of the police, who for most of their history were part of the military. He called for scrapping the new penal code because it embodied a "guaranteeist" approach that was meant for developed societies but was far too weak against Honduras's particularly virulent breed of crime. Believing that *mareros* were little more than irredeemable killing machines often under the control of vicious organized crime networks, Álvarez crudely dismissed NGOs' charges of rights abuse against the state.[47] Any law or set of legal standards so openly derided by the chief of security are unlikely to be followed by his subordinates. In fact, as one Cobra official stated confidentially, "people don't protest about human rights because they're too fed up with crime."[48]

Such views were followed up by means of legal action. In September 2002, for example, Álvarez put forth proposals through an interinstitutional security commission to "adjust" the penal process code to facilitate anticrime and antigang operations.[49] In June 2003 Congress deliberated on reforming the LOPN to help the police act "with firmness" against criminals, using a structure modeled after "the repressive police of New York" that provided "protection to officers who currently might be jailed for acting in

47. Óscar Álvarez, security minister, interview by author, Tegucigalpa, July 18, 2003; see also "Marero tenía su propio cementerio en un cerro," *El Heraldo,* April 6, 2005.

48. Anonymous, interview by author, Cobra Headquarters, July 11, 2005.

49. "Revisarán Código Procesal," *El Heraldo,* February 6, 2003.

their own self-defense against criminals."[50] A year later Maduro accused those filing a petition of unconstitutionality against Article 332 of "violating the human rights of hundreds of thousands of innocent Hondurans."[51]

This choice between guaranteeism and crime fighting was repeated in public as well. Supervising a January 2005 security operation, the president said, "My desire is to send all criminals to prison and then I'll worry about overcrowding in Honduran prisons, although always respecting the human rights of the prisoners."[52] Ignoring the fact that two of Latin America's worst prison massacres occurred during his administration and that well over half of all detainees were remaining unsentenced for years in massively overcrowded facilities,[53] the assumption being made—and largely accepted by society—was that imprisonment was the only solution. Porfirio Lobo, then president of Congress and presidential candidate, threw down the gauntlet when he proclaimed, "We are not going to recede one centimeter from the Ley Anti-Maras. . . . And to those who oppose this, all those who have threatened with going to international human rights tribunals, . . . are going to face the firm fist of our determination, the determination of a people who have said that we are not going to surrender, we are not going to permit a group of delinquents to rob us of security."[54] "Who has more human rights?" he asked, "the innocent person who represents the great majority of the people or the criminal who violates the rights of the rest?"[55]

Attacks on the rights of criminal suspects invariably lead to attacks on the penal process code that protects them. As part of its strengthening of due process, the CPP gave more powers to the MP and introduced public oral trials as well as new courts at the investigation and sentencing stages, such as the Juez de Ejecución to oversee pretrial procedures. Since coming into

50. "Congreso Nacional reformará la ley de Policía," *La Prensa,* June 23, 2003. This measure was based on a plan developed under Fonseca, who disavowed it because it was written by hard-line officials.

51. "Maduro defenderá legitimidad de la Ley de Propiedad y de la 'ley antimaras,'" August 9, 2004, http://www.CasaPresidencial.com.

52. "Llenaré las cárceles hondureñas de delincuentes," January 13, 2005, http://www.casapresidencial.hn/2005/01/13.

53. In 2004 Honduras's eleven to twelve thousand detainees were double the 1992 prison population and the intended capacity of the system's twenty-four facilities. Between 52 percent and 64 percent of prisoners were usually awaiting trial, over 90 percent of them for nearly two years. Centro de Documentación de Honduras (2004, 68, 96).

54. "No vamos a retroceder ni un centímetro con Ley Antimaras," *La Tribuna,* January 26, 2004.

55. "Sociedad ya no tendrá ese yugo de las maras," *La Tribuna,* August 8, 2003.

effect in 2002, the CPP has also sped up the slow criminal justice process through alternative resolution mechanisms such as mediation, which were credited with resolving 307 cases in the code's first two months, compared with 448 cases the entire previous year.[56] The code also has measures to fast-track cases stuck in the judicial process. Such measures were long needed. For example, of the 2,708 crimes reported in the first four months of 2002, just 295 were processed by the Fiscalía and presented to judges. Of those 295 cases, 128 had initial audiences and 67—limited to very serious crimes—led to detentions.[57]

As set out by the penal process code, the procedure followed in dealing with a crime has three principal stages: preparatory, intermediate, and debate. At a crime scene the *fiscales* (with the support of medical forensics) are supposed to carry out the first steps in the investigation, directing the DGIC officers in the collection of evidence and the questioning of witnesses. In many cases, however, neither a *fiscal* nor a DGIC official is available, leaving the work to the PN.[58] After the evidence and testimonies are compiled, the judge listens to the cases presented by the *fiscal* and the public defender in deciding whether to free the detainee for lack of evidence or to order detention for trial. The police are not allowed to order or carry out preventive detentions, except during the commission of a crime or under other exceptional circumstances. But the DGIC can ask the judge in charge of the case (*juzgado*) to extend the normal twenty-four-hour period of detention and investigation to up to six days (police may detain suspects incommunicado only under a *fiscal*'s orders and for no more than twenty-four hours, and must free anyone against whom the evidence collected is compromised). In areas without DGIC detention facilities, the PN may hold de-

---

56. The code has been fortified with international support, such as a 2002 IABD loan for a Justice Administration Modernization Program to strengthen the public defenders, the court inspectors (*inspectorías de tribunales*), and the judicial academy; to build ten municipal judicial centers; to train MP staff; and to reduce backlogs through an e-mail system for preparing and dispatching cases. Judicial reform has been supported by numerous international agencies, including the World Bank, the U.S. Agency for International Development, and the Japan International Cooperation Agency. Germany has provided about 300 million euros, and Sweden and Spain also send funds. Other countries have helped the police in particular—Taiwan, for example, has paid for much of the fleet of police cars.

57. "Honduras: Satisfacción por logros del Código Procesal Penal," La Prensa, April 10, 2002.

58. Procedures vary according to how the crime is committed and discovered. For example, if a person is arrested after being caught red-handed, the investigative police officer has six hours in which to present the case to a *fiscal*.

fendants instead, but in such cases it must hand over all information and report all actions to the DGIC. If the defendant cannot afford a lawyer, the *juzgado* can assign a court-appointed attorney (*abogado de oficio*). Only in some minor cases can the *juzgado* grant bail, and plea bargaining is not allowed. If warranted, the detainee is brought to the initial audience with the judge, *fiscal,* accuser, and all lawyers.

The intermediate stage consists of the formal accusation and trial preparation. After the DGIC completes the investigation, the *juzgado* determines whether there is sufficient evidence for trial. If warranted, the *fiscal* (usually the special *fiscal* on the particular problem involved) approves an official investigation and assigns it to a police agent, who must then present a preliminary report within twenty-four hours. Based on this report, the *fiscal* can then apply an alternative form of resolution, request preventive detention from a judge, or continue the investigation.

This process is littered with deadlines missed by the police, *fiscales,* and judges. The Fiscalía is unable to handle all the reports it gets in a timely manner and has to send back many incomplete police reports. Even after delays of six months or more, many of those reports are incomplete or insufficient. The biggest delays happen during the police investigation and later in the courts. One study revealed that of the outstanding cases at the time, 23.9 percent were in the courts and 37.3 percent under investigation—that is, nearly two-thirds were in the hands of either the police or the judges. Many judges blame poor police work for the delays, saying that 40 percent of the cases they receive must be absolved because of poor investigation.[59] In 2002, the CPP's first year, just 5,068 of the 23,644 crime reports sent to the DGIC were returned to the Fiscalía with completed investigations (Centro de Documentación 2004, 70).[60] Not only must officials free anyone against whom the evidence collected is compromised, but the *criterio de oportunidad* also allows the MP to refrain from prosecution for reasons such as the detainee's "personal circumstances" (CPP Article 28). The police, in turn, blame such regulations for "nullifying" their work.

The *fiscal* can also request a continuation of the investigation by the DGIC, the *juzgado,* the defendant's attorney, the *fiscal,* and the accuser's attorney. If granted, this "discovery" period is limited to thirty days but usu-

59. Alex Urrea, Penal Court Judge, interview by author, San Pedro Sula, February 24, 2004.
60. Although a lack of personnel is the usual complaint, the office with the higher average of cases did not have the longest delays.

ally takes much longer—often because judges, lawyers, and police deviate from established procedures.

The third and final stage is the debate, made up of the trial and sentencing. Although the more efficient oral arguments have now been adopted, judges still rely on written statements to the *juzgado* laying out the information obtained during the discovery. This practice, together with the lack of judicial staff, contributes to a backlog that stretches trials out for months and even years. Once a trial is complete, the court sends the verdict to the Court of Appeals (Corte de Apelaciones) for ratification, usually after any appeals by either the prosecutor or the defendant. Without time limits on these steps, delays are frequent at this stage as well.

Toiling under these conditions, one DGIC officer said that he and his colleagues have basically given up on being investigators. In San Pedro Sula, well over two thousand bodies are brought to the city morgue each year, 80 percent of which are gunshot victims. Yet the DGIC's office there employs only about a hundred officials, about eighty-five of whom are rookies, working in units that are supposed to cover, among other serious crimes, homicides, assaults, vehicle thefts and other robberies, and financial crimes. As in other countries in Latin America, officials' abilities to follow the procedures fully and correctly are hobbled by a lack of personnel and of the specialized and adequately equipped laboratories needed, for example, to detect water and air contamination or preserve the DNA evidence on which nearly 90 percent of criminal charges depend (Centro de Documentación de Honduras 2004, 85). Agents are able to conduct tests for narcotics, but they cannot conduct other investigatory tests because they have no photo labs, document testing equipment, vehicular reports, ballistics labs, or biological or chemical toxicology equipment (such as for tests to detect alterations intended to cover a vehicle's ownership). Some detectives may even be trapped at headquarters because no vehicle (or one with gasoline) is available to take them to the crime scene. In addition, many civilian officials charged with preparing cases lack sufficient training to do so. Analysis personnel, for example, are routinely criticized for their sloppy work on evidence.

One detective said on condition of anonymity that they have no real training in investigation or in citizen relations—basically they are just given a gun. When the DGIC was under the MP, its officials received extensive training by the International Criminal Investigative Training Assistance Program (ICITAP), a U.S. Justice Department program begun in 1986. Since then, however, they make do with little more than the rudimentary CIP course—essentially lowering them to the PN level. Many PN officers intimidate witnesses, inadequately protect crime scenes, and conduct their own parallel investigations while passing themselves off as investigative police.[61] Officers often plant or remove evidence, depending on whether they want to harm or benefit the accused. Overall, officials estimate that 90 percent of all serious crimes are not investigated, and one NGO says that 83 percent of homicides are unsolved.[62] Thus unless someone is caught *in flagrante delicto* (red-handed) or linked to a crime through strong evidence, such as a blood sample, there is little chance it will be solved.

But when and if more police or equipment are provided, they may be used just to ramp up the traditional and increasingly ineffective tactics. Describing his need for more officers, one police official said he would use them to support neighborhood "saturations." For example, after sending in a hundred agents and withdrawing most of them, he would leave twenty for a certain amount of time—say, eight or ten days—and then they gradually remove the rest until five are left.[63] If carried out in conjunction with social services and with adequate oversight, such a process could be an opportunity to bring in problem-oriented policing through traditional tactics. Encouraging community participation in the wake of an armed invasion is far from ideal, but many Honduran neighborhoods are robust enough to meet that challenge. Similarly, the long-term visions of several top officials, even if motivated by traditional goals, could also be a politically feasible way to integrate problem-oriented approaches. In an interview, the director of the country's Planning and Management Assessment Unit (Unidad de Planeamiento y Evaluación de Gestión, UPEG) described projects to improve policing by means of CompStat software, digital mapping, a crime observatory, and a new analysis center.[64] As noted in the first two chapters, part of the citizen security crisis is managing the police and the functioning of the criminal justice system. Therefore, an assessment of the limitations of the current police units should precede any restructuring. Before adopting

61. César Alexis Ruiz, chief of personnel, DGIC, interview by author, San Pedro Sula, March 2, 2004.
62. Andrés Pavón, president, Comité para la Defensa de los Derechos Humanos en Honduras (Committee for the Defense of Human Rights in Honduras), interview by author, Tegucigalpa, August 6, 2003.
63. Gustavo Adolfo Bustillo Salgado, subcommissioner, Policía Nacional, interview by author, San Pedro Sula, February 28, 2004.
64. Jorge Nery Chinchilla O., director, Unidad de Planeamiento y Evaluación de Gestión, interview by author, Tegucigalpa, June 14, 2006.

CompStat, for example, the Honduran government should investigate why, as one police officer stated, there is only sporadic internal communication on core issues such as drug trafficking and application of the CPP.[65] The national government must also increase the size and power of its Controlaría General (Comptroller General), the agency that oversees administrative and budgetary state procedures, because it is among the smallest and least powerful in the region.

When combined with the suspicions between the police and the Fiscalía and the lack of a functioning communications network, such poor coordination slows down and impairs criminal investigation. To improve interagency coordination on criminal investigation, the Public Ministry in November 2002 created the Integrated Center of Interinstitutional Work (Centro Integrado de Procesos de Trabajos Interinstitucionales, CIP). It is made up of *fiscales,* police, public defenders, and forensic doctors, divided into shifts and teams that work around the clock. When a crime is reported to the CIP, it brings the police and *fiscal* together to decide whether to move forward with searches, arrests, and alternative resolutions, and, if applicable, to release suspects in custody. CIP also pulls together evidence from crime scenes, helps prioritize cases, develops hypotheses, and standardizes procedures. According to many officers, however, CIP's contributions are neutralized by demands to solve crimes that push it to initiate charges without sufficient evidence. In other words, the stopgap measures of CIP are often too weak for the political pressures and institutional practices it must accommodate. Most discouraging, it has not yet been able to fully erase the discord between police and prosecutors. Many police officers complain that they have to track down *fiscales* about their cases, only to find out then that the evidence they presented was insufficient and that the *expediente* (a case's police report) is being returned to them. Beyond the annoyance and perceived lack of respect in not being notified directly, many of these officers add that the *fiscales* return *expedientes* for technical details not central to solving the case or are "too lazy" to make detailed comments that specify exactly what revisions are expected. (Some police officers also say that at times *fiscales* do not read their reports and instead punt them along to the courts, which causes problems later on.) *Expedientes* are also slowed down when military officials, who have no legal training, are involved in the response. In addition, according to the DGIC, each investigative agent juggles between a

---

65. Subinspector Daniel Molina, interview by author, Tegucigalpa, July 14, 2003.

hundred and two hundred cases at a time, which forces that agent to drop the majority of cases with leads but no clear evidence.

More *fiscales* and public defenders are needed. Most *fiscales* say they are often working on up to eighty cases at a time, which is particularly overwhelming because of the new CPP.[66] According to some estimates, there is just one public defender for every 6,000 persons and one *fiscal* for every 300,000. Reflecting the country's geographic divides, the scarcity is more pronounced in rural states. For example, Atlántida state has just eight defenders for the nearly thousand prisoners held there.[67] And detainees in the one of the country's largest prisons, Centro Penal San Pedro Sula, complained that they rarely meet the public defenders assigned to them.[68] *Fiscales* estimate that because of their low numbers they are directly involved in only just over a quarter of all cases. Within the Fiscalía, there are no consistent guidelines for the assignment or follow-up of cases, and so *fiscales* use varying criteria to determine the priority of their cases. As for public defenders, one of their directors says that each defender could handle a hundred cases under the old code, but no more than thirty under the new code's more stringent demands and time frames. Thus to carry out their jobs, he asserts, public defenders need forensic technicians, psychologists, and, most important, investigators under their own control instead that of the police. But these professionals are not provided on a permanent basis or even on loan for the majority of cases.[69]

Judicial Reform

The government has attempted to deal with these problems in criminal justice by instigating extensive reforms in Honduras's judiciary, including the creation of an independent judicial council to select most judges and judicial personnel, often with forums for public participation. Unreformed weaknesses in the judiciary, however, prevent it from building on such opportunities. Honduras's Judicial School (Escuela Judicial), with a curricu-

66. Walter Menjívar, *fiscal* coordinator of the northern region, interview by author, San Pedro Sula, February 27, 2004.
67. Victor Parelló, northern region human rights commissioner, interview by author, San Pedro Sula, February 20, 2004.
68. Detainees, Centro Penal San Pedro Sula, interviews by author, March 2, 2004.
69. Jorge Gutierrez Flefil, regional coordinator, Defensa Pública (Public Defense), San Pedro Sula, interview by author, March 13, 2004.

lum light on legal interpretation, does not produce judges disposed toward questioning policy. Almost uniformly, law school professors have a low opinion of the school. No mechanisms are in place to evaluate sitting judges, and they say they are often under pressure by their superiors to follow precedence (Romero and Salomón 2000). There is also a severe dearth of judges, just one for every 55,000 Hondurans, which is far below UN-established recommendation of one for every 4,000 (Caldera 2003, 167). The Supreme Court of Justice, made up of fifteen magistrates elected for seven-year terms,[70] is largely viewed as politicized. Although a judicial council opened up the selection process, nominations still reflect bargaining between the National and the Liberal parties. As demonstrated by the selection of new court magistrates in January 2009, it also reflects conflict between the executive and judicial branches. For the 2009–16 term President Zelaya sought to have Sonia Dubón, the wife of the presidency secretary, Enrique Flores Lanza, reelected to the Supreme Court and become court president, even though she was not among the forty-five candidates chosen by the nominating committee and presented to Congress. This clash led to a crisis as the January 25 deadline approached; Zelaya even met with the heads of the armed forces and threatened to use them against Congress. But with the National Party firm and the heads of Liberal Party in accord, a legislative majority voted to consider only the original forty-five nominees.

Supreme Court rulings often split along party lines, and the power of the court president to remove other magistrates—a practice condemned by international bodies such as the International Commission of Jurists—further compromises their independence. Decisions on security issues, however, usually yield strong majority votes. Although the Supreme Court exercises particularly strong police power through its right to vet congressional bills on the judiciary, it has been consistently supportive of the government's *mano dura* policy. Despite a few cautiously progressive rulings, such as obliging judges to be in charge of detainees during investigations, the court gave its stamp of approval to Article 332 and has refused to hear challenges to the constitutionality of presidential decrees such as 123-2002, which allows searches without a judicial warrant in residences in which there is suspicion of kidnapping or other illicit activity. The Government and Justice Ministry claims that this decree is validated by constitutional Article 99,

---

70. Three legal instruments set the judiciary's roles and powers: the Constitution, the Court Law (Ley de Organización y Atribuciones de los Tribunales), and the Judicial Career Law (Ley de la Carrera Judicial).

which allows for such searches in "cases of urgency," such as when there is a suspicion that a crime is being committed in the home. But such views require an open-ended interpretation of "urgency" that invariably erodes constitutional privacy and due process. Even though NGOs have put forth legal recourses in response to the LPCS, the Supreme Court has not struck down any of that law's provisions. Many writs of habeas corpus on behalf of minors in adult prisons have been rejected as well.

Since the political uncertainty of 2009 in which the Supreme Court played a central role, a renewed effort has been under way to get the judiciary back on track. With help from international agencies, judicial officials have introduced the Interinstitutional System of Digital Expediency (Sistema de Expediente Digital Interinstitucional, or SEDI) which allows judicial officials to better track cases, and the National Automated Case Management and Information System (NACMIS), a wireless communication system for filing criminal reports and giving investigators access to criminal files, arrest warrants, descriptions of stolen vehicles, and weapon registration. Court officers also plan to create jurisprudence websites with full case material, and to cooperate more with investigations by the National Anticorruption Council (Consejo Nacional Anticorrupción, CNA). Also supporting the courts, as well as the police, is the 2010 creation of a long-requested Technical Office of Criminal Investigation (Dirección Técnica de Investigación Criminal, DTIC) to support the Public Ministry, and in particular its *fiscal* for organized crime. According to Carlos Ortega, head of the Supreme Court's information system, such efforts are part of the judiciary's effort—when greater international scrutiny has made public relations more important—to buff up its image.[71]

Prisons

Probably the biggest challenges for the judiciary are the prisons, a lawless incarnation of the legal system's failure. The country's eleven-to-twelve thousand detainees are double the intended capacity of its twenty-four penal facilities. Since 1992, when the prison population was 5,717, it has been violently overcrowded. In part because of poor access to lawyers, between half and two-thirds of detainees at any given time are awaiting trial, and over 90

---

71. Carlos Ortega, executive director, Centro Electrónico de Documentación e Información Judicial (Electronic Center of Judicial Documentation and Information), Tegucigalpa, interview by author, April 5, 2010.

percent will wait up to two years.[72] Politicized changes in judges, say NGOs, also derail progress in many cases.[73] Basic rules—such as the CPP provision that prisoners must be separated by crime and be sentenced within four and a half years—are usually not enforced. Health care is poor, with hundreds of sick detainees held illegally (Zelaya 2004, based on DGSEP budgets). And there are no special provisions for people with HIV/AIDS or other illnesses, and most judges do not demand them.[74] Food is also inadequate; just $.44 is spent per prisoner per day for food.[75] All together, the costs expended by the state on each detainee amount to just $2.43 a day.

The few months of training that prison personnel receive leave them unprepared for the widespread violence, most common in facilities with a high number of *mareros,* who make up about 8.5 percent of the prison population. In April 2002, for example, sixty-nine inmates—sixty-one of them *mareros* —were killed in a fire at the El Porvenir Agricultural Penal Colony on the Caribbean coast, a three-hundred–capacity facility holding five hundred prisoners.[76] The massacre led to several reports, including an official one in which CONASIN participated and another by the Human Rights Commission. According to the official report, the killings were caused by a botched effort to disarm gang detainees that began when Cobra officials and the two prisoners in charge of internal security put certain *mareros* in punishment cells only days after the sudden transfer to the prison of the members of one gang without notification of the small twenty-person staff, even though members of the rival gang were being held there. After the *mareros* were released from the punishment cells, the gangs took up arms, killing the two prisoners in charge of internal security and attacking the police. In the chaos a large group of *pandilleros* took refuge in a cell. Officials then locked the cell, and the inmates burned in a fire. Soldiers apparently shot others trying to flee.

72. According to most estimates, between 50 percent and 70 percent of detainees are awaiting trial. Jaime Banegas, director general, Sistema Penitenciario de Honduras, telephone interview with author, July 9, 2005. Yoleth Calderón, delegada adjunta primera, Comisionado Nacional de Derechos Humanos (first adjunct delegate, National Human Rights Commission), interview by author, Tegucigalpa, April 6, 2010.

73. Lidia de Maradiaga, director, Pastoral Penitenciario, La Ceiba, interview by author, February 24, 2004.

74. Mario Cooper, Foro Nacional de SIDA, interview by author, San Pedro Sula, February 19, 2004.

75. In some prisons this amount is for both health and food. Mauricio Guardado, administrative director, Centro Penal San Pedro Sula, interview by author, March 1, 2004.

76. Officials at and prisoners in El Porvenir Agricultural Penal Colony and Penitentiary Barrio Inglés, interviews by author, La Ceiba, February 23–25, 2004.

This official version left unanswered many questions about why prisoners were given control of discipline, why those who burned to death could not get out, why the vast majority of them were in the *mara* 18th Street, and where all those firearms had come from. These questions revealed not only the lack of policy and control, but also state complicity in arms trafficking, drug trafficking, economic exploitation of detainee labor, and other abuses. And although fifty persons were accused of the actions that led to the massacre, the cleanup ordered immediately after the killings destroyed much of the evidence needed to try them in court. Nevertheless, in June 2008 a court convicted twenty-one of the forty-three officials involved, including a police commissioner and the police chief of La Ceiba, whose jurisdiction included El Porvenir.

Despite these preventable conditions, two years later an even deadlier incident occurred in Centro Penal San Pedro Sula, one of the country's largest prisons. A lack of health, legal, and other services had long made conditions there miserable.[77] The majority of its fourteen hundred prisoners, crammed into a space designed for four hundred, were *mareros* who had been placed in separate areas. "We don't get to leave this area, and they feed us through these gates—it's never enough, and there's a lot of competition to get what they have," said Melvin López, who later died in the fire.[78] "We only have a small space, and very few programs. Public defenders do not come regularly," said Óscar Jehovani Sevan, a survivor who did not belong to MS-13. In a windowless area of about 650 square feet where over 180 MS-13 *mareros* were held, a small fire broke out during the night of May 17, 2004. A scuffle then erupted when several prisoners tried to take equipment from firemen to rescue their compatriots, prompting the firemen to leave and the prison officials to deny help for those inside the cell. By morning, 107 inmates were dead. A report by the Human Rights Commission pointed to makeshift electrical equipment and the lack of escape routes, but clearly the lack of help was far more to blame.

With over 72 percent of the national penitentiary budget going to salaries, little is left for prisoner needs and safety in any of the prisons (Centro de Documentación de Honduras 2004, 101). In fact, ever since the LOPN shifted control of the prisons from the Government and Justice Sec-

77. Elías Canaca, director, Centro Penal San Pedro Sula, interview by author, March 1, 2004.
78. Melvin López, prisoner, Centro Penal San Pedro Sula, interview by author, March 1, 2004.

retariat to the Security Secretariat, prison conditions have not met the Minimal Rule for the Treatment of Prisoners.[79] The Penitentiary Cooperation and Control Committees (Juntas de Cooperación y Control Penitenciario), established in 1996, rarely meet. The El Porvenir and San Pedro Sula massacres, however, did finally prompt real reform efforts. In June 2003, in the wake of the El Porvenir fire, the president of Honduras proposed transferring penitentiary administration to an Interinstitutional Commission of Transition (Comisión Interinstitucional de Transición), and in 2006 Congress began deliberating a bill to create a Penitentiary Institute, under the Secretariat of Government and Justice, to train penitentiary officials, oversee budgets, and develop rehabilitation programs. After languishing for nearly two years in Congress, the law was finally enacted in June 2008. And despite the law's administrative overhaul and rights guarantees, even its sponsors acknowledge that it will mean little without money to build new prisons and efforts to break up the organized crime networks that control several of them. Combined with the legal conflation of potential and actual *mareros* and the judiciary's failure to create an information system that would establish a *marero*'s status, such slow change impedes rehabilitation as well. In short, as in other areas of criminal justice, reforms do not work without an honest diagnosis of the laws and institutions they replace.

NGOs provide some alternatives. For example, when its inability to handle the swelling prisons attracts negative media attention, the government tends to promote church-affiliated rehabilitation for gang members. In fact, religious institutions are one of the few refuges for those who try to leave their *maras*.[80] According to the director of one such program, however, these institutions have only a limited impact amid the state's ongoing abuses and failure to apply the Rehabilitation Law, which it regards as little more than "a piece of paper."[81] The 1984 Law of Delinquent Rehabilitation (Ley de Rehabilitación Delincuente), which includes treatment programs geared toward different types of offenses and offenders, is not implemented adequately. Nor is the 2001 Law for the Prevention, Rehabilitation and Social

79. According to the Comisión de Reforma del Sistema Penitenciario (Commission for Reform of the Penitentiary System), 2003.

80. "Honduras: Evangélicos preparan a policías para educar en valores a los jóvenes," *Ekklesia viva: Tu Foro Cristiano Evangélico*, March 8, 2003, http://www.foroekklesia .com.

81. Ondina Murillo, director, Paz y Justicia, interview by author, La Ceiba, February 24, 2004.

Reintegration of Persons Belonging to Gangs (Ley para la Prevención, Rehabilitación y Reinserción Social de Personas Integradas de Maras y Pandillas), which established a national program that has only been partially enacted. Like other security laws, these measures have become part of the ongoing debate over a policy of *mano dura* versus human rights. The press heavily criticizes the laws for allowing inmates time outside prison, and officials called for the law's "revision" after two prisoners were arrested for assault in 2006 while on leave. Many officials, from Álvarez on down, have said directly that rehabilitation is a waste.

Offenders under 18 years of age do not fare much better. Judges can send underage offenders to a juvenile detention center for one to eight years. These centers (three for boys and one for girls, with a total of about three hundred youth) are operated by the Reeducation and Social Reinsertion Program of the Honduran Childhood and Family Institute (Instituto Hondureño de la Niñez y la Familia, IHNFA). They have many dedicated personnel and several rehabilitation programs, from intensive counseling to professional vocational workshops run by the National Vocational Training Institute (Instituto Nacional de Formación Profesional, INFOP). Such programs are supported by additional educational, therapeutic, community service, and labor centers for youth, as well as an intrainstitutional commission to coordinate them. For example, through the Security Secretariat's 2004 UN-supported Small Arms, Security and Justice Project, fifty young people who were incarcerated but who left their gangs received training in baking and metallurgy at the Centro Penal in Comayagua. Such efforts, however, are obviated by the incarceration of some of these youths in adult prisons, where they are subject to physical and sexual abuse. Although such practices violate international norms recognized by Honduras, in 1995 the Supreme Court issued a ruling that allowed them.

Like adult prisons, juvenile detention centers are generally characterized by poor conditions and inadequate services. For example, the Renaciendo Center in Támara holds up to two hundred youth in a space meant for seventy. The center is controlled by a twenty-five-member security unit that, divided into three shifts, provides no more than ten on-duty officers at a time, along with some unarmed IHNFA guards. Physical mistreatment, sexual abuse, and trading in arms and drugs are rampant, but instead of pushing the armed police to take control, many INHFA officials suspect them of complicity and understandably want to get rid of them. IHNFA guidelines call for one counselor for every fourteen youths, but in Renaciendo there are only eight counselors for two hundred youth.[82] *Mareros* sent to these centers, most of them captured in raids, are placed with their fellow *mara* members. They receive very little education or rehabilitation and are left to form their own social structures. The whole program lacks sufficient personnel, and, because the IHNFA office is located outside of the youth center, case workers have limited contact with those inside and complain that they spend most of their time "shifting around papers." To keep up with its current workload, the agency says it needs two or three times the current budget of 100 million lempiras (a little over $5.5 million). Without increases, broader preventive steps cannot be taken. For example, there is no analysis of the country's high school drop-out rates, and school officials barely notice or do not have the means to act when students are chronically absent from class.

Decentralization and Privatization

The state's uneven presence also limits the provision of security services that rely on a range of agencies. The criminal justice system's presence varies widely in Honduras, and particularly that of the public defenders, Human Rights Commission officials, and others focusing on due process protection. Because small towns suffer a dearth of *fiscales* and judges as well, the police have disproportionate power. In Latin America one cause of such irregular provision, even amid decentralization, is the ongoing weakness of local governments. Honduran mayors could create and fund many local security committees to take on some policing functions, but because of the lack of money few have done so. Similarly, the Municipal Department of Justice could mediate conflicts among citizens, but once again it is limited to areas that can afford it.

To deal with these limits, sometimes mayors decide to band together. For example, seventeen Sula Valley mayors formed a Peace and Coexistence Program that has helped reduce violence but is limited by a lack of funds in the region and backing from the capital. In response, these localities are organizing citizen forums *(mesas ciudadanas)*, which were heavily promoted by the Zelaya government. The *alcaldes auxiliares* (auxiliary mayors) of municipalities also promote local action in security and judicial matters, usually by working with judges of the peace *(jueces de paz)*. Judges of the peace,

---

82. Carla Luque, coordinator, Program of Reeducation and Social Reinsertion, Instituto Hondureño de la Niñez y la Familia, interview by author, Tegucigalpa, June 12, 2006.

who are not required to have law degrees, handle civil cases in which the demand does not exceed 50,000 lempiras. The judicial reach of such officials is limited, however, and indicates to local officials that the federal government intends to replace real devolution with a limited form of deconcentration or delegation that retains real power in the capital. Although many initiatives have spelled out the powers that local governments should have, commissions to establish rules have become bogged down in political and regional competition (see Sosa 2007). So even when new initiatives help improve security, such as in La Ceiba, local officials are frustrated by what they regard as an insufficient national commitment to long-term support. In response to Security Secretary Álvaro's comments that local actions should be geared toward helping the police rather than vice versa, La Ceiba's mayor called out Álvaro—"What planet does the Minister live on?"—for misconstruing the police's obligations and spurning the role of local officials.[83]

Although the big cities tend to have high concentrations of police, the smaller but fast-growing cities are falling far behind. The Valle de Sula metropolitan area, for example, has two million residents—700,000 in the city of San Pedro Sula and the rest in nineteen medium-size cities such as Choloma, discussed later in this chapter as a community policing model. But together these cities have fewer than four hundred police officers, or fewer than one for every two thousand residents (local officials claim it is more like one for every four thousand), even though these areas are notorious for *maras* who outnumber and outgun the police. Honduras's constitution allows municipalities to form their own police forces, but the ones that have been established are limited mainly to maintaining order in parks and open market areas. The only significant ones are those in San Pedro Sula, which has over a hundred officers for its modest mandate, and Tegucigalpa, where the Municipal Police has sixty agents working in three shifts. Because the only prerequisite to join is past service in the armed forces or police, the capital's force is composed mainly of retired officers, with only some refresher training for preparation. Their authority is similarly circumscribed, at least on paper: they do not carry out special operations, and anyone they detain must be handed over to the PN. With only two vehicles and two motorcycles, they largely help keep order in the parks, the city's central plaza, and the public markets (particularly among street merchants).[84]

83. Pablo César Zapata, "No quieren ayuda," *La Prensa,* September 29, 2007.
84. Capt. Francisco Javier Díaz Colidonio, chief, Policía Municipal, interview by author, Tegucigalpa, June 14, 2006.

Because they have experience in security, the Municipal Police chafe at their limited role as well as at the frequent fights with vendors, whom they are constantly shooing away. Many officers talk longingly about real policing, such as working with the Cobras. Because of the weak accountability, such comments may be more than just wishful thinking. Many reports on anti-*mara* raids mention the Municipal Police as part of the operation, indicating that the unit has a bigger role in practice than in law.

The country's march toward decentralization, however, will force it to confront local limitations. In 2010 President Lobo introduced bills to divide the country into six districts—a move regarded positively by most officials and state reform specialists. Most change is likely to fall to the country's 299 municipalities, which have already taken on more responsibility and are represented in their politically influential association, AMHON. But corruption and capacity at the local level vary wildly in Honduras. There is "great weakness in the vast majority of municipalities," asserts an Inter-American Development Bank official working closely with the government, echoing a belief of most officials.[85] The head of an NGO working with local government on sustainable development underscores the point, describing "serious political, technical, and administrative weakness in the great majority of municipalities."[86] According to international officials, such weakness is regarded as the main reason for the "total failure" of the promising antiviolence IADB loan in the Valle de Sula, the metropolitan area of the city of San Pedro Sula. A leading security specialist, Julieta Castellanos, has bluntly asserted that mayors "contaminated" the project with politics.[87]

More reflective of security's fragmentation and failure is private security. LOPN Article 21 prohibits assigning or contracting out police for paid work with private entities without the express permission of the secretary of security. The government publishes a regular report on private security agencies, but with no clear guidelines. Honduras has 189 legal private firms: 116 are registered with the police's Unit of Registration and Control of Private Security Enterprises, set up in 2005, and the rest are formed by individual businesses and *colonias*. Laws and regulations require private firms to register, pay a fee of 100,000 lempiras (a little over $5,000), and report

85. María José Jarquin, state modernization specialist, Honduras Office, Inter-American Development Bank, interview by author, Tegucigalpa, April 6, 2010.

86. Isaac Ferrera, executive director, Fundación Vida, interview by author, Tegucigalpa, April 6, 2010.

87. Julieta Castellanos, rector, Universidad Autónoma de Honduras, and Honduran Truth Commission member, interview by author, Tegucigalpa, April 9, 2010.

on their arms inventory. The Association of Firms of Security and Private Investigation of Honduras (Asociación de Empresas de Seguridad e Investigación Privada de Honduras, ASEMSIPH) estimates that the country has up to four hundred private firms. They have nearly seventy thousand employees, of whom only about twenty thousand work for the 189 legal firms (Palacios 2007). Many of the extralegal firms are known as "suitcase businesses" because they have no fixed address and do not make public their owners' names, how their personnel are selected and trained, or the types and sources of their weapons. The Zelaya administration took additional steps to regulate private security, such as through commissions and laws to register more firms, to enforce the prohibition of automatic weapons, and to restrict possession of the rest to one per officer.

Despite the 2006 Law of Transparency and Access to Public Information, the government refuses to answer questions about why many firms operating around the country remain unregistered and are able to obtain AK-47s, M-16s, and Uzi-22s. Part of the reason stems from the links between officials and these firms. In 2003 the UN Development Programme launched a project on registering private police that was to be extended to documenting control of arms and other issues. Everyone at the top level, in both the government and police, was in favor. But then several elements in the police itself told the police chief they would kill him if the project continued. Because many arms seized by the police are laundered by officers through private companies, any disruption to that cycle, say officers off the record, would cut their incomes in half. The project then came to an abrupt end three months after it began.

Acountability

Although the international community has continued to support disarmament, the 2003 UNDP project demonstrated the difficulty in taking that third step in full accountability—addressing the causes of abuse. As discussed throughout this book, the legislative and judicial branches do not fully check the executive. For example, the president of the Honduran Congress's Defense Commission said he had only one staff person to investigate the range of national security issues.[88] In the area of internal security,

88. José Rodolfo Zelaya, president, National Defense Commission, National Congress, interview by author, Tegucigalpa, April 7, 2010.

trying to fundamentally alter such feeble accountability was an objective of Honduras's 1990s reforms, whose accountability mechanisms were stronger than those in most other countries. Since then, however, this critical channel has been drastically narrowed. When the Secretariat of Security was established in 1997 and given control over nearly all police agencies, there was initially a sharp drop in internal investigations of wrongdoing in the DGIC, as well as follow-up to specific accusations by CONASIN. At the Human Rights Commission, which also hears rights accusations against any state official, the three state agencies topping the list of those agencies with complaints lodged against them have been the PN, the DGIC, and the Transit Police. Less constrained by membership consensus, as well as by expectations of actual power, the commissioner has been more unequivocally critical of both the policies and declarations of the government. One reason the commission wields little influence in the government is that the complaints it receives are supposed to shape policy through CONASIN. But CONASIN cannot carry out this or its other functions if it is not convened, and the security secretary, CONASIN's head, is the only official empowered to convene it. In doing so only when needing political cover during institutional crises (such as after El Porvenir), the secretary has effectively excluded CONASIN from policy, planning, and internal control. Thus although CONASIN, much like the Human Rights Commission, conducts in-depth reports critical of criminal policy, its primary function of accountability has been largely neutralized. Internal police controls are also weak. Despite regulations in the LOPN and government claims that it has punished hundreds of officials for abuses—Álvarez said that 307 officers of all ranks were suspended for illegal activity in the first half of 2003—the disciplinary processes are not made public. In addition, according to CONASIN and UAI officials, many of the officers whose names CONASIN presented to the UAI for rights violations were not investigated because of a lack of investigators and resources.

Such limited accountability does not bode well for the control of police corruption, whose forms in Honduras range from routine motorist shakedowns to unreported decommissioned vehicles. But it is drugs that most corrupt officials, from first-year patrol officers up to members of Congress and the executive cabinet. In May 2006 in one of the few force-wide drug tests, the results of one in five officers were positive. Even big police actions against traffickers are often tainted, with suspects managing to flee the country even when their goods are confiscated. Infiltration of the police by organized crime runs deep; most police units are linked to networks of car robberies, kidnappings, and narco-trafficking. Such levels of corruption make reformers hesitant. Programs are "not sustainable," in the words of a high-ranking U.S. official stationed in the country, because "nearly the whole political elite is corrupt, [most] tied to narco-trafficking."[89] Although many of the country's *fiscales* work on corruption, about nine in every ten corruption cases in the Fiscalía are rejected for lack of evidence or are transferred to other agencies (UNDP 2003, chap. 7). Within the police academies, the discussion of corruption appears to be far milder than its reality. When asked about expanding the discussion, the directors often refer to the "professionalization" courses taught by specialists from Spain.

Such responses do not stem from a lack of instruments against corruption. One such instrument is the 2006 Law of Transparency and Access to Public Information (Ley de Transparencia y Acceso a la Información Pública), which is supported by seven million lempiras (about $380,000) in World Bank funds and by training for public employees by a group of civil society organizations called "Alianza 72."[90] But such laws often bark up the wrong tree, because access to information means little if the information is suspect. A more frontal attack against police corruption is internal purges, which have been a part of every security reform in Honduras. When he was security secretary, Fonseca created an intelligence unit made up of retired military officials to investigate the police. The unit's investigations led to the dismissal of 2,500 officials in 2000–2001, a whopping 30 percent of the force, mostly for connections with organized crime.[91] However, the processes and causes of the dismissals were not made public, and the vast majority involved no charges or trials. The purge came to a halt not because it rid the force of all corrupt officers, but because of a change in officials at the top, who then reinstated many of the officers who were fired. The DGIC lost 150 agents during this time, many of whom later got their jobs back, particularly after the Supreme Court's Constitutional Chamber ruled the purge unconstitutional for not following the police law's guidelines and for "transgressing constitutional precepts."[92] Although technically accurate, this decision was a politicized use of rules over principles. In addition, many

89. Interview by author, Tegucigalpa, July 8, 2005.
90. "Sociedad civil capacitará funcionarios públicos en aplicación de Ley de Transparencia," *Conexión,* no. 80, July 1–15, 2007.
91. Serapio Umanzor, "Honduras al frente de la lista de corrupción policial en Centroamérica," *La Prensa,* February 13, 2002.
92. Supreme Court president Vilma Morales, quoted in Centro de Documentación de Honduras (2004).

police claimed that the purge caught up many officers who were slandered unfairly as corrupt, and the government calculated correctly that, amid high crime rates, most of the population was uneasy with a shake-up that might reduce police presence.

The lightning rod of controversy on policing in Honduras has been the Internal Affairs Unit. Since its formation, the UAI has been debilitated by a weak structure, insufficient resources, and open-ended regulations. From its single office in Tegucigalpa, the UAI's twenty-member staff depends administratively and financially on the Security Secretariat, which has never given it an adequate budget. When there is an "irregularity" by a police officer, such as a homicide, the officer "gives everything over to the UAI—it does its part," claim government officials. Although the UAI can receive reports from any citizen or group, it is not allowed to take preventive action, such as investigating officers with disturbing behavior or assets that are disproportionate to their salaries. The UAI has also been undercut by the continuing existence of the Office of Professional Responsibility, which investigates the Preventive Police with little transparency, and of the Office of the Inspector General, which disciplines the DGIC. These units conduct internal investigations of police misconduct and can recommend sanctions against those found guilty, but only the accused officer's immediate superior can actually punish him or her. In 1996 the MP created the ORP within the then-DIC to monitor the behavior of its agents. It reported to the attorney general as well as to the agency's human rights section. Accused by the MP and human rights groups of not pushing for more objective investigations of police wrongdoing, the ORP was slated for elimination by the LOPN. But it was saved by the DIC's move to the Security Secretariat.

What led to the most controversy over accountability was the UAI's focus on the accelerating number of youth killings. Undisputed off the record by state officials, the NGO Casa Alianza reports that 3,200 children and youth were killed between 1998 and June 2006, with an average of over forty killings a month during Zelaya's term—a rate exceeding that of the authoritarian era. Of the more than 1,600 extrajudicial killings of young people under the age of 23 reported between 1998 and 2003, 61 percent were inadequately investigated, and 39 percent had evidence of police responsibility.[93] In 2002 no perpetrator was identified in 60–70 percent of the

93. Casa Alianza, http://www.casa-alianza.org/EN/about/offices/honduras/. See also Amnesty International (2003). According to press reports and Casa Alianza, 549 persons ages 23 and under were killed in 2002 and 557 in 2003—often with AK-47 machine guns.

killings, and gangs were suspected in 15–20 percent of them. Such killings take place in a perpetually menacing atmosphere against youth. Young people complain of continual harassment and attack, often by unmarked gray vans roaming areas such as the basketball courts where they congregate.[94] According to one victim's mother, he and a friend were beaten in front of his house by unknown assailants, who then set fire to their bodies. "But the police don't do anything," she said, "not even punish those responsible."[95] Rights groups and many former police and government officials claim that the government turns a blind eye to police killings. Fonseca summed up many officials' beliefs when he said, "The shortest road to terminate crime is to terminate criminals."[96] But responsibility goes beyond the police. The UN Special Rapporteur on extrajudicial, arbitrary, or summary killings has sharply criticized the judiciary for its inaction and the media for inciting and even praising such killings.[97] Many officials, on condition of anonymity, also confirm accusations that the police's roughly twenty death squads—particularly "The Magnificents"—control most of the activities of CEINCO, the Department of Analysis and Information, the Frontier Police, and the Anti-Kidnapping Office (Sección de Antisecuestros). Such accusations, repeated independently and often without prompting, do not convey much confidence in the veracity of criminal information or in the strength of the internal control of police misconduct. Meanwhile, NGOs talk about an "enormous social indifference to the killings" and, despite the new penal process code, very limited access by poor Hondurans to the courts.[98]

In September 2002, after several years of careful investigation, UAI chief María Luisa Borjas, a police veteran with twenty-five years of service, charged the Security Secretariat and National Police officials in at least twenty extrajudicial executions of children and youths. She immediately began to receive telephone death threats, her office support staff was reduced, and two months later she was suspended, allegedly for having failed to present proof of her claims (in violation of LOPN Articles 8 and 22). Members of the police hierarchy then piled on, demanding legal action

94. Street youth, interviews by author, Tegucigalpa, July 16–17, 2003.

95. Felita de Jesús Peralta, interview by author, Tegucigalpa, July 17, 2003.

96. Guatama de Fonseca, former security secretary of Honduras, interview by author, Tegucigalpa, July 21, 2003.

97. "Relatora de naciones unidas pide a gobierno poner coto a las ejecuciones extrajudiciales," Equipo Nizkor, August 16, 2001, http://www.derechos.org/nizkor.

98. José Gustavo Zelaya, legal director, Casa Alianza, interviews by author, Tegucigalpa, August 4–5, 2004, and February 15, 2005.

against her for "staining and provoking irreparable deterioration of the country's image" abroad.[99] "When we began to investigate the participation of police in the deaths of youth, we obtained the names of several of the officers who formed these groups," she recounted. "But the Minister, far from supporting us, asked for my resignation. I did not pass on the information to him, since we realized [the information] was going directly to those involved in these deaths."[100]

But Borjas's firing only drew greater attention to the problem. As a response, the PN began expunging officers, and in September 2002 the Security Secretariat formed a Special Unit to Investigate Children's Deaths (Unidad Especial de Investigaciones de Muertes de Menores), which documented 967 violent deaths between 1998 and 2004, 24 percent of which were connected to security officers. Of those cases, the unit investigated 470 and presented 120 cases to the Fiscalía.[101] But only three of those cases led to a conviction. A lack of evidence and witnesses impeded prosecution of the others, and the unit chief denounced the interference of DGIC officials, some of whom were carrying out parallel investigations. After the unit ran out of money at the end of 2004, it no longer had the financial wherewithal to overcome such obstacles.

Honduras's Fiscalía can investigate police wrongdoing as well, but it lacks the institutional and political power to instigate change because "there are neither human nor logistical resources," a former youth prosecutor said, to handle "the enormous quantity of cases."[102] A human rights prosecutor whose investigations demonstrated "systematic killings by a specific group" complained that investigations of the police faced constant delay and obstruction —criticism that led to death threats against her and public accusations by the security secretary that she acted "subjectively and with suspicion" against the police.[103] In fact, in January 2002 the *fiscal* topped the list of those accused by the security secretary of usurpation of powers.[104] Since

99. "Oficiales enfilan 'batería' contra Borjas," *La Prensa,* June 23, 2003.

100. María Luisa Borjas, ex-chief of internal affairs, Policía Nacional, interview by author, Tegucigalpa, July 18, 2003.

101. "Policías detrás de ejecuciones," *El Heraldo,* January 3, 2005; Róger Lindo, "Ex jefe policial afirma que agentes también participan en ejecuciones," *La Opinión,* October 10, 2004.

102. Eduardo Villanueva, fiscal de la Niñez, interview by author, Tegucigalpa, July 15, 2003.

103. Aída Estella Romero, interview by author, Tegucigalpa, July 22, 2003; "Álvarez molestó con fiscalía de Derechos Humanos," *La Prensa,* February 26, 2004, 14.

104. Comisionado de Derechos Humanos, Bulletin No. 1638, January 14, 2002.

then, the conflict between the *fiscales,* on the one hand, and the attorney general and the executive, on the other, has only worsened. Evidence of that deterioration was the April 2008 hunger strike by *fiscales* protesting the dismissal of colleagues working on cases of corruption involving political figures.

Meanwhile, the UAI has been relegated to mediating minor disputes and civilian complaints. It receives about three hundred complaints a year and resolves about seventy-five of them, mainly through its daily conciliation sessions. The UAI has the "full cooperation" of other judicial entities, points out Elia Ramírez, Borjas's replacement as UAI chief. But she adds that many cases that begin in the UAI are not tried, often because of lack of evidence, which "is frustrating because sometimes we work hard on those cases."[105] Although the UAI insists on its autonomy, asserting that the security secretary has "never said to do something," its limitations are apparent. "We investigate," the chief says, "but don't blame." Although the unit has specialists who help officers avoid repeating abuses, it never grapples with larger patterns of misconduct because most of its time is spent on conflicts whose resolution, as in judiciaries without *stare decisis,* have no legal binding on related cases. Many top officials conjecture that what keeps the UAI in such a position is the lack of support from either the state or society. The post-Borjas UAI thus suffers from the worst of several worlds—a lack of power needed to confront the government, a lack of results needed to gain societal backing, and even a lack of confidence from at least some of the police, which is needed to gain their cooperation and information.

Such roadblocks demonstrate the pattern of accountability discussed in chapter 3 in which answerability and punishment do not lead to uncovering the root causes of abuse. Aware of the need to take those steps, the Zelaya administration promised yet another police purge and formed committees to handle police wrongdoing, such as forums and a Misdemeanor Commission (Comisión de Faltas). In other positive developments, it stressed police officer rights and created an internal affairs office whose personnel would follow a separate track and so could not be transferred without their consent. In June 2008, Congress reformed the police structure through a revamped Ley Orgánica de la Policía Nacional, which gave the minister greater power over the Direcciones Generales, and, theoretically, more ability to purge the agency. But the law reduced the official powers of CONASIN,

105. Elia Ramírez de Zelaya, chief, Unidad de Asuntos Internos, interview by author, Tegucigalpa, June 16, 2006.

handing its policy formulation role to a strategic directorate composed of police officials. It also failed to make the improvements needed to strengthen and clarify the main steps in police promotion and discipline. María Luisa Borjas, now a CONASIN member, criticized the law for giving the police a military structure and for not allowing civil society participation. The Human Rights Commission argued that the law would hand the country over to narco-traffickers by giving too much power to police administrators.[106] And a group of twenty civil society organizations criticized it for allowing greater discretion, downplaying the contributions of municipalities, and, more broadly, failing to promote community policing, regulate police-military relations, oversee police intelligence, or improve the MP's investigative capacity. But in giving the security secretariat direct power over the heads of the divisions, it also brought more administrative coherence to the police. Óscar Álvarez, reappointed security minister by President Lobo, added that it also allowed him to restructure a "passive" and "demoralized" force.[107]

Community Policing and Honduran Society

The citizen participation so fundamental to problem-oriented policing was integrated into Honduras's initial reform through CONASIN at the national level, the Development Commissions (Comisiones de Desarrollo Departamental) at the department level, and the Development Councils (Consejos de Desarrollo Municipal) at the municipal level. Citizens were also given a chance to shape policy through the grand-sounding and much-heralded National Convergence Forum (El Foro Nacional de Convergencia, FONAC). Originally created under the Flores administration but revived in 2002 by Maduro, FONAC was designed to develop policies that advanced governance and development through dialogue between the government and civil society sectors such as teachers and indigenous groups. However, despite many meetings on citizen security, most of FONAC's long-term plans were cut short by the government's insistence on short-term results. Although the government exerted too much control over these channels of citizen partic-

106. Marcos García, "La nueva Ley de Policía entregará el país a narcos," *La Prensa*, May 19, 2008.

107. Óscar Álvarez, security minister, interview by the author, Tegucigalpa, April 9, 2010.

ipation, in other ways it did not exercise enough. Citizens could get involved in daily security in many ways, including through their neighborhood councils (*juntas de vecinos*), through their *patronatos,* which were officially nonpartisan committees elected by the community, and through their local security councils, which had elected presidents and focused on both prevention and police support. Soon after it was formed, the Security Secretariat also created Citizen Security Committees, which worked with police in surveillance, patrols, and detentions. Nearly six hundred committees were formed throughout the country over a short period of time. However, because they were often equipped with high-caliber weapons, they attracted a lot of people with questionable backgrounds and personal agendas. The lack of a clear and uniform national legal status added to their abuses. As a result, when Fonseca became security secretary he reined in the committees.

Such false starts led to a reevaluation of community policing and the police structure. In San Pedro Sula, for example, the police divided the city into six sectors with teams of police to patrol them. This change, local officials claim, has led to a 70 percent drop in crime.[108] In other areas of the country the police have created special units with positive impacts. For example, the heads of the units on family and children said that patrols exclusively focusing on domestic violence have significantly increased reporting. Although the unit heads could not cite raw numbers, they estimated that the rate of reports on domestic violence jumped from fewer than half to three out of every four.[109] In the national survey described shortly, women were more than twice as likely as men to see cooperation with the police and police visits in the home as central to community policing. "Having women officers walk down our street every afternoon" as part of the community policing program, said one woman in the low-income *colonia* of El Pedregal, "has helped give us some sense of recourse."

Much of this approach was integrated into the 2002 national community policing program Safer Community (Comunidad Más Segura, CMS), which has turned out to be one of Honduras's most successful and durable citizen security reforms. Hampered by weak organizations and socioeconomic instability, residents in poor neighborhoods say that most power falls to the *patronato* and the police. And if an area's assigned police officer "exercises

108. José Luis Muñoz Licona, subcommissioner for the northern region, interview by author, San Pedro Sula, February 28, 2004.
109. Julián Hernández Reyes, head, Dirección Infantil (Children's Office), and Lincoln Pacheco Murillo, head, Dirección de la Familia (Family Unit), interviews by author, July 11, 2005.

discretion" to build citizen relations, said one community activist, "he becomes a leader." The CMS takes advantage of this natural base of police power through its three basic components: (1) assigning officers to improve community relations by means of foot patrols, (2) implementing special programs and education seminars on issues such as drugs, and (3) organizing community councils and meetings. In its first year of operation in which 126 police officials were working in seven cities, the program claimed that it "benefited" 264,000 people.[110] In 2005 community policing chiefs said that crime declined even in the toughest areas.[111] Although such numbers are exaggerated, independent observations point to marked reductions in homicides, robberies, and domestic violence in CMS areas. The government also said the program "rehabilitated" 2,500 gang members.[112] Even though this number has not been independently verified, the CMS has been used to launch and boost anti-*mara* actions based on the education and rehabilitation of young offenders. As a result of the range of its advances, the CMS has expanded to thirty of Honduras's most crime-ridden *colonias.*

Such success seems to be mainly attributable to citizen involvement and police autonomy, both of which the CMS has encouraged, probably more than intended. At one level, local commissioners have been given more leeway. In neighborhoods infested by powerful narco-traffickers, for example, commissioners can declare curfews, and officers can alternate shift schedules and house visits to avoid having anyone targeted as cooperating with the police. Other innovations are in infrastructure, such as providing or replacing street lighting lost to neglect, vandalism, and robbery. San Pedro Sula, for example, used the CMS to get thousands of streetlights repaired.[113] When integrated into larger municipal planning and local politics, the social service dimension of community policing can give the CMS program a big boost. After attending a local security meeting, for example, the mayor of Choloma emphasized how city services such as education and housing are "part of our goals for human security."[114]

110. "A un año de su implementación," *La Prensa,* January 8, 2004.

111. Ramón Martínez Hernández, chief, Community Division (police), interview by author, Tegucigalpa, June 20, 2005.

112. "Comunidad Más Segura ha rehabilitado a 2,500 mareros," *La Prensa,* October 13, 2003.

113. These efforts have been funded and organized by Honduras's legislature, the National Electric Energy Company (Empresa Nacional de Energía Eléctrica), and the Central American Bank of Economic Integration. Many residents have provided metal cages to protect individual lights.

114. Sandra Deras Rivera, mayor, Choloma, interview by author, February 17, 2004.

Community policing also owes its continuation to public support. Up to 75 percent of the respondents in some polls recognize its "favorable effect."[115] Meanwhile, in a survey of 237 citizens in CMS neighborhoods in four cities—Tegucigalpa, San Pedro Sula, Danlí, and Choluteca—respondents generally expressed approval.[116] In that survey, which took the form of both a general questionnaire and individual interviews, over 90 percent of respondents said that the police were listening more to residents, 89.9 percent said their confidence in the police had increased, 75.9 percent said that communications between police and citizens were better, and 78 percent said that their opinion of the police had improved. Police officers interviewed reported their own higher professional satisfaction, as well as higher crime reporting. Such increases were verified by residents, who were asked to evaluate the impact of community policing on different crimes as very, somewhat, more or less, or not successful. On violent crime, 19 percent reported that community policing was "very successful," and 55.7 percent said it was "somewhat successful." Evaluations of the impact on gang activity were also positive: 32.9 percent said community policing has been "very successful" at controlling gangs, and 30.4 percent said it was "somewhat successful."

The reasons for such opinions are on view in the Valle de Sula. Long saddled with the country's highest levels of violent crime, many of the valley's poorer areas have stopped or reversed crime rates through community policing. The CMS *barrio* of Choloma, for example, showed quick results soon after adopting community policing: the area had nine murders in January 2002 but only four a month in the first four months of 2003, and it had seventeen robberies in January 2002 but none at all in the first four months of 2003.[117] Part of that success was attributable to the bimonthly community policing committee meetings, which attracted about twenty-five residents.[118] In the eight months following the killing of nine persons on Au-

115. "A un año de su implementación," *La Prensa,* January 8, 2004.

116. This survey was carried out by the Centro de Documentación de Honduras (Cedoh) and Mark Ungar as part of the project "Community Policing in Latin America," a collaborative effort funded by a grant from the City University of New York and directed by Mark Ungar and Desmond Arias in 2004 and 2005.

117. Sandra Deras Rivera, mayor of Choloma, interview by author, Choloma, February 19, 2004.

118. At a meeting in the San Pedro Sula neighborhood of Choloma, for example, those attending one of the program's regular meetings discussed the many social programs that have dramatically reduced the area's crime rates. Interviews by author, community policing meeting, Choloma, February 19, 2004.

gust 5, 2002, Rivera Hernández reduced its level of violence dramatically; the monthly tally of violent incidents dropped from forty-five to three. In what was one of the most dangerous towns in Honduras, such declines earned the program the reputation of a national model. Much credit was given to the regional director, detective Óscar Gámez, who worked with a security committee made up of churches, city councils, sports leagues, youth groups, and private businesses. Before he took on this role, Gámez said, the *maras* were responsible for 70 percent of the area's crime and organized criminals for 10 percent, but the program reduced those statistics to 10 percent and 8 percent, respectively.[119] He attributed the success not just to the resident committees, but also to the power granted to him by the LPCS. In particular, he declared curfews frequently and put 90 percent of the police on the street (instead of in police stations). The result, Gámez claimed, was a near-complete reversal in insecurity, with 98 percent of the neighborhood feeling insecure before the program, and 93 percent feeling secure after it was in place.

Despite such promise, entrenched obstacles remain, not the least of which is the convoluted government response to the country's severe socioeconomic conditions. The resulting deprivation can be seen throughout the twin cities of Tegucigalpa and Comayageula, both of which have CMS programs (see Map 4.1). One of the largest CMS programs is in the Tegucigalpa area of Kennedy, whose 38 *colonias,* with 162,140 residents spread out over almost 13 square miles, are run by the *patronato* and six citizen security committees, one for each of the area's *supermanzanas* (large residential blocks). Because it has plenty of citizen groups, many with connections to the capital's political institutions, Kennedy is in a good position to benefit from community policing. More broadly, its vibrant community is able to overcome many of the limits discussed in chapter 3. In addition to the CMS, in fact, the area has extensive educational programs against *maras,* sexual exploitation, domestic violence, and drugs.[120] But for both residents and police their problems remain far more formidable than their programs. According to one CMS officer, the area's unemployment rate is at least 40 percent, which she says inflames violence by men against their wives and children. And another police officer claimed that a high level of drugs was being brought into the area by Kennedy's 2,500 *mareros.* Gangs bring in large

119. Óscar Gámez, Rivera Hernández police inspector, interview by author, San Pedro Sula, February 18–20, 2004.

120. Mainly through the drug program DARE (Drug Abuse Resistance Education), which began in the United States and now operates in forty-three other countries, most of them in Latin America.

amounts of money as well by charging residents for general "protection," making them even more difficult to dislodge. Although it is far better off than other Tegucigalpa *colonias* such as Pedregal and San Miguel, Kennedy lacks the kind of infrastructure that facilitates community policing. For example, the *colonia* has sports leagues, but no field on which they can play.[121]

Such conditions cause great frustration among the police. In Kennedy's main police station, the three starkly furnished rooms have little more than a few desks; collective information is kept in a log book that is often misplaced. Lower-level officers often use these conditions, along with the pressures of their job, as an excuse to brush off civilians trying to file a crime report or provide information. For those higher in command, the law is the main problem. Kennedy's police commissioner says that the "very guaranteeist" CPP makes it difficult to find all the persons suspected of a crime within the time frame allowed to do so—particularly because obtaining a police vehicle can take up to two hours.[122] Meanwhile, the *colonia's* CMS officers complain that many of the painstaking advances they make in community relations are often wiped out by uncoordinated, unannounced, hamfisted special operations and raids by different police and military units that needlessly abuse and antagonize residents.

Officers may be divided over where to place blame, but, as in other countries, the bulk of them are skeptical of community policing as a solution. Those working in the CMS, from its directors down to its patrol officers, feel that their ability to prove such views wrong are constrained by limited budgets and immediate demands. Scheduled rotations make it particularly difficult for them to demonstrate results, thereby enhancing the innovation and reputation of community policing. Changes at the top, such as the transfer of a regional director to the national community policing unit, also deflate the momentum behind community policing in several areas. Many CMS officers are frustrated as well with media coverage. Óscar Gámez, who headed the successful CMS program in the Sula Valley area of Rivera Hernández, vehemently criticized the press "for putting it on the front page when the police kill someone but not when someone kills a police officer."[123] More serious, according to several human rights and community critics, the

121. María Sierra and Elena Medina, officers, Colonia Kennedy, interviews by author, Tegucigalpa, June 2006.

122. Rolando Carcomo Piura, subcommissioner, Colonia Kennedy, interview by author, Tegucigalpa, June 2005.

123. Rivera Hernández residents and police inspector Óscar Gámez, interviews by author, San Pedro Sula, February 18–19, 2004.

Map 4.1. Tegucigalpa and Comayaguela (clockwise from upper right: the *colonias* of San Miguel and Kennedy in Tegucigalpa, and El Pedregal in Comayaguela)

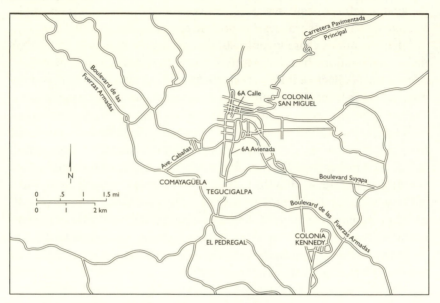

Source: Google Maps.

program had become a channel for abuse by participating citizens. This was a partial legacy from the citizen security committees that began in 1994 and often were dominated by former military and police officers who used them for extrajudicial killings. In fact, prosecutors and human rights commissioners estimate that thousands of unreported vigilante attacks since 2002 have been connected to community policing.[124] In the poor *colonia* of El Confite, which has La Ceiba's main community policing program, the head of the citizen CMS group described how citizens use it to attack local delinquents.[125] And in one of the biggest blows to community policing in Honduras, police detective Gámez was arrested in connection with the 2004 killing of two suspected *mareros,* bringing his "model" program to a swift end.

124. Victor Parelló, northern region human rights commissioner, interview by author, San Pedro Sula, February 20, 2004. All three officials agree that vigilantism has gotten out of hand, but do not want to estimate the number of cases.

125. Céleo Santo Sosa, Colonia El Confite, La Ceiba. Atlántida Department, interview by author, February 25, 2004.

The vast majority of residents, however, are dedicated to community policing that respects individual rights. But many are held back in supporting the CMS by their doubts over how far the police and the government are willing to apply the program. Of the six biggest problems identified by residents in the survey described earlier, four of them were the following: too little logistical support, 31.6 percent; too little economic support, 27.8 percent; too few personnel, 9.3 percent; and too little community support, 5.6 percent. Although police personnel also had a very positive view of the CMS (predictably—the interview pool was skewed toward CMS supporters), they too stressed its lack of financial and logistical support. For example, two CMS areas had just one vehicle, and most others had none. "There is not enough consideration of regional needs in national budgetary planning," said one PN commissioner of operations, "leading to frustration among our cops in certain areas."[126]

Officers and citizens alike are also aware that community policing may not address underlying practices. Contrasting views of the impact of community policing on different crimes reveal awareness of how police corruption has limited the CMS. Although homicides and robberies had decreased, a fact widely recognized by program area residents, only 26.6 percent of respondents in the four-city survey felt that the CMS was very or somewhat successful against narco-trafficking. On police abuse, equal numbers reported both progress and lack of it. Choluteca, a city known for high levels of police corruption, reveals other CMS weaknesses. When asked to describe the functioning of community policing in their area, the responses from Choluteca residents were strikingly different than those in the other cities. Just 3.8 percent of residents said that one role was "protecting the community" (compared with 12 percent in Tegucigalpa and 26.1 percent in San Pedro Sula), and only 9.5 percent (compared with nearly 50 percent in other cities) said that residents should involve themselves in citizen security.

But the survey results reveal a dearth of citizen involvement. Asked about their participation, the residents of Choluteca reported less kinds of participation than did those of the other cities, except for providing "logistical support" (50 percent). Although nearly everybody in the other cities said that "police listen more to citizens," most tellingly nearly one-third in Choluteca said they did not. As in Tegucigalpa, meetings with residents re-

---

126. Marcos Arnaldo Herrera Rodríguez, commissioner of operations, Policía Nacional, interview by author, Choluteca, June 16, 2006.

vealed low citizen participation and trust in the CMS. Meetings were frequently canceled, and those that did take place involved little more than police officers updating residents on the program's future plans. When survey respondents were asked to describe their participation in community policing in fact, the largest response, 29.8 percent, was "none," followed by "logistical support," 22.6 percent, and "patrols," 10.7 percent. Asked to describe their roles, those who did participate answered vaguely about helping the police, but gave little indication that they should actually help develop policy. In many areas a domineering and sometimes intimidating police presence causes such self-restriction. As long as the police decide when and how citizens participate, the right citizen–police balance will never be struck. Many community policing meetings in Tegucigalpa's Kennedy *colonia,* for example, consist almost entirely of showing scratchy videos with no real discussion beyond having attendees follow the text in comic book form.[127] Nor can citizens turn easily to other agencies to help them get organized. Over 54 percent of survey respondents said they knew of no participation by other government agencies, and 62 percent said that no NGOs participated. The only exception was Danlí, where the nearly opposite findings of 71 percent indicated some sort of NGO involvement. This marked difference stems from the origins of Danlí's program. After physical confrontations with the police, the city's residents decided to organize their own security groups. And although most of those groups have been absorbed into the CMS, the city's community policing program is far more independent and robust because it maintains a local staff, budget, and set of neighborhood programs.

In most of the country, though, efforts to boost citizen participation will be complicated by the fractured nature of Honduras's low-income communities. Honduras is the Western Hemisphere's third poorest country, with a 2009 per capita GDP of just $1,921. Its cities comprise sprawling areas of extreme deprivation. Despite annual macroeconomic growth of about 3 percent since 1998, which has helped Hondurans at all income levels, 59 percent of the entire population (and 75 percent of those in rural areas) was impoverished in 2008.[128] About 44 percent of Hondurans live on less than $2 a day (half of them on $1 a day), and official unemployment reaches up

127. Comunidad Más Segura meeting, June 29, 2005.
128. Central Intelligence Agency, *The World Factbook,* https://www.cia.gov; International Fund for Agricultural Development (IFAD), "Regional Agricultural Development Project in Central America," http://www.ifad.org/media/success/honduras_2.htm.

to 27.5 percent. The high rates of poverty are matched by the high rates of inequality. In Honduras, whose Gini coefficient for income is 55, the richest 20 percent of households receive 54.3 percent of national income, while the poorest 20 percent receive only 3.2 percent. Because about half of the seven million Hondurans are under 19 years of age, such conditions aggravate youth misery and portend poorly for the future. Of every one hundred children entering school, only sixty complete their secondary education, and just three of them graduate from a university. Of low-income youth, only 8 percent finish high school (Arriagada 2001). Young people head 10 percent of Honduran households, and 68 percent of these households are below the poverty line.

Beyond the daily suffering, such conditions open up fissures that are hard to close. In particular, the constant heavy emigration has been a big drain on society. According to most estimates, about eighty thousand Hondurans try to get to the United States each year to join the estimated half-million Honduran men working abroad (Sladkova 2007). But only a quarter of them make it. Feeling they have let down their families, most continue trying to leave instead of finding work locally. Such outflows have left very few families and neighborhoods intact. It also leads to the incorrect assumption that the young men who do not leave must be *mareros* operating in the area. As some youth organizers point out, however, about two-thirds of the youths who are killed do not belong to any *pandilla* or *mara*.[129] But the vicious tactics and territorial divisions of the *maras* that do exist have succeeded in getting society to close itself off in its own self-imposed geographic divide and fear-driven isolation. Such divisions only reinforce themselves. A poll by the national Human Rights Commission revealed that insecurity has led nearly 50 percent of respondents to stop using public transport, about 33 percent to stop using taxis, and over 40 percent to stop visiting family and friends.[130]

The impact of such conditions is evident in the bigger crime drops in areas with more citizen participation and more supportive commissioners. Such progress prompted the Zelaya government to come out, at least rhetorically, for expansion of the CMS. It reintroduced the citizen security groups (*mesas de seguridad ciudadana*) through which begins, said CMS executive director Carlos Chinchilla, "the process of creating new parameters . . .

129. Ernesto Bardales, director, Jóvenes Hondureños Adelante–Juntos Avancemos (JHA-JA), interview by author, San Pedro Sula, June 27, 2004.
130. "Autoridades Inician Fuertes Operativos Contra la Delincuencia," *La Prensa,* February 1, 2008.

to change the reactive attitude" of the entire police, particularly its middle ranks. "Up until now, the course was on detentions and repression," he described. "Now, it will be working with the community."[131] Similar views were expressed by actors whose strong connections to the police and presidency could integrate such views into the security system. Mario Perdomo, a police general who was appointed security vice secretary in 2008 and who headed an internationally sponsored effort to write a security report of reform, emphasized the need for deep changes in the police's basic outlook.[132] Similarly, presidential adviser Ramón Romero, despite an arguably misplaced desire to have the president more forcefully impose community policing, personally supervised CMS meetings, and he conveyed his personal stake in the program to the president.[133]

The worry was that if they became politicized, co-opted, or underfunded, the groups (*mesas*) spearheading this change might begin to resemble little more than the disastrous 1990s *comités*. Thus the *mesas* had to begin by addressing people's fears of the police. But in doing so they did not get off to a good start. Of the small minority of meeting attendees who spoke, nearly all seemed to view the police far less critically than most Hondurans, indicating a lack of outreach. The meetings themselves were not designed to overcome residents' passivity. For example, the first forums at Choluteca were very formal, failing to pose real questions or stimulate meaningful discussion. Planning strategies to recruit citizens included no mention of their fear of working with the police, which was particularly important in Choluteca, where surveys showed that community policing had little impact on police corruption. Danlí, which now offers a diploma in community policing after a six-month course, is a better model of how to switch the source of citizen security from officials above to citizens below. But even a program with such a strong beginning will peter out without changes in the rest of the police force. After three years of community policing, Police General Perdomo said resignedly, there was a lack of "awareness" of it among the top brass.[134] In high-crime areas even community policing officials often expressed either impatience or indifference toward that approach.

131. Carlos Chinchilla, executive director, Comunidad Más Segura, interviews by author, Tegucigalpa, July 22, 2003, and Choluteca, June 2006.

132. Mario Perdomo, police general and former director, ISEP, interview by author, New York, November 10, 2006.

133. Ramón A. Romero Cantarero, interview by author, Tegugicalpa and Choluteca, June 2006.

134. Mario Perdomo, police general, interview by author, Tegucigalpa, July 12, 2006, and April 6, 2010.

Indeed, despite the favorable reputation earned by community policing in the area, the chief heading the program in the Sula Valley district of Chamelocón showed little enthusiasm for it while dealing with serious crime.[135] And although newer police officers by and large are more amenable to problem-oriented policing, many academy recruits seem unclear on the concept of community policing. After a day of workshop discussions on community policing, one of the first questions raised by an ANAPO cadet in the concluding session was: "Is it okay to bring attack dogs when visiting a resident's home?"[136]

Any improvement in community policing will also require a real look at gender. The Feminine Auxiliary Police was formed in 1977, and in 1995 women were allowed to matriculate into the National Police School (Escuela Nacional de Policía) to become officials. But fewer than four hundred officers, less than 5 percent of the total, are women, and only fifteen of them are in the top ranks. As in most other countries, chronic sexism is a large and largely unaddressed issue in the Honduran police force. The only unit in which women constitute a substantial proportion is the CMS, where they make up nearly half of the corps. This is a positive trend in the sense that community policing is the most promising of Honduran reforms and women are more trusted by the community. But underneath is a thinly veiled attempt to marginalize both women and community policing, which, in turn, deepens stereotypes, creates separate trajectories of professional development, and engrains traditional policing. One of the regular roles of the CMS is to make presentations at schools, but just about all of the presentations in Tegucigalpa are done by women. Meanwhile, violence against women, Honduras's most serious and hidden form of violence, demonstrates the potential and challenge of problem-oriented policing. The MP's Technical Unit of Penal Reform (Unidad Técnica de Reforma Penal, UTR) and the MP's Office for Women (Fiscalía de la Mujer) reported a nearly fourfold increase in reported attacks against women between 2002 and 2003, which probably reflected better access to reporting mechanisms but was still only a fraction of the total. The growth continued through 2008, when nearly ten thousand cases were reported.[137] For many years, unclear government guidance curtailed aggressive enforcement and an integrated response by

135. Raúl Martínez, inspector, Comunidad Más Segura, and director, Chamelocón San Pedro Sula, interview by author, Chamelocón, February 18, 2004.

136. Honduras Investigative Police (DGIC) Academy, July 6, 2005.

137. Fiscal Especial de la Mujer, Tegucigalpa; "Preocupante aumento de violencia doméstica en Honduras," *Prensa Latina*, May 12, 2008; "Se acrecientan casos de violencia doméstica en Honduras," Radio América, October 9, 2008.

the courts, police, and hospitals. But better-publicized campaigns against this scourge, many developed in 2010, have helped.[138]

Future Policy Outlook

Perhaps the greatest promise, though, comes from recognition by officials under both the Zelaya and Lobo administrations of how the dilemma between traditional and problem-oriented policing has slowed progress. The Zelaya government began responding to that dilemma through a series of reforms that reversed many of his predecessor's practices and policies. The Strategic Plan of Integral Public Security, which laid out the goals for 2006–10, recognized the range of police weaknesses, from low institutional transparency to high personnel turnover. Although it soft-pedaled police corruption and abuse as a "lack of credibility," it addressed them with twenty-five separate plans at a cost of 272.8 million lempiras (about $15 million) in the first of its three phases. Along with expansion of the *mesas,* according to the vice security secretary, the government wanted to strengthen social services, statistics collection, and the DGIC. To improve accountability, he wanted a stronger UAI, ORP, and inspector general.[139] The Office of the Inspector General proposed in 1998 was intended to be transparent, but the one that was actually formed conducted most of its investigations confidentially. Most ambitiously, Zelaya wanted to restructure the police with a hybrid structure that combined centralized control with a network of posts and mobile units. The largest mobile force, with about two hundred officers each, would roam Tegucigalpa and San Pedro Sula.

The Lobo administration has continued in this direction and, despite the controversy surrounding its election during the de facto government, its rightist political position may give it more credibility and success in reform. Óscar Álvarez, the former security minister and the top vote-getter in the 2009 congressional elections, was reappointed security minister and has embarked on a critique of the policy of *mano dura.* Realizing its limits, he is now promoting more preventive initiatives, such as Barrio Saludable (Healthy Neighborhood), which strengthens social services in high-crime areas. Responding

138. Carlos Ortega Medina, executive director, Centro Electrónico de Documentación e Información Judicial, interview by author, Tegucigalpa, April 5, 2010.

139. José Roberto Romero Luna, police commissioner and vice secretary of security, interview by author, Tegucigalpa, July 13, 2006.

to a long-demanded support, the Technical Office of Criminal Investigation (Dirección Técnica de Investigación Criminal, DTIC) is being created to support the Public Ministry, and in particular its *fiscal* for organized crime. Such a move will respond to a long-term demand while significantly improving investigation. Indeed, over 80 percent of cases are not investigated at all,[140] and because of their complexity "the most serious crimes are the least investigated," observed the MP's director general, Danelia Ferrera.[141]

To have a lasting impact, though, such advances will also need to include an honest assessment of state functioning. First, the role of the military in internal security must be clarified. Many officials involved in human rights abuses in the 1980s found posts in Honduras's various police units.[142] Sparking unease within the police and protests from NGOs, both Zelaya's first security secretary and his vice secretary (and successor), retired colonel Jorge Rodas Gamero, were military officials. Rodas was a member of the notorious DNI, which carried out rights abuses in the authoritarian era, but his expertise in terrorism was thought to be useful in relations with the United States. He and other top officials relied on traditional policing actions that brought the armed forces into law enforcement, such as the 2008 "Five Stars" Operation, which involved ten thousand police officers and ten thousand soldiers, and plans to move into the police force one thousand military officers. With antinarcotics funding from the United States an ongoing major source of aid, and with narcotics central to both national and internal security, the government will continue to face the challenge of clarifying the line between the police and the armed forces.[143]

140. Interview with Yoleth Calderón, April 6, 2010.

141. Danelia Ferrera, director general, Ministerio Público, interview by author, Tegucigalpa, April 7, 2010.

142. Juan Almendares, executive director, Centro de Prevención, Tratamiento y Rehabilitación de las Víctimas de la Tortura y sus Familiares, interview by author, Tegucigalpa, July 2003.

143. U.S. funds for police and military antinarcotics operations rose from $1.17 million in 2001 to $3.62 million in 2004. The lack of rights conditions attached to such aid, says Commissioner Leonel Sauceda, often means that abuses do not necessarily prompt reductions in funding (interview by author, Tegucigalpa, July 14, 2003). Since the mid-1990s, Honduran military and police personnel have been trained at the School of the Americas, a U.S. Army training facility; the U.S. Navy Small Craft and Technical Training School; the Inter-American Air Forces Academy; and the U.S. Defense Department's Center for Hemispheric Defense Studies. Honduras received almost $5 million in foreign military financing between 2000 and 2006—$620,000 from Section 1004 Counterdrug (a Defense Department program), and other funds from International Narcotics Control. Between fiscal years 2000 and 2003, Honduras also received $1.93 million

Officials will also have to study why many problem-oriented programs go nowhere fast. As the next chapter describes in Bolivia, long-term plans are usually misaligned with institutional and financial realities, causing large chunks of them to be discarded. Even the most worthwhile projects will fall flat without an analysis of what is wrong with the ones they replace and why officials do not see them through. Similar to the Sula Valley antiviolence programs, for example, the much-vaunted Pandilla Prevention Program (Programa de Prevención de Pandillas), based on NGO services and education for youth, was effectively abandoned despite the European Union's promise of 20 million euros in support. Along with assessing the actions of top officials, training for lower officials will also be needed. For example, although over four hundred officials have been trained in NACMIS, the criminal case tracking system described earlier, international aid officers regard it and other programs as "too sophisticated" for most police officers, who lack basic education.[144]

Both of these weaknesses in the state require better accountability, particularly as state officials acquire greater legal powers. Although Álvarez and other Lobo officials stress prevention, they also want tougher laws, and accountability mechanisms must be strong enough to check them. Most broadly, a campaign backed by judges, members of Congress, and the *procuraduría general* (who represents the state in legal cases) proposes making Article 332 "much more severe." And in addition to longer prison terms, the Security Secretariat wants to introduce conspiracy and racketeering charges, as used those in the United States against the mafia. Such requests reflect organized crime's tremendous power in Honduras. Narcotics predominate, but syndicates are also trafficking stolen goods, cars, persons, and psychostimulants such as amphetamine. More recent developments are networks of prostitution, kidnapping, deforestation, and land acquisition. Nearly every area of economic activity in fact seems be considered by officials as "controlled" by organized criminals. Thus even

---

from ICITAP (Source: Center for International Policy). Worried that Honduras may become a recruiting ground for terrorists, the United States also stepped up funding to bolster the government's ability to fight terrorism, such as through the State Department's International Military Education and Training program. In August 2003 Honduras declared a national terrorism alert after receiving information that Al Qaeda was trying to recruit Hondurans to attack foreign embassies. The Security Secretariat said a Saudi terrorism suspect sought by the United States was spotted in Tegucigalpa.

144. María Isabel Gil, Spain's Technical Office of Cooperation in Honduras, Embassy of Spain, interview by author, Tegucigalpa, April 7, 2010.

though more powerful laws may be necessary to fight them, their likelihood for abuse also requires more powerful judicial monitoring. One step toward that goal came in March 2010 when the minister of governance and justice announced plans to have CONASIN meet once a month, or far more often than the total of two or three times it had met in the previous four years.[145] However, in order to reach the third stage of accountability by addressing the causes of abuse, it will need more powers to go along with those meetings.

Such accountability is particularly important because, in addition to much of the economy, organized crime controls much of the state. Zelaya's security secretary, Romero, said that they had begun to attack the problem, in contrast to the Maduro government, which "didn't touch organized crime, only *pandillas*." This spin on Zelaya's policy, though, has been roundly repudiated in light of the many scandals reaching the highest levels of that government. As before, many accusations against officials around the country were halted as soon as they started pulling in others, such as a 2006 investigation of the police chief of Roatán that implicated a large cast of local and high-level national officials. By most accounts, today the infiltration has only become deeper. Most damning, the director of the National Anti-Narcotics Council (Consejo Nacional contra Narcotráfico), a consortium of the top twenty-five state and nonstate antidrug agencies that coordinate national antidrug policies, says unequivocally that "all of the state organizations working on drugs are infiltrated by drug traffickers."[146]

Conclusion

Notable and promising in both Zelaya's and Lobo's plans were the acceptance of a theoretical dichotomy between the dominant reactive policing and the hoped-for preventive policing. Unlike other countries' review of their initial security reforms, Honduras did not hold back on its list of the effects of repressive police actions, including deterioration of the rule of law, social intimidation, radicalization of delinquents, and "partial security" in urban areas.

Diario Tiempo, one of Honduras's newspapers of record, congratulated

145. "Instalado el Conasin para apoyar la lucha contra la criminalidad," *La Tribuna,* March 12, 2010.
146. Mirna Andino, executive secretary, Consejo Nacional Contra el Narcotráfico, interview by author, Tegucigalpa, April 8, 2010.

itself at the end of Maduro's term for having never failed to point out "the disastrous action" of that government on citizen security. It noted the administration's "enormous budgetary applications, squandered on false publicity and leaving a disarticulated police, tremendously infiltrated by narco-trafficking, and in general, by organized crime, or dominated by corruption."[147] Indeed, there is nothing quite like regime change to bring out 20/20 hindsight. The leaders of the 2009 government overthrow, for example, did not fail to point out that conditions had not changed under Zelaya. In addition to the series of corruption scandals tarring Zelaya, de facto foreign minister Enrique Ortez charged the overthrown government with facilitating shipments of drugs on Venezuelan-registered planes. This heightened politicization of security extended to the security forces, from daily policing to long-term reform. The use of police officers to violently break up pro-Zelaya protests demonstrated, on one level, how abruptly political change can alter routine functions. On another level, the rift among reformers set back change on security policy, according to Mario Perdomo and Víctor Meza, two of the leading and most knowledgeable reformers, who were also prime sources for this chapter. But Perdomo continued on as vice security minister of the de facto government of Roberto Micheletti, and Meza, a minister of governance and justice under Zelaya, became the ousted president's chief negotiator, distracting them from reform and aggravating divisions that will take time to bridge. Even human rights groups were pulled into the political divisions. In particular, Ramón Custodio, who long provided the country's most consistent and unbiased guidance on constitutionalism as human rights commissioner, became mired in controversy through his support of Zelaya's ouster.[148]

Continuation of such conditions will eventually wear down even the toughest reform-minded police officials, such as the community policing officer Reina Grazzo, who have put up with the conditions in the expectation of something better. Despite an entirely new police force, a set of accountability agencies, and a well-designed new penal process code, citizen security reform has been hindered in Honduras through societal fear of *maras,* political attacks that link accountability with leniency, institutional obstruction of the monitoring of police activities, and a lack of reliable information. But community policing, the CPP, and other changes have given

147. "Nueva Policía" (editorial), *Diario Tiempo,* June 14, 2006.
148. Ramón Custodio, national human rights commissioner, interview by author, Tegucigalpa, April 7, 2010.

problem-oriented policing a foothold in the country, which, by continuing to show demonstrable results, may begin to gradually break down many traditional policing approaches. Even the acrimonious end of the Zelaya administration in June 2009 may lead the police to distance themselves from federal officials and the armed forces by moving away from national action and toward local action. As described in the next two chapters, even such ruptures can turn into opportunities for change.

Chapter 5

Bolivia

"Our security depends on us—we do what the community demands," said a police volunteer confidently during his patrol in El Alto, a sprawling Bolivian city perched above the capital of La Paz. El Alto's vibrant civil society is taking on an expanding range of self-appointed security activities, from conducting community justice forums to hanging effigies of suspected criminals, demonstrating the potential of citizen action in Bolivia, as well as the weakness of the state it is trying to supplant.

Since Bolivia's 1982 transition to democracy, reforming citizen security has been a goal of the government that ongoing economic and political crises have not allowed it to achieve. Decentralization and a series of legal and judicial reforms in the 1990s laid a foundation for overhauling and strengthening the National Police (Policía Nacional). But the opportunity to do so was lost in the subsequent instability fueled by labor disputes, police strikes, an intensive coca eradication campaign, increasing socioeconomic inequality, territorial tensions, and the massive protests that brought down constitutional governments in 2003 and 2005. The presidency of Evo Morales, elected in December 2005 with a decisive 54 percent majority (the biggest of any candidate since the transition to democracy), provided another chance for comprehensive reform, most broadly through the country's 2009 constitution. But the changes enveloping nearly every aspect of life in Bolivia may not extend to policing. Is it even possible, reformers ask, to transform a citizen security structure that has become steeped in corruption and administrative decay, that is distrusted by a divided society, and that is caught up in the often violent feuding among the country's nine increasingly assertive departments (provinces)?

History

The police have always been at the center of Bolivia's history. Amid social unrest, economic crisis, and frequent changes in government, the police have been used to maintain order and carry out policy. During Spanish rule, poorly trained and abusive militias enforced the law in the Viceroyalty of Peru, which covered the western sliver of modern-day Bolivia, and the Viceroyalty of La Plata, which accounted for most of the remaining territory (most notably the wealthy silver-producing areas of Sucre and Potosí). Policing was largely a local affair comprising ad hoc and unaccountable activities geared toward keeping order. The locus of police power shifted to the department and national level after Bolivia became independent in 1825. The new republic's 1826 constitution centralized most state powers, but created police forces at the department level, backed up by military squads. To further specify police responsibilities, the government adopted regulations governing the police in 1831 and in 1845. In 1830 it created a National Guard, also at the department level, with penal and civil codes enacted the year after.

However, the failure to build on such laws by professionalizing the police allowed old practices to continue during these first decades of independence. The police became even more unaccountable and militarized during this time. In 1862 and 1874 the force was placed under the War Ministry, and in 1884 the army was given control over police discipline. Thus by the time the 1886 Police Regulation turned the police into a civilian institution separate from the armed forces, regional loyalties and military traits were ingrained in the police. Meanwhile, the ongoing political turmoil continued to dilute the measures taken to stabilize it. Defeat by Chile in the 1879–83 War of the Pacific, in which Bolivia lost access to the sea, led to a drawn-out struggle between the traditional Conservative Party and the La Paz–based Liberal Party, which represented an emerging middle class. The Liberals won a civil war between them in 1898, and while ruling from 1899 to 1920 rewrote the constitution to create a balance of power among the three branches of government. They also took steps to make the police more efficient and better integrated into the state, such as through the 1910 formation of a General Office of Police in the Government Ministry.

Bolivia's defeat and further territorial shrinkage in the 1933–35 Chaco War with Paraguay precipitated the next major security sector overhaul when the returning soldiers, a mass of potentially destabilizing armed men, were transferred hurriedly into the police. The police force itself was reorganized in 1937, when the Military Police, the Gendarmerie (Cuerpo de Gendarmería), the paramilitary Security Police (Policía de Seguridad), and the army's Carabineros (Regimiento de Carabineros) were merged into National Corps (Cuerpo Nacional de Carabineros) regiments similar to those of the military. The government also established a professional training institution, the Police School (Escuela de Policía), later renamed the National Police Academy (Academia Nacional de Policías, or Anapol). These changes—which made the police even more militarized, disciplined, and hierarchical—are now regarded by many of its officers as the origin of the authoritarian practices that followed. The police formally adopted military training and organization in 1950, which was institutionalized further with the 1951 Organic Law of Police and Carabineros.

The Chaco War also precipitated major societal and political shifts, the most significant of which was the alliance of the middle and rural working classes that led to the formation in 1941 of the National Revolutionary Movement (Movimiento Nacional Revolucionario, MNR). After it took power in the 1952 National Revolution against a U.S.-oriented oligarchy, the MNR brought far-reaching change by nationalizing the tin mines, dividing agrarian estates among former tenants and peasants, granting universal suffrage, and financing big social development programs. These reforms extended to the police, which had long been controlled by the Defense Ministry. Because most top police officers supported the 1952 National Revolution, the MNR transferred the National Police to the Interior Ministry and rewarded it with many of the drastically reduced authorities and resources of the military.

After leading the 1964 military coup, Vice President Rene Barrientos Ortuno continued most MNR policies, and his death in 1969 generated a short-lived leftist resurgence. But after taking over in a 1971 coup, army general Hugo Banzer banned left-leaning parties, suspended the powerful labor union Central Obrera Boliviana, exiled or killed thousands of political opponents, and eventually prohibited all political activity. After Banzer was forced out in 1978, the eight authoritarian regimes that ruled the country until 1982 continued to rely heavily on police power to control the population amid coups and disputed elections. But there were a few positive developments during this otherwise dismal period, such as the 1973 creation of the Feminine Police Brigade, which led to the naming of the first women officers in 1978, a year after similar steps in Honduras (Policía Nacional de Bolivia 2002). But most governments—such as that of Luis García Meza, who, in less than a year in office, turned the state security forces into a vast drug-trafficking operation—managed to lower the already low standards of Latin American politics of the time.

Citizen Security Reform

The 1982 democratic transition stopped this downward spiral and imposed a clearer organization and rules on the police, mainly through the 1985 Organic Law of the National Police (Ley Orgánica de la Policía Nacional, LOPN). Run by the executive branch's Government Ministry, the centralized Policía Nacional was put in charge of crime prevention, investigation, and prison administration in all of the country's departments (see figure 5.1). At the center of the force's wide range of bodies are four sets of national agencies (see appendix B for the full list of agencies). The first set comprises central command and control, headed by a commander general appointed by the president. The main control is the Superior Disciplinary Tribunal (Tribunal Disciplinario Superior), led by a commander general appointee but with autonomous regulations and procedures. The second set is made up of surpport units specializing in areas such as training and dangerous substances. The third set is the "decentralized" and independent units, which have been prone to corruption. The fourth set is the operative and specialized agencies, most of which the General Command has the power to create and eliminate (LOPN Article 10). One of the most important but recently formed of these national units is the Technical Judicial Police (Policía Técnica Judicial, PTJ), which depends in part on the judiciary and is responsible for processing suspects and investigative procedures such as evidence collection. One of the more unusual of Bolivia's police units, the Battalion of Private Physical Security (Batallón de Seguridad Física Privada, BSFP), is also among this set. Unlike other countries, Bolivia officially provides private security through the battalion's seven thousand officers, who had police uniforms but not police status until they went on strike in January 2007 to demand full integration and receive the corresponding salaries.

Also at the national level, Bolivia's many antiriot, antinarcotics, and antiterrorist units have been placed in several of these sets over the years. The Special Security Group (Grupo Especial de Seguridad, GES), in charge of reestablishing public order and responding to attacks against property, was used widely to control large public gatherings and protests, but also was known for rights abuses against vulnerable groups such as street children.

Figure 5.1. National Police Structure, Bolivia

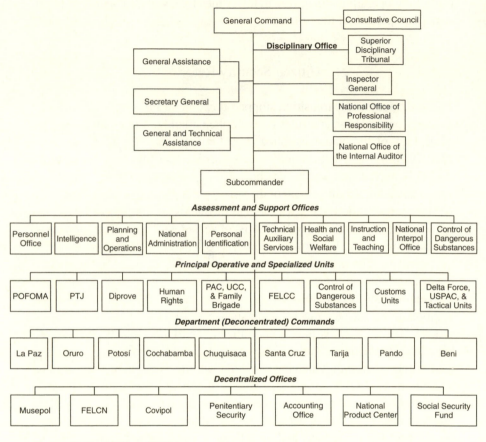

Source: National Police of Bolivia.

The GES was central to strikes against the government in 2003, and so in 2006 it was replaced by the Tactical Police Operations Unit (Unidad Táctica de Operaciones Policiales, UTOP).[1] Organized crime was fought by means of the U.S.-formed Special Crimes Investigation Task Force (Grupo de Tarea de Investigación de Delitos Especiales, GTIDE) and the Immedi-

---

1. GES antiterrorism courses led to the creation in 1987 of the Multipurpose Intervention Brigade (Brigada de Intervención Polivalente, BIP) to handle "uncommon" acts such as kidnapping, hostage taking, and subversion. In the 1990s the government of Jaime Paz Zamora gave primary antiterrorist authority to the Special Elite Antiterrorist Force (Fuerza Especial Antiterrorista de Elite, FEAE).

ate Action Group (Grupo de Acción Inmediata, GAI). The GAI was dismantled by the United States in 2004 after being accused of participating in political upheavals, and in late 2007 it was replaced by the elite rapid-action Delta Force (Fuerza Delta).

Since the police were brought into antinarcotics operations in 1983, the creation of anticoca forces—which together employ to six thousand officers—has been the biggest single change to the security structure in the democratic era. The main narcotics unit is the Special Anti-Narco-trafficking Force (Fuerza Especial de Lucha Contra el Narcotráfico, FELCN) created in 1987, which has led operations in the three largest coca regions—Beni, Chapare, and the Yungas. FELCN, which has had about fifteen hundred officers, constitutes about 4 percent of the national police. In 1989 it created its own intelligence service to gather evidence on suspected traffickers. FELCN also oversees the fifteen-hundred-strong Mobile Rural Patrol Unit (Unidad Móvil de Patrullaje Rural, UMOPAR), which is known as the Leopards (although FELCN also claims that mascot). Formed in 1983 as part of four narcotics treaties signed between the United States and Bolivia, UMOPAR is based in Chapare and run by the Government Ministry through the Social Defense Secretariat (Secretaría de Defensa Social). The United States provided most of UMOPAR's funds in its first decade of existence, and those funds were not included in the published state budgets. As the source of about 95 percent of the materials for FELCN, the United States also oversees most of the selection, administration, and other services of that unit.[2] Much like the armed conflicts of previous eras, this extended antidrug campaign has made the "militarization of police" an ingrained part of the country's security system (Gamarra and Barrios Morón 1996).

Daily policing is the responsibility of the departmental divisions, whose structures are similar to those of the National Police to which they are subordinate. Most departments have about twenty units (see appendix B for full list), and are roughly divided between urban and rural forces. The urban force, divided into patrol and criminal investigation sections, operate police stations and local jails. Much of the rural force, including the Customs Police (Policía Aduanera), is assigned to border posts to combat smuggling and illegal crossing. Over half of all police personnel are placed in the three

---

2. Proportionally, Bolivia has a higher level of international involvement in its security than most countries because of its low income level and its production of illegal narcotics.

departments with the largest cities: La Paz (about 23 percent), Santa Cruz (about 16 percent), and Cochabamba (about 14 percent). La Paz and some other departments have additional units such as an Explosives Brigade (Brigada de Explosivos) and a Women's Police Brigade (Brigada Policial Femenina). Municipalities are entitled to form a police force for enforcing local ordinances, but only a few have done so, such as the Municipal Police in the capital of La Paz (Policía Municipal de La Paz). However, many other cities have formed specialized law enforcement agencies with citizen participation. Protective of their limited role in security, many mayors have gone on the defensive by opposing national plans such as the Law of the National Citizen Security System (Ley de Sistema Nacional de Seguridad Ciudadana), discussed shortly, for contradicting Bolivia's "process of decentralization and municipalization." This stance has set the stage for conflict with police officials, who say that the constitution, which centralizes the police, trumps any form of local power. Lacking the kind of steady direction to steer clear of Bolivia's volatile regional tensions, citizen security has not avoided the politics of decentralization described in chapter 2. With battles between national and regional forces, it has instead exemplified and fueled them.

During the democratic era in Bolivia, the number of police officers has more than tripled, from about ten thousand in 1982 to nearly thirty-five thousand by 2009 (CEJA 2010),[3] of which about three thousand are civilians in technical, auxiliary, or identification units or civilian investigators working in detection, forensics, and logistics.[4] The national population was 8.3 million in 2001, and the ratio since then has been one officer for every 500 persons, or just over 230 officers for every 100,000 persons. The police are divided into two levels. At the lower level, making up between 78 and 85 percent of the force, are the subcommissioned officers, who can rise only as high as superior subofficial. The top set comprises the superior officials, whose ranks are identical to those of the military, from general to sublieutenant (see appendix B for a full list).

The 1985 Organic Law of the National Police altered the structure of the police, and a series of political and legal reforms in the mid-1990s altered

3. No statistics are available on how many are in the PTJ. But even the increase since 1982 has not matched the rise since independence, when there were only 11 per 100,000 persons.
4. Civilians are classified as superiors (*funcionarios superiores*) and subalterns (*funcionarios subalternos*).

its legal and political context. Bolivia revised its constitution in 1994, establishing a Judicial Council to select and oversee judges, and a Constitutional Court to rule on the constitutionality of laws and decide on high-level cases. It also created a public advocate/ombudsman (*defensoría del pueblo,* DDP) empowered to investigate all state agencies, including the police, and send cases to the Fiscalía for prosecution. The other main agency of police accountability, the National Office of Professional Responsibility (Dirección Nacional de Responsibilidad Profesional, DNRP), is within the Policía Nacional. It was formed in 2003 to investigate wrongdoing and send cases with sufficient evidence to the Superior Disciplinary Tribunal (Tribunal Disciplinario Superior, TDS), which tries and disciplines the accused.

Along with the 1999 New Penal Procedure Code (Nuevo Código de Procedimiento Penal, NCPP), many other new laws have a direct bearing on citizen security. A 1994 law that abolished imprisonment for nonpayment of debts and a 1995 law on domestic violence were among the many steps taken to strengthen basic rights. In the area of governance, new possibilities opened up with the creation of the 1994 Law of Popular Participation (Ley de Participación Popular, LPP) and the 1995 Administrative Decentralization Law (Ley de Descentralización Administrativa), followed by the creation in 2000 of local government units, Unidades Políticas Administrativas, which together made government in Bolivia more decentralized than it had ever been. Such measures were part of a neoliberal streamlining of the state bureaucracy and national economy, which included liberalization of monetary policy and, through a law on capitalization, the privatization of many public services.

Such policies in Bolivia were also an attempt by national officials, who felt constantly harassed by department governments, to give those governments a taste of their own medicine by empowering the municipalities to lodge demands from below. Although the national government retained the authority to appoint departmental governors (prefects), these laws generated more change than federal officials wanted or anticipated. Before the LPP, most of the country was made up of rural areas that fell outside municipal control, in which a group dating from the precolonial era, the *ayllu,* often helped oversee local affairs. Thus the new laws brought whole swaths of the country into the national structure for the first time. Meanwhile, the LPP transferred 20 percent of the national budget to the country's 327 municipalities and, in one stroke, increased the number of local officials from 262 to 2,900. Along with the 1996 electoral law, which allocated half of the seats in the Plurinational Legislative Assembly to local races (the other half are department-wide), the LPP also led to a new crop of indigenous leaders who began wresting control from the large political parties. As discussed in chapter 2, decentralization can be a double-edged sword by giving local governments more responsibility than they can handle fiscally or politically. The LPP's quick creation of hundreds of municipal governments aggravated corruption by empowering less accountable local officials.

The laws also led to a surge in local citizen organizing. Most municipal governments were overseen by committees composed mainly of grassroots territorial organizations (GTOs), 13,827 of which were recognized by the government in just the first three years after passage of the LPP. In some areas GTOs jumped into tasks such as participatory planning and fiscal oversight, which were two of the LPP's strengths. The *ayllu* also become stronger and more organized, particularly after the two main *ayllu* networks[5] formed a national council, Consejo Nacional de los Ayllus y Markas del Quollasuyo, or CONAMAQ (Pacheco 1992, 225–235). Meanwhile, although privatization increased foreign investment, it also led to interest rate hikes, which, combined with a lack of visible improvement for the poor, generated massive protests. In summary, because all these legal and administrative changes brought out long-standing tensions between Bolivia's indigenous majority and its elite minority, they could not contain the pent-up demands they were supposed to channel. The national government, caught off guard, ended up more destabilized than shored up by the reforms it had brought forth.

Crime and Criminal Policy

These political tremors heightened the already growing public pressure over the rising crime and violence in the country.

Crime Rates

Bolivia's crime rate quadrupled between 1993 and 1999, to more than 200,000 cases in 1998 alone. Between 2000 and 2004 there were 21,477 registered aggravated robberies (*atracos*), or 1.4 a day.[6] Despite a reduction

---

5. The Consejo Nacional del Aymaras, Kechuas, Tupi-guaranies Unido por Ayllus y Comunidades (AKTUPAC) and the Confederación Única de Ayllus-Comunidades-Capitanías del Kollasuyo-Bolivia (CUAKK-B).

6. El Instituto Nacional de Estadística, as reported in "El rojo sangre tiñó a la gente," *La Prensa,* December 25, 2005.

in crime from 2001 to 2003, some officials calculate that the overall rate of common crime rose between 235 percent and 360 percent in the 1990s, and that crimes against property and persons have increased by at least 60 percent since 2000.[7] But the varying estimates of crime, detailed in table 5.1, cast some doubt on the veracity of reported statistics. For example, the PTJ received just 114 homicide reports in 2000, which was clearly a gross underestimate.[8] More contradictory of official reports, and probably more reliable than them, are victimization surveys. In 2005, for example, one in every three citizens reported that someone in their family was the victim of a crime (UNDP 2006, 8–9). Measured in citizen polls, rates of perceived insecurity are also very high, increasing by up to 10 percent each year. About 40 percent of respondents in most surveys say that crime is rising, and over 70 percent feel insecure or somewhat insecure in their own neighborhoods.[9] In another poll two out of three respondents said that the city in which they lived was insecure and only getting more so (UNDP 2006, 8–9). But such numbers probably tell only part of the story, because police say that only about three of every ten crimes are reported. Even the numbers that are reported (see table 5.1) are unreliable, with sharp fluctuations since 1992, often from year to year.

The inability of the National Police to bring down these crimes rates— even with a 340 percent increase in budgets during the 1990s (Mollericona 2007)—is attributed to many causes, which tend to fall into two categories. The first category includes the socioeconomic or external conditions emphasized by the police: poverty, unemployment, alcoholism, mass migration to the cities, deterioration of the family, and, apparently most vexing to officers (even those stationed far from the borders), the constant "infiltration of Peruvian criminals" into the country. The other category is structural and is highlighted by civilians: the police force's bureaucratic internal management, half-hearted recruitment and training, wholesale corruption, and

7. The estimate of 235 percent is between 1995 and 2001 (Telleria Escobar 2004, 22). The 360 percent figure covers the full 1990s decade and is from Quintana (2004, 25). Of the 161,358 registered crimes in 2003, 33,600 were common crimes (*faltas*) and 73,141 were misdemeanors (*contravenciones*). Policía Nacional, "Casos policiales registrados en el año 2003." The 60 percent figure was furnished by Gloria Eyzaguirre, Comisión de Reforma Policial (Police Reform Commission), interview by author, La Paz, December 22, 2004.

8. Policía Técnica Judicial, "Cuadro estadístico de incidencia de casos, 2000" (sheet from Observatorio).

9. "Bolivia—Encuesta sobre dimensión subjetiva de la inseguridad," Instituto Latinoamericano de Seguridad y Democracia, July 17, 2006, http://www.ilsed.org/index.php.

Table 5.1 Crime Rates in Bolivia, 1992–2007

Year	Total crimes	Crime rate per 100,000 persons	Homicide rate per 100,000 persons (number of cases)[a]
1992	28,303[b]	410.5	n.a.
1993	58,222[c]	824.0	n.a.
1994	76,450[c]	1,056.4	n.a.
1995	68,163[c], 139,690[e]	921.1; 1,887,7	68[d]
1996	75,096[b], 241,470[e]	989.7; 3,182.3	78[d]
1997	142,706[c]	1,837.3	n.a.
1998	201,520[e]	2,534.9	28[d]
1999	13,200[f], 162,700[e]	162.3; 994.1	n.a.
2000	47,311[f], 209,210[e]	571.3; 2,570.8	37.7 (3,078)
2001	43,783[f], 298,600[e]	529.1; 3,662.6	35.7 (2,957)
2002	19,973[b]–36,577[f]	233.8–428.2	30.6 (2,610)
2003	22,875[b]–36,162[f]	259.7–410.6	29.1 (2,565)
2004	36, 015[f]	380.2	39.6 (3,748)
2005	32,150[f]	317.2	n.a.
2006	35,463[f]	337.7	n.a.
2007	38,817[f]	357.3	9.3 (1,013)

Note: "n.a." indicates reliable data are not available.
[a]2000–2004: based on numbers of homicides reported to the PTJ; and in various copies of the Instituto Nacional de Estadística de Bolivia's annual report, "Situación de Salud: Indicadores Básicos."
[b]1992, 1996, 2002: Policía Nacional and Instituto Nacional de Estadísticas, cited in "La delincuencia se dispara en Bolivia," *La Prensa,* September 5, 2004; 2003: Policía Nacional, "Casos Policiales Registrados en el Año 2003."
[c]*Verde Olivo—Boletín Informativo Policial,* no. 1, 1997.
[d]1995, 1996, 1998: Camara and Salama (2004, 159–81).
[e]Telleria Escobar (2004, 22). These figures include misdemeanors.
[f]Based on author's calculation of number of reported crimes and national population, excluding misdemeanors.

inability to control alcohol sales. Such socioeconomic and structural problems cross over and compound each other. For example, police officers' resentment of low pay and poor training limits their willingness to deal with social problems outside the scope of their written responsibilities. As the former commander of the La Paz police put it, officers are expected—without much backup from other agencies—to deal with social conditions as they "deteriorate into different criminal acts."[10]

This division in criminological diagnosis—fed by the combination of socioeconomic underdevelopment and unstable politics—runs particularly deep in Bolivia. The repercussions are evident in relatively straightforward

10. "Juan del Granado pide descentralización también en esta área," *La Prensa,* January 24, 2004.

problems such as alcohol abuse, in which the different targets of blame, from the focus of the police on social conditions to the civilian focus on policing, lead to policy deadlocks. The repeated mention by top officials of an alcohol-fueled "culture of excess" reveals a deeper dimension of that division: the ingrained stereotypes and the discrimination directed by the predominantly European elite in Bolivia at the indigenous majority.

Security Plans

As successive policies fall through, public confidence and government officials fall with them. Bolivia has had twenty-six government ministers, which is more than one per year, since the democratic transition in 1982. The only consistency has been the amount of time in office; most ministers have spent about a year in their position, giving nearly every administration an equal number of ministers and years in power. Most of those ministers left as part of a presidential "fresh start" on security, or felt hindered during their times in office. Thus even though President Carlos Mesa's government minister made it through his boss's truncated term, he complained of constant "negative interference from the political sector."[11] Even more numerous than government ministers have been police chiefs; twenty-three have served in that position since 1982. This frequency compounds instability in the ministry by severing continuity in the two top levels of security policy and practice.

These revolving doors have also led to a large number of citizen security plans—at least twelve since 1990. Most of these plans have embraced a wide range of goals, such as rooting out corruption, reorganizing structures, and improving education. Such ambition has often reflected the multiparty makeup of most governments, which are often the product of forced negotiations among the leftist Revolutionary Left Movement (Movimiento de la Izquierda Revolucionaria, MIR), the MNR, and the Nationalist Democratic Action Party (Acción Democrática Nacionalista, ADN). Not very sturdy to begin with, many security policies then crumbled along with those shaky coalitions. Because most plans were initially prompted by a specific scandal, often the only specific proposal in them to be executed was a personnel shake-up. Under the government of Hernán Siles Suazo in the early 1980s, corruption and a lack of internal controls led to a strengthening of

11. Saúl Lara Torrico, minister of the interior, interview by author, La Paz, December 16, 2004.

discipline and the dismissal of a few dozen officers. In the late 1980s and early 1990s police abuses during detentions and incarceration led the Human Rights Commission of the House of Deputies to propose prohibition of detention without a judicial arrest (except in cases of *in flagrante delicto*) and the creation of judgeships to ensure due process. Such abuse also resulted in the prosecution of twelve officers for killings and torture.

More comprehensive reforms were proposed during the 1989–93 government of Jaime Paz Zamora, again spurred by corruption scandals such as the forty officers fingered by the U.S. Drug Enforcement Administration for their involvement in narco-trafficking. Such reforms included decentralization; higher salaries; reorganization of the radio, investigation, transit, and other units; and improvements in discipline, internal affairs, and cadet education. New and increasingly creative forms of corruption—such as police charging for nonexistent supplies as well as nonexistent police ordering actual supplies—spurred another leadership change during the 1993–97 government of Gonzalo Sánchez de Lozada. Some of Lozada's attempted structural reforms, such as his 1994 proposal to create police modules to "deconcentrate" the force, never got off the ground. But his series of judicial reforms, as this chapter discusses, turned out to be transformative for the criminal justice system and had far more of an impact on policing than earlier plans focusing on citizen security.

Even more audacious outbreaks of corruption prompted even more ambitious reform under the elected 1997–2001 government of Hugo Banzer. Early in the new administration the chief commander of the police force was accused of dipping into the Cooperative Police Mutual Fund (Mutual de Cooperativas de la Policía, Mucopol), and his acquittal and return to the police prompted an exodus by top police officials. To assuage them, in 1997 Banzer modernized the police's administration and gave them many new vehicles. This development led to the Government Ministry's 1997 Citizen Security and Protection Plan for the Family, and to complementary laws that created a new transit code, new regulations for private security, a law on arms possession, removal of some police from administrative duties, and structural deconcentration to increase the police presence in the *barrios*. Most significant, the Citizen Security and Protection Plan aimed to bolster citizen participation through formation of the School Brigades, the Neighborhood Security Brigades, and the Group of Civilian Support for the Police (Grupo de Apoyo Civil a la Policía, GACIP), discussed later. In 1998 the police floated a "Strategic Plan" to better target crime through Immediate Action Police Units (Unidades Policiales de Acción Inmediata) and more regional flexibility in policy implementation.[12] Because it improved police efficiency, this proposal laid the groundwork for Decree 25477 of August 1999, grandly dubbed a "Restructuring of the National Police," which advanced early plans through changes such as salary increases and a new accounting system. Also in 1999, the Integral Plan of Security and Community Participation moved forward on deconcentration of policing, and the Plan of Community Participation tried to strengthen discipline in order to address the mounting complaints of "irregularities" in police activity.

But, as before, most of these proposals ran aground, and one of the few provisions actually carried out was another purge of the top ranks. In contrast to such efforts at greater transparency and accountability was a greater militarization, such as through the 2000 Plan Ciudadela (Citadel Plan), which brought soldiers into the policing of major cities around the country and likely inflamed regional resentments in areas such as Santa Cruz, as discussed shortly (Bolivia Press 1999, 6). More community-minded but equally militarized was the 2001 Plan Tranquilidad (Tranquility Plan), which brought the army and police together to attack "factors that generate neighborhood lack of tranquility," such as alcohol consumption by minors (Telleria Escobar 2004, 24). Even the 1999 Integral Plan of Security and Community Participation brought the military into this wider (and arguably more intrusive) realm of law enforcement.

Although many plans provided a lot of new equipment and some included long-needed salary hikes, few dealt with training or other underlying weaknesses. Furthermore, despite the new powers and material, higher officials were frustrated by what they regarded as the government's sluggish responses to crime, such as the long delays in passing the Citizen Security and Protection Plan.[13] They also resented being shut out of policymaking, including proposed revisions of the Organic Law as well as officer expulsions. For example, when five generals and a vice minister kept a planned 1999 purge tightly under wraps to avoid condemning to "civilian death" the officers slated for dismissal, their secrecy triggered opposition that neutralized otherwise strong support for the citizen security plan (CEDIB 1999).

After President Banzer resigned because of poor health in August 2001, citizen security policy grew both more comprehensive and more militarized under his successor, Jorge Quiroga. Following policies such as the Plan of

---

12. Juan Alfaro Velásquez, "Plan de Seguridad Ciudadana," *Bodas de Plata,* no.1, April 1998.
13. Editorial, *La Gaceta Jurídica,* July 28, 2000.

Reinforced Citizen Security (Plan de Seguridad Ciudadana Reforzada), the Quiroga administration gave the military many new police authorities, mainly by incorporating the Military Police (Policía Militar, PM) into street policing. Although PM officers were proscribed from being armed or holding suspects in military facilities, they could make arrests in the presence of the police. The ministers of government and of defense formed a Committee of Citizen Security Policies to evaluate the plan, which reflected an emphasis on traditional policing. Such approaches led to operations and policies such as the 2002 Citizen Security Emergency Plan, which deployed hundreds of police officers and army soldiers to La Paz, Cochabamba, and Santa Cruz.

Other proposals developed under Quiroga were carried forward after Sánchez de Lozada was elected again to the presidency in 2002. In early 2003 the new government's 34 million boliviano ($4.25 million) Integral Plan of Citizen Security and Public Order was put into effect. It included a 40 percent increase in the police budget, a National Citizen Security Fund (Fondo Nacional de Seguridad Ciudadana), a 15 percent increase in the number of police officers (and more of them on the streets), changes in the police academy curricula, better coordination, and, to round it off, a citizen security "system" made up of a hundred different programs. Councils from the country's departments were involved in forming the plan, but, in a major strategic error, local governments were not. Municipal officials soon criticized the plan for not empowering departmental and district security councils to implement it, and the Federation of Municipal Associations of Bolivia (Federación de Asociaciones Municipales de Bolivia) and the mayor of La Paz, along with the department heads, rejected any possibility of earmarking part of their budgets for security or the purchase of equipment for the police.[14] Meanwhile, the police complained about the lack of resources to implement the plan. But the armed forces rejected the plan outright. This should not be a problem in a stable democracy, but in Bolivia it was a setback because of the military's growing police powers.

Nevertheless, much of the plan got past these institutional and political blows and culminated in the August 2003 National System of Citizen Security Law 2494 (Ley de Sistema Nacional de Seguridad Ciudadana 2494). This landmark law established a National Security System to develop and coordinate policy through national, departmental, and provincial citizen security councils that brought together representatives of the police, civil so-

14. "Alcaldías no tendrán que pagar el plan de Seguridad Ciudadana," *Correo del Sur,* November 1, 2002, http://www.correodelsur.net/2002/1101/w_nacional17.shtml.

ciety, and three government branches. It established a National Council of Citizen Security and Public Order (Consejo Nacional de Seguridad Ciudadana y Orden Público) to reduce corruption, strengthen internal police communications, and gradually reintroduce neighborhood police stations. The council would also emphasize better cooperation between the police and the armed forces in rural areas (a legacy in part of the Committee of Citizen Security Policies) and the development of pilot programs in urban areas (see Mollericona et al. 2007, 31). Amid subsequent institutional failure and political uncertainty in the country, many of the plan's programs were transferred to the 2003–7 Institutional Strategic Plan (Plan Estratégico Institucional 2003–7),[15] whose lineup of objectives included better education, housing, and health services for the police; improvement of the police's public image; modernization of the National Office of Personal Identification; creation of a Police Treasury (Tesoro Policial) to centralize and control police finances, with authority to audit all of their sources; an Institutional Practices Unit (Unidad de Gestión Institucional); a 40 percent increase in officers and a distribution of them through new evaluations; economic incentives and rewards for officers; a new Disciplinary Regulation (Reglamento de Disciplina); and rigorous application of the Career Regulation (Reglamento del Plan de Carrera) and Law 1178, known as Ley Safco, which laid out financial oversight of state agencies. As with earlier efforts, however, these plans were too ambitious, but the more technical provisions did survive those that were either very general or focused on institutional change. For example, the number of police officers had jumped to 29,000 by 2006, though with few of the improvements in their professional lives promised by these laws. Carlos Mesa, who assumed the presidency after Sánchez de Lozada was forced out of office in October 2003, had expressed his commitment to police reform as the 2002 vice presidential candidate. But once Mesa assumed office, his need to control rather than improve the police took precedence, because police strikes had triggered Lozada's downfall. Scaling down expectations, Mesa pushed to strengthen the internal disciplinary system as well as the academy curricula, primarily through more emphasis on legal education. With his presidential term cut short as well, this approach proved to be a prescient one.

Evo Morales's electoral mandate loosened these constraints, allowing him to lay out a new citizen-oriented paradigm of law enforcement rooted

15. "7 políticas del Plan Estratégico de la Policía 2003–2007," *La Razón,* May 16, 2003.

in legislation such as the LPP. Signaling a policy commitment to citizen security, Morales also elevated the General Office of Citizen Security (Dirección General de Seguridad Ciudadana), created in 2000, to the rank of a vice ministry. But as the president questioned the practices of the police and other political institutions through his efforts to "re-found" the Bolivian state, smoldering regional tensions came to the forefront, often erupting in armed confrontations over departmental control of the police. Policing was also central to the rebellion of the four eastern departments—Santa Cruz, Beni, Tarija, and Pando—which are whiter and richer than the highland departments in the West. After declaring autonomy from the central government in December 2007, the departments ground the legislature to a halt and voted for autonomy in 2008. Leading the rebellion was Santa Cruz, which covers over a third of national territory, contributes 40 percent of the nation's tax base, and earns over half of its GDP.[16] Santa Cruz also complains about the fact that the only police academy is in La Paz. Moreover, the La Paz Department has over 12,000 officers for a population of 2.35 million, whereas Santa Cruz has just 2,700 officers for nearly 2.39 million people and a territory three times as large as La Paz (Quintana 2004, 42). Santa Cruz provides about 46 percent of the National Police budget, but just 30 percent of the funds sent find their way back to Santa Cruz;[17] the lion's share of the rest stays in La Paz. According to statistics provided by the Santa Cruz members of the national legislature, the department's police force receives about three million bolivianos a year, amounting to under 10 percent of the 35–45 million bolivianos in annual police earnings nationwide. Human resources are marked by a similar imbalance. Two-thirds of officers are from La Paz Department, and only 5 percent are from Santa Cruz (although Santa Cruz politicians claim it is just 1 percent). Thus the lack of clarity in police finances stokes not only corruption but also departments' perceptions that they are being cheated.

As a result of such disparities, Santa Cruz wants its own force, or at least many of its own policing agencies, such as a separate department police academy. It has also proposed creation of an external control unit comprised

16. The eastern and southern departments of Santa Cruz, Beni, Pando, Chuquisaca, and Tarija, which together have been demanding more autonomy from the central government, make up over two-thirds of the national territory.

17. These budget numbers are disputed. Some Santa Cruz congressional delegates assert that their department receives about three million bolivianos a year, which is about 10 percent of all police income. "La policía desnuda su pobreza y admite que hay corrupción," *El Nuevo Día,* November 20, 2002.

of judges who would investigate allegations of corruption in the police administration and operations.[18] In 2004 the Santa Cruz legislative delegation announced its intention to push through the Law of Budget Deconcentration and Collected Resources (Ley de Desconcentración Presupuestaria y de Recursos Recaudados), which would have permitted each departmental commander to administer resources for his or her department. A lot of resources find their way from the national treasury to unknown recipients, who are not known "because corruption is institutionalized," said one legislator. Moreover, in Santa Cruz the police complain that, because they often have no funds, they have to plead with the electric and water companies to provide service to their stations. Thus a central demand of Santa Cruz is a deconcentration of national funds to allow payments to be coordinated between the local government and the police, which Santa Cruz officials hope would also prevent delays in payments from the national treasury to the police. Although the budget deconcentration bill was approved by the House of Deputies and sent to the Senate, it was never enacted, primarily because of political instability and the fact that any change would reduce funds for the rest of the country.

Reform and Political Change

Bolivia's large physical size and ethnic diversity have long made centralization ineffective, and more recent political changes have made it outdated as well. The president's Movement to Socialism (Movimiento al Socialismo, MAS) Party lacks the two-thirds majority in the legislature to completely halt the push for decentralization by the eastern departments,[19] whose referendum votes for autonomy require Morales to compromise with them. The Constituent Assembly that formed the 2009 constitution kept the national police force intact, but it entertained different levels of police decentralization, from a nominal administrative deconcentration to a complete division into autonomous state forces, as in federal countries. Such proposals continue to aggravate federal-department relations, because little short of complete autonomy would satisfy powerful sectors in many departments. More decentralization thus appears inevitable, but it will not necessarily be beneficial. Under such politicized conditions, any arrangement would prob-

18. Movimiento Autonomista: Nación Cambia, "Policía y Seguridad Ciudadana," http://www.nacioncambia.net.

19. MAS won half of the vote in the July 2006 election of a Constituent Assembly, giving it 135 of the 255 seats.

ably be rushed, multiplying the weakness of the existing system and almost certainly leaving poor states such as Potosí and Oruru with diminished police services. Not surprisingly, most top police and government officials are against any kind of decentralization at all. Several oppose it because of the difficulty of implementation, and one colonel at the Escuela Superior de Policías said the police are against it mainly because of the inequalities it would produce. However, just as with community policing, that stance often clashes with those of officers on the ground. As those officers point out ceaselessly, the requirement that all decisions be approved centrally slows down effectiveness and responsiveness to the highly changing and localized problems of citizen security. As one officer put it, "If you have a problem in an outlying department like Beni, you have to go to the center to resolve it." By the time support does materialize, he adds, the problem has worsened, leading to yet more drawn-out requests.

Like his predecessors, Morales also faces a restless citizenry and volatile police-society relations. The police continue to be ranked as the country's most (or second most) corrupt and untrustworthy institution. In a 2001 poll, 65 percent of respondents said policing was poor, 30 said it was regular, and just 5 percent regarded it as good.[20] Five years later, less than one-third of Bolivians approved of the police's performance, and fewer than 40 percent could ascertain how the police was responding to insecurity in their neighborhoods. As a result, about half of all citizens said they do not report crimes and turn instead to a growing range of alternatives (UNDP 2006, 9–11). "We just know how to deal with these problems a lot better," said one El Alto resident at a community justice meeting. "How can we trust a police that just comes to break up our demonstrations? Where are they at other times?"[21] Facing expectations for broad and participatory problem-oriented reform, Morales's commitment to change must be accompanied by concrete improvements that do not lessen daily security.

Even though the police are aware of society's frustrations and expectations, they often view themselves as the victims. Three-quarters of police acknowledge society's lack of confidence in them, but nearly the same proportion also reports being assaulted by a citizen (UNDP 2006, 3). As in Buenos Aires and other areas with high police death rates, officers often turn questions about citizen confidence into discussions about citizen antago-

    20. "El desempeño policial se mide por los resultados," *La Razón Digital,* April 28, 2005, http://www.la-razon.com.
    21. Community Justice Council, El Alto, July 28, 2007.

nism. Officers say that state agencies and rights groups, in their zeal to document violence by police, ignore its use by citizens. Grieving over officer deaths in the line of duty, one official asked, "How has [society] responded to this holocaust of the servants of law and order? With a dense and heavy silence. It seems that no one cares that a police is killed. Human rights organizations, which raise thick dust clouds when an anti-social is eliminated in a police operation, have [been] desperately mute."[22] Informally, many officers say that the daily grind of social conditions and hostility sends them on a descent into increasingly violent tactics. Many admit that they often respond to an "ungrateful" population with "brutality, authoritarianism, and violence."[23] Forms of such abuse include forced entries without warrants, illegal confiscations, extrajudicial shootings, and beatings. And the most common targets are poor women, youth, detainees, *campesinos,* and community activists. Reflecting the kind of socioeconomic singling out practiced in many countries, often such abuses are based on officers' assessments of citizens' statuses and their corresponding proclivity to dispute police action. As part of their daily policing, for example, subcommissioned officers in Bolivia routinely extort money from small businesses, entertainment halls, brothels, criminal gangs, detainees, and street merchants. Even many street officers who acknowledge that they take out their job frustrations on residents in "chaotic" neighborhoods such as Pura Pura in La Paz (see map 5.1 later in this chapter) put themselves last on their list of those responsible for violence during policing—after their bosses, politicians, citizens themselves, and human rights groups.

Explaining a lot of these police-citizen tensions are officers' work conditions. Exploitation and low pay, in particular, have led to frequent and very violent police strikes, walkouts, and takeovers of government buildings. Seventeen strikes were held between 1982 and 1997, twelve just between 1997 and 2002, and six in 2002 and 2003 (Quintana 2004, 29). These strikes grew in political threat as they grew in frequency. On February 12, 2003, in one of the biggest outbreaks of civil disorder since the 1952 revolution, the government was nearly toppled when military troops tried to stop youths from breaking presidential palace windows during protests against spending cuts and a new income tax. When the protesters were joined by police officers on a wildcat strike, soldiers used tear gas, and the police responded

22. Miguel Vásque Viscarra, *Verdo Olivo—Boletín Informativo Policial,* no. 9, 1995, segundo semestre.
23. Col. Jaime Gutiérrez Terrazas, director of human rights, Policía Nacional, interview by author, La Paz, July 13, 2000.

in kind in an armed confrontation that injured hundreds of people and killed twenty-seven. In October 2003 another flare-up of unrest stemming from similar conditions forced the president out of office.

The involvement of police officers in such unrest, along with the feeble institutions that it has overwhelmed, makes it difficult for any police force to handle new challenges to public order in Bolivia. Such violence has also boiled over into the issues of coca and gas. Because coca was one of the few relatively secure sources of rural income during the economic liberalization of the 1980s and 1990s, its eradication was limited. However, the year after he was elected president in 1997, Banzer put forth a U.S.-funded Dignity Plan (Plan Dignidad) that created a new batch of military police units to eliminate illegal coca in targeted areas. Among them were the U.S.-funded Joint Task Force (JTF), a joint police and military operation formed in 1998, and the Expeditionary Task Force (ETF), a fifteen-hundred-member joint police and military operation formed in 2001 and backed by existing police units such as the Unidad de Policía Ecológica (Ecological Police Unit). Supported by separate drug courts and prisons, these new forces militarized and complicated the country's fragile judicial system and its police structure. As Plan Dignidad expanded, it cost the economy about $500 million each year (Farthing and Kohl 2001, 36), and its clumsily applied crop substitution programs provided few of the promised alternatives for coca growers (*cocaleros*). It also incited even greater violence, because the JTF and other security forces responded to protests with states of siege, mass detentions, and armed battles with *cocalero* self-defense committees, which accounted for most of the 150 killings by police since 1990 (Quintana 2004). As a result, the JTF forces were downsized, and the ETF was liquidated in July 2002 after losing U.S. funding.

On the heels of these problems emerged another one. More directly destabilizing to Bolivia's democracy were the massive and unrelenting protests over plans to build a gas pipeline through Bolivia's historical enemy, Chile. These protests hastened the collapse in 2003 of the government. Whereas the drug war blurred policing with military operations, the gas protest blurred it with political protests. Most police were moved from their regular duties to help break up and prevent the road blocks, demonstrations, and other forms of physical protest that were bringing the country to a halt. There was little choice but to physically deploy officers at that point, and yet the government's failure to anticipate the protests also made such a response inevitable and ineffective.

Applying a wider critique, many Bolivian police officers say that there has never been an effort to define *internal security* in ways that allow a distinction among the many causes of violence, from economics to internal emigration, and therefore promote the development of different policies. In one officer's view, the "Doctrine of National Security," in which a repressive response is applied to threats against public order, is the only one that exists. The failure to develop alternatives has thus allowed this Cold War relic to continue as a convenient off-the-rack response for blocking forms of societal agitation that, channeled into less confrontational forms, might help the police find ways to prevent them from building in the first place. President Morales and his cabinet ministers involved in security agree that such embedded approaches are a major challenge, but they struggle to find compelling and workable frameworks to replace them without risking political instability.[24]

Police Training

The foundation for workable new approaches is education. Curricula and training improvements not only help incorporate criminology, but also help transform the police from below. Bolivia has three main police education academies. The first is the Universidad Policial "Mariscal Antonio José de Sucre" (Unipol), created in November 2006 as the successor to the officer-level National Police Academy (Academia Nacional de Policía, Anapol).[25] Unipol is composed of three academic centers. One provides basic police training degrees (*grados de técnicos medio*) for entry-level ranks (*tropas*); another gives superior-level degrees (*grados de técnico superior*); and the campus in La Paz grants a bachelor's degree in police science—students choose to specialize in criminal investigation, transit, or order and security. Unipol also offers courses in criminal law, penal and civil investigation, criminology, ballistics, laboratory science, narcotics, traffic, counterinsurgency, and human and public relations.

The second academy is the Basic Police School (Escuela Básica Policial, Esbapol) founded in 1994 for subcommissioned officers. Its courses range from patrol to investigation. Officers in the lower ranks can also attend classes at the School of Perfecting and Specialization of Police Classes (Escuela de Perfeccionamiento y de Especialización de Clases de Policías) in Cochabamba.

24. Evo Morales, president, and Juan Ramón Quintana, minister of the presidency, interviews by author, La Paz, September 18, 2006.
25. Based on two semesters for one of four specializations: judicial policing, order and security, transit, or intelligence.

The third academy is for higher officials holding the ranks of lieutenant colonel and above. The Superior Police School (Escuela Superior de Policías, ESP) was established in 1973 for training in managing departments, operational units, and educational institutes. The ESP offers postgraduate courses and one-year programs for serving officers so they can specialize in areas such as laboratory science, intelligence, administration, and command. Both civilian and police professionals serve on the faculty, though budget restraints have created a permanent imbalance in that ratio in favor of police insiders.

Overall, recruitment standards for the academies have steadily improved since the days when admission depended on political connections. Medical, physical, and psychological examinations as well as general knowledge tests for applicants were introduced in the 1980s. In 2004 the government's "new police education system" (Resolución Suprema 222297) not only created Unipol, but, along with the police's 2003–7 plan, expanded course offerings and standardized curricula that had long been subject to uncoordinated changes by both government reformers and police chiefs. While needed, such efforts are still just a beginning. For one thing, recruitment remains highly unrepresentative—that is, it does not reflect Bolivia's sharp socioeconomic and racial divisions. Eighty-one percent of officers and higher civilian employees are from the middle or upper classes, whereas 82 percent of subofficials are from middle or lower classes, and a majority are from the indigenous groups that constitute three-quarters of the population. An estimated 60 percent of the lower ranks are Aymara, the main ethnicity in Western Bolivia. The poor pay, lack of prestige, and often insufferable working conditions at this level attract few people outside of these low-income sectors, and lead to high turnover among those who do join. Unipol graduates can theoretically be promoted to the top rank of general, but an Esbapol graduate can rise only to *suboficial.* Meanwhile, most of the entrance requirements to Unipol, which vary according to specialization and level, remain out of the reach of most Bolivians. By contrast, officers are commissioned by means of graduation from Unipol, by transfer from the army, through direct political appointment for demonstrated ability, or through outright patronage. Most civilians are also political appointees, and they usually but not always have some relevant experience. Seventy-seven percent of lower-tiered officers have said they considered entering Unipol/Anapol, and 70 percent said they would still do so if given the opportunity (UNDP 2006, 5).

Ethnic, hierarchical, and other divisions in the police are mirrored by the gap between the police academies' actual functioning and their potential. Although each school received relatively good assessments (77 percent for

Anapol, 67 percent for Esbapol, and 57 percent for the ESP), 86 percent of serving officers believed it was important or very important to reform the educational system through measures such as better synchronization with actual police work and between upper- and lower-level training (UNDP 2006, 5). Training has in fact been gradually strengthened since the late 1990s, such as through more flexible scheduling and integration of the police's educational system into the Superior Studies level of the National Education System, which have made it more open and academically rigorous. But police education remains inadequate. For example, although Unipol is divided into specializations, it is criticized for its paucity of offerings in areas such as penitentiary administration, accountability, community policing, and public relations. And even though Unipol has continued to scale down emphasis on physical preparation, a process that began at Anapol, training remains centered on arms use and violence control. Stalled in many predemocratic conceptions, education overall is thus still largely regarded by police and civilian officials alike as militarized. The legal education that cadets receive is based on rote and formalistic readings of the law, giving short shrift to critical thinking and social issues. For example, human rights are not discussed in any real depth in any of the Organic Law's 138 articles, and so the subject is not well integrated into coursework. Thus even a concerted push from the outside to improve police preparation on rights, such as the DDP's efforts to strengthen course material and to open human rights offices within police stations, has had a limited impact.

Any narrowing of the gap between lower-rank and upper-rank education may end up coming not from improvements for lower-ranked officers, but from the deterioration of the higher police academy. Almost since Unipol's inauguration, hopes for improvements have been crumbling along with its infrastructure. The academy's students are crammed into crowded dormitories where they sleep in triple bunks, eat food with no nutritional value beyond its calories, and queue every morning in long lines for the bathroom.[26] "By the time we get to class, we're exhausted," confided one cadet on condition of anonymity. Because of the reputation Unipol is acquiring, many students and instructors suspect, applications dropped in 2008 and are unlikely to go back up. Conditions at Esbapol are not much better. Its cadets complain that the food and equipment budgets are stretched beyond capacity, often to accommodate the sixty or so extra students admitted each year through politically connected *padrinos* (local godfathers).[27] More serious,

26. Unipol officers and cadets, interviews by author, La Paz, July 24, 2007.
27. Esbapol officials and cadets, interviews by author, La Paz, July 30, 2007.

physical abuse of cadets has become an expected part of the Esbapol experience. One cadet there mentioned regular beatings and other forms of hu-
miliation, but investigations by the DDP and other agencies seem to catch
only the worst offenders. Conversations with current students and recent
graduates invariably turn to the assaults they have suffered, but they and their
superiors often excuse and tolerate such abuse as fitting preparation for a life
of policing. Students who put up with such ordeals are thus particularly resentful to find themselves directing traffic ten hours a day. And mistreatment
does not usually stop once they get onto the force. In a study by the UN Development Programme, just 13 percent reported they had never been sub-
jected to insults, 23 percent said they had never been unjustifiably arrested
or sanctioned, and 23 percent said they had never been overworked. Of those
who complained of such treatment, only one in four was satisfied with the
process of redress. Conditions are particularly bad for women; one in three
reported being sexually assaulted, and three-quarters of the time by their direct superiors. More than half of the police, at all levels, did not have confidence in their leadership and felt unrepresented by the General Command.
Overall, between 75 percent and 85 percent of officers said their work conditions were decidedly substandard and precarious (UNDP 2006).

Officer Promotion Policies

This discontent extends to procedures of ascension in the ranks. As in other
Latin American countries, promotion in both the commissioned and subcommissioned ranks is far clearer and fairer on paper than in reality. Administered not by the Office of Instruction and Training (Dirección de Instrucción y Enseñanza) but by the Personnel Office (Dirección de Personal),
promotion differs among ranks but is based primarily on two areas. The first
is exams, which most officers can take after completing a minimum time in
their rank of between four and six years.[28] The second area is a point system; officers gain points for different tasks and contributions.

Similar standards and promotion tests also apply to subcommissioned officers. In reality, though, as several officials claim, because of entrenched

28. Since 2000 officials have asked for this period to be extended to seven years. Officers are tested on statistics, crime laboratory science, intelligence, planning, penal
process law, shooting, and physical education. About 25 percent of Anapol graduates
reach the ranks of major or lieutenant colonel. Officers who do not ascend within the
slated time stay in the police until completing thirty years of service. Subcommissioned
officers are given exams on subjects such as police procedures, physical security, and
criminal investigation.

favoritism each year's promotion process is a "total war" that is "contaminated by disputes."[29] Despite efforts by the Morales government to make promotion to the top ranks more transparent, three-quarters of police officers believe that the system is neither honest nor consistent (UNDP 2006, 7). In addition to the well-known practice of paying for good grades on the exams, the number of ways in which to earn points has grown so large as to render merit nearly meaningless. "Even participation in an event, no matter how insignificant, has points," says one official. And a bumper crop of points is awaiting those who have or can develop connections at the Personnel Office "because there you can arrange things for your friends and allies." As a result, many promotion files are filled with a "very impressive" number of points. "But when you do a more rigorous analysis," say officers who have tracked promotion, "it's garbage."[30]

Helping to inflate the artificial point bubble is the lack of opportunity to earn real ones. Mundane and often mind-numbing routines waste the first crucial years on the job. Just as many new police officers in countries like Argentina stand on a corner all day (see chapter 6), many of Bolivia's street police spend most of their shifts directing traffic. In La Paz Department, for example, new officers are put on the street, either on foot patrols or in traffic duty, with little chance to develop citizen relations. Many of those who endure those tasks are then rewarded with more exciting motorized patrols, which by their nature limit the kinds of citizen contacts on which problem-oriented policing is built. With enough seniority, officers then move into administrative work in areas such as identification or finance.[31] But even at these higher levels the constant rotation prevents officers from developing the expertise in geographic or technical areas that helps improve both their own work and that of their units. Built into the promotion process, then, is an association of street policing with the lower-level ranks and desk jobs with the higher-level ranks. The result is an administration-heavy security force. The estimates of employees working in administration vary widely—the police report 15 percent and DDP personnel estimate 36 percent. Differences in how "administration" is defined—which seems to be a bone of contention practically everywhere—explain much of this disparity. Some

29. Officials on condition of anonymity, interviews by author, La Paz, December 2004 and July 2007.

30. Alfonso Ferrufino, former government minister and current executive director of FUNDAPPAC (Fundación de Apoyo al Parlamento y a la Participación Ciudadana), interview by author, La Paz, December 16, 2004.

31. Col. H. James J., comandante, Policía Nacional, Departamento La Paz, interview by author, La Paz, December 22, 2004.

officials define administration as tasks carried out only by actual administrators, while others try to calculate the administrative time put in by all officers. Supporting the latter approach, nearly all officers say they spend far
too much time fulfilling administrative requirements. The solution for most
of them begins with installing more decentralized police operations and replacing the officers who are doing administrative work with civilians. In
2003 the new police commander announced a "rationalization" to send ten
thousand police officers working primarily in administration into the streets
—particularly into those taken over by criminals because of the absence of
the police.[32] But onetime "rationalizations" are not much help if they do not
address the deeper set of internal incentives and how they continue to widen
splits between street and office work on top of the already rancorous division between officials and subofficials.

As in other countries, they will also have little impact without changing
the rotation practices. Because ascension in the ranks requires a certain
amount of time in different units, personnel rotations halt accumulation of
the expertise needed to overcome material limitations. Even mid-ranking
PTJ officers, who seem to appreciate the chance to work in different areas
of policing, say that a resulting lack of expertise is the one of their biggest
staff defects. Their bosses in the agency, who want their officers "to begin
and die in the PTJ," have pushed for revision of the promotion system to
encourage investigative expertise and to minimize lateral movements.[33]
Such plans, however, have yet to be incorporated in actual legislation. Without such changes and without supportive technology such as crime maps,
the PTJ remains reactionary not by choice but by necessity, thereby considerably slowing any move toward problem-oriented policing.

Police Management

Poor management marks other areas of the policy as well. A proliferation
of agencies within the force has created much duplication and overlap (see
figure 5.1). Many units work in the same areas, and, more often than in other
countries, additional ones are formed to deal with new security issues. At
times such expansion and flexibility are needed. For example, the Multipurpose Unit (Unidad de Polivalentes) is usually ensconced near the U.S.

32. "Vientos de cambio en la Policía," *La Razón,* September 20, 2003.
33. Rolando Fernández, chief, Policía Técnica Judicial, interview by author, La Paz,
December 20, 2004.

Embassy in La Paz to deal with street protests, but it has been moved out to residential neighborhoods such as Pura Pura that suffer from at least a dozen violent crimes each day. However, the Polivalentes seem to be of limited help there, in part because they are frequently moved with other units back to the city center and main roads to break up protests. More important, their lack of both permanence and community policing also limits any positive impact they might have in residential neighborhoods.

Smaller and newer police units are usually spared from such continual shifts, but only because they lack the personnel to be moved around. Their bare-bones staff, however, subjects them to other problems, such as being forced to be appendages to other agencies. Because the Human Rights Office had has only one official and one secretary for many years, it has been slated for integration into the Personnel Office. Other new offices struggle to carry out their basic tasks. Even the small 150-member Tourist Police (Policía Turística), which has the straightforward mission of providing security for foreign travelers (usually through prior agreement with tour groups), is rife with problems. Although this unit has taken concrete remedial steps such as setting up kiosks at bus stations and other transport sites, it lacks foreign language capacity, equipment, and coordination with other state tourist services. It is also known for its delayed responses to calls for assistance and its poor knowledge of the streets and tourist spots. If it was not burdened by such limits, however, this unit could test the notion of combining traditional and problem-oriented policing by helping to identify tourism-related patterns of crime. Instead of dispersing responsibility, the functional proliferation discussed in chapter 2 could be used to test ideas in policing by letting new units take innovative approaches.

Such an approach could also shore up criminal statistics, which have long been patchy. After years of demand, the police created a Kardex Archive to consolidate crime statistics and related information. But officers say that a poor information-gathering capacity in many parts of the country, particularly in rural areas, makes these numbers unreliable. The source of such unreliability is the spectrum of capacity among stations: some have only paper, some have only typewriters, and many of those with computers lack statistical software. As a result, complete and dependable information gathering by and sharing among the PN's disparate units, beyond their separate submissions to a central archive, remains a long way off. And no one wants to guess at the *cifra negra* (unreported crimes), although the Government Ministry's very conservative estimate is well over 50 percent. Officials maintain that the lack of information is not a technical problem but a political one: the police do not want information to be public because it would expose failures and create unattainable expectations. For example, with the justification that it would sow confusion, in July 2004 the commander general ordered all units to withhold information unless approved from the top. Many officers would like to see a more concerted effort, ideally in conjunction with the judiciary, to bring together information on individual crime records, previous arrests, sentences served, and chronic offenders, with that on businesses, arms registries, wanted persons, prison records, and drivers' licenses. Such cross-referencing would support both policing on the ground and processing in the courts. In addition, although the number of cases reported to each division is made public, the number resolved is not. That additional piece of information could help diffuse the endless debate over accusations about the release of dangerous criminals.

Affecting any kind of improvements in statistics gathering as well as other areas of police functioning is money. Although the hard numbers vary, properly directed funding is inarguably low, as the condition of police facilities and services demonstrates. Health and other social programs, according to one chief, are in a state of "putrification." Better technology is the first problem cited by the La Paz Department chief, who says he needs basic equipment such as radios. Officers in nearly every other unit and station also emphatically point out the low supplies of materials. Stations in El Alto, Sucre, and Santa Cruz all lack typewriters, paper, vehicles, uniforms, and other daily necessities. As an example of their desperation, some officers even buy candles for the wax they need for stamps on administrative forms. Successive directors of the PTJ, arguably the most important single police unit, constantly bring up material limitations. The PTJ lacks its own operational budget, and all of its funds come out of the General Command, which they legitimately claim makes it subject to politicized and unanticipated alterations that complicate planning. At PTJ headquarters in La Paz, equipment is outdated, the physical plant is deteriorating, and officers must work in cramped small rooms. One former PTJ chief says that his regular allowance for 1,000 liters of gas falls well short of the 2,500 needed—with the difference coming out of his officers' pockets.[34] The PTJ is virtually absent in much of the country's rural areas, and even lacks personnel in many urban centers. Its chiefs say they need twice as many staff members in cities such as Santa Cruz, where the police also complain about the lack of *fis-*

34. "La Policía desnuda su pobreza y admite que hay corrupción," *El Nuevo Día,* November 20, 2002.

cales during their night and weekend shifts. Another PTJ director pointed to the lack of experts in different areas of investigation, from crime scene protection to forensics. As discussed in previous chapters, such an uneven presence of different agencies skews the kind of security that citizens receive, mainly by limiting the civil rights and investigative components of criminal justice.

In such stultified police structures, police finances are wasted and opaque in part because of centralization. The commander general controls everything in La Paz, and the departments lack their own operative budgets, forcing many local chiefs to cultivate their own corruption networks and *padrinos* (local godfathers). Not surprisingly, department officials have long demanded their own budgets, and 93 percent of police believe that each department should have them as well (UNDP 2006, 8). In addition, over half of police officers do not regard the management of money as transparent, and say that they do not know what their chiefs do with the money (UNDP 2006, 8). Along with weak oversight and evaluation, both external and internal, the frustration resulting from such limits brings out the worst tendencies in police practice. For example, the PTJ and criminal justice officials lose documents, fabricate evidence, and routinely skirt due process procedures. Instead of simply blaming penal process code requirements, many say they cut these corners just to get through the day.

As in Honduras and other countries, privatization stands out in contrast to such shortages. Within Bolivia's police, many chiefs assign their officers to private concerns, a large number of which are owned by police officials. In addition, many officers supplement their low salaries with off-hours work for private businesses. But unlike other countries, Bolivia officially provides private security through the police's Battalion of Private Physical Security. As mentioned above, the battalion's officers lacked official police status until a 2007 strike that, by threatening to expose practices the government preferred to keep under wraps, succeeded in achieving their demands.[35]

Although private firms are crowded out of the market by the battalion, and have even gone on strike to protest the fee of 20,000 bolivares to obtain a license, their numbers have also mushroomed. About a hundred have formed in La Paz since 2000, and the second-largest city, Santa Cruz (where

35. In February 2002 some La Paz officers denounced the commander general for renting out police officers for private businesses and homes, with the earnings going to the police chiefs.

the first private firm was formed in 1982), has about twenty-two such agencies. Cochabamba has over sixty firms, but fewer than twenty belong to the Security Enterprise Association (Asociación de Empresas de Seguridad). Officials and analysts agree, however, that the actual numbers are much higher in view of the fact that an estimated 30 percent of the population uses private agencies (García Soruco 2003, 12). Whatever the numbers, because of the lack of formal regulations until 2002 the government did not accurately document or oversee these businesses. And the Security Enterprise Federation scoffs at the regulations that have been adopted, such as a prohibition on carrying arms, saying that the regulations are only intended to prevent private firms from competing with the battalion.[36] Finally, even though they are clearly filling a gap, private security firms also open up another channel of corruption through favoritism by public officials toward private clients.

Acccountability, Corruption, and Discipline

All of these financial distortions, from a lack of gasoline to an overabundance of private police, are just part of what Bolivian police officers uniformly but anonymously view as a "profound" and "systemic" corruption that essentially constitutes a form of "organized extortion."[37] All three of the principal types of police corruption discussed in chapter 2—extortion among the lower ranks, illegal practices in particular police agencies, and the misappropriations pervading financial transactions—plague the Bolivian police. At the top, of the over twenty police commanders between 1982 and 2004—almost one for every year of democracy—eighteen were forced out because of crime, cover-ups, or other forms of malfeasance.[38] Under

36. The April 2002 Regulation on Private Security Enterprises (Reglamento de Empresas Privadas de Seguridad) and the Supreme Resolution 221126 on Private Security Enterprises prohibit the use of arms by private security enterprises.

37. Members of the Police Reform Commission, interviews by author, La Paz, December 22, 2004.

38. Between 1999 and 2004 four former police commanders were prosecuted after being relieved of their duties in response to accusations of corruption: Ivar Narvaez Rocha (1998–99), who was part of the accusations against the former president of the Cooperative Police Mutual Fund (Mutual de Cooperativas de la Policía Mucopol) for allegedly stealing $435,000; José Luis Medina (1999–2000) for stealing $500,000; Wálter Osinaga (2001) in the Prosegur case; and Wálter Carrasco, commander general of the police, who was investigated in 2002 for a firearms purchase of $1.8 million. In September 2004 Jairo Sanabria, another commander general of the police, resigned in the

their loose watch many agencies have integrated corruption into their operations, such as overcharging "up to a million dollars, easily" in contracts with companies providing arms or other provisions.[39] At the lower levels, seven out of ten officers report corruption in their own units, and 65 percent say that denouncing it would have negative repercussions on their jobs (UNDP 2006, 8).

Police control over its own finances has allowed corruption to penetrate the core of security budgets, not just skim their tops. In fact, the details of police accounting are "not known" to the Government Ministry.[40] Even the minister does not receive full income reports from the police.[41] And the police chief claimed in 2002 that he does not know where all the money actually goes.[42] Although nearly every official complains about how much higher the military budget is compared with the police budget, the Government Ministry receives the second biggest chunk of the national budget, after the Defense Ministry.[43] Of that ministerial budget, a little over 80 percent goes to the police each year.[44] That police budget increased from 106 million bolivianos in 1982 to nearly 1.10 billion bolivianos in 2005 (about $136.85 million by that year's exchange rate of eight bolivianos to the dollar) and to 1.34 billion bolivianos in 2009 (a little over $192.66 million by that year's exchange rate of 6.95 bolivianos to the dollar).[45] Most of the

---

face of accusations—less than a month after the newly appointed government minister ratified his position while announcing plans to eliminate police corruption. *Bolivia—FBIS Report,* August 19, 2004; Quintana (2004, 27).

39. According to a high-ranking Interior Ministry official on condition of anonymity.

40. José Arancibia Mollinedo, retired police official, interview by author, La Paz, December 15, 2004.

41. Juan Palacios V., "El Gobierno fiscalizará las recaudaciones de la Policía," *La Prensa,* December 13, 2004, 6a.

42. "Instituciones piden la descentralización del dinero de la Policía," *El Nuevo Día,* November 21, 2002.

43. Despite allocations such as the $26 million Citizen Security and Protection Plan in 1999, and even though the police have 70 percent more personnel than the armed forces, the police budget in the democratic era has been on average only about 60 percent the size of the military budget. The military received $240 million in 1995, compared with the $140 million for the police the same year.

44. Of the rest, the ministry's administration uses 14 percent, the Immigration Service 1 percent, and the Vice Ministry of Social Defense, in charge of antitrafficking policy, an additional 3 percent (Treasury Ministry, Vice Ministry of Budget and Accounting [Ministerio de Hacienda, Viceministro de Presupuesto y Contaduría]; FULIDED 2004).

45. Figures for 1982 and 2005: Ministerio de Hacienda, Viceministro de Presupuesto y Contaduría; FULIDED (2004). Figure for 2009: "Rada desmiente a Costas sobre pre-

money, amounting to between 66 and 81 percent of the Government Ministry's budget, goes to personnel services, which cover salaries and "social contributions."[46] The 56 percent growth in the police budget in nominal terms between 2000 and 2004 in fact stemmed primarily from a 96 percent increase in personnel expenditures that was driven by a 50 percent rise in both the number of police officers and their salaries; the expenditures on nonpersonnel services fell by 21 percent between 2000 and 2005 (FULIDED 2004, 11, 14).

So even accounting for inflation (which has ranged from 5 percent to 95 percent), it is clear that the security budget has risen steadily and substantially in the democratic era. Less clear to outside accounting and potential internal whistleblowers alike is where all that money has gone. Specifically, there is a serious discrepancy between official expenditures and actual salaries. Roughly, the personnel budget amounts to $2,445 per police official. In the upper ranks a sublieutenant starts out with a monthly salary of about $200, rising to about $300 a month six years later. The annual salary for the police chief is about $20,000; top officials earn $6,000–12,000 a year, and a detective earns about $3,200 a year (García Soruco 2003). Subject to one of Latin America's lowest rates, lower-ranking officials earn well

---

supuesto para seguridad ciudadana y le insta a dejar las 'palabrotas,'" *Los Tiempos,* June 25, 2009, http://www.lostiempos.com/diario/actualidad/nacional/20090625/rml. The National Department of Control and Income (Departamento Nacional de Fiscalización y Recaudaciones), established in June 1986, is a decentralized agency in charge of carrying out Article 117 of the Police Law, which details the destination of funds. Between 2000 and 2004, primarily because of a 96 percent increase of expenditures in personnel services, the Government Ministry's budget increased by 56 percent in nominal terms (FULIDED 2004, 11–14). Between 2001 and 2005 the police budget rose by just under 62 percent, from 516 million bolivianos to 838 million bolivianos.

Budget numbers vary according to the source. The police budget for 2004, for example, ranged from 812 million bolivianos ($103.5 million), according to some officials, to 930 million bolivianos (about $115.7 million), according to the Ministerio de Hacienda, Viceministro de Presupuesto y Contaduría, and FULIDED (2004). According to the DDP, the public security budget rose 165 percent between 1993 and 2003, and according to the police, its budget rose 47 percent from 2002 to 2006. In 2000 the police budget was 479 million bolivianos (about $79 million). It rose by 47 percent to 704 million bolivianos in 2006 ($87 million). Adjusting for inflation, the increase was just 9 percent. There are differences between the "security" and "police" budgets, but they closely approximate each other.

46. In 2001, 81.3 percent of the total security budget was devoted to personnel services.

under $2,400 a year.[47] Many street officers in the capital are paid as little as $1,300 annually. Put together, these salaries do not add up to that line item in the annual budget. Based on the number of police each year on which these budgets are allocated, salaries for subcommissioned officers (at an average of $2,000 each) add up to $52 million at most and for the officers and civilians (at an average of $9,000 each) to $8.5 million at most. All together, then, actual salaries amount to a maximum of just over $60 million, well below the average of $70 million allocated each year since 2000.

Outside of the main budget, the finances of particular police agencies constitute a second form of corruption. About 10 percent of the police budget is earmarked for equipment, but several mid-ranking officers say that these funds are dwarfed by monies from nonbudgetary sources that are free from rigorous accounting, such as ID cards and fines. And as they outstrip the official budgeted funds for materials, these additional sources have been turned by certain units into lucrative rackets. Investigations into the Customs Control Unit (Unidad de Control Operativo Aduanero) exposed officers receiving salaries after being fired and contraband-laden trucks crossing bridges without police checks—lax supervision that has allowed international car smuggling networks to take root in Bolivia.[48] Four notoriously corrupt agencies appear to be the headsprings of most corruption: the Police Housing Council (Consejo de Vivienda Policial, Covipol), which receives 12 percent of funds collected by the police and is in charge of obtaining home improvement and mortgage loans for its members; the Benevolence Society (Mutual del Seguro Policial, Musepol), whose thirty thousand members (mostly active police and retired police and their families) support the country's some six thousand retired officers; Mucopol, which helps its nineteen thousand members acquire provisions at "reasonable" prices; and the Anti-Car Theft Unit (Dirección de Prevención contra el Robo de Vehículos, Diprove), which is in charge of preventing and investigating motor vehicle theft. The security battalions of five cities—La Paz, Cochabamba, Santa Cruz,

47. Luis Pedraza, Government Ministry official, interview by author, La Paz, December 17, 2004. "La Policía desnuda su pobreza y admite que hay corrupción," *El Nuevo Día,* November 20, 2002. These salaries are constantly eroded by inflation. Proposed income tax increases in February 2003 ranging from 7 percent to 13 percent that would have further eroded that minimum salary triggered violent strikes by the police unions. "10 Die as Bolivian Troops Fire on Striking Police and Protesters," *New York Times,* February 13, 2003.

48. "El contrabando no deja de actuar pese al escándalo," *La Razón,* September 22, 2004; "El escándalo no cesa en la Policía, revelan sueldos fantasmas," *La Razón,* September 24, 2004.

Tarija Sucre, and Oruro—are corrupt as well. Against these agencies alone complaints of about a hundred significant "irregularities," ranging from illegal charges to criminal heists, are lodged each year.

Such unruliness has motivated many attempts to bring these entities under control. But the most ambitious one, a 2000 effort to fuse Musepol, Mucopol, and Covipol into one bureau responsible for police officers' social welfare, went nowhere. These units are all particularly resistant to such restructuring because each of them, unlike the departmental police, manages its own budget, which includes both official and unofficial income sources. The LOPN delineates fourteen forms of police income, officially directing 15 percent to a Government Ministry account and 85 percent to a special National Treasury account.[49] But in practice many charges not specified in the LOPN, such as for parking spaces and firearm licenses, bring in millions of unreported dollars. On top of that is money taken from police raids, "contributions" from communities, PTJ charges to issue police records and residential registrations, and sundry fees charged by Diprove, the Tourist Police, and the Road Police (Policía Caminera). According to police and state officials, most of those funds do not arrive at their intended destinations and remain unaccounted for at the discretion of their respective units' chiefs.

As bad as these agencies are, they do not hold a candle to the Office of Personal Identification (Servicio de Identificación Personal), which each year charges citizens to issue, renew, and replace about eighteen million drivers' licenses, ID cards, registrations, firearms licenses, certificates of good conduct, and other documents.[50] The police do not make public the amount that they make from the documents. But according to government records, 384,000 persons apply for a new ID card each year. In La Paz alone, over 230,000 people—six out of every ten residents—lose their ID (the majority more than once) every year and go to the ID office to request a new one.[51] At 17 bolivianos each, all these new and renewed cards bring in a hefty 6.5 million bolivianos (nearly $1 million) annually. With so much cash at stake,

49. Of the money in that account, 58 percent goes to a Complementary Fund, 30 percent for maintenance of police buildings and equipment, and 12 percent to Covipol. Articles 117 and 118, Ley Órganica de la Policía Nacional; Movimiento Autonomista: Nación Cambia, "Policía y Seguridad Ciudadana," http://www.nacioncamba.net.

50. Article 27 of the Organic Law says that "the National Office of Personal Identification is in charge of granting ID cards, exercising control of migration, maintaining the registries of criminal records and of residence."

51. Of them, only 20 percent—about 76,000 persons—are going for the first time. A roughly similar number of people renew expiring cards each year. According to one press investigation, about 1,600 cards are issued daily.

battles rage continually between the police and the National Identification Registry (Registro de Identificación Nacional, RIN), created in 1998 as an autonomous agency under the Ministry of Justice and Human Rights, to take control of national identifications. This protracted struggle has exposed irregularities, such as duplications of nearly 650,000 ID cards, which RIN said was proof of the current ID system's "inefficiency, inefficacy and corruption."[52] In 2002 former police chief Ívar Narváez (who was confirmed as police chief in 1998 despite objections based on corruption charges) was held responsible by the Comptroller General of the Republic (Controlaria General de la República, CGR) for 4 million bolivianos in missing funds, and in 2004 Musepol's former president was charged with appropriating 20 million bolivianos. Neither case, however, led to any trial or discovery of the funds. In March 2005 the elections for Musepol chief were canceled amid rancorous accusations of corruption. The two leading candidates revved up the accusations again four months later, just before elections, with one accusing the other of mishandling $6 million and the other saying his rival did the same with $3 million.

Only a complete break of police control over their finances, say officials, can end the "climate of institutional cannibalism."[53] For two-thirds of police officers and three-quarters of citizens, in fact, citizen security reform must be centered on the eradication of corruption (UNDP 2006, 13). Toward that end, the Sole National Registry (Registro Único Nacional, RUN) project was created as an alternative accounting system that would exclude police from the management of citizens' personal data. In 1993 the Interior Ministry strengthened the Civil Registry system and the data bank of the Electoral Court. But the RUN plan did not lead to actual changes. In 2003 Law 2152 moved RIN into the National Electoral Court, but the police's Identification Office retained technical operations. Article 14 of Law 2152 authorized RIN to establish an ID system to provide a single, secure ID card to every citizen—ordering the transfer to RIN of all of RUN's archives and data. This move triggered very strong resistance by the police, and in the end neither RUN nor RIN lasted. Since then, steps to change the system have managed to complicate it without wresting control from the police. The Mesa government's Law 2616 allowed for "exceptions" to obtain a birth certificate—a requirement for getting an ID card—by allowing a per-

---

52. "La Policía ofrece un sistema de identificación sofisticado," *La Prensa,* July 30, 2000.

53. Luis Ossico Sanjinés, former vice president, interview by author, La Paz, December 16, 2004.

son to simply present two witnesses before a Civil Registry notary to obtain a birth certificate. In early 2007 the Morales government enacted Supreme Decree 28626, part of the Government Ministry's "I exist, Bolivia exists" program, which grants free ID cards to undocumented citizens based on "just the verification of the Civil Registry database without the need to physically present a birth certificate." But the program only covers new IDs, and its director admitted it would be difficult to prevent people from being registered under both systems. The director of the ID office heavily criticized this decree, saying that it allows foreigners to obtain IDs and others to have two of them.

Police corruption is also individual—not just institutional. Most officers agree with the estimate by one former air force colonel who worked with different police units that 90 percent of police officers are corrupt and together rake in millions of unaccounted-for dollars each year.[54] High-ranking officers in the PTJ and other units regularly extract money for speeding up or slowing down court cases, covering up crimes, and ignoring illicit activity by powerful people. Police at all levels are also involved in kidnapping, robbery, organized crime, contraband, and the trafficking of drugs, arms, and cars. Many minor charges against citizens are often trumped up. Although punishment for most misdemeanors is limited to a fine, many police arrest and fine violators in a manner often proportional to their incomes.[55] Arbitrary and unjustified detentions by the PTJ, Transit Police, FELCN, and the Citizen Conciliation Unit (Unidad de Conciliación Ciudadana) are, according to the DDP, the principal type of complaint against the police. Even police officers have pointed out the lack of guidelines for these units (Mancilla Cárdenas 1998). Related forms of abuse are detentions without food or legal access, often after mass roundups that are campaigns to "clean the city" before a holiday. The extent of corruption was demonstrated in 2003, when, literally days after the Interior Ministry purged the 290 officials running Palmasola Prison for taking about $200 from prisoners to leave the prison for weekend jaunts, the same practice was up and running under an entirely new staff. A network of car traffickers operating out of the same prison was exposed a whole year before the government shut it down.

Mutual protection among officers against these and other outside accusations may actually be reinforced by the Bolivian police's dual rank divi-

---

54. Freddy Camacho, interview by author, La Paz, July 28, 2007.
55. "Infractores son doblemente sancionados: Arresto y multa," *La Prensa,* October 9, 2003.

sion. In addition to the police's blanket denials, officers in the lower corps have created another line of defense against accusations from their superiors. One police general wrote in the police bulletin *Verdo Olivo* that "many honest police, because of a false sentiment of 'solidarity' and 'esprit de corps,' extend a protective veil to protect comrades discovered in illicit activities, [thereby] making themselves inoperable" in terms of promoting clean policing.[56] Poor remuneration exposes as well as causes corruption, with many police officials maintaining a lifestyle that could not be possibly supported by their salaries.[57] Unpunished, such practices become only more appealing to other officers.

For most of the last two decades, inquiries into such abuses lacked teeth, and even investigations into twenty-five of the police's seventy-seven senior commanders were not concluded. Requesting anonymity, many officials say that financial officials in the Government Ministry either are corrupt or have "no control" over police finances. But targeted efforts by the three main accountability agencies have led to some improvements. The Office of the Comptroller General can oversee police income through its authority to audit the financial, administrative, and operational functions of any public entity virtually without conditions, as stipulated by Articles 41–48 of Ley Safco. But by most accounts, including those of officials of the Internal Audit (Auditoría Interno), the CGR's primary investigative unit, the CGR has not exercised its powers with any real effectiveness.[58] Fed up with the police force's free financial ride, the Government Ministry announced in late 2004 its intention to hire a private firm to reorganize the "disorganized and chaotic" financial system of the police. Although the focus was on IDs and drivers' licenses, some of the plan's sting was taken out by the ministerial assurance that the police would remain in charge of their finances. In early 2008 a bolder step was taken when the police commander requested a CGR audit of Musepol over the last ten years. As in other areas of reform, this request may prove more effective by having the police itself investigate past practices before moving on to a new system.

Similar advancements have been made in the accountability over police abuse. The biggest agency authorized to act on this issue is the DDP, whose

56. Gen. Willy Arriaza Monje, "En la hora de la prueba," *Verdo Olivo—Boletín Informativo Policial,* no. 9, 1995, segundo semestre.

57. Luis Pedraza, Government Ministry official, interview by author, La Paz, December 17, 2004.

58. Members, Police Reform Commission, interviews by author, La Paz, December 2004.

extensive public outreach and education programs have been accompanied by a high level of popularity. The *defensoría del pueblo*'s meticulous documentation of abuses and corruption has laid the groundwork for improvements in human rights protections. The agency also has helped the country overcome a political crisis by facilitating negotiations among political parties and between the government and protestors. Based primarily on following through on the hundreds of complaints it received, the agency assessed its work between 2001 and 2006 to be between "good and optimal" (Defensoría del Pueblo 2006, 4). On citizen security, however, the DDP has been constrained by obstruction and stonewalling by the executive and the inefficiency of the courts, which are slow to take up the problems the DDP exposes. Ana María Romero de Campero, the *defensora* who served from 1998 to 2003, complained of having to constantly undertake legal recourse against unconstitutional state actions such as intrusions on citizen privacy and the use of clandestine agents. Her demands for lists of prisoners helped force the police to stop holding prisoners for more than the legal twenty-four-hour limit. In public opinion as well as in policy this stance often put her on the unpopular side of the division between human rights and citizen security. For example, she was greeted at a neighborhood meeting by a crowd jeering "*defensora* of delinquents!"[59] Toward the end of her term she charged the legislature with "dirty tricks" and the executive of blocking her reelection. Her successor, Waldo Albarracín Sánchez, a longtime human rights leader, has more cooperative relations with the government, but he does not pursue as many kinds of abuse as Romero did.

Within the police are several layers of oversight of general and individual officer functioning. The Inspector General (Inspectoría General de la Policía Nacional) uses investigations, monitoring, and other instruments to check police services and finances. The Office of Professional Responsibility (DNRP) investigates wrongdoing and send cases with sufficient evidence to the Superior Disciplinary Tribunal, which tries and disciplines the accused. The DNRP had been known as the place "where complaints die," and most efforts to strengthen it tended to fall short.[60] In 2002, for example, the police chief fired the entire staff of the Personnel Office as part of an effort to facilitate corruption reporting and to ensure that the points for promotion actually meant something. Although the point system gained some legitimacy, reports

59. Ana María Romero de Campero, ombudsperson, interview by author, La Paz, July 12, 2000.
60. Alfonso Ferrufino Valderrama, interview by author, La Paz, December 16, 2004.

of corruption did not exactly begin to flow. But prodding by the United States led to modification of the police Disciplinary Code with new guidelines and to funds to increase efficiency and strengthen due process—for example, by prohibiting preventive detention. As a result, in 2004 the number of cases processed by the TDS doubled and the time in which complaints were processed plummeted from up to ten years down to under ten days.[61] Moreover, the average number of annual discharges resulting from the disciplinary process nearly tripled, from twenty-eight to seventy-nine.

Within the judiciary, action against police has also grown bolder. Encouraged by the government firing of four police chiefs for corruption and involvement in crime in 1997, the Fiscalía became more willing to prosecute high-level corruption cases, including the first-ever conviction of police generals. A serving colonel and two former generals were sentenced in December 2004 to four years in prison for failing to prevent the holdup of a Prosegur company security truck, in which three people were killed, or to arrest the perpetrators. One reason for this rare legal success was that it was part of a longer investigation into a band of bank robbers led by a former police colonel. The prosecutor had obtained false documents and questionable testimony by the generals. This conviction demonstrates the importance of enabling police officers to follow information leads that may be valuable for both specific cases and security in general (see chapter 7).

Although the DDP has publicized abuses and the DNRP and Fiscalía have prosecuted them, even an accumulation of cases does not mean a reversal of underlying practice. Aside from the few high-profile prosecutions, in fact, the vast majority of cases handled by the internal disciplinary system—seventy-four of the seventy-nine in 2006—have been for desertion among the lower ranks, along with misdemeanors by officers, which are handled by internal Police Courts (Juzgados Policiales). This situation again reflects and deepens the two-tier system biased against the lowest ranks. The police's internal code of sanctions has only furthered this tendency by targeting individual over institutional practice. For example, the controversial 2000 code limited officers' access to the media and forbade a range of behavior such as political militancy, "forming groups within the agency," homosexual relations, and "living with someone with a bad reputation."[62] A 2003 revision backpedaled a bit through measures such as in-

---

61. Officials requesting anonymity, interviews by author, La Paz and Sucre, December 2004.

62. Resolución Suprema 220080, November 1, 2000; "El Defensor del Pueblo y

troducing oral trials and strengthening due process for accused officers.[63] Wanting to bolster more formal accountability units as well, many officials recommend forming an ombudsman within the police and returning sanctioning power to the Judicial Council.

Criminal Justice

In Bolivia, as in other countries, the failure to put the courts into good working order has also undermined citizen security. The judicial reforms of the 1990s attacked some of the judiciary's worst problems, such as by designating a special court to hear constitutional issues and by ensuring more social protection for the rights of women and children. In addition, the MP Law of 1993 gave the Fiscalía authority over criminal investigations. But continuing inefficiency and chaos in the criminal justice system, marked by chronic strikes by judicial personnel, led the Ministry of Justice and Human Rights to take the bigger step of enacting the New Penal Procedure Code in 1999. A landmark reform that began operating in May 2001, the new code replaced written trials with oral trials, moved investigative authority from the police and judges to the *fiscales,* and set up a process of four judicial stages: preparatory, oral trial, appeals, and sentencing. The investigation and trial preparation are carried out by prosecutors under the investigative court's supervision. Detainees must be turned over to a *fiscal* and an instruction judge (*juez de instrucción*), who determines detention or release. The *fiscal* has six months to investigate, and then may propose an alternative sentence, ask for a plea bargain, or present the case before a sentencing court judge. The trial is then carried out in a sentencing court, led, in cases in which the penalty is more than four years' imprisonment, by two sitting judges and three citizens. Preventive judges (*jueces de instrucción cautelares)* may intervene in the preparatory stage and may decide on alternatives (usually called *medidas cautelares*) to trial, and Juzgados de Ejecución Penal oversee the postverdict processes.

The benefits of the NCPP became clear very quickly. The average time devoted to a case fell from between two and six years to about a year, and

---

DD.HH. critican las nuevas reglas aprobada por el gobierno," *La Razón,* December 2, 2000.

63. Reglamento de Faltas Disciplinarias y sus Sanciones para la Policía Nacional, Resolución Suprema 221886, July 31, 2003.

from 2002 to 2004 the number of convictions rose 63 percent and the number of processed cases quadrupled, from 306 in 2002 to 1,300 in 2004.[64] Aided by U.S. and internationally funded training, the number of oral trials rose from 480 in 2002 to 594 in 2003 and to 764 in 2004.[65] Public Ministry (Ministerio Público, MP) and DDP staff members also say that the number of cases rejected by the MP for defects in investigation has been reduced, the rate of MP requests for alternative measures has increased, and the number of detentions exceeding the legal time limit has been halved. Most judicial officials also believe that corruption in the judiciary has been reduced under the NCPP. Although they cannot cite specific evidence or studies, almost all of them mention a noticeable reduction in bribes and forms of preferential treatment during the criminal justice process. In the experience of public defender Ramiro Molina and several of his colleagues,[66] the reduction in such obstacles has, in turn, reduced the length of time between clients' arrests and hearings. As discussed in chapter 7, identifying such points of tension can go a long way toward unclogging the long criminal justice process.

Despite an abundance of training for police and prosecutors as well as educational programs for the public, implementation of the NCPP has been slowed by inadequate funds, interagency coordination, judicial infrastructure, and political support. Internal agencies overseeing criminal procedures, such as the MP Inspector General's office, have been weak, causing many judicial districts to lag behind on implementation. The creation of implementation councils was delayed in La Paz, where local authorities balked at what they regarded as an imposition. As a result, the promising results produced in the NCPP's first years slowed, stretching out the forty-

64. At the end of 2002, 291 sentences were passed down, rising to 408 in 2003 and 764 in 2004. Comisión Nacional de Implementación de la Reforma Procesal Penal, Comité Ejecutivo de Implementación, Avances en la Justicia Penal—Informe Estadístico (June 2001–June 2002). The average duration of the investigatory stage is 336 days and that of the accusation and oral trial is 134 days (Riego Ramírez 2005).

65. Most U.S. training was conducted by the Illicit Crop Monitoring Program of the UN Office on Drugs and Crime through Management Science for Development (MSD) and the U.S. Agency for International Development. According to ICITAP's director, the program's work in Bolivia has changed, not "only from training to development but also in the development of the whole judicial system—not just the police." ICITAP was "trying to change the whole focus" by training judges and prosecutors (Executive Office for United States Attorneys 1996). There has also been extensive U.S. support for institutional strengthening of the judiciary (MSD 2003).

66. Ramiro Molina and colleagues, interview by author, La Paz, December 18–22, 2004, and July 28, 2007.

five-day maximum for a trial into months. The percentage of unsentenced prison inmates also increased, jumping nearly 7 percent just between 2006 and 2007 (Riego Ramírez and Duce 2008). In most years about 20 percent of criminal charges are resolved, with rates far lower for crimes against vulnerable sectors such as women. Quarrels over who or what is culpable for such delays only extends them. Most agree that a primary cause is the poor cooperation between *fiscales* and police, which leads to a confused mix of the old and new codes or continuing use of the inquisitive approach exclusively, which, in turn, allows many delinquents to "escape trial."[67] Several police chiefs say that "things disappear" at the MP and that the *fiscales* do not follow up or direct them well. Distortions in human resource management at the MP also undermine implementation. With just a few *fiscales* assigned to the property crimes that constitute nearly half of all charges, some *fiscales* have six hundred cases, while others have under a dozen (Ledezma Inchausti 2005). The police also say that the public defenders in the PTJ offices focus only on securing provisional liberty for detainees "above the interests" of society and victims, and that judges, in an often "arbitrary" manner, detain the accused only in high-publicity cases, but release others without taking into account "the evidence supplied, the dangerousness of the detainee or his record."[68] Such actions then force the police to deal with additional crimes committed by released suspects, halting or reversing the NCPP's quicker pace. *Fiscales* throughout the country have been assigned to night shifts since implementation of the code, but the police complain that they are not there at times of high crime. Many NGOs working on judicial reform also criticize the MP, primarily for not developing a strategy for implementing the code or even offering practice in the basic defense and accusatory procedures of oral trials.[69] As in other countries, the NCPP absorbs much of the blame by being "very guaranteeist" and lenient on detainees. And once charges of releasing criminals are brought into the mix, the debate moves from the procedural to the political, halting the arc of criminal justice reform before evaluation of practice can be used to improve it.

Meanwhile, public defenders, *fiscales,* and others claim that police officers are not willing or able to act outside of their own institutional hierar-

67. Gen. Oscar Molina, interview by author, La Paz, December 18–22, 2004.
68. José Velarde, "El Nuevo Código de Procedimiento Penal," *Revista de la Policía Nacional,* no. 230-2002, 8–9.
69. Ximena Vázquez and María de los Ángeles Loayza, Centro de Estudios sobre Justicia y Participación (Center for Justice and Participation Studies), interview by author, La Paz, December 14, 2004.

chy. Instead of coordinating with *fiscales,* the pressure is simply too strong on lower-ranking officials to communicate only with their chiefs, who, after all, are the ones who control their promotion and salary. As some judges acknowledge themselves, the police have a lot of influence on judges, and together they often resist applying the new code's presumption of innocence. Asserting that the Fiscalía has "no control" over the police, one prosecutor said that "access to information is precarious" and that the judicial police often delay sending it to prosecutors. Because "*fiscales* depend on the current government in power, there is no independence," he added.[70] "Although the *fiscal* is in charge of cases, the police officers send their material to their bosses instead. We ask for sanctions against them, but often times they are not taken. Sometimes the police even shut the *fiscales* out physically from police stations. Sometimes the police extort those reporting the crime." In addition, as a legislative investigation documented, pressure is routinely put on the *fiscales* who are investigating police and military involvement in drug trafficking (Human Rights Commission 1995). Police chiefs, who are in the best position to correct such actions, often answered interview questions about such issues by focusing on procedure. Above all, they said that the real problem was that their personnel were simply not trained sufficiently to implement the new code rules on gathering evidence, interviewing suspects, and protecting crime scenes. Some officials tried to be more objective, seeing problems on all sides. Most of his colleagues, said one *fiscal,* "will get the crime report, read the final part and provide an opinion of about four lines. However, the police manage the whole file. As a result, the same culture continues, the same as the old system, with the majority of officials [and their practices] not changing."[71]

Like accountability, better performance by the NCPP is most likely to flow from specific measures that show concrete results by shoring up relations among police, judges, and *fiscales.* Examples are providing more and better-managed PTJ resources and giving judges more time to conduct "careful and exhaustive revision" of PTJ investigations.[72] The Institute of Forensic Investigations (Instituto de Investigaciones Forenses, IDIF), which often does not complete its work because of a lack of resources, and which often illegally charges families for its services, also needs more personnel and oversight. Police officers merit greater support as well. The law mandates that a

---

70. William E. Alave Laura, public prosecutor, interview by author, La Paz, 17 December 2004.

71. Ibid.

72. *Bodas de Plata,* April 1998, 74.

police officer carrying out an investigation cannot be pulled into other activities that delay it, but in fact officers are often sent at short notice to provide security at a soccer match, prevent the building of blockades by protestors, or (a perennial complaint of Bolivian officers) do traffic duty. Such practices, which are the individual-level equivalent of moving units around (as discussed earlier in relation to the Polivalentes), also inflate administration by creating paperwork and other processes that officers have to fulfill.

Meanwhile, more of three main sets of criminal justice officials—*fiscales,* defenders, and judges—are needed. In El Alto some court dockets are filled with up to eight hundred cases each, and many La Paz *fiscales* have about a hundred cases at any given time.[73] One member of the legislature concurred that "there is not sufficient capacity among current *fiscales* to implement the NCPP."[74] Public defense—whose budget for many years was provided almost entirely by the United States—long has been at the "point of collapse," according to NGOs, with far too few public defenders to serve the many defendants who need them, despite efforts such as the 1995 Public Defense Program aimed at strengthening public defense or creating public defense offices in underserved neighborhoods.[75] The NCPP itself needs more administration. It has few instruments for transparent tracking of cases or communications with other agencies; the Police Reform Commission estimates that the status of about 70 percent of cases is unclear at any given time and that only about one in every five cases reaches trial. Resolution rates are particularly low when victims are from more vulnerable sectors. For example, the Family Protection Brigade receives over forty reports of domestic violence each day, but the courts resolve only a few of them each year. Receiving more media attention are the reports of rejections of criminal charges, which heighten the public's perception of impunity for criminals and deepen its suspicions of due process. Three out of four police and nine out of ten citizens believe that serious criminals such as drug traffickers and murderers do not deserve the same rights as other citizens. And six out of ten police and seven out of ten citizens approve of physical or psychological violence against delinquents during arrest or interrogation (UNDP 2006). Moreover, about a third of citizens consider it

73. "Las condenas aumentan 63 por ciento con el Nuevo Código Penal," *La Prensa,* June 1, 2005.

74. "Exigen una política nacional de seguridad ciudadana," *El Nuevo Día,* November 21, 2002.

75. Law 2496 of August 2003 formed the National Public Defense Service (Ley de Servicio de Defensa Pública).

reasonable to break laws in certain circumstances, and seven out of ten police agree with them.

Conditional liberty has been a big bone of contention, and probably has resulted in the declining use of alternative sentencing since enactment. As one judge put it, "Before, the rule was detention and liberty the exception. Today, it is the reverse. Society asks, 'Why do the code's *medidas cautelares* [preventive measures, in this case to protect due process] only favor the accused and not the victims?'"[76] Responding to a backlash against the NCPP, in 2003 the heads of the three branches of government met to adjust the code to the "national reality" by "better punish[ing] crime."[77] In doing so, they mainly restricted its *medidas cautelares* in order to prevent repeat offenders from benefiting from measures that substitute for preventive detention.[78] They also modified five NCPP provisions and eleven penal code provisions to increase the punishment for different crimes, particularly the crime of erecting the blockades associated with political protest. Another NCPP provision criticized for undermining rights allowed the use of masked agents— a practice adopted by FELCN in acting against drug trafficking networks.[79]

Such hostility to civil rights is evident in Bolivia's high rate of vigilantism, as well as in the courts' and media's treatment of it. Many police officers, as well as the citizens who volunteer with them, blame the penal code for contributing to frequent lynchings by overlooking them. For example, although the 110 lynchings reported from January 2001 to January 2003 were a record number to date, none was prosecuted.[80] The number has only increased—71 lynchings were reported in 2009 alone[81]—but the likelihood

76. Róger Valverde Pérez, penal instruction judge, interview by author, La Paz, December 22, 2004.

77. "Los tres poderes acuerdan modificar el Código de Procedimiento Penal," *Bolivia Hoy,* June 13, 2003.

78. "El Gobierno refuerza a la Policía con dinero, equipos y proyectos," *La Razón,* July 19, 2003; "Aumentan las penas para evitar varios delitos," *La Razón,* January 8, 2003.

79. "Los agentes encubiertos ya operan contra narcos," *Los Tiempos,* January 7, 2004. Antidrug laws often encourage such practices.

80. See Permanent Human Rights Assembly and Acción Andina, http://www.cedib .org/accionandina/index; "El Estado debe enfrentar a la inseguridad," *La Razón,* March 4, 2002. Thirty-six of these cases (60 percent of the total) occurred in Cochabamba and eighteen cases (30 percent) in Santa Cruz. "60 linchamientos ocurrieron en 15 meses. Pese a la cantidad, ninguno de los homicidios fue esclarecido por la Policía o Fiscalía," *La Razón,* January 9, 2003.

81. "Preocupa a ONU aumento de linchamientos en Bolivia," FM Bolivia, June 11, 2010, http://www.fmbolivia.com.bo.

of prosecution has not. Parallel with the lack of legal action against vigilantes is the lack of prosecution of petty criminals, who are vigilantes' primary targets. On "minor crimes, the courts let them out, and the circle repeats itself," neatly concluded one top police official. "This causes lynchings."[82] To such charges judges have grown tired of responding that poor investigation and management are much more culpable than the NCPP. They can bring in anyone suspected of being involved in an attack, say PTJ and MP officials, but must let them go when there is no evidence to keep them. The high rate of lynchings underscores the lack of confidence in the police to maintain order, but this lack of evidence underscores the inability of the police to prosecute even cases with a lot of perpetrators and witnesses.

In the meantime, as social change outpaces state action, lynchings have become more politicized. As Goldstein (2004) and others point out, vigilantism has grown along with citizen activism in Bolivia, showing how civil society can undermine democratic standards. Thus although there were fifty-seven actual and attempted lynchings in 2007, which is about the same rate as in earlier years, there were well over a hundred media stories about them (Vaca 2009). Beyond the grisly and often sensationalistic details, such reports more and more associate lynchings with formal community justice forums and trials, which have become one of Bolivia's biggest deliverers of justice. And instead of seeing vigilantism as filling a vacuum left by the state, journalists see it as being facilitated by the state. By maligning one of Bolivia's major areas of legal reform, their reporting then diverts attention from the real judicial and socioeconomic roots of *auto-justicia* around the country.

That interdependence among new laws, judicial practice, and social pressures afflicts even laws that are limited in scope. For example, the 1994 Blattman Law, which prohibited anyone from being jailed for debt or detained for an extended period without a formal indictment, was one of the key legal reforms of the 1990s because it directly addressed inequalities in the judicial system. But it may have inadvertently allowed crime to rise because police began to not bother catching criminals that the courts were likely to release. A few months after the law began granting prisoners provisional liberty, the population in many of the country's largest detention facilities dropped by a third or more. But amid political pressures and bureaucratic hurdles, application of the law began to fade, to the point at which

82. Juan Carlos Saa Manzanata, director, Nacional de Instrucción y Enseñanza, Escuela Superior de Policías, December 15, 2004.

the prison population ended up even higher than before the law. About 55 percent of prisoners were being held for narcotics crimes, and over 70 percent of all detainees were awaiting trial. In addition, even with the NCPP the low application of alternative sentencing continues to fill up the prisons.

As they become increasingly overcrowded (eight thousand people are crammed into a system with a capacity of five thousand), the prisons are characterized by violence, inhumane conditions, and a lack of services such as rehabilitation centers for minors or psychiatric hospitals. Despite reforms —such as release of debtors and untried detainees, new bail laws, and more public defenders—between 60 and 75 percent of inmates have not been charged or sentenced, according to estimates by officials in the Ministry of Justice and Human Rights. In La Paz's San Pedro Prison, all but the small number of inmates who "buy" individual cells are forced to sleep on patios and stairs. "It's like another city in here," said one inmate, "a real survival of the fittest."[83] The National Penitentiary and Supervision Office (Dirección Nacional de Régimen Penitenciario y Supervisión), part of the Government Ministry and the police, runs the country's prisons, assigning about four hundred officials to run them. The police do not want to be there, but the Law of Penitentiary Security (Ley de Seguridad Penitenciaria) puts them in charge. As in Honduras and other countries, rights groups then blame the police for prison conditions, and the police blame a shortage of funds.

These are just some of the reasons why officials talk about a "total loss of credibility in the judiciary."[84] However, a foundation for responding to them has been laid. A *Police-Prosecutor Functions Manual* as well as a Criminal Records Registry have finally been completed. An office that offers twenty-four-hour service to receive complaints and help crime victims, the Platform for Attention to the Public (Plataforma de Atención al Público), opened in 2007. To avoid lengthy criminal proceedings, the Unit of Immediate Reaction (Unidad de Reacción Inmediata, UDRI) conducts mediation for victims, the accused, and their lawyers to find acceptable alternatives. Using both the judicial and PTJ officials assigned to it, the UDRI also helps facilitate interagency coordination more generally.

External actors continue to help implement judicial reform as well. The Center of the Study of Justice of the Americas set up Integrated Justice Cen-

---

83. San Pedro Prison, interviews by author, La Paz, July 19, 2000, and August 1, 2007.

84. Franz Zilvetti Cisneros, Dirección General de Seguridad Ciudadana, interview by author, La Paz, December 2004.

ters (Centros Integrados de Justicia, CIJs) in Bolivia that offer free legal information and orientation, as well as conciliation services. It also helped form the Center for Information, Orientation and Citizen Training (Centro de Información, Orientación y Capacitación Ciudadana, CIOCC), which provides support for educating citizens on human rights and providing training on the NCPP. However, like problem-oriented policing, small-scale efforts zeroing in on the bottlenecks in the process have proven the most effective. For example, the internationally funded "Support Project for Penal Process Reform" has reduced by 30 percent the number of criminal reports rejected by the MP for errors and by 40 percent those rejected by superior courts in the main cities, and it has increased by 20 percent the number of requests for alternative forms of resolution.

Community Policing

Because local efforts are often the nucleus of change in citizen security, hopes for improvement in Bolivia are riding on the many small security and justice programs being developed around the country. With its highly multicultural and mobilized citizenry, community policing is even more promising and appropriate in Bolivia than in most of Latin America. Through laws, police restructuring, and community justice forums, the government has both directly and indirectly promoted citizen-based responses since the 1990s. For example, most national citizen security legislation has prioritized citizen participation by forming councils at the national, departmental, and provincial levels through the National System of Citizen Security Law 2494 described earlier.[85] Many of these programs, however, have been compromised by politics. Although many of the citizen councils are up and running, they are heavily criticized in the communities for being composed almost entirely of government officials. The country's Neighborhood Council Federation (Federación de Juntas Vecinales, FEJUVE) has demanded more participation by grassroots organizations in these councils. Because of the growing power of local officials, along with the federal government's calls on FEJUVE to support it in times of political disturbance, such de-

85. Provinces fall under departments. The Law of Organization of the Executive, No. 2446, incorporates the General Office of Citizen Security and Crime Prevention (Dirección General de Seguridad Ciudadana y Prevención del Delito) into the Government Ministry.

mands must be taken seriously. Even so, the sheer size and variety of Bolivia's municipalities will make it a challenge to do so, particularly with the increase in these councils and the reactions that their formation can touch off. The mayor of El Alto even organized protests against the law's penalization of protests and blockages, as well as the fact that monies for public lighting go to the Electricity Superintendence while the city government must pay for lighting fixtures and residents will face higher charges.[86] Although El Alto has always been at the forefront of protests in Bolivia, it illustrates the risks of decentralization discussed in this book. Decentralization is often initiated because the central government is not strong enough, but then it must quickly demonstrate that it is strong enough to withstand the political pressures that ensue.

Because of this instability, concerted plans for community policing have not yet materialized. Although they are often inspired by national change, most programs around the country have been ad hoc local initiatives. Though usually lacking outside accountability, as discussed shortly, this bottom-up approach may actually prove more productive in the long run. The first of them emerged out of the LPP. It led to the formation of Vigilance Committees (Comités de Vigilancia), which express community concerns in general, and community security forums, which try to resolve citizen concerns in particular. The Support and Citizen Cooperation Patrol (Patrulla de Auxilio y Cooperación Ciudadana, PAC) was set up in 1994 and is led by Anapol graduates to "support citizens" through better handling of youth delinquency, homelessness, and drug addiction. The Plan of Participatory Security put forth in May 2002 was too ambitious, but the broader Participatory Vigilance Program (Programa de Vigilancia Participativa)[87] of June 2002 aimed to improve the diagnoses of the causes of crime by both police personnel and the nine thousand so-called Lookout Pairs (Parejas de Vigías) connected through cell phones. In La Paz the Citizen Security Pilot Project (Proyecto Piloto de Seguridad Ciudadana)[88] was launched in May 2004 to coordinate daily police-government inspections of places that sell alcohol. Other citizen-based units have formed in cities and departments

86. "Con la ley, al alumbrado le costará más a los vecinos," *La Razón,* August 16, 2003.

87. "9.000 celulares conectarán para la seguridad vial. El Proyecto de vigilancia vecinal empieza hoy con 4.200 serenos," *La Razón,* March 5, 2002.

88. Subalcaldía Centro (Central Submayor's Office), "Alcaldía paceña impulsa proyecto Piloto de Seguridad Ciudadana con participación vecinal," La Paz, May 19, 2004.

around the country, such as the Neighborhood Security Brigade (Brigada de Seguridad Vecinal), typically involving the heads of neighborhood councils (*juntas vecinales*), municipal officials, and the local police commissioner. La Paz's brigades are composed of volunteers under the direction of the PTJ and the Transit Police. Cochabamba's brigade includes about 130 families, mainly to keep order during public festivities. One of the more common groups is the School Brigades (Brigadas Escolares), composed mostly of student volunteers who help with the afterschool neighborhood policing as well with cultural and sporting events. "The school brigades allow us to get close to the parents of the students involved. Through the youth, we can get to know the parents, the big brothers, the neighbors," says the La Paz Department police chief. "This is the best way of being close to the community."[89]

Structural changes within the police have also advanced community policing. One such change in many areas of the country has been construction of police modules—small kiosks for officers in areas with a low police presence. In 2000 the police's Citizen Security Plan began with the installation of about fifty police modules around La Paz and El Alto, with round-the-clock staffing. With the support of PAC, similar "green houses" were planned for Santa Cruz and Cochabamba. In addition, Cochabamba assigned many of its new officers to foot patrols and special units such as the Operative Transit Agency.[90] In La Paz, construction was approved in 2010 for new police stations to provide a range of services in high-crime areas. According to many police officers, they would like to use these changes to develop better coordination with umbrella grassroots groups, but members affiliated with those groups say that the police have not really tried. The city's multiple ethnicities and numerous citizen groups, as El Alto community policing activist Daniel Atahuichi points out, makes such coordination difficult, even for citizens and police intent on trying.[91]

Since the mid-1990s these programs have been complemented by the community justice councils and forums that have proliferated in Bolivia through constitutional provisions and legislation augmenting decentralized local administrative and juridical autonomy and indigenous legal norms. These forums have been part of a reassertion by the Aymara, Quechua, and Guaraní

89. Col. H. Jamés J., comandante, Policía Nacional, Departamento La Paz, interview by author, La Paz, December 22, 2004.

90. "Plan de Seguridad Ciudadana: Policía instaló 'casetas verdes,'" *La Prensa,* July 30, 2000; "Dos camionetas y un soporte humano para hace funcionar los módulos," *Los Tiempos,* January 7, 2004.

91. Daniel Atahuichi, community policing activist, interview by author, El Alto, December 2004 and July 2007.

peoples, the country's largest indigenous groups, of their legal, cultural, and political identities amid economic uncertainty, a weak state, and massive urban migrations. Among these projects is the Justice Ministry's Justice of the Peace (Justicia de Paz) network; it has been formed in about 40 percent of the country's municipalities to carry out traditional forms of conflict resolution, directed by judges of the peace. Backing up this network are the Integral Justice Centers (Centros Integrales de Justicia) formed to "de-judicialize" local conflicts. Six of these centers have been established in high-crime El Alto and others in the coca regions of Chapare and Yungas. In addition, since Morales's election many local officials around the country have revived the National System of Citizen Security Law by forming citizen security committees and by modifying that law to facilitate participation by societal groups.[92]

Although such efforts are a step toward problem-oriented policing and improved police-community relations, most have been short-lived because of weak funding, institutional assistance, and citizen confidence. For example, many of the civilian night patrols, the *serenazgo vecinal,* did not have the equipment needed, and the police officers in charge were not trained in how to prepare volunteers. As a result, some programs were never launched, and the volunteers in others ended up quitting.[93] Primarily because of the government's desire to maintain as much control as possible, the most durable "community policing" programs are those directed by police or geared toward specific objectives. Such control, though, has not been sufficient to head off abuses against citizens. Although formed mainly to provide local search and rescue services, many GACIP units morphed into cliques of powerful citizens who acted with police authorization but without the appropriate training or oversight by the specially trained Anapol graduates who nominally head them. PAC, also led by Anopol graduates, has similarly been linked to rights abuse—often with the backup of police units such as Radio Patrol 110. One probable cause of such abuse is a lack of regulation. Some police units geared toward community relations, such as the Citizen Conciliation Unit (Unidad de Conciliación Ciudadana, UCC), have been singled out for lacking clear guidelines in police laws and regulations such as the Misdemeanor Code (Código de Faltas y Contravenciones) —see Mancilla Cárdenas (1998). Beyond their own irregularities, such units have overrun some of the areas that should have been filled by citizens. In particular, the drawn-out effort to

92. "Implementarán nuevas estrategias para mejorar seguridad ciudadana," *El Diario,* April 7, 2008.

93. "El Plan de Serenazgo Vecinal empieza con fallas de coordinación," *La Razón,* April 30, 2002; "25 vigilantes renuncian al plan de serenazgo vecinal," *La Razón,* June 11, 2002.

pass a Community Justice law, which began in the mid-1990s, undermined community policing by depriving localities of much-needed forums for locally led security initiatives, which, as discussed in other case studies, can help resolve causes of crime by addressing claims for justice.

El Alto, the low-income city of 650,000 mostly indigenous rural immigrants, embodies the inherent tensions between citizen and police control in the more hastily developed community policing programs. It also exposes the deeper struggles over civil society and public space. On the one hand, the city's vibrant politics has generated a host of innovative and successful programs. In response to the city's high levels of domestic violence, for example, in June 1995 it received one of the first deployments of the Family Protection Brigade.[94] The mayor has touted the success of his city's *serenazgo vecinal* groups and the creation of a "red zone" to prevent nightlife businesses—and the crimes that accompany them—from propagating. The city is also constructing police modules as part of the Safe City (Ciudad Segura) program. One of the city's police chiefs has planned an additional series of programs such as surveys of students and cultural events, so that "the police are a part of the population."[95] Meanwhile, many El Alto communities have set up a wide range of justice and security forums that have strong popular support because they are elected, utilize indigenous customs, and act rapidly.[96] Most disputes taken to these forums center around the lesser charges of violence.

On the other hand, a high level of violence often leads to actions that cut short such plans and channels. Several of El Alto's police officials estimate that about eighty people are killed each month in the city, which would translate into an astounding homicide rate of 147 per 100,000 persons. According to the national police statistics, between 2001 and 2005 an average of 3,442 crimes were committed in the city each year, which translated into a rate of 530 per 100,000 residents, or over 70 percent higher than the national average. In the face of such violence, residents have restyled potentially problem-oriented programs into instruments of violent action. Even the city's community justice forums have become channels of abuse, such as the illegal seizure of private property.[97] In some

---

94. *Verde Olivo—Boletín Informativo Policial,* 1995, 6, segundo semestre.

95. Maj. Hugo Morales, interview by author, El Alto, July 29, 2007.

96. For example, the Villa Bolívar "D" neighborhood junta usually solves over half of its cases in a week or less.

97. El Alto neighborhood council meetings, interviews by author, August 2000, December 2004, July 2007; Ministerio de Justicia y Derechos Humanos, República de Bolivia y Centro de Asesoramiento Social y Desarrollo Legal, 1998.

El Alto neighborhoods, justice council members even use whistles to alert each other of "criminals," whom they then beat up or kill. Those suspects have fair warning, said one forum member in Villa Adela Conavi, pointing to the signs attached to effigies clearly announcing that "petty thieves will be lynched by vendors and neighbors." Some vigilante groupings draw inspiration from the Armed Self-Defense Brigades (Brigadas de Autodefensa Armada), formed mainly in El Alto during the protests that toppled the government in October 2003. Directors of the city's 562 neighborhood councils were urged to convince "volunteer residents" to form such brigades to fight state repression with "Molotov cocktails and explosive booby traps (*cazabobos*)."[98] Although the brigades disbanded and most residents say they reject the brigades' tactics, they seem to agree that the brigades provided a model of organized citizen forces that is still needed. Some working-class El Alto areas such as Huayna Potosí aim to attain "collective security" through neighborhood brigades whose actions and authorities are kept deliberately flexible. More middle-class El Alto areas such as Ciudad Satélite have turned to private police, which, while more limited, have still altered the neighborhoods' public space and general atmosphere (see map 5.1).

Despite these and other practices loosely associated with community policing in Bolivia, many police officials see such practices as one way to make up for their own shortcomings. But to do so, they often add, these practices must be centered on cohesive responses to citizen-identified problems. For example, when asked about the causes of insecurity, residents in La Paz's high-crime Pura Pura complained not just about criminals, but also about the local stores that were selling alcohol to violent individuals and the small factories that were polluting the air and the streets. Among the more long-term residents, such conditions mark the neighborhood's descent into "chaos." In revealing residents' true concerns, such questions also reveal the difficulty of responding to so many issues. After all, one of the police's biggest fears about community policing is that citizens will expect a response to each problem articulated. At the same time, residents still envision practical change, starting with more police kiosks and rehabilitation centers for offenders.[99] Less political violence at the national level may allow such projects to go forward and evolve into forms of problem-oriented policing. In fact, despite their low confidence in police officials, Bolivians

98. "FEJUVE Instruye Crear Brigada de Autodefensa," Indymedia, October 17, 2003.

99. Residents, La Paz neighborhoods of Pura Pura, Villa Victoria, and La Portada, interviews by author, July 2007.

Map 5.1. La Paz and El Alto, Bolivia (counterclockwise from top left: El Alto areas of Huayna Potosí, Villa Adela Conavi, and Ciudad Satélite; La Paz areas of Alto Tejar, Cementerio General, Max Paredes, and Pura Pura)

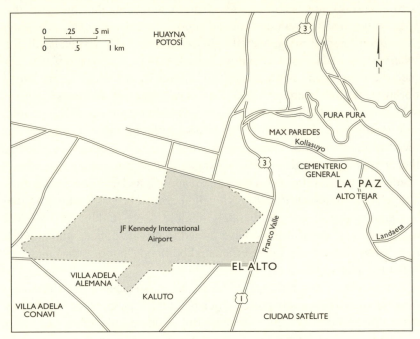

in general seem willing to at least consider working more closely with them. Most citizens say they feel more secure with the police nearby, and only 4 percent equate police with insecurity (UNDP 2006, 12)—a negligible number that sharply contrasts with surveys in countries like Brazil and Venezuela. However, clearer and better enforced standards and procedures are needed to prevent community policing from enabling the police to avoid its responsibilities or needed reforms. One way to institute these standards would be through a "System of Citizen Security Information and Alerts" that allows citizens to identify areas and times of crime risks.[100] This idea seems to be well received in neighborhood meetings, because it appeals to citizens' desire for direct involvement that brings direct benefits.

100. Luis Cayujra, "Opinión: Políticas públicas en seguridad ciudadana y construcción institucional," *La Prensa,* January 23, 2005.

Cities and neighborhoods around Bolivia, in part reflecting the lack of national guidance, have been taking up this challenge in earnest since at least 2005, attempting to form systematic community policing. Santa Cruz launched a community policing program that year, and Cochabamba followed a year later. Though different than the program in El Alto, the Santa Cruz program also reflects inherent tensions over community policing. Most officials from the department want a "community police" in terms of an autonomous force geared toward its "distinct" population, but some areas have implemented less politicized programs. Plan Tres Mil, a sprawling low-income area in the southeastern section of the city with a large Guaraní indigenous population, created a security council with the participation of neighborhood groups, the police, the mayor's office, and the district *fiscal*. Like El Alto, the Plan Tres Mil has encountered political turmoil, but its creation of a security council prior to potentially competing efforts such as justice councils has allowed community policing to focus on citizen-based prevention.

In 2006 a national deconcentration plan set up eight police districts around the country, with one hundred officials assigned to each one. These districts have been given many tasks, including "recuperating" citizen confidence, ensuring rapid arrival at crime scenes, forming citizen security brigades, and supporting citizen security schools. In La Paz the pilot Community Police Project was launched in May 2006 to build ten police centers in the Max Paredes district (see map 5.1), fund "social education" programs, and form neighborhood brigades with the participation of residents and eighty-seven police officers.[101] FELCC provided training on how to conduct conciliation and prepare a crime report, and the Family Protection Brigade—a police unit that supports and protects the rights of victims' families—held seminars on family unity and violence. By the end of 2008, according to most estimates, crime had dropped in that area by about half. Such progress probably stemmed from the citizen participation that the initial drops in crime attracted. The reduction also attracted the attention of other high-crime zones with weak citizen groups, such as Alto Tejar and those near the Cementerio General (see map 5.1). In 2008 it also led the La Paz government to establish modules based on Max Paredes in thirty other areas of the city, and to begin supportive services via a free telephone line. Community policing also expanded in Santa Cruz and other cities in 2008 and 2009, giving it stronger roots in different parts of the country.

101. This $119,000 project was financed by the British with the cooperation of the police and mayor's office.

In August 2006, La Paz's municipal government held a competition for proposals for the Neighborhoods of Truth Program (Programa Barrios de Verdad). The competition was aimed at the city's poorest areas to stimulate the participation of the citizens themselves in program priorities.[102] As in Honduras, Argentina, and other countries, interviews revealed positive attitudes and a growing confidence among citizens and police that could sustain such efforts. In the UNDP survey in fact, 97 percent of police officers said they felt proud to be a part of their agency, and 70 percent expressed confidence in their agency (UNDP 2006).

That said, the country's socioeconomic conditions are both a vehicle and an impediment to community policing. On one level, improvements in health, education (the proportion of children in school has risen from about 25 percent to nearly 90 percent), and other areas have given Bolivians a greater ability to take part in security and other social service efforts. But there is still a long way to go. Despite steady improvements, the percentage of Bolivians living in poverty ranges from 38 percent to 63 percent, significantly higher than the regional average of 36 percent (CIDA 2007). The unemployment rate is 7.8 percent, but involuntary underemployment is estimated to be as high as 40 percent. Bolivia is far and away Latin America's most unequal country in terms of income distribution, and perhaps the most unequal in the world. Among the UN-calculated ratios of the richest 10 percent to the poorest 10 percent, Bolivia has a score of 168.2, followed by Namibia at 128.2. The second most unequal country in Latin America is Paraguay, with a ratio of 65, less than half of Bolivia's. Bolivia also leads the region in its Gini coefficient of 60.1, followed by Colombia at 58.6.

Bolivia has one of Latin America's youngest populations; over 40 percent of the population is under the age of 15 (Reed 1998), which magnifies the future impact of socioeconomic deprivation (Klein 2003, 251). Between 1970 and 1990 the percentage of its population living in its cities swelled from 36 percent to 60 percent, giving Bolivia one of the region's highest rates of urbanization (Hopenhayn 2004). Like other Andean countries, Bolivia is an exception to the correlation between GDP and urbanization, with GDP rates similar to those of Central America and yet an urbanization rate of 62.5 percent that is far higher. Such patterns aggravate the tensions and instability characterizing urban life. For example, officials estimate that about 60 percent of residential property is under unknown ownership,

102. "Último día para las propuestas al programa barrios de verdad," *El Diario,* September 18, 2006.

which feeds the long-running disputes between long-term residents and local state agencies about who determines use of the land underneath. In short, as long as these and other indicators of socioeconomic stability lag so far behind participatory pressures in Bolivia, community and problem-oriented policing will not be able to achieve the predictability it needs.

Conclusion

In conversations, top officials around Bolivia talk about the police's "absolute" resistance to or "functional incapacity" for reform. But as historical changes yank them forward, the police will not have much of a choice. Amid Bolivia's growing levels of citizen mobilization, they will first have to become more engaged and integrated with the population. Police repression, from routine patrols to political protest, has served less to subdue than to antagonize a society increasingly able to resist it. The police will also have to repair internal fissures, from ethnic divisions to systemic corruption, if they are to remain a cohesive force. Despite steps to improve the rights of police officers, and the promise of more under Morales, reversing professional exploitation will require a real assessment of the police force's structure. "This generation of police is totally beaten down," as one official summed up the prevailing mood, "with very little possibilities of rising up."[103]

President Morales's strong reelection in 2009 gave needed political stability to the citizen security reform. But without a corresponding reinforcement of the country's economic, geographic, or societal foundation, Bolivia's reform path remains more precarious than those of most other countries. If they are not done carefully, changes in areas such as structural reorganization and control mechanisms risk fracturing the security system even more. But if they are done too reluctantly, changes are unlikely to alter the patterns in daily policing and institutional relations that have allowed the security crisis to fester. This dilemma is most evident in the standoff between the national and departmental governments that may mean the end of the National Police itself. Since the colonial era, centralization has been viewed as essential to keeping this weak state intact, particularly in the aftermath of losing wars with Chile and Paraguay. But the many financial, administrative, and policy drawbacks of a centralized police, as for most state agen-

103. Ximena A. Prudencio Bilbao, director general, Seguridad Ciudadana, interview by author, La Paz, December 21, 2004.

cies, have been increasingly apparent since democratization. Until this question is resolved, the centrifugal strain on Bolivia's unitary structure will destabilize the country. But if the police force is broken up regionally, its ability to make the transition to efficient and organized structures in contrast to its present competing and fragmented factions will depend on the ability of regional and local authorities to take advantage of the new beginning by carefully implementing the CPP and adopting problem-oriented approaches based on current community policing experiments. The consensus among reformist officers to alter traditional practices often does not lead to the next step of agreeing on what change is most needed.[104] But, as the next chapter discusses, regional autonomy and a concern about rights can form a foundation for lasting reform.

104. "Prudencio quiere romper los 8 fracasos de la Seguridad," *La Prensa,* November 15, 2003, http://www.laprensa.com.bo.

Chapter 6

Argentina

On a routine patrol through his neighborhood, a police officer in La Rioja Province rapidly ticked off his needs. "If health services worked with the police on substance abuse, if neighborhood centers worked with us on documenting 'uncivil' behavior, and if the courts processed cases more quickly," then, he was sure, his district's residents would feel and be more secure. Although such cooperation remains way off, awareness of it by the police signifies a sea change for citizen security in Argentina. In a country that spent the twentieth century under repressive dictatorships and tumultuous democracies, a move toward problem-oriented policing has been welcome but fitful. Indeed, contemporary Argentina is a patchwork of police practices and changes. From its twenty-three provinces have emerged some of the world's most advanced legal codes and some of its worst police abuses. Such diversity makes Argentina among the most instructive examples of police reform in Latin America.

This chapter analyzes the political, functional, and legal obstacles to some of the key changes that have been under way in different regions of the country since the 1983 transition to democracy. In the years since the ambitious but politicized and largely unsuccessful reforms of the 1990s, only a handful of provinces have enacted major citizen security reforms, each of which has been dealt major and ongoing reversals. But these difficulties reflect the willingness of the provinces to confront directly the conditions discussed in chapter 2 by restructuring police forces and putting citizen participation front and center. Together, those experiences have helped reformers anticipate obstacles and learn how to steer clear of them.

The reigning citizen security paradigm up through the 1990s in Argentina was a centralized, arrest-based response to crime. But as this approach became increasingly removed from the socioeconomic conditions that caused crime, problem-oriented reforms were gradually enacted. Those changes fall into three main categories. First, many provinces restructured their police forces to make them more efficient and less militarized, such as through flatter hierarchies and decentralization. Second, most provinces also enacted new penal process codes to transfer investigative power from the police to the prosecutors, replace written trials with oral trials, and create new courts. In the third and most ambitious change, community policing programs were tentatively developed at the local level to empower citizens to work with police in identifying and addressing the causes of crime through citizen councils, neighborhood police modules, and community justice centers. In addition to their basis in earlier failures and weaknesses, one common characteristic of these otherwise different reforms is that they have opened up policing and security to public scrutiny and debate. Thus even as these changes are slowed by political, financial, and institutional obstacles, the citizen participation they have encouraged will help the country move past the division between traditional and problem-oriented policing.

This chapter is divided into two parts. The first part is an overview of citizen security at the national level, which begins by describing the course of federal policy since 1983. It then turns to changes in Argentina's Federal Police (Policía Federal Argentina, PFA), which is responsible for federal crimes (such as drug trafficking) throughout the country and for all law enforcement in the autonomous federal district of Buenos Aires (hereafter Capital Federal). The second part of the chapter describes citizen security reform in the provinces, which are often overlooked despite being active laboratories of policy innovation. After an overview of patterns and obstacles around the country, this section then turns to the three provinces—Buenos Aires, Mendoza, and La Rioja—that have adopted the country's most comprehensive citizen security renovations, but with outcomes that reflect the institutional and political pitfalls of most kinds of reform in Argentina.

Along with Brazil and Mexico, Argentina has attracted a substantial number of studies of polices practices and reform. For example, Donato (1999), Burzaco et al. (2001), and Ragendorfer (2002) have described the extensive corruption and violence among the police, particularly in the province of Buenos Aires, while others, such as Sain (2001) and Vallespir (2002), have used reports of that abuse to develop recommendations for change. Few studies, though, incorporate and tie together trends in crime and criminal policy at the provincial and local levels around the country. Rather than point out the problems of a specific police force or security plan, this chapter looks at how provincial and local citizen security initiatives are helping to push the country toward problem-oriented policing. Because the innovations of and obstacles to police reform are clearest at the subnational level, they best reveal the prospects for change in Argentina as a whole.

Citizen Security at the National Level

In a national history shaped by internal strife, Argentina's police have been pivotal. In the colonial era and the civil wars following independence from Spain the police were boosted by regional strongmen (*caudillos*) in their endless battles with each other. Even as constitutional rule was established in the mid-1800s, the police gained more discretionary power, such as through the 1868 and 1888 penal codes that gave the PFA the power to detain people based on suspicion of criminal intent. At the turn of the twentieth century, police agencies again became a key instrument of political and social control. Amid industrialization and a huge wave of immigration, the police were used to crack down on the country's increasingly active unions and socialist organizations. For example, the infamous "Tragic Week" in 1919 in which a violent army crushed a metalworkers' strike began with police intervention in a labor strike. After the military took power in 1930, it widened and institutionalized police authority through executive decrees, ordinances, and "regulations." Most of these edicts were applied as well during periods of constitutional government, such as those of Juan Domingo Perón (1946–55) and the brief Radical-led administrations in the 1960s over which the military held much sway. Police abuse then reached a climax during the 1976–83 military dictatorship (a period commonly known as El Proceso, short for the military's self-proclaimed title of El Proceso de Reorganización Nacional), which killed or "disappeared" up to thirty thousand people, utilizing a repressive security apparatus that included provincial and federal police agencies (Rock 1985, 363; CELS and Americas Watch 1991, 7).

Because of such repression, human rights were the primary target of reform after the 1983 transition to democracy. The Radical Party government of Raúl Alfonsín (1983–89) strengthened civil rights protections while improving police training, tightening internal discipline, and replacing top PFA officials. During those first years of democracy, several provinces adopted new penal process codes, streamlined police hierarchies, and enacted police-community measures such as civilian boards. Many provinces also purged their police forces. San Luis conducted a "deep depuration" that rid the force of more than a hundred officers involved in the dictatorship's abuses and retired a further six hundred, according to the minister who helped oversee the process. Like other provinces, it also overhauled education in order to demilitarize and "democratically professionalize" the police.[1] Aside from such actions, however, the police as institutions were spared from major scrutiny in most provinces. Their structures and authorities remained largely intact, and in some cases fortified by military officials finding postdictatorship positions within their ranks. In addition, mainly because of Peronist obstruction in the National Congress and the economic crisis of the mid-1980s, early reforms of the police were not used as a platform for long-term structural change.[2]

The 1989–99 government of Peronist Carlos Menem then moved in the opposite direction by building up the national security apparatus and encouraging a policy of *mano dura*. For example, in the wake of the 1994 bombing of the Jewish Community Center, it created by decree—despite opposition from the police themselves—the powerful but short-lived Secretariat of Security and Community Protection (Secretaría de Seguridad y Protección a la Comunidad), which brought together all federal forces under direct executive control with greater powers such as formation of special units. The government also named former Proceso officials to top positions and promoted wide powers for police agencies, such as allowing them to stop crime in the "pre-criminal" state.[3] Even after nearly a decade in office the president insisted that a policy of *mano dura* was the only way to respond to crime. "Zero tolerance. Iron fist. There is no other option, no other," he insisted, adding that "human rights organizations may scream to the sky, but here I believe that delinquents have more rights than a police officer or the people."[4] With the president and his party dominating national politics for most of the decade, Menem's approach was copied by most governors at the time as well. Legal controls over the police usually came only in response to specific incidents of abuse or as part of larger political deals

1. Héctor Torino, former minister of government and education, San Luis Province, interview by author, San Luis, August 5, 2002.

2. Jorge Bacqué, Supreme Court magistrate (1985–90), interview by author, Buenos Aires, December 6, 1996.

3. For example, Carlo Aurelio Martínez, principal assessor to Emilio Massera, a leader of the dictatorship, was named head of immigration, and Col. Óscar Pascual Guerrieri, who operated several detention centers, was named head of the intelligence service. A detailed description of Menem appointments can be found in Andersen (2002).

4. Agenda Abierta, "Menem: No queda otra salida que la mano dura frente a la inseguridad," *Clarín,* September 13, 1998.

between the parties.[5] However, substantial changes were made in the judiciary. In particular, the penal process code received a long-needed overhaul in 1992 that simplified criminal procedures and strengthened the Fiscalía.

The government may have tightened its grip on security, but it loosened control in most other areas. Menem's neoliberal policies, among Latin America's most extensive, fundamentally altered the traditionally patronistic Argentine state through deep spending cuts, privatization, decentralization of basic services, and a fixed exchange rate. As the decade wore on, though, this approach led to record rates of unemployment, poverty, inequality, and crime.[6] Between 1991 and 2004 the percentage of people under 18 below the poverty line rose 30 percent, reaching a high of 67.9 percent in 2002.[7] In 2002 nearly 77 percent of students did not finish high school, and only 40 percent completed primary education.[8] Meanwhile, the crime rate doubled between 1992 and 1999, and violent crimes rose 65 percent between 1994 and 1999. In 1980 there were 800 crimes per 100,000 inhabitants, and in 1999, 2,904 (more specifically, the crime rate per 100,000 persons was 1,484 in 1991, 1,650 in 1993, 2,043 in 1995, 2,288 in 1997, 2,904 in 1999, 3,712 in 2001, 3,356 in 2003, 3,127 in 2005, and 3,095 in 2007).[9] Although few Argentines wanted to return to the dictatorship ruling the country in 1980, rising insecurity during democratization fueled pres-

5. In 1991 the death of a 17-year-old in a police station prompted the legislature to modify the PFA Organic Law (Ley Órganica de la Policía Federal Argentina) to allow detention only for a reasonable suspicion of criminal activity (or inability to produce identification), and to reduce from twenty-four hours to ten hours the maximum time allowed for such detentions. Menem vetoed the modification, arguing that ten hours was not enough time for an adequate investigation, but his veto was overridden by the legislature. Passed in November 1994, Law 24390 prohibited preventive detention for more than two years—a limit that continues to be routinely superseded.

6. The percentage of Argentines below the poverty line rose from 22 percent to 43 percent between 1990 and 2000, and the number of homes lacking some basic needs rose from 7.1 million in 1980 to 8.56 million in 1991. After the 2001 economic collapse, 58 percent of Argentines were below the poverty line and 28 percent were in extreme poverty. Daniel Muchnik, "Una herencia difícil de resolver," *Clarín,* April 27, 2003. Of the country's ten million people between the ages of 14 and 24 (35.6 percent), 70 percent were poor (Dirección General de Prevención Comunitaria de la Violencia 2004).

7. National Institute of Statistics and Census (Instituto Nacional de Estadísticas y Censos, INDEC), June 2004.

8. National Office of the System of Information, Evaluation, and Monitoring of Social Programs (Sistema de Información, Evaluación y Monitoreo de Programas Sociales, SIEMPRO), 2002, http://www.siempro.gov.ar.

9. MJDH, "Evolución Anual de Hechos Delictuosos registrados," http://www.jus.gov.ar/areas-tematicas/estadisticas-en-materia-de-criminalidad.aspx.

sures on elected officials to clamp down. In 2000, 39 percent of the population reported being victims of crime, and violent robberies rose from 12 percent to 15 percent of crimes between just 2000 and 2001 (Sain 2004, 131).

With majorities of up to 86.2 percent reporting feeling insecure, demands for tougher policing also grew during this period (Dammert 2000, 11). In response, the police made more arrests, mainly for property crimes and misdemeanors.[10] But these arrests had little impact because of a lack of general improvement in the criminal justice system. Less than 2 percent of violent crimes led to convictions, and less than a fifth of federal prison inmates at the time were incarcerated for serious offenses. In fact, a 2005 government review revealed that over fifty of every hundred cases in federal court were drug crimes, almost all of which were less serious than unresolved cases of corruption.[11] And while the crime rate zoomed up in the 1990s, the number of criminal sentences rose only gradually, from 16,049 in 1989 to 18,377 in 2001 (INDEC 2000, 38). Agencies such as the Justice Ministry's Office of Criminal Policy were hampered by poor information and infrastructural support. Because "the larger criminal policy and its normative and sociological approach have not changed" since the predemocratic era, its director pointed out, "those who commit minor crimes are the only ones caught in the penal process's selectivity."[12] Such ineffectiveness was further highlighted by the rapid growth of crime, which nearly tripled from 498,290 crime reports in 1993 to 1,218,243 in 2007. Crime increased in complexity as well. In the Capital Federal, for example, the PFA struggled with sharp increases in arms use as well as of violent carjackings, the latter becoming one of city's principal causes of homicide. Ad hoc measures such as personnel changes had little effect, because the police "themselves demonstrated an enormous capacity to reproduce patterns that perpetuate their own corruption and inefficiency" (Senado de la Provincia de Buenos Aires 2002, 238, 242).

Not surprisingly, citizens grew less confident in the police over the 1990s, with police officials in the three provinces examined in this chapter (Buenos Aires, Mendoza, and La Rioja) estimating that only about 30 per-

10. In 1988, of the 480,617 criminal charges, 317,239 (66 percent) were for crimes against property; in 1992, 247,666 (59.6 percent) of the total 416,125 criminal charges were for property crimes (Instituto Nacional de Estadísticas y Censos 1994, 763–69).

11. Paz Rodríguez N. and Gabriel Sued, "La justicia, saturada por delitos menores," *La Nación,* February 21, 2005.

12. Mariano Ciafardini, national director of criminal policy, interviews by author, Buenos Aires, October 18, 1994, and June 18, 2004.

cent of victims were reporting crime. As elsewhere in Latin America, rising crime fueled two contradictory pressures: for more *mano dura,* on the one hand, and for more accountable police, on the other. The *mano dura* usually came first, stoked by the public's fear and by the country's slow criminal justice systems.[13] But when it did not lead to the expected results, this tough approach itself came under scrutiny, often leading to more preventive policies that also were slow to demonstrate results.

As the media began reporting on police abuses and scandals more assiduously, Argentines began to believe that the police were too corrupt, complacent, and violent to be effective. Those beliefs fed society's larger rejection of the state policies accompanying the political and economic collapse in December 2001, when police killings of protesters precipitated the resignation of President Fernando de la Rúa. Four interim presidents then took office in quick succession, and relations between provincial and federal officials broke down. In response, grassroots civil society organizations began to take up the slack on issues ranging from poverty reduction to gender equality. Governors, desperate to distance themselves from the chaotic national scene, began to encourage (and be affiliated with) community participation and institutional accountability on policing. But the country's dire economic straits often caught up with them quickly. Even with strong backing, most reforms adopted at this time were undermined by financial limitations, police resistance, lack of training, and ongoing citizen suspicion of anything sponsored by political elites. In many provinces the disappointing results then led to calls for both a deepening of these reforms as well as a return to a policy of *mano dura,* taking them back to square one of the dilemma between the two approaches.

National Crime Prevention Plan

In this environment of policy stalemate in most provinces, and as the 2001 economic collapse heightened fears around crime, much of the pressure for change fell on President Néstor Kirchner, who entered office in 2003. Trying to forge new ground on policing and criminal policy, Kirchner purged 107 top PFA officers during his first year in office—and pressured the province of Buenos Aires to do the same. In April 2004 the administration breathed new life into the National Crime Prevention Plan (Plan Nacional

13. Despite the rise in crime after the 1980s, criminal sentences in Argentina declined from 19,764 in 1983 to 18,377 in 2000.

de Prevención del Delito), an ambitious fusion of social programs, tougher punishment, state agency overhaul, and problem-oriented law enforcement that would be implemented through accords with cities and provinces. Its proposals included a new crime mapping system, a twelve thousand–officer Federal Investigations Agency (based on the U.S. Federal Bureau of Investigation), citizen boards to evaluate police promotions, and the replacement of many police chiefs with elected civilians. But the plan's main thrust, say its directors, was prevention, centered on poor urban areas, such as through the Vulnerable Communities Program, and on support for at-risk groups, such as through scholarships to bring an estimated fifty thousand teenage dropouts in "critical areas" back to school.[14] Many of these plans had been run out of the Ministry of Labor and the Ministry of Social Development, which were now working with the Ministry of Justice, Security and Human Rights (Ministerio de Justicia, Seguridad y Derechos Humanos, MJSDH) on the plan. The plan also included judicial reforms, such as creating new juvenile courts, introducing jury trials in many criminal and corruption cases, and moving some judges and prosecutors out to the neighborhoods. In addition, out of the spotlight the federal legislature was being more diligent about forging long-term plans. For example, several members of the Senate wanted to use their legislative power to push for national models and standards.[15]

These and other projects continued under Cristina Fernández, Kirchner's wife and successor, who was elected president in 2007. Such continuity was facilitated by evaluation mechanisms included in the initial plan, which, as the next chapter discusses, are central to making the adjustments that any reform needs. Policies also incorporated broad social concerns such as public space and youth, which, as chapter 3 discussed, are often left out of legislation. Through this combination of prevention, structural overhaul, and attention to social conditions, the plan's ultimate goal was nothing less than "the transformation of the police" and creation of a "new culture of urban security," which were larger than the sum of the plan's otherwise disparate parts (MJSDH 2004, 5).

Although the National Crime Prevention Plan has been the country's boldest and most comprehensive security plan since the democratic transi-

14. Officials, Subsecretaría de Política Criminal y Asuntos Penitenciarios, Ministerio de Justicia, Seguridad y Derechos Humanos, interviews by author, Buenos Aires, August 22, 2002.

15. Senators Marita Perceval of Mendoza, Rubén Giustiniani of Santa Fe, Vilma Lidia Ibarra of Federal Capital (Ciudad Autónoma de Buenos Aires), and Diana Beatriz Conti of Buenos Aires, interviews by author, Buenos Aires, August 3, 2005.

tion, it has faced deep political, legal, and functional obstacles. First, support by even popular presidents like Kirchner did not translate into support for the plan because, as in other countries, an impatient public is more inclined toward proposals that appear tough and immediate. In a bout of bad timing, an upsurge in the demand for such proposals came on the heels of the government's 2004 rollout of the plan. In March of that year the kidnapping and killing in Buenos Aires Province of 23-year-old Axel Blumberg led to a protest rally in the Capital Federal that drew nearly 200,000 persons. In response, the legislature enacted a series of hastily drawn-up laws that, among other things, lowered the age for criminal liability and toughened the sentences for murderers, kidnappers, and rapists. Because the government had not yet announced its own long-term plan, it went back to the drawing board, thereby fomenting perceptions that it was being unassertive and unclear. It was also upstaged by a wave of robberies that led the city to demand two thousand more officers, opening up a channel for criticism of the government's earlier purges that reduced the size of the force. The growing frequency and tensions of the protest marches by the unemployed and other social movements—whose confrontations with the police hastened the downfall of the two previous presidents—also put the government on the defensive. Although 97 percent of those polled said that the April protest was not directed at Kirchner, disagreement between the police and the government led to the resignation of the PFA chief and the president's dismissal of the minister of justice, security and human rights, who headed up the plan's formulation. Reform was further delayed and confused by the transference of the PFA between the MJSDH to the Interior Ministry, along with the political isolation of the officials behind the National Crime Prevention Plan. Executive politics also played an outsized role. One of Fernández's appeals as a candidate was association with her husband's popular record but not with the political enemies he acquired. On security, though, the opposite was true: the first lady, who as a senator had been involved in national politics far longer than her husband, had been a key figure in security policies since 2003 and had been central in the PFA purge.

The National Crime Prevention Plan and other federal initiatives were set back further by reluctant provinces, whose cooperation was needed for any country-wide policy. As Eaton (2008) and others have pointed out, competition and sabotage among the different levels of government are a perennial obstacle to change in Argentina. In fact, soon after the MJSDH announced the government's security plan, eighty security officials from all the provinces complained that it would intrude on their autonomy by allowing federal forces in localities—a situation they were not disposed to allow. The provinces also objected to the creation of a Federal Investigations Agency that would have power throughout the country and to the plan's financing—despite the minister's assurances that the federal government would foot the bill—based on suspicion that it would come out of the "co-participating" funds through which the provinces received federal money.

Policía Federal Argentina

Reflecting the power and priorities of the federal government, the PFA has been one of the country's more consistently competent security agencies.[16] But, according to officials such as a Proceso-era police chief, many of its repressive predemocratic tendencies survived the transition in the 1980s and were revived during the Menem administration.[17] In a pattern seen in other provinces this continuation was facilitated by a lack of external control. The national Subsecretariat of Human and Social Rights had a limited impact on actual police practice, and the national legislature's bicameral commission overseeing the PFA did not monitor police practices much beyond investigations into particular abuses (Martínez et al. 1999). Starting in the mid-1990s, however, political pressure on the PFA increased after the Capital Federal attained provincial status, putting more progressive politicians in office. Combined with crime's growing extent and complexity, the newly minted province made the PFA one of the first police agencies in Argentina to face the larger choice between traditional and problem-oriented policing.

The initial focal points of these pressures—and of the PFA's power— were the twenty-three edicts that the agency acquired over its long history, giving it wide discretionary power largely free of court oversight. Allowing detention for behaviors ranging from "scandal" to "drunkenness," these edicts became a basis of the PFA's daily policing. Well over half of PFA activity involved edict violations. For example, of the some 240,000 annual detentions in the Capital Federal in 1995, the last year the edicts were fully in force, over 150,000 were for edict transgressions, 50,000 for verification of identity, and 40,000 for suspicion of an actual crime (*delito*).[18] A lack

16. Along with smaller federal forces, such as the Gendarmería, officials estimate Argentina has about 140,000 national police personnel.

17. Valentín Espinosa, top-ranking PFA officer until his retirement in 1983, interview by author, Buenos Aires, August 21, 2002.

18. "Se cuadruplicaron las detenciones por edictos," *La Nación,* September 8, 1996, 15.

of juridical control enhanced the edicts; less than 1 percent of arrests under them were appealed, and of that number almost all were repealed.[19] But when the Capital Federal became a province, its 1996 constitution abolished the edicts and instantly deprived the PFA of its operational foundation. Amid the growing rivalry between the national Peronist government and the city government headed by the opposition Alianza and Radical Party mayor Fernando de la Rúa, the president and the PFA vociferously opposed the change. In particular, they attacked the city's 1998 Código de Convivencia (Coexistence Code), enacted to replace the edicts, and they condemned it for tying the police's hands as well as for promoting vices such as prostitution and drug use. Such criticism resonated strongly with the fearful middle class, and more broadly, it associated reform with immorality, violence, and cultural change. Using his powers of decree, the president then reinstated the edicts through decree, thereby making the federal dominance clear but further straining national-local government relations. The edicts "were very effective," insisted one officer from the PFA's public outreach Office of Police Agreement (Oficina de Convenio Policial), and he blamed the "great ideological differences" with the city government. "This problem of guaranteeism," he insisted, has been "overcome in other countries."[20]

When de la Rúa was elected president in 1999, he initiated change by enacting new anticorruption laws and by backing community policing programs. As in the 1980s, though, a mounting economic crisis put long-term reform on the back burner. Political and economic stabilization since 2002 have opened up new spaces for reform, but they have been accompanied by some of the same obstacles that earlier slowed down the national plan. First, the concurrence of crime patterns and functional jurisdiction in the Buenos Aires area has obscured their connections and neglected the needed cooperation. The city of Buenos Aires, which has about three million residents, has a lower crime rate than the surrounding urban belt, known as the *conurbano*. That belt, which is in the province of Buenos Aires, contains about nine million people who suffer from high poverty rates and a homicide rate that is about four times than that of the Capital Federal.[21] Although the capital and the *conurbano* form a single urban area with similar patterns of crime, the three mutually suspicious governments that run them have not

19. Ibid.

20. Anonymous officer, interview by author, Buenos Aires, May 26, 2004.

21. "Solá anunció que bajó el delito, pero le preocupa la sensación," *Diario La Unión* (La Plata), July 15, 2004.

sufficiently developed common criminal policies and operations.[22] There is also scant coordination between the police and social services on problems such as drug abuse, a basis of problem-oriented policing. Finally, even though official homicide and overall crime rates declined after 2003, casting doubt over that figure is the estimate by officials that about 70 percent of crime victims in metro Buenos Aires do not file police reports. Nearly half of those who did file reports said they believed that nothing would be done anyway (Sain 2001, 137), reflecting but also perpetuating criminal justice's lethargy.

Such inadequacies, along with the national economic disintegration, prompted an assertion of local power. Since the late 1990s federal authority had gradually given way to local moves toward problem-oriented policing, including the formation of an unarmed "Urban Guard" and a network of security coordinators and forums in each of the city's eight administrative districts to allow residents to identify and respond to sources of insecurity. The Capital Federal's first official community policing program was launched in 1997 when the city government promoted the formation of neighborhood Crime and Violence Prevention Councils as part of the city's Program for the Prevention of Crime and Violence. These councils would allow residents to translate their security concerns into policy. Following suit, and responding to continuing demands for community policing, in 2004 the PFA, MJSDH, and city government created a Community Police Office (Dirección General de Policía Comunitaria) to oversee and develop community policing operations. A Buenos Aires City Community Police was created at the end of 2004. It began with a force of five hundred officers, with plans to expand to two thousand within four years. But the plan called for the entire force to consist of recent academy graduates and to put them in plazas and other public spaces. This program seemed designed for failure by marginalizing it to a particular sector of the police, staffing it with inexperienced personnel, and not empowering citizens in any real way.

As in Honduras, Bolivia, and other countries, a far more substantial move toward community policing has been society-driven. Much of that effort in Buenos Aires has gone toward forming neighborhood consortiums (*consorcios vecinales*) that cover almost the entire metropolitan area. The

22. After the 2004 rally Kirchner said that Buenos Aires Province had to go deeper in its police reform, prompting its governor, Felipe Solá, to assert that he would need "an extra one billion pesos" from the federal administration to deploy more police, but that he would go ahead on his own if the Kirchner government did not cooperate.

fifty consortiums formed have produced an impressive quantity of information about security issues, from public lighting to police corruption. The local government's Citizen Security Program (Programa de Seguridad Ciudadana), based on a 1997 decree, also began moving the basis of security from a police response toward citizen prevention, mainly through the establishment of Support and Participation Centers (Centros de Gestión y Participación) that initiated two problem-oriented initiatives. The first initiative was made up of Neighborhood Councils of Crime and Violence Prevention (Consejos Barriales de Prevención del Delito y la Violencia) composed of residents, business owners, NGOs, and institutions such as schools and hospitals in the zone, along with representatives from the Support and Participation Centers, the Citizen Security Program, and city social services. These councils help residents document and correct the causes of crime in their area, improve relations with the police, reduce conflict, help at-risk groups, and, using different sources, draw up crime maps. The second initiative was composed of the Body of Neighborhood Auxiliaries (Cuerpo de Auxiliares Vecinales), which work closely with the centers and councils to direct crime victims to the appropriate services, submit requests to the city government on behalf of residents, pass along information about infractions and conflicts, and publicize helpful information.

The initial responses to these programs were positive, which lowered the percentage of residents with negative views of the police and further encouraged participation (Dirección Nacional de Política Criminal, Ministerio de Justicia de la Nación 2001). One of the program's directors, by publicizing creative solutions to insecurity, provided a particularly strong boost of citizen trust in the program.[23] But as time went on, programs started to fray along geographic and class lines. In particular, the citizen security councils diverged in ability and influence, depending on the strength of neighborhood organizing. In areas with local groups, the councils became part of preexisting local networks experienced in making collective claims. In well-off areas such as Palermo, where long-established local groups already enjoyed good relations with the police and knew how to push demands through the city bureaucracy, the program fortified existing actions. By contrast, councils in areas without strong organizations or political connections complained that their efforts to convince the police to address problems specific to their areas were not making headway. For example, in

23. Claudio Súarez, Jefe, chief, Programa de Seguridad, interview by author, Buenos Aires, May 27, 2004.

the partly industrial zones of Constitución one kiosk owner who had been trying to organize others to reduce nighttime robberies said that the local station had not been particularly responsive. Officers at the local station, Comisaría 8, responded that their hands were tied by headquarters, which controlled resources and sent their own officials to conduct investigations. Such a response was in part an excuse, because police in other low-income areas, such as Comisaría 32, said that they could act freely. What seemed to be a more accurate underlying explanation was that most police lacked guidance from above on how to deal with residents. In a 2004 citywide evaluation, described shortly, Comisaría 8 was rated one of the ten worst *comisarías* in terms of residents' sense of insecurity, and nearby Comisaría 18 was also ranked among the ten worst. But two other *comisarías* in the vicinity, 10 and 20, scored in the top ten. This proximity of areas with similar socioeconomic conditions but different resident opinions would have been a good basis for a comparative study of PFA activity. As the next chapter emphasizes, such an evaluation is central to problem-oriented policing, but is often the most neglected stage of reform. And without the consistency that evaluations help bring, the common response from residents of these working-class and commercial areas was then withdrawal from participation or renewed claims for traditional policing.[24]

The PFA's weak grasp of problem-oriented policing originated in its academies for both top and subcommissioned officers. These schools are better than most provincial academies, but, like them, tend to focus more on physical preparation and formalistic knowledge than on analysis and discussion of criminal policy and social conditions. Moreover, according to several PFA officers, heads of the subofficial police academies (Escuela de Suboficiales and Escuela de Cadetes) embezzle many of the funds earmarked for firearms, so that cadets graduate without sufficient training in this basic necessity. This situation accounts as well for the capital's high rate of killings of police and civilians.[25] Indeed, just fifty-four PFA officers were killed between 1990 and 1999, but well over a hundred were killed in each

24. Milko Radzic, interview by author, Buenos Aires, August 19, 2002; officers, PFA Comisaría, interviews by author, Buenos Aires, August 20, 2002.

25. Police officials, Academia de la Policía Federal Ramón L. Falcón (Ramón L. Falcón Federal Police Academy), interviews by author, Buenos Aires, May 27, 2004; Escuela Federal de Suboficiales y Agentes, Comisario General Alberto Villar (Federal School of Suboficial and Agents, Commission General Alberto Villar), interview by author, May 28, 2004.

of the three following years.[26] In the capital, between 1996 and 2002 the number of civilians killed by police rose by 89 percent, and the number of police killed rose by 132 percent. Reflecting the particular insecurity of youth, 522 persons under the age of 21 were killed by security forces in the Buenos Aires metro area between 1996 and 2004, 36.4 percent of them by the PFA and 58.6 percent by the provincial police (López et al. 2005, 6). Rather than poor training, vague use-of-force regulations are cited more often by top officials to explain such high rates.[27] Nevertheless, the government has generally expanded the PFA's use-of-force power, such as its approval in 2008 of the use by elite PFA officers of "dum-dum" bullets, which have been criticized by the UN as dangerous and by other city police as ineffective. Thus, although changes such as CompStat have helped city *comisarías* better track crimes in their neighborhoods, a dependence on force often overshadows their ability to use those statistics to better discern and integrate analysis of crime's causes and patterns into their daily work.

This combination of police violence and inadequacy is particularly marked in the Capital Federal's twenty-one *villas* (shantytowns)—often referred to as *villas de emergencia*—which often have noticeably fewer "incident" pins on many *comisaría* crime maps, even though they clearly have higher crime rates than the surrounding areas. Local officers also seem to downplay some of the larger patterns of insecurity. At an informal meeting in the low-income Illia district, residents recited a long litany of problems such as poor health clinics, illegal construction, and "putrid streets filled with piles of garbage." One resident who commented on all-night drunken revelries said that the Fiscalía would use the Código de Convivencia to come in and disperse offenders, but that there was no real preventive intervention or follow-up.[28] As in La Paz and other cities, people in poorer areas presented a larger picture of insecurity in which they could identify the most dangerous streets, practices, and hours of the day. However, the police assigned to the area preferred to talk about particular suspects or incidents. In some cases, this lack of engagement was rooted in the same frus-

26. Policía Federal Argentina and Juan Carlos Li Rosi, high commissioner, PFA, interview by author, Buenos Aires, August 20, 2002.

27. Article 97 of the PFA Organic Law says that police may use force "each time it is necessary to maintain order, guarantee security, impede the perpetration of a crime and in all other acts of legitimate exercise."

28. Residents, Illia district, interviews by author, Buenos Aires, June 22, 2004, and July 19, 2007.

trations that citizens faced. For example, one police officer in Comisaría 32 talked about how many of the blocks in the high-crime Zona Zabatela were unmarked and dark, making patrols too hazardous, and how the constant influx into an already overcrowded area had made community relations too difficult.[29] In a reflection of the police's low profile, residents in these areas talked about how they usually saw officers only during special operations or when operating their own corruption schemes.[30] Residents in Ciudad Oculta said police would come in only once between the high-crime hours of 6:00 p.m. and 12:00 a.m.—and then only because of a change in shift.

In this fertile ground the roots of crime sink deep. One of the most evident causes of criminal violence in the city's *villas* is the highly doctored, smokable form of cocaine known as *paco*. Since early 2003 much of the cocaine being smuggled into Argentina from Peru and Bolivia has been mixed with toxic chemicals and sold for a little over a dollar a hit. As a result, the addiction rates among young people and the levels of property crime have skyrocketed, from 327,722 crimes in 2001 to 711,987 in 2007.[31] And yet despite many meetings with concerned-looking officials, a coherent policy response has been slow to form, forcing many residents to seek out social services outside the area to help addicts, victims, and their families. Like a complementary form of traditional policing, residents also band together to attack or expel *paco* traffickers and dealers.[32] In early 2009 a group of residents convinced the federal government to conduct a series of raids that both seized large stores of *paco* and closed many of the residential kitchens that produced them. But without concerted efforts to coordinate policing with social services, the short-term results of such traditional policing tactics will eventually lose out to *paco* networks learning how to evade them. The same is true for other forms of violence. In Ciudad Oculta, for example, some residents proudly proclaimed their membership in the Amazons, a group of women who gather and clap loudly in front of homes where domestic violence is known to take place. But without social service intervention or police protection, the results are likely to be short-lived.

29. Comisaría 32, interviews by author, Buenos Aires, June 23, 2004.

30. Padre Luis Farinello, Fundación Farinello, Quilmes, Buenos Aires Province, interview by author, May 22, 2004.

31. MJSDH, "Evolución anual de hechos delictuosos registrados," http://www.jus.gov.ar/areas-tematicas/estadisticas-en-materia-de-criminalidad.aspx.

32. Author meetings with neighborhood groups in Ciudad Oculta, Buenos Aires, May 23–24, 2004, and July 18, 2007.

For police officers, using the city's community policing network to address such problems would be a good opportunity to develop innovative power. Many of the needed elements are in place, from willing residents to a supportive local government. But promotion in the PFA downplays such initiative. Rather than positive actions or specific skill development, moving up in the ranks of the PFA depends almost entirely on an officer's academy exam score and whether he or she has done anything that might offend, overshadow, or otherwise bring uninvited attention to higher-ups. Street officers largely monitor a single corner, without proactive law enforcement training from their supervisors.[33] Several officers said that even though they are relieved that their superiors only occasionally check in on them during their shifts, the sporadic and cursory nature of those interactions also leaves them feeling directionless and unprotected. Even when a crime occurs, officers are shunted aside. We are just "garbage men to clean up crime scenes," concluded one *subcomisario* in Comisaría 11. Among the lower ranks, formal promotion mechanisms are not much clearer. The form used for ascension is just a single page, without questions about the agent's real policing work. As a result, officers are exposed to very little skill development in their stations.

Human resources are also poorly managed. Less than one-third of PFA officers are in the street at any given time, leading to sparse coverage in many areas.[34] And officers complain about the lack of financial and logistical support, especially about salaries that average just 500 pesos (under $200) a month for the lower ranks and 1,700 pesos (under $600) for a *comisario*. But the misdirection of funds appears to a bigger problem than their absence. As in other countries, police control over budgets and procurements has long generated corruption networks in the PFA. In the stations, street agents collect funds for station commissioners, who give part of the proceeds to the regional commissioner.[35] Police control over the legal side of internal affairs leads to similar problems, especially slow or nonexistent investigations into police wrongdoing. In fact, the head of the main legal affairs office, General Autonomous Office of Judicial Affairs (Dirección General Autónoma de Asuntos Jurídicos) says he does not have sufficient

33. Commissioner, subcommissioner, and two subcommissioned officers, Comisaría 32, interviews by author, Buenos Aires, May 25, 2004.

34. Fernando Simón, Subsecretaría de Coordinación e Innovación, interview by author, Buenos Aires, May 26, 2004.

35. Police officials, Escuela Policial Falcón de Oficiales PFA, interviews by author, Buenos Aires, May 27, 2004; Villar, interview.

personnel for the constant backlog of cases. Even judges—who also have little trust in the judiciary—continually send him additional cases to investigate.[36] Indeed, many top executive officials say off the record that well over 80 percent of top officials are corrupt, but that they lack the information and power to prosecute most of them.

Most accusations of abuse by lower-ranking PFA officials are handled by their superiors, who respond with warning, arrest, dismissal, or exoneration. Although many officers say these rules appear fair on paper, their application often violates due process. For example, in the PFA and in the police forces of other provinces, accused officers complain that they are not given access to all the documents and that their own defense does not pull together and present all the possible supportive evidence. Hidden punishments outside the disciplinary code are also widely used by the higher ranks, such as undesirable assignments to violent neighborhoods or mass events. Lower-ranking officers say that any charges they manage to bring against either their superiors or civilian officials are not received in an impartial manner.

The upper ranks also feel aggrieved. For example, almost the entire top echelon of the PFA was angered by Kirchner's dismissal of 107 of their colleagues.[37] Some of those who were fired "were very good police, but we do not know why they left," said one official, concluding that the president's action was a "political response to a political problem without really knowing the causes." (Executive officials responded that at least 30 percent of those fired were processed through Internal Affairs.)

Despite this tension, the PFA has been promoting specific and effective solutions. The chief of one of the training schools, acknowledging that "we have lost a lot of time" because of a lack of courses in areas such as prevention and drugs, said that the schools were creating tougher entrance requirements, carrying out detailed individual reviews during academy training, and offering more opportunities for serving officers to study. Perhaps most significant, greater attention has been given to use-of-force practices —"to shoot only in extreme conditions"—and to arranging meetings with

36. Alejandro Hayet, chief, Dirección General Autónoma de Asuntos Jurídicos (General Autonomous Office of Judicial Affairs), interview by author, Buenos Aires, May 24, 2004.

37. Author meeting with top-ranking officers (Plana Mayor) of the PFA, Buenos Aires, May 26, 2004. In that meeting each top official claimed that he could be fired next without knowing why.

38. Comisario Inspector Andrés Valentín Schmitz, chief, Escuela de Suboficiales y Agentes, interview by author, Buenos Aires, May 27, 2004.

victims of police violence.[38] Other PFA heads said that they had consolidated databases with officers' financial records, were improving cooperation with the provincial police, and, to make promotion more stringent, were carrying out "more profound" interviews and wider evaluations. Such evaluation has also been applied to policing overall. The MJSDH began an evaluation of the PFA's fifty-two *comisarías* using citizen surveys in June 2004, in particular offering both financial and professional incentives for those *comisarías* that brought down crime rates. The government also began to investigate wayward police officers using new methods—such as through new citizen channels or by not reassigning an accused officer to a position, which would force that officer to retire after two years. However, institutional and political obstacles reemerged to derail such initatives. With the changes in minister and in the PFA's affiliation, the financial incentives for *comisarías* were ended. But the biggest change in Capital Federal policing was the formation in October 2008 of the Metropolitan Police under city control. Under Mayor Mauricio Macri, a conservative opponent of the Kirchners who was elected in 2007, the Metropolitan Police may finally give the city the edge in the long-standing metro tug of war over security. But it will still require navigating a difficult political and institutional terrain—a terrain also faced by reformers in most of the country's provinces.

Citizen Security Reform in the Provinces

Because it is a federal nation of highly autonomous provinces with their own police agencies, Argentina has more opportunities for reform than centralized states with only one police agency. It also has taken fuller advantage of those opportunities than the region's other federal nations—Mexico, Brazil, and Venezuela—where national and provincial politics have hampered change even more than in Argentina. As discussed in chapter 2, regional governments are smaller and closer to the population, and so theoretically they are better able to provide security and act as models for each other. But such a virtuous cycle is slowed in a federal system by politics that is usually more clientalistic and laws that usually are weaker at the provincial level than at the national level.

In Argentina, along with society's distrust of the entire political class, such an environment has stymied reform in all but a handful of provinces, and in those few change happened only after repeated failures and reversals. Change imposed from above is also unlikely. Although Argentina's national government has rarely refrained from wielding its power, it lacks the direct policy controls wielded by executives in countries such as Mexico, as well as the legal legitimacy to enforce standards like that enjoyed by the executive branch in the United States. However, after Argentina's 2001 economic collapse, changes in leadership opened up paths for pioneering reforms in different parts of the country. But the lack of financial and institutional support for these changes, as discussed earlier, resulted in frustration and second thoughts that mired many of these provinces in the same debate between traditional and problem-oriented models. Nevertheless, the surge in citizen participation around the country has sustained reform and helped some provinces emerge from the shadow of that debate.

Argentina's provinces are diverse. The four most populous ones—Buenos Aires, Santa Fe, Córdoba, and Mendoza—are heavily urban. Many in the Patagonian south are sparsely populated and dependent on natural resource extraction. The rest are largely rural and poor, concentrated in the north of the country. They have small political elites and largely state-employed labor forces. The per capita income of those provinces is only about half that of the urban provinces such as Córdoba and a third that of the Patagonian provinces such as Santa Cruz. Despite such differences, nearly every province experienced record rates of crime and insecurity as the country's economic crisis deepened during the 1990s. The number of crimes for every hundred thousand persons, which was fewer than two thousand during the mid-1980s in most provinces, nearly doubled between the late 1980s and 2003. The ever-increasing prison population, rising from 26,690 in 1997 to 55,423 in 2005, did not make much of a dent in the crime rate (Dirección Nacional de Política Criminal 2005). Police impunity also continued: of the 435 documented killings by police officers between 1993 and 1998, only 10 percent were fully prosecuted.[39] Criminal justice and policy invariably came under greater scrutiny as a result of these trends, exposing the effects of low remuneration, poor training, weak discipline, and corruption among the police. But policy responses straggled behind. Political officials in most provinces had withdrawn from direct oversight of the police, often in an unspoken pact with the police to stay out of each other's business. In the absence of external oversight, policing practices and procedures were determined more by internal relations than by legal or state

---

39. Of these killings, the majority were in nine provinces: Buenos Aires, 105; Santa Fe, 54; Capital Federal, 44; Córdoba, 30; Mendoza, 27; Neuquén, 13; Corrientes, 11; Río Negro, 8; and Entre Ríos, 7 (CORREPI 2002).

guidelines. When pressure mounted to take action, officials who wanted to reengage then found it difficult to move things forward. Many provinces thus found themselves in one of reform's binds, with pressure on political officials to bring change peaking during a political crisis that diminished their ability to do so.

Despite these difficulties, policing based on centralized and repressive power gradually began to give way in different parts of the country to decentralization, institutional transparency, and community involvement. These changes began tentatively in the early 1990s and picked up steam toward the decade's end. Civil rights abuse in particular catalyzed change in Santa Fe, Mendoza, Neuquén, Córdoba, San Luis, and the city of Buenos Aires, spurring the establishment of internal affairs units, disciplinary bodies, ombudsmen, investigatory police units, and regional divisions for underserved areas. Most provinces also overhauled their security structures, often by creating civilian-led Ministries of Justice and Security and flattening militarized hierarchies. Provincial police agencies were often broken up into functional divisions—either into preventive and investigatory units or into separate security, judicial, transport, and specialized units. Others were further divided to correspond to the province's judicial districts, such as in Buenos Aires and Mendoza. Others took on long-avoided politicized controversies. For example, in 2005 in a move that defused serious internal strife, Chubut Province ended "extraordinary" promotions in its police force. Education was also rewired. Córdoba gave its academies new curricula and entrance requirements, and Buenos Aires, San Luis, and Mendoza created new police academies that stressed human rights and were administered by civilian specialists. Santa Fe has been a leader in advancing merit-based promotion, and several areas, such as the Capital Federal and Buenos Aires Province, have also followed the international trend of adopting computer crime mapping.

Thirteen provinces significantly reformed their judiciaries as well. Nine of them formed judicial councils to select and oversee judges, taking these powers away from the executive. In the early 1990s Córdoba enacted a highly rigorous selection process for judges and placed the judicial police under the Supreme Court, giving it some needed distance from the executive's political agenda. Most significant, eleven provinces revised their penal or penal process codes. Like other codes adopted around Latin America, those in Argentina's provinces limited police responsibilities to investigation under the direction of a strengthened Fiscalía, replaced long-standing written inquisitorial trials with oral accusatorial trials, and gave more investigatory power to judges, often in newly created courts for detainee rights and sentencing.

An even more extensive and innovative area of reform during this period was community policing. Together with the Capital Federal, seventeen provinces adopted community policing programs, most of them composed of citizen councils, neighborhood watches, and social programs for at-risk groups such as youth.[40] Buenos Aires, Chaco, Chubut, Córdoba, Entre Ríos, La Pampa, La Rioja, Mendoza, Río Negro, Santa Fe, and San Luis centered their community policing on security forums or other channels of community input.[41] Many also incorporated forms of community or problem-oriented policing in their education. In 2008 Córdoba raised educational expectations for police academy cadets, while placing them in the *policías caminera* (foot patrols) during their first year on the force. Entre Ríos Province began offering community policing courses in 2001 for both the police and officials from municipal, education, and youth agencies. Some have made corresponding institutional adjustments—for example, Santa Fe created a municipal community policing council within its Government Ministry.

Such programs fare best when supported by structural alterations in both the government and police. In the late 1990s, for example, Santa Fe began forming Neighborhood Community Security Committees (Juntas Barriales de Seguridad Comunitaria) to promote discussion between police and residents, beginning in the capital city of Santa Fe and expanding into smaller municipalities (Rosúa 1998). The government created seven provincial offices headed by political appointees to oversee the police, improved recruitment through a more transparent selection process, and strengthened training through accords with universities for specialized education. It also eliminated the division between official and subofficials, held public forums to enable merit to replace internal favoritism for promotion to higher ranks, and inverted the top-heavy hierarchy by hiring more lower-ranking police and putting more of them on the street.

In many provinces, however, these changes were not followed through with the political push needed for institutional integration. As a result, they were often left to the mercy of new officials and unexpected events. For example, through a turbulent decade Salta managed to keep alive plans for

40. The following provinces have some kind of citizen security forum: Chaco, Chubut, Córdoba, Entre Ríos, La Pampa, La Rioja, Mendoza, Río Negro, Santa Fe, and San Luis. For Buenos Aires, see Martínez et al. (1999).

41. In Buenos Aires (Articles 11 and 12 of the Provincial Public Security Law) and Capital Federal (see Martínez et al. 1999).

structural changes such as combining the commissioned and noncommis-
sioned ranks and strengthening cadet training. But these plans were scuttled
when the main advocate of the changes, Vice Governor Raúl Wayar (1995–
2007), lost the 2007 governor's race.[42] Alternative plans were developed
the next year, however, when Peronist members of the provincial legislature, criticizing the police for their approach to social conflicts, proposed a
community police unit with the involvement of a wide range of agencies,
and when the security secretariat turned a *comisaría* known for abuses
against youth into a Unit of Minor Protection. Critics in the province argued
that such changes would be cosmetic unless accompanied by a more in-
depth analysis of criminal justice practices such as spying on political protesters, overcrowding the prisons, and bringing people to the police station
just to check their police record (*averiguación de antecedentes*). Still, the
idea of reform was strong enough to endure through changes in government
and even in legislation itself.

Executive-level politics both stimulates and stalls security reform in
many other provinces as well. In San Luis Province, a spurt of change took
place in the 1990s under Gov. Adolfo Rodríguez Saá (1983–2001). Among
the significant reforms enacted were the appointment of an ombudsman and
a human rights commission, the fusion of the police into one unit, and the
establishment in 1999 of a progressive new police academy, the University
Institute of Integral Security (Instituto Universitario de Seguridad Integral,
IUSI), under the Education and Culture Ministry to provide a three-year improved law-based curricula. The ombudsman made great headway on matters that contribute to insecurity, such as poor street lighting and high levels of air and water pollution in poor areas.[43] But, as elsewhere, a lack of
backing dissipated the momentum initially behind such changes. San Luis's
small political elite and the rigid hierarchies of the police, the Fiscalía, and
other criminal justice bodies left little room for these new agencies to make
policing more transparent. Within the police, the lack of salary increases
and improvements in work conditions, symbolized by an obsolete schedule
(twenty-four hours on the job followed by twenty-four hours off) led to
strikes and depressed morale. Moreover, the flattening of the police hierarchy from eighteen to six levels entrenched resistance, particularly by officials with more years of service and higher salaries who lost out in the new

---

42. Wálter Raúl Wayar, vice governor, Salta, and Gustavo Ferraris, security secretary, Salta, interviews by author, New York, November 29, 2006.
43. Jorge Aníbal Sopeña, ombudsman, interview by author, San Luis, August 7, 2002.

structure. Many police lacked the third year of their education, and the rights-oriented curriculum changes made at the IUSI by its first postreform director—reforms intended to make community-oriented policing its "praxis" —were mostly discarded after she left that post.[44] The widespread resentment at being left out of policy formulation itself also produced resistance. In a collective meeting the entire top staff of the police said that the government did not include them in criminal justice policy. On problems such as domestic violence and the influx of "immigrants" from other provinces (a common object of blame), one police chief said, "Congress does not consult with the police," and, as a result, there was no long-term citizen security plan to deal with them.[45]

As in the other provinces, in the face of a real or perceived lack of state support the police can easily justify their illegal actions. In one informal conversation with four new police officers and IUSI's director, one officer said it was normal for those in the *comisaría* "to hit people," and another agreed, adding that "the police will deny it" and "the judges don't do anything." Yet another said he saw a child being beaten up in the street, but felt he did not have the training or support to respond. As an earlier chapter discussed, corruption or abuse by low-level officers often takes place in a context of inaction from above, thereby demonstrating the need for accountability mechanisms that go beyond specific incidents. But in San Luis accountability has been limited by a weak political opposition and a *defensor del pueblo* too closely connected with elected officials. Meanwhile, the lack of public defenders undermines due process within the courts, helping to fill up the provincial prison beyond capacity. And yet policy deliberations and decisions often remain limited to the higher levels. Especially controversial was the naming of former military and police officials, some with suspected roles in the Proceso, to top IUSI and Security Ministry posts. Contrary to the official history, a significant number were apparently not forced out of office after 1983. The government usually does not realize the combined effect of all these problems until after politicization makes it more difficult to act objectively. Politics helped lead to a 2006 law that declared that San Luis's security system was in a "state of emergency" and that tried to jolt the police force by creating several additional agencies, in-

44. Adriana Algarbe, director, Instituto Universitario de Seguridad Integral, interview by author, San Luis, August 6, 2002.

45. Manuel Objeta, commissioner general, and Carlos Machiavelli, commissioner major, interviews by author, San Luis, August 5, 2002; Plana Mayor, Policía de San Luis, author meeting, San Luis, August 5, 2002.

cluding an internal affairs unit. But established practices and insular political relations, as before, diluted the effect of the law.

When otherwise conservative political establishments are railroaded into reform, such as in the province of San Luis, the foundation for its incorporation is shaky. Even with government support, its successors (even from the same party) often want to move away from reforms associated with a particular former governor or party, particularly amid the factionalization common to Argentina's parties, legislatures, and state agencies. Throughout the country, even viable proposals have come up against such political and institutional obstacles, which range from a lack of support for start-up programs to the depiction of reform as a threat to crime fighting. Discussion of change is then channeled into easier or *mano dura* ideas, which never lack a vocal public constituency that goads politicians. For example, the 2008 Senate hearings on security policy in Santa Fe Province were interrupted by citizen protests that "there are no human rights" for detainees and demands that the police "directly kill" them.[46] Such sentiments are also apparent in the growing support for reducing the age of legal responsibility to 14 years (a proposal favored by up to 70 percent of poll respondents),[47] to place more restrictions on probation, and to increase the punishment for adults who use minors in criminal activities.

And yet one of the benefits of Argentine federalism is the many realms in which such debates can be inserted into policies and laws that attempt to balance competing views. For example, Santa Fe formed militarized Special Operations Troops and Crime Victim Centers in 2008, and earlier, in 2007, Córdoba announced plans for both a heavily armed and tough-sounding Immediate Persecution Command (Comando de Persecución Inmediata, CPI) and a community policing program. How those units perform and interact would serve as good case studies of the relationship between traditional and problem-oriented policing. Federalism also means that the more substantial of those changes has a fair chance of taking root somewhere. Not many provinces have been able to introduce ambitious reforms and see them through the ongoing setbacks as well. The three that have—Buenos Aires, Mendoza, and La Rioja—are discussed in the rest of this section. Although the progress and results of these reforms remain tentative, these

46. "La seguridad en debate tras un acto polémico en el Senado provincia," *DERF-Agencia Federal de Noticias,* June 9, 2008.
47. Centro de Estudios Nueva Mayoría, May 2002; poll sampled 842 residents of greater Buenos Aires.

three otherwise different provinces provide evidence of Argentina's larger potential for change.

Buenos Aires

Buenos Aires Province has been the setting for one of the biggest show-downs between traditional and problem-oriented policing in Latin America. Though not a country, it has exhibited nearly all the complexities described in chapter 2 of national reform. By far Argentina's largest province and home to one-third of the national population, Buenos Aires also has its largest police force—the 55,000-strong agency commonly known as the Bonearense. Since the mid-1990s the Bonearense has undergone turbulent change, beginning with an overhaul that collapsed and was then revived with strategies to avoid its earlier policy and political mistakes. Reflecting the country's larger difficulties with democratization, the drama in Buenos Aires Province was nothing new. Since the country's independence in 1983, its police force, which has a long history of corruption and abuse, has required ongoing reform. As governor from 1829 to 1852, Manuel de Rosas held most of the country under his dictatorial sway through a centralized state and a secret security force, the Mazorca, which terrorized the population. A half-century later, in the early 1900s, police units were central in crackdowns against unions, immigrants, and other agitators. The province's police became integral to the repression when national governments used it to gain and maintain power, beginning with the country's first modern military regime in the 1930s, continuing through the democratic intervals, and culminating in the 1976–83 dictatorship, when the Bonearense ran eight clandestine detention centers.

Since the return to democracy, the agency's officers have been implicated in drug trafficking, torture, bribery, extrajudicial killings, extortion, drug trafficking, "trigger-happy" shootings, and the 1994 bombing of the Argentine Israelite Mutual Association (Asociación Mutual Israelita Argentina, AMIA). As in the Federal Capital, the police have drawn much of their power from their wide range of edicts, including fifty in the 1970 Misdemeanor Code (Código de Faltas) that allowed for arrest. In addition, as Ragendorfer (2002) and Sigal, Binder, and Annicchiarico (1998) detail, the police were linked with all major criminal rings in the province, from drugs to prostitution. Thousands of officers were dismissed during the 1990s for crimes such as homicide, assault, torture, and drug trafficking. But the lack of accountability and action by the top ranks allowed extensive criminal justice abuses—such as a lack of due process protection and harsh prison conditions—to continue. External oversight bodies such as the provincial Human Rights Commissions were weak, as was the education on human rights offered by the police academies. Keeping these agencies on the defensive was the government's *mano dura* policy, which had widespread support as the rate of violent crime rose from 39.7 reports per 10,000 persons in 1987 to 111.4 in 1995 and 212.4 in 2000. Crime was particularly violent in the *conurbano,* which registered 156.5 crimes per 10,000 persons in 1997 (Sain 2001, 85). Support for *mano dura* hardened during this period, driven in part by former Proceso figures who were now police officials in local *comisarías.* Although backing for the hard line then diminished as it failed to reduce crime, officials were unable to take advantage of this shift to try to make changes to an inefficient administration that weighed down the police. In particular, up until the 1997 reform about half the force was thought to be working mostly on legal procedures and incarceration. Very little effort went into prevention, even as economic conditions called for more effort in this area. This lack of planning, administrative rationale, and officer specialization together turned the force, in the words of one official, into a "de facto penal system."[48]

Action was finally taken when this untenable combination of rampant crime, abuse, inefficiency, and corruption began to impinge on the presidential candidacy of Gov. Eduardo Duhalde. After the legislature, at his request, declared a state of emergency in December 1996, the government split the unitary police force into preventive and judicial bodies, fired over two hundred officers, and formed a judicial police. A new penal process code altered the slow, biased, and inaccessible criminal justice system by shifting the control of investigations to the prosecutor through a Law of Public Ministry (Ley de Ministerio Público), thereby creating a new level of judges (*jueces de garantías*) to oversee detainee rights and bolster individual liberties such as by prohibiting information-gathering on citizens that was unrelated to criminal investigations. But the reform was immediately resisted and diluted by the police, mayors, local officials, and Peronist party operatives. The victory of the opposition Alianza Party in the October 1997 elections created a second front of opposition from the political left, which asserted that the reforms did not go far enough. The governor was then forced back to the drawing board.

In December 1997 Duhalde unveiled a more expansive reform that effectively dissolved the entire police force. He dismissed nearly five thou-

48. Anonymous police official, interview by author, La Plata, August 22, 2002.

sand officers, established a Secretariat of Justice and Security, and named León Arslanián to lead it as the civilian secretary of justice and secretary. Arslanián, a judge in the historic 1980s trials against the former military dictators, was serving as chief of the Security and Criminal Policy Institute (Instituto de Política Criminal y Seguridad, IPCS), which oversaw the changes. In addition to forming transport, investigative, and criminal detainee units, the reform distributed the core police body—the preventive 35,000-officer Security Police—among the province's eighteen judicial departments, each run by an official directly accountable to the province's civilian secretary of justice and security. The reform dissolved special brigades such as the one on narco-trafficking, whose relative autonomy fostered abuse. Thus, unlike under the old structure, in which a police chief headed a single hierarchy of nine departments, the new force was divided into five separate entities run by a civilian chief. Perhaps most significant, Law 12.154 of July 1998 created citizen forums at the neighborhood, municipal, and departmental levels. The neighborhood forums (*foros vecinales*) were designed to encourage participation, channel complaints, and formulate preventive actions. The municipal forums, focusing on policy development, were composed of representatives of the mayor's office, the city council, the neighborhood forum, and other local and religious organizations. The other new position created was the *defensor municipal de seguridad,* a local official elected by the municipal forums to coordinate activities. The provincial legislature also formed a Congressional Bicameral Commission (Laws 12.068 and 12.069), Office of Control of Corruption and Abuse (Oficina de Control de la Corrupción y Abuso Funcional), and Office of Evaluation of Information for Crime Prevention (Dirección General de Evaluación de Información para la Prevención del Delito) to develop intelligence and crime prevention policy and to investigate police abuses.[49]

But these changes did not reach into the inner workings of the police. As Dutil and Ragendorfer (2005) describe, the governor provided diminishing cover for his own reforms as the threat the security issue posed to his political career ebbed. Reflecting the shallow institutional reach of the reforms was a lack of basic follow-up. For example, the police force's particularly powerful and corrupt special units (such as those for narco-trafficking,

---

49. The Oficina de Control de la Corrupción y Abuso Funcional comprised an Internal Affairs Auditor (Auditor de Asuntos Internos) and an Ethics Court (Tribunal de Ética). The Operative Group of Complex Investigations and Narco-criminality (Grupo Operativo de Investigaciones Complejas y Narcocriminalidad) was formed to reengineer drug policy, such as by focusing police action on consumption as well as sales.

fraud, and the AMIA investigation) were dissolved and replaced by the Complex Investigations Unit (Unidad de Investigaciones Complejas, UIC). But the UIC's organizational regulations were not put into place, and, as Annicchiarico (1998, 78–79) points out, continuation of poor training and confused laws undercut UIC's functioning. Above all, upon the enactment of reform the top officers, angered by the mass dismissals, began organizing against it. Aided by Peronist officials, they exposed internal rifts within the party, as well as its connections to networks of corruption. Violent retributions among the police spread to the population, and the number of civilians killed by the police shot up from 120 in 1998 to over 200 in 1999. Poor administration also slowed down change. Between 30 and 35 percent of officers continued to work on administrative and minor matters, and only 47 percent were assigned to the *conurbano,* even though it had 64 percent of the population and 67 percent of reported crimes. Meanwhile, the executive never sent the legislature the promised bill that would have replaced the police personnel law that was created during the Proceso. Only 22 of the province's 134 municipalities elected *defensores municipales de seguridad,* only 102 of 330 *comisarías* established neighborhood forums, and not a single departmental forum was formed. In the criminal justice system the lack of material and human resources slowed the transference of power to and the training of prosecutors, allowing police control over criminal investigations to continue. The Office of Evaluation of Information for Crime Prevention was not established, preventing adoption of crime mapping and related approaches. The Auditor de Asuntos and the Tribunal de Ética were created, but they were duly ignored by the police. In short, many of the police's most corrupt and dysfunctional agencies had been dismantled, but, lacking better oversight, more training, and bigger budgets—at least six times bigger, analysts recommended—their practices were not.

Within a few years the police and political resistance latched onto climbing crime rates to bring the reform crashing down under Duhalde's successor. The antireform backlash had gone all the way to the top, fueling the victory in the 1999 governor's race of Peronist candidate and national vice president Carlos Ruckauf. Ruckauf ran on a campaign platform of "Bullets for Murderers" and justified police killings with the assertion that "the bullet that kills the delinquent" is "society's response to the bullet that kills innocent people."[50] Duhalde's implicit acceptance of Ruckauf's attack on progressive change prompted the resignation of Arslanián, whose replace-

---

50. Eduardo Oteiza, "Consecharás tempestades," *Clarín,* August 8, 1999.

ment was associated with the dismissed police officers. Thus just a few months after the forums began meeting in October 1999, security policy took a complete about-face. Ruckauf even appointed Aldo Rico, a right-wing former military official who led a military uprising against the trials of the former junta leaders in the 1980s, as chief of security. As a provincial police official in the 1990s, Rico had the support of many other former dictatorship officials cum *comisarios* with his position that "it is necessary to kill [delinquents] in the street without any doubt and without having pity."[51] Amid continuing jumps in crime, with robbery and assault rising 46 percent between 1997 and 1999, the new administration rode a popular wave of support for a return to a policy of *mano dura*. Among other things, it restricted bail and widened the powers of the police to question prisoners and to conduct random searches.[52] The 2001 economic implosion and subsequent political changes again shook up the province. Amid rising criminal violence, angry mobs attacked police stations and killed officials suspected of involvement in kidnappings and other abuses. Disillusionment among the police also grew, prompting a *conurbano* police chief to publicly accuse President Duhalde of leaving the force "in rags."[53]

But with economic stabilization and the election of reformers in 2003 (despite the presidential candidates backing the right-wing candidates), the government of Felipe Solá (2002–7) regained the initiative. Arslanián, the architect of the ill-fated 1997–98 reform, was reappointed security chief, and he reintroduced the reform in April 2004 through a "new paradigm" based on citizen empowerment and a radically different police structure. He proclaimed that the structure amounted to nothing less than "the abandonment by the heads of the province in the formulation of security policies."[54] First, the police force was completely restructured (again). The official and subofficial hierarchies were fused and the number of ranks compressed from seventeen to nine. More radically, the police's entire structure was turned on its side when operative control was transferred to its thirty-two

51. "El carapintada por la boca muere," *Página/12,* March 10, 1998, 12.

52. "Quieren usar custodios privados para prevenir y reprimir delitos," *Clarín,* July 28, 1999, 38. In February 1999 the provincial government formulated a plan to increase from twenty-four hours to forty-eight hours the time the police could hold someone detained for identification, and to make it easier for the police to carry out inspections without court authorization.

53. Julio César Frutos, commissioner major, Jefe Departamental de Quilmes, "Carta abierta de un policía al Sr. Presidente," letter provided by police officers on condition on anonymity, July 2002.

54. Interview by author, Lima, Peru, April 1, 2007, and Buenos Aires, July 26, 2007.

departmental headquarters. Law 13.210 created the Communal Police (Policías Comunales) and placed it in charge of all *comisarías* in municipalities with populations under seventy thousand. Resolution 1625/04 created Security Districts and District Police (Policías de Distrito) for municipalities with populations of over seventy thousand. The District Police are now run by a chief and an Evaluation Cabinet composed of police officers from different operational areas, such as investigation. To respond to the *conurbano*'s particularly high levels of criminal violence, Law 13.202 of 2004 created the Buenos Aires 2 police to work exclusively in the area of criminal violence, paying greater attention to violent crime and providing stricter oversight in areas such as human rights, thereby giving this unit more freedom from distracting responsibilities such as guarding specific persons or buildings.

Human and material resources were reorganized as well. Civilians were incorporated into the hierarchy, and long-denied personnel payments such as for overtime were brought into the salary scale (through Laws 13.201, 13.202, and 13.210). An emergency line and a telephone connection to the Subsecretariat of Community Participation were also set up. Education was strengthened through formation of the Center for Advanced Studies in Police Specialties (Centro de Altos Estudios en Especialidades Policiales, CAEEP), composed of six schools in the province working with local universities and Departmental Retraining Centers (Centros de Reentrenamiento Departamentales). In 2004 the province established the Technological School in Public Security for more advanced training for graduates of the Juan Vucetich Police School, the main academy for provincial officers, which itself was revamped under the Solá government. Finally, to facilitate the use of crime mapping, a CompStat system—System of Geographic Information (SIG) and System of Special Analysis for the Construction of Maps —was installed.

Accountability, critical to any Bonaerense reform, was strengthened by means of an internal affairs office (Auditoría General de Asuntos Internos) empowered to receive and investigate citizen complaints. Under this system, police superiors decide on misconduct directly related to an officer's duties, such as tardiness or failing to obey orders, whereas the Auditoría investigates cases of corruption or abuse, deciding whether a formally accused officer, who has thirty days to present a defense, continues in the force.[55] Its staff of

55. Máximo Zitti, director, Apoyo Tecnología y de Análisis de Información, interview by author, La Plata, July 20, 2007.

about two hundred civilians receives about fifteen reports a day (about a third through e-mail) of police misconduct. Based on investigation of those reports, an increasing number of officers have been expelled, the majority for corrupt acts such as extortion, physical coercion, and bribes. The unit also undertakes accountability actions that are broader and more preventive than those undertaken by most other units in Argentina and the rest of Latin America. For example, it conducts patrimonial investigations of officers' finances, and uses its Automatic Vehicle Location system to monitor the 4,500 police cars in the *conurbano*. Using this power, the Auditoría is able to extend accountability beyond answerability and punishment to actual eradication of the root causes of abuse. Compared with the evaporating accountability of the 1997 reforms, most residents, when asked, say that under these reforms the police are more restrained or are at least circumspect about their illicit activities.

With such controls in place, the government has been able to carefully expand some of the police force's authority. In December 2005, for example, the province disregarded federal opposition and responded to a great "social demand for a quicker response" to drugs by giving the Bonaerense control over detentions for minor drug violations.[56] In fact, because of the *conurbano*'s high crime rate, traditional policing has been unavoidable. In November 2003 President Duhalde ordered security forces into three of the province's highest-crime areas. In an unprecedented show of control in the democratic era, 400 Bonaerense officers occupied the *villa* Carlos Gardel, 350 National Prefect officers took over the *villa* La Cara, and 500 gendarmes moved into the *barrio* Ejército de los Andes. Although residents complained of police abuses, as they do in other *villas,* the operations did eliminate illegal drug trafficking and other crime in these areas. "We were resentful of the police when they first came," said one resident in Carlos Gardel on condition of anonymity during a meeting with federal civilian officials in June 2004. "But we are glad that they got rid of the delinquents—our lives are more peaceful now." According to the police, though, this and other provincial *villas* continue to be crime hot spots, particularly for kidnapping and car robbery. Many officers acknowledge that, as in the *villas* in the Capital Federal, preventive social services are clearly needed for lasting change.

Most of all, reform in Buenos Aires boosted citizen power and participation beyond that associated with almost every other regional reform. Based

56. Roberto Silva, comandante and head of drug operations, Policía de la Provincia, interview by author, La Plata, July 2007.

on this potential, many forums continued to meet during the four years in which reform remained on the back burner, helping to galvanize new ones after 2004. The "rights" of citizens to participate in the "elaboration, implementation and control of public security politics," as guaranteed in Article 11 of Law 12.154, began to be exercised through the neighborhood, municipal, and departmental forums, as well as through the municipal security *defensores* elected by the municipal forums to coordinate activities. Instead of serving merely as an extension of the police or a sop to community activists, as in other countries, these forums have substantial legal authority. In particular, the neighborhood forums were given a great deal of control over evaluation in four broad areas of citizen security: (1) identifying the causes and locations of crime; (2) controlling and monitoring policing; (3) pursuing situational prevention by developing programs on school safety, public space, family violence, and other socioeconomic problems; and (4) improving criminal justice by forming committees that correspond to the province's eighteen judicial departments. In the first area, the causes and locations of crime are documented in reports, meetings, and crime maps drawn up for the Subsecretariat of Investigations and Criminal Intelligence (Subsecretaría de Investigaciones e Inteligencia Criminal) and CompStat meetings. In the second area, policing is controlled and monitored mainly by developing criteria, issuing reports, and writing evaluations of officers that become part of the annual review of the Professional Certification Unit. As part of that responsibility, the municipal forums help the police chief oversee the Communal Police and to design Integral Plans of Municipal Security. The third area of forum action, linking situational prevention to economics, is one of the reform's most predominant and catalyzing features. The Security Secretariat is constantly referencing the province's excluded sectors—youth, the critically poor who make up about 12 percent of the population, and the informal sector, which makes up about 40 percent of laborers.[57] In the fourth area, the committees formed that correspond to the province's eighteen judicial departments[58] have markedly increased citizen access to justice by helping to decentralize the Fiscalía and simplifying the process of filing a crime report.

A host of programs support these areas of work. In 2005 the program Control and Evaluation of the Response, Quality, and Attitude of the Local

57. Martha María Arriola, subsecretary of community participation, Ministerio de Seguridad, Provincia de Buenos Aires, interview by author, Buenos Aires, July 19, 2007.
58. Districts are divided into civil, commercial, family, labor, administrative, penal, and minors areas.

Police Service (Control y Evaluación de Respuesta, Calidad y Actitud del Servicio de Policía Local, CERCA) began to train citizens in evaluation methodologies, and the province's Multiple Response Program (Programa de Respuesta Múltiple, PRM) helps communities develop prevention-based strategies focused on social conditions in the province's poorest areas. But the main areas for citizen action, which are widely regarded as the heart of the province's reform, are the Schools of Community Participation in Security (Escuelas de Participación Comunitaria en Seguridad). The first school opened with two hundred students in August 2005 in Quilmes, a low-income municipality south of the Capital Federal known for its killings and abuse by police. Since then, five other schools have opened around the province, bringing together 350 community organizations, nearly 450 forum members, and hundreds of additional participants. During a year of instruction using different modules, the schools educate citizens in policy, pedagogy, and policing.

Beyond their specific policy and evaluation tasks, the appeal of the forums is that they serve as open spaces of civil society to increase citizen confidence, enable general analysis of government functioning, and facilitate the exchange of experiences. They are something profoundly new, emphasizes one of their chiefs, aiming at no less than the "reconstruction of the social fabric."[59] They try to get people to "think in the first rather than the third person," in the words of one participant—that is, to claim ownership of the security issue through diagnosis, planning, execution, and policy evaluation, while minimizing political interference and strengthening the existing community power and resources. The forums, then, are designed to solve rather than simply respond to problems—an approach, in the wake of the 2001 crisis, perfectly attuned to the prevailing national mood.

How this fusion of policy power and open-ended participation plays out is on view at forum events. At one meeting in Lomas de Zamora, an impoverished high-crime district, engagement was both wide and strong, with residents from different walks of life exhibiting detailed knowledge of crime trends and social conditions. "A photocopy of Law 12.154 arrived in our hands, and when we read it we were very surprised," said one resident to explain the area's high turnout. We realized that "we found something quite distinct." Many studies of participatory budgeting in Latin America see socioeconomic differences as a hindrance to participation. But the vis-

59. Néstor Borri, executive secretary, Centro Nueva Tierra (New Land Center), interview by author, Buenos Aires, July 18, 2007.

ible signs of such division have been minimized in Buenos Aires Province —in part because of the extent to which the 2001 crisis diminished everyone's economic standing as well as the social standing of anyone with "experience." Bringing together citizen forums with groups such as the chambers of commerce, the Lomas de Zamora area held an extraordinary 998 meetings from the beginning of 2006 to the middle of 2007.

What residents have found particularly useful about these meetings is the ability to put into place multiple responses to security problems. For example, a citizen-initiated study of detained youth revealed that a majority of them had not completed elementary school, leading to the enactment of new education programs. The citizens' forum also updates crime maps and places notebooks at different locations along officers' routes for them to sign, helping to ensure that they keep to their assigned patrols. Perhaps most telling of the reform's impact, residents now say that they are more inclined to call the police station when there is a problem—a big change from the past and a basis for the connection between such a citizen initiative and actual policy that has been absent in many reforms. For example, the robbing and dismantling of cars—one of the area's most persistent forms of illegal activity—has been reduced through raids on car shops, often as a result of anonymous calls. Nearly a hundred of these shops have been closed, and, more important, they have not been replaced.

The combination of structural decentralization and citizen organizing has also greatly enhanced the power of municipal governments and opened the way for local efforts beyond provincial laws. In smaller cities, the chiefs of the communal police have been chosen since 2007 through local elections —an unusual but very powerful tool of citizen power. In addition, many of the province's larger cities have devoted more resources to prevention. Morón, La Plata, and Ituzaingo have responded to social demands with programs such as youth centers, free telephone lines, and the placement of law student interns in police stations.[60] The city of Ituzaingo also opened a Municipal Center of Assistance to Victims of Insecurity (Centro Municipal de Asistencia a Víctimas de la Inseguridad) that included medical and legal facilities. Most notably, Morón's mayor Martín Sabbatella—who was from the Frepaso political coalition and upon election in 1999 became one of the province's few large-city mayors independent of the Peronist party machine —allowed city facilities to be used for after-school youth programs and civil

60. Police officials and youth, Morón, Ituzaingo, and La Plata, interviews by author, June 2004, February 2005, and July 2007.

rights seminars. Like "violence interrupters" in the high-crime neighborhoods of Chicago, discussed in the next chapter, much of the impact of these
centers has come from their ability to end cycles of retribution by helping
defuse tensions. For example, nearly everyone at a meeting of teenagers in
Morón could recount recent confrontations with police officers, but said that
having this space helped them either to file formal complaints or at least to
let off some steam.[61]

In other areas local leaders facilitate ongoing meetings. Most of the
Almirante Brown municipality, for example, is divided into sectors, each of
which has a neighborhood team and a police team that hold monthly or bimonthly meetings to discuss area problems.[62] Many *barrios* within the municipality have developed security plans that take on a full plate of issues,
from discrimination to drug trafficking, through policy innovation and
mechanisms of evaluation. Most notably, these plans do not seem to shy
away from actions that might upend long-standing social or institutional relations. For example, they talk about violence among residents, which always carries the potential for embarrassment or discomfiture, and the lack
of police response to information provided by residents, which challenges
police power. In a reversal of traditional policing and even many community policing forums around the region, one resident used large maps to il-
lustrate for the *comisaría* how drug use was spilling over from one neighborhood to the next.

Widening citizen action, however, invariably bumps up against a triad of
politics, economics, and bureaucracy, which tends to be stronger in the industrialized urban settings that make up most regions such as Buenos Aires
Province. For example, forum analysis of "situational prevention" has
pointed to the provincial train system as a major source of insecurity, characterized by the physical deterioration of and the ongoing criminal activity
in both the stations and the trains. Because the railroad is run by metropolitan concessionaires (*concesionarios metropolitanos*) and not by the municipalities or even the provincial government, citizens had to go through
different channels to exert pressure for change, which required more work.

In the criminal justice system, persistent problems include confusion
over judicial processes, unclear administrative responsibilities, and delays
in warrants for raids and for preventive arrests. "When we file a crime re-

61. Municipal officials and youth, Morón, interviews by author, May 21, 2004.
62. Karina Valegas, lieutenant, Almirante Brown, interview by author, Almirante
Brown, July 23, 2007.

port," complained several citizens at a meeting, "we also become victims of the bureaucracy." They cited, for example, the problem that several *comisaría* jurisdictions overlap in certain blocks, creating confusion for their residents about whom to contact. Many goals of the local projects, admitted one police official, were far from being reached because of such bureaucratic impediments and the resulting dissuasion among residents.[63] Even efforts with strong local support and government money are obstructed by local politics. In the San José area of Almirante Brown, for example, residents who developed a disarmament program were surprised by the lack of will by local officials, who, they say, were too "tied in" to local police officials who were resistant to sharing responsibility on this issue with citizens.[64]

The broader economic conditions are even farther beyond citizen control than the political conditions. Buenos Aires Province has about one-third of the national population, but most of its poverty and over half of its homicides. The general unemployment in metro Buenos Aires is higher than in all of Argentina's other urban areas (Ministero de Economía 2002). Youth unemployment and delinquency continue to be huge burdens for both society and the criminal justice system. Between 1992 and 2002, for example, the court cases involving minors in the provincial judiciary—which has forty-six minor courts—rose 92 percent.[65] In an attempt to deal with these increasing numbers, in 2007 the province dissolved the minor courts and replaced them with thirty-five Courts of Juvenile Penal Responsibility (Juzgados de Responsabilidad Penal Juvenil) and forty-three Courts of Youth Guarantees (Juzgados de Garantías del Joven), each with teams of social workers and the provision that anyone detained for over 180 days without trial must be freed.[66]

Argentina's wide gap between rich and poor is also on clear display in the province, perhaps most visibly in the growth of private security and

63. Roberto Castronuovo, district chief, Lomas de Zamora, interview by author, Lomas de Zamora, July 27, 2007.

64. Margarita Gandolfo, president, Foro Vecinal de Seguridad Almirante Brown, interview by author, July 24, 2007.

65. Most of that increase is attributed to a corresponding rise in unemployment, from 19.7 percent in 1990 to 34 percent in 2000 for the 15–19 age group (Encuesta Permanante de Hogares, Instituto Nacional de Estadística y Censos, Ministero de Economía). According to SIEMPRO, 47 percent of minors are impoverished, nearly double the 25 percent of the overall population (Dirección General de Prevención Comunitaria de la Violencia 2004).

66. "No va más para los Tribunales de Menores en la Provincia ante puesta en vigencia del Fuero Juvenil," noticiasmercedinas.com, February 3, 2007.

gated communities. About 80 percent of the 450 suburban gated communities in Buenos Aires were built since 1995, when crime began to spike. Among the largest and newest of them are the "garden towers," which house up to 600,000 residents. Between 1991 and 2001 up to 90 percent of both new urban housing and single detached suburban homes were in gated communities, which made up over 10 percent of the suburban share and about 25 percent of upper-income residences (Janoschka 2002). A large percentage of these and other residences hire private firms or are built with private security as a main draw. The province has nearly 900 registered private security agencies with over 45,000 employees, although most estimates put the number of private officers at 70,000, about 25,000 of whom work illegally or as independent contractors.[67]

The ongoing shortfalls in public security have increased citizens' reliance on private security. For example, in the late 1990s cities such as La Matanza hired private firms for basic patrols (Lozada 1998, 51), and in December 2006 the provincial legislature passed a law allowing only private security guards to guard bars and nightclubs—primarily, many observers say, because of the high levels of corruption found when the police guard such businesses. Such legislation is rooted in Law 12.297 of 1999, which regulates the province's private security firms but explicitly promotes a central role for them in crime prevention. Even the tenants in many middle-class buildings who cannot afford to hire a firm will pool their money to pay local officers for protection—in effect, a privatization of public security.[68] Although violent crime has fallen in many areas, highly publicized incidents such as armed robberies of crowded restaurants keep public fear of crime high. Believing such crimes are possible only with police collusion, more businesses, especially services such as markets and banks, have turned to private firms.[69]

Because it frees up some responsibility for the public police, private security also allows better-off areas to solidify their generally positive relations with the police. The wealthy Buenos Aires provincial enclave of San

67. "En la Provincia de Buenos Aires, solo los agentes de seguridad privada podrán custodiar boliches y bares," *Clarín,* December 22, 2006. In the Capital Federal many public officers also work in paid private law enforcement.

68. Ibid.

69. Private personnel in the city are paid up to 50 percent more than the state police. Roberto Sausa, president, Seguridad Magnum, interview by author, Buenos Aires, October 24, 1994. See also Cámara Argentina de Empresas de Seguridad e Investigación, http://www.caesi.org.ar.

Isidro, for example, has a community participation group, weekly meetings with the police, and formal agreements of collaboration among municipal services on security issues. By contrast, some poorer *conurbano* districts have seen few changes in the course of provincial reform. In the middle of San Isidro, for example, is Barrio La Cava, a *villa* of carton houses, open sewers, and very tense relations with the local police. Another poor but more organized low-income area is Quilmes, which embraced reform early on and formed the first School of Community Participation in Security. But its residents still complain of ongoing police violence and anemic citizen participation, saying they have seen little improvement. Since their formation, in fact, Buenos Aires 2 agents have shot unarmed youths on several occasions. Many citizens say that such "trigger-happy" incidents, one of the biggest abuses of the Bonaerense and a main target of the reform, cannot be ended simply by a new agency whose agents receive only sixty-four hours of rights training. Moreover, many people in Quilmes and other areas fear becoming involved in any forum, because they say it would identify them, to both police and criminals, as possibly being complicit in corruption. Thus even broad structural and judicial reform may leave corruption intact. Many residents also dismiss those who are active in the forums as interested in using them only to get involved in local politics. "One of our biggest challenges is how the citizens organize," says one Quilmes resident, "since without organization is it impossible to change politics."

Mendoza

Like Buenos Aires, other provinces have had to confront long-standing tensions, patterns, and injustices as they try to move their security systems in a new direction. Mendoza, an Andean province and Argentina's fifth most populous, long had the country's second-highest crime rate and one of its worst records of police abuse in the postdemocratic era. According to one estimate, Mendoza's crime rate tripled between 1991 and 2001 (Arland 2002); another estimate says it more than doubled between 1993 and 2003.[70] Between 1986 and 1996 Mendoza had four times the number of reported cases of police violence per capita than notorious Buenos Aires Province and nearly seven times the number of nearby Córdoba Province.[71] Within its

70. Based on 2004 reports by the MJSDH, as discussed in Pérez (2004, 78–83).

71. Mendoza had one police killing of civilians per 48,676 residents, Buenos Aires Province one per 212,371, and Córdoba Province one per 325,526. *Revista Noticias,*

Table 6.1 Number of Crimes per 100,000 Inhabitants, Mendoza Province, Selected Years, 1987–2005

	1987	1989	1993	1994	1996	1997	1999	2000	2004	2005
Total	132.1	209.0	282.1	312.0	387.8	427.6	566.3	570.3	552	594.2
Capital	n.a.	n.a.	657.8	656.8	921.2	1,112.6	n.a.	n.a.	n.a.	n.a.

Sources: 1987–2004: Gorri, Lecaro, and Repetto. (2003); 2004–5: http://www.indec.gov.ar/nuevaweb/cuadros/8/z030601.xls.
Note: "n.a." indicates data were not available.

highly militarized structure established in 1983, the 6,297-strong provincial police was divided into a command force, an administrative support force, and several special units.[72] But there were serious rifts within the police, caused, as one of the chiefs at the time explained, by citizen distrust of the force that grew along with the crime rates (Vargas 1995). For its part, the province's hapless judiciary was plagued by a perennial overload of cases, poor salaries, and a lack of training and technology.[73] The combination of police and judicial inefficiency also led to greater recidivism, whose rate rose from 21 percent in 1992, which was 4.5 percent less than the national average that year, to a rate that was well over the national average by 2006—although the police, judges, legislators, and the governor's office have different estimates. In addition, at any given time about half of the province's criminal detainees were awaiting trial in its two antiquated and inhumanely overcrowded prisons. After some physical improvements in 1983, there were none again until the legislature approved in 1994 the construction of a new facility, which quickly become overpopulated. Not surprisingly, Mendocinos' evaluation of their government's security record is withering. In a 2004 poll that asked about the most problematic part of the government,

---

November 8, 1997, 1–26. In April 1990 Adolgo Garrido and Raúl Baigorria "disappeared" and were killed by the police; in 1992 Armando Neme, Carlos Ross, and Paulo Guaradatti were killed by the police; in 1993 Egardo Muñoz was killed by a police agent after a football party; in 1996 Luis Gómez died after being pursued by the police, and Hugo Gómez Romagnoli was shot in the back by a "trigger-happy" agent.

72. Laws 4697 and 4747. The command force is responsible for security and functioning as an auxiliary to the judiciary, and the support force serves as an auxiliary to the command force. Under increasing pressure for more security by society, in 1997 the government revived the Special Security Group (Grupo Especial de Seguridad, GES), a twenty-five-officer division with commando training for especially serious conflicts.

73. Up until the mid-1990s the average criminal trial lasted twenty months (Tappatá, Binstein, and Farhi 1997).

53.78 percent of respondents cited security, followed a distant second by salaries (12.89 percent).[74]

By maintaining control over all areas of citizen security—from criminal policy to the police and prisons—governors and the Government Ministry were able to head off attempts at reform for many years. But in 1995 crime began to top corruption and even record unemployment as Mendocinos' biggest worry; about 60 percent of those polled felt unprotected and underserved and blamed the police and courts.[75] As public trust in the police rapidly eroded, it took the convergence of more abuse, a crime wave, and police rebellions to finally push through actual reform. In October 1997 the death of Sebastián Bordón, a Buenos Aires youth on a graduation trip to Mendoza, exposed cover-ups, hidden evidence, public deception, and possibly homicide by the police, prompting Peronist governor Arturo Lafalla (1995–99) to dismiss the government minister, the police chief, the subchief, and various top officers.[76] Lafalla was particularly incensed by the police's fabricated evidence that the young man was not in the province.[77] Faced with unfavorable national attention and just one more year in office, in early 1998 Lafalla formulated the Strategic Plan of Security and Prevention of "Anti-Social" Conduct (Plan Estratégico de Seguridad y Prevención de Conducta Anti-Social), which envisaged a clearer penal code, a stronger Fiscalía, and community policing programs around the province. In October, along with increase in the criminal justice budget, bills to reform the penal and penal process codes were introduced.

74. "Las opiniones políticas de los mendocinos," *Los Andes,* July 20, 2004.

75. Telesurvey, Opinión Pública, Empresa Heriberto Murano, 1995. In a June 1998 telephone poll of a 1,200-person cross section of the province, crime was the biggest concern expressed (Gorri, Lecaro, and Repetto 2003). In another June 1998 poll 14 percent of respondents said that crime and insecurity were their biggest concerns, followed by education with 13 percent, corruption with 12 percent, and unemployment with 9 percent—even though the provincial unemployment rate had reached nearly 15 percent (Telesurvey, Opinión Pública, Empresa Herberto Murano).

76. "Cómplices del silencio," *Revista Noticias,* October 18, 1997, 132.

77. Arturo Lafalla, governor, Mendoza Province (1995–99), interview by author, June 3, 2004. Public outrage at Bordón's death led the government to reopen the case of Paulo Christian Guardatti, a young man who was detained by a police officer in the province on May 23, 1992, after an altercation between the two, and then he was never seen again. Lafalla's government subsecretary revoked an earlier resolution declaring a "lack of merit" in the initial accusations against eight officers involved in Guardatti's disappearance, and the governor acknowledged the state's responsibility. See also Almada and Licht (2001).

Few steps were taken toward structural reform of the police, however, because the rising crime rate—which jumped by a quarter in some years in the late 1990s—made legislators cautious. Meanwhile, most top police officials opposed the penal reforms as an attempt to limit their authority, and they were not mollified by increases in their budgets. Following an assault on a police contingent in a failed bank robbery, the legislature approved two executive bills to increase punishment for carrying illegal arms and to strengthen criminal witness protection laws, and the executive released five hundred of the some twelve hundred police personnel working in administration.[78] But, as often happens in attempts at police reform, the situation had become too politicized for either side to step down unilaterally. Grievances had been building for years among an underpaid, overworked, and poorly equipped police force that was feeling increasingly squeezed by a society and state demanding better results but unwilling to commit the resources to provide them. Their resentment was fully manifested in October 1998 when a large contingent of officers marched on the provincial legislature, impelling all officers to walk off the job and hand the government a long set of demands that included a salary hike, more equipment and personnel, an eight-hour workday, compensation for overtime and seniority, participation in any reform (a perennial grievance in many provinces), suspension of protection of private businesses, and a more formalized personnel hierarchy (Salomón 2008, 3).

After an uneasy agreement brought the police back on duty, the province's main political parties—the Peronists, the Partido Demócrata Mendoza (Mendoza's Democratic Party), and the Alianza—forged a strategic plan that emphasized citizen participation and victim rights. Despite its lofty principles, the agreement was nevertheless a closed one among the parties, without any direct participation of police, criminal justice officials, or NGOs. Although a restricted set of negotiators might reduce the impediments facing reformers, in the long run it can undermine change by giving major actors like the lower ranks little stake in it. At the end of December 1998, the agreement materialized into Laws 6642, 6651, 6652, and 6653, which created a civilian-led Ministry of Justice and Security over all security and criminal justice issues. The positions of police chief and subchief were abolished, and they were replaced in part by the Council of Public Security (Consejo de

---

78. The government, according to a senator, "could not be seen to be out of step with the social demands channeled through the media and the opinion polls." Alfredo Guevara, senator, interview by author, Mendoza, August 13, 2002.

Seguridad Pública). A year later the legislature approved a Public Security and Police Law (Law 6721, Sistema Provincial de Seguridad Pública de la Provincia de Mendoza, and Law 6722, Ley de Policías de la Provincia de Mendoza), which decentralized the police into four district police units, corresponding to the province's four judicial districts (Gran Mendoza, Valle de Uco, Sur, and Este). Each was headed by a government-appointed district security chief.[79] A Liaison Unit (Unidad de Enlace) was created to coordinate actions by the four districts. The reform also established a judicial police force centered in the Department of Criminal Analysis (Departamento de Análisis Criminal), whose five divisions were devoted to misdemeanors, property, persons, economics, and narcotics; a Department of Inspection (Departamento de Inspección) to help carry out criminal investigations in Gran Mendoza; a Scientific Police (Policía Científica) to work with the courts on criminal investigation; a transport police; a twenty-member Detective Body (Cuerpo de Inspectores); and six special units (including motorized, bicycle, mounted, and aeronautic).

Because a central objective of the restructuring was to regain citizen confidence, the reform put nearly a thousand extra officers on the streets of Gran Mendoza and adopted programs such as Policía a Mano and Policía Puerta a Puerta that organized new officers into teams of block-by-block prevention. The reform also eliminated the distinction between the official and the subofficial corps, and it reordered the basis for promotion, placing efficiency and aptitude before seniority (Repetto and Simón 2001). It established as well a congressional bicameral security commission; neighborhood criminal justice committees, *foros vecinales;* a coordinator of security to coordinate police-society relations; and Security Councils (Consejos Departamentales de Seguridad) of municipal officials, police, and citizens. To investigate police wrongdoing, the reform created the General Inspector of Security (Inspección General de Seguridad, IGS) within the Ministry of Justice and Security.

With the weakness of the Buenos Aires reform in mind, reformers gave their structure wide powers to address public concerns and to control police behavior. The IGS is authorized to report criminal activities among the police, conduct regular inspections, receive and investigate reports of wrongdoing, assess police regulations, participate in the promotion of police offi-

---

79. The district chief heads up operations personnel and the district hierarchy, comprising a *jefatura* (top staff), *subjefatura,* and *comisarías,* as well as special units, normally answerable to the minister, working on particular operations in the district.

cers, monitor police finances, and develop new policies of police administration. In these efforts it is supported by the Disciplinary Board (Junta de
Disciplina), which prosecutes errant officers. In its first six months the IGS
made full use of these powers, receiving over one hundred reports of abuse,
conducting thirty-seven inspections, and initiating over eight hundred investigations (Arland 2000). Aiming to prevent as well as to respond to police abuse, the agency has also trained mediators and placed them in police
stations.[80]

The reform also regeared police education by replacing the Escuela de
Oficiales and the Escuela de Cadetes with a new academy, the University
Institute of Public Security (Instituto Universitario de Seguridad Pública,
IUSP), a joint effort of the government and the National University (Universidad Nacional de Cuyo) that offers a six-month training course for basic policework, a two-year technical degree, and a four-year bachelor's degree. Training for new and serving officers also has been expanded through
seven satellite academies, special IUSP courses for judicial police, and cooperative programs with other police.

The reform had the foundation for success: it was comprehensive, covered each stage of criminal justice, enjoyed at least an elite political consensus, and gave the police civilian leadership that could theoretically neutralize internal opposition.[81] The *foros vecinales* that were up and running
became a source of projects and ideas that furthered the reform, such as
alarmas comunitarias, which alert all the homes in a community about a
neighborhood robbery or other crime. Many nonpolice state programs that
also strengthened the reform included an anti–family violence project, local health centers, and an experimental School for Fathers geared toward
building parental self-esteem. The reform also led the way to greater professional support for the police, such as a new Personnel Law that made way
for the training of prison officials and so relieved the police of much of this
responsibility. Because half of police personnel do not own their own homes
and most live in high-conflict areas, one program helps them secure bank
loans at favorable rates. Even more important, say police, promotion has
become fairer. It is now based on a score of 0–20, calculated by using spe-

80. Andrés Miranda, inspector general of security, interview by author, Mendoza,
June 3, 2004.
81. As Lafalla asserted, "The more we see, the more convinced we are that this is a
plan that will have to work for all Mendocinos, as well as this and future governors." "A
pesar de la opinión de la gente, Lafalla está más convencido que nunca sobre el plan de
seguridad," *Diario Los Andes,* October 17, 1998, 2.

cific criteria such as community relations, awards, and sanctions. Seniority counts as just 30 percent of the score, which is far below the official and unofficial rates in most other provinces.

When it was first implemented, the reform spurred "ferocious resistance"[82] by a police force that, like the one in Buenos Aires, was largely left out of formation of the reform and so saw it as an attack on the force's institutional interests. More significant, the reform was eroded by the Radical Party government that was elected in 1999 and had no intention of paving the way for a policy associated with the previous Peronist administration. Although officials did not admit to deliberate sabotage, their resistance was supported by pro–*mano dura* blocs in all three government branches. Interviews with judges indicated a particularly strong resistance in the courts. For example, even though the hundred-year-old prison was built for no more than 700–900 inmates but held over 2,200, many judges dismissed both alternative mechanisms and human rights concerns by continuing to send detainees there regardless of the severity of the charges.

Equally or perhaps more damaging to the reform was the lack of visible improvements in police officers' work. Although bureaucratic rationalization was one of the primary bases of the new laws, that goal was scuppered by disputes over how many officers actually worked in administration. The Senate Security Commission, flexing its new authority over security policy, said that 40 percent of officers worked in administration, but the government security chief countered by accusing the commission of "lying" and stating that only about 5 percent did (about 300 of the province's 6,700 officers).[83] At the root of the disagreement was a dispute over methodology, because such an estimate depends on whether administrative work is measured by official tasks or by time spent on them. Another goal on which the reform and subsequent Senate proposals fell short was enlarging the force to 9,500 officers.[84] Money problems continue to hold the police force well below that number; it had reached about 7,000 by 2007. Although some of those difficulties could not be anticipated—for example, the country's fi-

82. Alejandro Salomón, secretary of security, interview by author, Mendoza, August 15, 2002.

83. Carlos Abihaggle, senator, interview with author, Mendoza, June 1, 2004.

84. In 2003 the Senate Security Commission put forth a $400 million plan to bring the police up to nine thousand officers, "apply a new judicial system," and expand the prisons to accommodate six thousand inmates. While popular, these goals were out of sync with the province's financial capacity. Sen. Carlos Abihaggle, "Plan Quinquenal," unpublished proposal, Security Commission, Senate of Mendoza.

nancial meltdown required a hiring freeze for most of 2002—the goal was still clearly unrealistic when the reform was enacted. As discussed in other chapters, it also drew attention from the more significant issues of human resources management. In Mendoza, fewer than 850 officers—just 12 percent of the force—are on patrol in any twenty-four-hour period. In addition, the police complain about a lack of basic equipment and the bureaucracy involved in trying to get more. Many *comisarios* claim that they have just one bulletproof vest for every four officers and just four radios for every one hundred.[85]

In response to the perceived political need to boost the police presence, in 2000 the provincial government did so cheaply and quickly by forming an auxiliary police, which sent its officers into the street after a rather slap-dash twenty-four-week training course. Because they were not sufficiently prepared, however, the province had to backtrack and open a school for the auxiliaries. But as the force swelled from twelve hundred to about two thousand officers, the school had a hard time correcting its practices. Another solution, then, was to steer auxiliaries toward the regular police. But those who began the process of entering the regular police were required to attend the IUSP while maintaining their regular work schedules. Because it was difficult to do both, the few dozen auxiliary officers who actually matriculated into the IUSP often did not show up for work. Between that development and the poorly trained municipal and community police, the security structure became even more chaotic.

Bringing more security officials onto the street did not, however, dent the appeal of private security. The movement toward private enterprise was already well under way in the 1990s, and between 1994 and 1997 the number of companies increased by 60 percent at the provincial level (Repetto 2002, 184). By 2007 eighty-eight private security companies, with their 5,570 officers—amounting to a parallel force—were serving 1,460 businesses and residential neighborhoods in the province. Although their sizes and specializations vary, they all seem to charge high rates. Small-business owners in the capital districts of Godoy Cruz and Guaymallén have complained about steep charges for just a basic custodian, and many of the province's well-known wineries have paid the equivalent of 55,000 bottles a year for their services (Andes Wines 2007). Despite their growth, though, the oversight of these services is irregular. The 1997 law that first set out

85. Author meeting with provincial police commissioners, Mendoza, February 21, 2006.

general regulations for private security was modified in 2005 to strengthen them, such as by allowing radio contact with state police. Since 2006, about eight firms have been closed each year for various irregularities. Only about 20 percent of the firms in operation have been accredited by the Private Enterprise Registry, and, according to a union of private guards, no more than 60 percent of them are adequately trained.[86] One guard in front of a store in the municipality of Guaymallén said that even though he tried to stay awake on the job, he often slept during his training sessions because—much like the auxiliary police officers—he was exhausted from working for "different police." Although it is common knowledge in Mendocino neighborhoods, public and private officials seem to have no idea that many of the public police are violating the prohibition against working for private firms. In one case, a woman working for both the public police and private security was finally caught after twenty years, and her case was sent to the IGS. More serious, many firms not authorized to possess firearms do so anyway. Part of this lax approach by the state certainly stems in part from its perceived need to rely on private sector. In 2007 the government signed an agreement of cooperation with the Association of Private Security Agencies.[87] And among those asked to work on the government's "anticrime plan" was the private agency headed in part by an intelligence official in Mendoza police headquarters, which had a secret detention center that "disappeared" hundreds of people during the Proceso.[88]

Criminal policy did not help reduce such confusion. Despite the creation of the Ministry of Justice and Security, citizen security policy continued to be confused, polemic, and often makeshift. In 2002 the government proposed two strong *mano dura* laws: the first to permit searches and seizures by the police without the approval of a judge, and the second to restrict release from prison in a way that would risk the "total collapse of the penal process system."[89] Although opinions by majorities of the Penal Law Commission of the Bar Association declared the two bills unconstitutional, they received strong

---

86. Marcelo Arce, "Afirman que no está capacitado el 50 percent de los vigiladotes privados," *Diario Uno,* April 23, 2007.

87. Mariana Carvajal, "Las polémicas definiciones y proyectos del Gobernador Cobos en Mendoza," *Página 12,* May 6, 2007.

88. E-mail correspondence, Pablo Salinas; Carlos Rodríguez, "Mendoza Convoca a agencias cuestionadas por sus directivos la seguridad a manos de represores," *Página 12,* May 13, 2007.

89. Diego Lavado, human rights lawyer, e-mail correspondence with author, March 21, 2003.

popular and political support. Not to be outdone, opposition party members in the legislature, citing a "collapse" of the police, petitioned to have the national gendarmes patrol the province. One national legislator demanded lowering the age of legal responsibility to 16 and advised Mendoza to follow the tough policing approach of New York City where, he claimed, people "were not allowed to walk on the main avenues after 5:00 in the afternoon."[90]

Meanwhile, the province's policy was rudderless because of the revolving door of ministers. Gov. Julio Cobos went through five security ministers during his 2003–7 administration, with each change moving policy in directions that were not thought out. In 2004 the government considered allowing municipalities to create their own armed police forces. In 2007 Cobos proposed tough new methods of law enforcement such as wiretapping, saying that "we are going to privilege life over the laws" and put "limits on rights" to combat crime. But his anticrime plan was heavily criticized for involving officials with connections to past abuses, such as the Bordón killing and the Proceso, all of which again pulled security policy into longstanding political schisms rather than keeping it above the fray.

Rights groups and opposition legislators were able to quash these proposals. But their posture remained essentially defensive, deflecting harmful laws instead of promoting progressive ones. Just as with controversial issues in any country, legal opinions and legislative debate may clarify the law, but they often do little to resolve the political tensions over it. This lack of clarity is often caused by officials who hammer away at due process and accountability as harmful to the fight against crime. Nowhere were the consequences of that attitude displayed more clearly than Mendoza's hundred-year-old prison, built for 900 prisoners but holding over 2,200 and where overcrowding, inhumane conditions, and continual riots and killings have prompted international condemnation. However, in response to a ruling by the Inter-American Court of Human Rights in 2004 in behalf of Mendoza's prisoners, the vice minister of security attacked the human right lawyers sponsoring the petition for "not being there for the victims of crime."[91]

Such administrative, political, and institutional conditions also overwhelmed the new accountability agencies. The IGS quickly became inundated with minor complaints, personnel disputes, and other cases that ex-

90. "Más sobre delitos juveniles," *Diario Uno,* August 12, 2002, 21.

91. Pablo Salinas, a lawyer who works with detainees, interviews by author, June 2004 and August 2005. See also Jorge Fernández Fojas, "No hay que politizar o usar partidariamente a la cárcel," *Los Andes,* August 14, 2005.

ceeded its capacity to process them. But efforts to separate minor administrative charges and serious accusations, which would have lightened this
load, were blocked by the government and police. The original blueprint for
the IGS included training civilian investigators, but because of the lack of
resources about 90 percent of investigations of police misconduct were carried out by police officers working in the IGS.[92] Furthermore, the IGS's
structure allowed it to become a conduit for political interference. The agency
was run by three commissioners, each named by one of the province's three
main political parties. One former IGS commissioner pointed out that these
commissioners were often going to the press and contacting legislators from
their respective parties.[93] For example, several members of the Junta de
Disciplina said that the Peronist commissioner—rewarded with the appointment after losing an election—was in constant contact with the party
during investigations, thereby compromising the integrity of both the commission and its work. Meanwhile, citizens were suspicious of the IGS not
only because of such compromises but also because they could not easily
access it—the police housed it deep inside police headquarters, which in-
timidated anyone coming with complaints. Meanwhile, because its job is to
follow up on the IGS cases, the Junta de Disciplina did not carry out much
work. In view of such institutional weakness, according to one top official,
the police chief did not feel the need to follow through on IGS actions or
recommendations. With no independent evaluation to address these concerns or to follow up on recommendations to create support mechanisms,
such as a disciplinary court or internal affairs auditor, most IGS and Junta
members have had short stints in office. Without the experience and autonomy that longtime commissioners build up, both agencies have had trouble
gaining the accountability they need.

In Mendoza, police preparation and police work need to be better integrated. As the IUSP's director acknowledges, the institute is strong on theory but weak on the types of practical questions and training that prepare
officers to prevent the existing and evolving forms of crime. In part because
of this weak education and in part because of the lure of the private sector,
only 25.5 percent of IUSP graduates work in professional police operations
(Instituto Latinoamericano de Seguridad y Democracia, 2005, 105). As a

92. Gustavo Lucero, serving IGS commissioner, interview by author, Mendoza,
June 3, 2004.
93. Jorge Vicchi, former IGS commissioner, interview by author, Mendoza, June 4,
2004.

result of all these problems, claims one official, the pool of annual IUSP applicants dwindled from the usual six hundred to fewer than one hundred.[94] And for those who do pursue long-term police careers, poor human resource management forces them to cover many aspects of policing all at once, putting them "always behind crime instead of in front of it."[95]

As for the promotion process, despite the very substantive improvements for individuals, said many officials, the lack of incentives or evaluations tied to district results has been a weak link in the overall ascension process. Several districts do publish crime maps, but even with an Office of Victim Assistance there are no comprehensive, province-wide victimization surveys. And even with a Department of Criminal Intelligence, information remains disorganized—finding a detainee's record requires going to the different courthouses, as many judges grumble.

Adding to the frustration in the courts is the stalled penal process code. The cause is mostly financial, leading one judge to deem the code a "First World reform with Third World money."[96] As in the police academies and other agencies, tight money also has exposed generational differences. According to the president of the province's Supreme Court, criminal judges and prosecutors who have been in their positions for fifteen to twenty years resist any kind of change.[97] Many others blame the police. For example, the province's district attorney said that the police are simply incapable of carrying out an investigation.[98] But police officers, by all accounts, were handed a new set of roles without enough preparation for structural change. The slow and erratic transfer of investigative responsibility to the Fiscalía, in particular, left them with continuing but unofficial control over most criminal investigations, causing a great deal of bureaucracy and frustration. Complaining that they typically were spending an entire day completing the paperwork for a dossier, many officers say that they began to back off from this role, thereby leaving this key step in the criminal justice process without clear control.[99]

94. Hugo Alberto López, subcommissioner, Policía de Mendoza, interview by author, Mendoza, August 15, 2002.

95. Hugo Duch, director, IUSP, interview by author, Mendoza, May 31, 2004.

96. Daniel Correllio, judge of instruction, interview by author, Mendoza, June 1, 2004.

97. Jorge Nanclares, president, Mendoza Supreme Court, interview by author, Mendoza, June 1, 2004.

98. Rodolfo González, attorney general, Mendoza Province, interview by author, Mendoza, June 1, 2004.

99. Carlos Puebla, subcommissioner, interview by author, Mendoza, August 16, 2002.

Community policing has also fallen behind expectations. Most of the province's high-conflict areas do not have community or other innovative forms of policing, and the citizen committees set up in other areas rarely meet. The security councils established by the 1999 provincial reform rarely meet as well, and less than half of the projected number of department security councils were set up after eight years. Rotation of officers also prevents the police-citizen bonds that underlie real community policing, particularly in view of the differences in municipal policy. As in Buenos Aires Province, mayors can have vastly different approaches to policing, so that officers moving just within the capital area may have to adjust to very different expectations. In May 2004 the lower chamber of Mendoza's legislature proposed allowing municipalities to form their own armed police forces —without mandatory training or reform—which would have multiplied the problems of poor police accountability. The mayor of the capital city pushed for this proposal, citing polls that "73 percent of people are demanding greater security," but opposition by the provincial governor eventually killed it.[100] However, reflecting the lack of control and clarity from above, the mayor of Mendoza city still went ahead and created his own "community police," who were just another poorly trained group that seemed to do little more than harass teenagers and street vendors.[101] Although they were boosted by public support and slick public relations, the community police were disbanded in 2005 after their officers killed two civilians. But since then the city and many other areas have formed new community police agencies using money received in the Emergency Law of 2008.

Nevertheless, community policing remains the pivot for change. Building their own versions of problem-oriented policing, several municipalities have enacted extensive social programs to back up the security forums and other citizen-centered provisions of the 1999 reform. For example, the mayor of the municipality of Las Heras (250,000 residents), which is the poorest part of Mendoza, enacted a set of wide-ranging changes responding to the security concerns identified by residents. Programs targeting youth truancy, alcohol consumption, and bus stops were among the municipality's well-conceived responses.[102] Each one of these projects is based on data

100. "Los intendentes radicales se pelean por el proyecto de dar armas a policías municipales," *Los Andes,* May 30, 2004, 1A-2A.

101. Author observations on patrol with the Policía Municipal, Mendoza, May 31, 2004.

102. Rubén Miranda, mayor of Las Heras, interview by author, Las Heras, June 4, 2004.

reported directly from the community (Guzmán et al. 2002). Thus both policy evaluation and citizen participation are incorporated into the reforms. Various links to the mayor's political operations led to some criticism, but this joint effort did help to publicize activities, galvanize volunteers, and bring in other social services.

Together, such local developments may also help tip the balance in Mendoza's continuing swings between traditional and problem-oriented policing. Despite its vacillation, the Cobos administration boosted police accountability by transferring the IGS into the province's main administrative office (Dirección de Procesos Administrativos). As part of this move the IGS staff more than doubled, with civilian inspectors taking over most investigations from the police. The IGS also received more vehicles and an information system that enabled it to be in continual contact with *comisarías*. In retrospect, however, some of that contact was presumably not appreciated by some officers in those stations. In late 2009 the agency began investigating reports that police had been holding orgies in various stations. It is certainly a public relations boon for the IGS to share headlines with "sex parties," and such publicity may bring it the kind of public awareness that gives it a stronger hand in accountability. Such awareness might be useful as the growing number of crimes and youth gangs persuade officers to fall back on traditional practices. Checking a person's police record is still a common basis for detention, and more youth are being sentenced to life terms.[103] Linked to this approach is the continuing lack of services for released inmates—a situation that, society is increasingly realizing, is a cause of crime in the province.[104]

According to Arturo Lafalla, the governor who set the reform train in motion, the essential problem was that the government did not provide leadership or hands-on direction for the police. Instead, it named the police chief and then left it all up to him. Despite rampant deficiencies and incompetence, he said, the press, society, and political opposition did not pressure the government to improve policing. Up against such political and institutional conditions, "we were never able to implement the changes."[105] Since

103. Author meeting with heads of the Mendoza Penitentiary System, Mendoza, February 21, 2006.
104. Aida Kemelmajer de Carlucci, minister of justice, Mendoza Supreme Court, interview by author, Mendoza, June 1, 2004.
105. Arturo Lafalla, governor, Mendoza Province, interview by author, Mendoza, June 3, 2004.

then, however, public pressures may have ended that hands-off approach for good. Celso Jaque, elected governor in 2007, was determined to fortify and expand the reform. But one of his first concrete plans, the September 2008 Social Accord for Security, was a repertoire of many *mano dura* approaches and rhetoric, triggering fallouts with rights and community organizations that had backed his candidacy. Many of those organizations and the officials they support have worked to keep the 1999 reform in the public eye and develop projects to support it through the many political changes since then. The drop in killings by police on the street and in police stations indicates that their efforts have not gone unrewarded. Thus even though reform has shown its lasting power by putting problem-oriented policing on the ground, it still needs to stay one step ahead of the political and institutional obstacles that mount along with the crime rate.

La Rioja

La Rioja is a province typical of northern Argentina—poor and rural and where nearly three in every four workers are employed by the government. Home of the Menems, it has its own powerful family dynasty. Unlike other provinces, though, it has developed conditions amenable to citizen security reform such as low crime rates and a government that, with a detailed policy blueprint and written manual, has been attempting to recast the provincial police force based on a community-oriented model (Montbrun and Berton 2005). Although such efforts have had more consistent political support than those in Mendoza, as in Buenos Aires reformers' reliance on that support leaves them vulnerable to turnovers in officials. In addition, as in Mendoza they also face a limited institutional and financial capacity.

These efforts began in 2000 when the country's building economic crisis led to a police work stoppage and other disruptions that prompted the government to restructure the force by placing a new Security Secretariat and a police Office of Strategic Planning on top. Despite many subsequent changes in government after provincial elections, this effort led the way to the 2003 strategic plan that envisioned a radical transformation of the police based on a community policing model. According the security secretary, this change was designed to give citizens "responsibility" and police officials clearer expectations.[106] To start off, the governor and government

106. Jorge Viñas, security secretary, La Rioja Province, interview by author, La Rioja, July 25, 2005.

minister created a support network in the provincial government.[107] The effort itself was spearheaded by four coordinating bodies: a Strategic Government Coordination Committee (Comité de Coordinación Estratégica In-
tersectorial Gubernamental), Intersectional Operational and Coordination
Councils (Consejos Operativos de Coordinación Intersectional Zonal,
COCI), a Community Policing Planning and Implementation Team (Equipo
de Planificación e Implementación de la Policía Comunitaria), and Neighborhood Community Policing Councils (Consejos Barriales de Policía Comunitaria). Although it sounds like bureaucratic overkill, these four entities
were focused on two of the weak points of problem-oriented policing: a lack
of coordination among state agencies and variable application of policies in
the neighborhoods. In response, these entities brought together security officials with social services and central actors such as schools and churches
with the explicit objective of identifying and alleviating the local sources
of insecurity.

The plan was sustained, like the forums in Buenos Aires Province, by pilot community policing programs in the capital city's *comisarías*. Aimed at
improving police-community cooperation and problem resolution, these efforts were a mix of traditional and preventive approaches. Specific initiatives included home visits by the police, crime mapping, registries of uncivil behavior, and educational seminars on issues such as domestic violence.
Those efforts were implemented most widely in two of the capital city's
seven *comisarías,* the fourth and the fifth, which were restructured to further encourage problem solving through foot patrols, neighborhood meetings, and incentives to develop neighborhood projects. These changes were
popular among both residents and police officers, prompting other communities to ask for such programs or to set up prototypes such as the collective
warning *alarmas comunitarias* that were also established in Mendoza and
other areas. These changes also led to wider acceptance of this approach, as
evidenced by its adoption by other provincial cities, as well as by the police
academy's addition of community policing courses in 2006.

Even with its wide programmatic scope, the focus of the reform was on
youth, regarded as the main source of insecurity in the province. The first
step in fact was the formation in 2003 of the Community Prevention Brigade
(Brigada de Prevención Comunitaria, BPC), composed of twelve police of-

107. Ángal Maza, governor, La Rioja Province, interview by author, La Rioja, July
26, 2005; Alberto Paredes Urquiza, government minister, La Rioja Province, interview
by author, La Rioja, July 2005; New York, November 2006.

ficers who worked with young people at risk in twenty-five to thirty *barrios*. In an unusual step for a police personnel process, these officers were selected on the basis of their interests, experiences, and awareness of the issues most affecting young people. Within a few months these officers had drawn up a map of the territories of the city's fourteen major gangs (an estimate), educated people on the services available, and developed strategies to deal with some of the social dysfunctions of youth. The number of groups with gang characteristics jumped from 53 in 2006 to 127 in 2007 (Ibáñez forthcoming). Although this increase reflected better documentation more than an actual increase, it did bring greater attention to the problem through a range of special programs. The Integration Program (Programa Integrar) gives stipends to youths who participate in the "Ecological Brigade," a work program that focuses on gang leaders and trains twenty youths in environmental fields such as maintenance of potable water systems (Celis 2005). According to the program's staff and participants, the training has led to real jobs in the sector, because most of La Rioja is arid desert and so is always in need of water maintenance.[108] There is also an education center for former gang members and a treatment center for youth offenders. In the otherwise desolate neighborhood called Antártida Argentina (named after the country's claimed territory in Antarctica), teenagers in these programs talked excitedly about their textile and other projects. By bringing together policy, action, and education on gangs, this approach avoided the disparate and politicized actions that render most gang policy ineffective.

This policy approach also owed some of its success to the effort to integrate state services. In particular, COCI facilitated interservice programs on school reintegration, support for parents, and antidrug projects such as "You Choose" to help keep kids away from drugs and crime. In fact, COCI was conceived primarily as a "space" for discussion and policy development, which, in some areas, led to concrete strategies such as focusing on the parents of delinquent youth. In an attempt to redirect both social relations and channels of local power, COCI also intends to enlist cooperating youth to serve as a link between the police and the community. In addition, the Provincial Coordinating Council of the Juvenile Problem (Mesa Coordinadora Provincial de la Problemática Juvenil) coordinates provincial agencies to carry out four types of intervention based on the level of risk of the targeted population: youth who have been arrested repeatedly for crimes

---

108. Nito Brizuela, staff member, and youth participants, interviews by author, La Rioja, July 27, 2005.

and misdemeanors, youth who commit crimes occasionally (as well as some gang heads), youth who are in a state of vulnerability, and youth who have been exposed to different levels of risk. Responses to each category were tailored by a Matrix Team (Equipo Matriz) composed of police, youth violence agencies, and representatives of ministries ranging from those devoted to education and employment to health and sports.

This collective approach maximized expertise by avoiding the kinds of preset responses likely when just one agency is in charge. One of the more successful initiatives to come out of the Matrix Team was the Education and Work Program that placed a thousand young people in schools or jobs. Together, officials estimate, this range of programs reaches up to 90 percent of the three to four hundred youths at risk of violence and drugs (mainly marijuana, glue, and alcohol). And in areas where such programs have been established, most residents say that the noticeably diminishing crime has reduced their fear of it. With satisfaction, many officials involved in community policing report that parents actually reach out to them for support with their kids. At one meeting at the fifth *comisaría*, the level of trust between local police and activists allowed them to plunge right into a discussion about how to deal with various security issues.

Unfortunately, obstacles throughout La Rioja's state, police, and society are preventing such concrete programs from fully reorienting the provincial police toward following a problem-oriented model. The biggest obstruction is the police. Many of its chiefs flatly assert that they have neither the time nor the resources even for reforms that might make their work easier and more effective. Despite the fact that complaints over resources are endemic in most police forces, the insufficiency of resources in La Rioja is evident. One *comisaría* has just one vehicle to patrol dozens of neighborhoods. Of the six officers on each of the three shifts, only three are actually out on the street because the rest are assigned to guard prisoners or political officials. A community policing project that established small police modules staffed by one or two officers failed when there were no personnel to fill them. Even the community policing fourth *comisaría* has just fifty-eight officers for thirty-one *barrios* inhabited by 35,000 residents, when, according to its personnel, it needs at least 108. Police officers in other capital city districts say they spend up to 60 percent of their time on administration. Most of the ten officers who answered a survey conducted by Aconcagua University and the City University of New York rated human resources, administrative budgets, vehicles, and educational material on community policing as "greatly insufficient," and equipment as "nearly sufficient."[109] Because of their low salaries—about $250 a month for a street officer and $400 a month for a *subcomisario*—most officers also work an extra eighty to ninety hours for banks and other private business. Thus requests for police personnel to spend more time talking with citizens and attending neighborhood meetings, but without corresponding salary or schedule benefits, are neither welcome nor feasible. Such conditions may explain why, according to the informal survey just cited, only about a fifth of officers unequivocally favor community policing, with very few top officials among them.

Such frustration in the lower ranks is used to bolster resistance to change in the upper ranks, even if under closer examination the lack of resources at the root of these complaints is not an indomitable characteristic. As in other provinces, La Rioja's thin, nontransparent—and, to the police, unjust —distribution of personnel stems from poor planning and evaluation by the Human Resources Department. No regular studies are made of whether the current distribution reflects the city's overall needs or those of particular neighborhoods. Each *comisaría* always has the same number of personnel, reflecting the lack of management planning and flexibility. Amid disaffection over hierarchies and promotion, the fact that the salary of one retiring officer could pay for two new ones is not lost on any officer. In addition, the police force underutilizes the specialists it does have. Of the 10–15 percent of provincial officials who have received special training, such as in financial crimes, only 3 percent are actually using it.

As discussed in previous chapters and in more detail in the conclusion, the implementation of community policing is often out of sync with a problem-oriented approach. As in Bolivia, many police in La Rioja cannot resist the temptation to use community policing in service of preexisting goals. Because it focused on undercover work and information and, above all, on cooperative public projects, the province's well-regarded Community Prevention Brigade was rebuffed by many of the at-risk sectors that were supposed to cooperate with it. The responses by police chiefs to the first community policing training, based on a series of courses, were also discouraging. Many chiefs sent groups to the first course and others to the sec-

109. This survey was funded by the CUNY Collaborative Project on Community Policing of the City University of New York (CUNY) and carried out by Nancy Barrera and Jorge Galleguillo under the direction and auspices of Universidad Aconcagua (Aconcagua University) in Argentina.

ond, with the result that many officers missed large parts of the training. Or chiefs would send some groups at the last minute, overcrowding classrooms and diluting the effect of the courses. Although hundreds of police officers eventually received the bulk of the training, community policing was not integrated into the three police academies (Escuela Superior [Superior School], Instituto de Formación Superior [Institute of Superior Formation], and Escuela de Suboficiales y Agentes [School of Subofficials and Agents]) until 2006. Combined with the militarized approach to other issues—most of Argentina's academies still use curricula created during the Proceso—La Rioja's reform has not done enough to dent officers' perceptions of delinquents as "enemies" and therefore to lessen their suspicious and often aggressive treatment of young suspects. Education and curriculum in general have paid far more attention to civil rights over the last twenty years, but of the forty-two courses that La Rioja's officers take over the three years of their education, only one is devoted to human rights and only one is on social relations. However, other courses do incorporate these issues, and the curriculum is supplemented by a three-day course by the Human Rights Commission on UN principles. But when human rights are presented primarily or exclusively in a course outside of practical training, they are sidelined in daily practice.

Training and support for police geared toward crime prevention in general are also weak, precluding many opportunities to earn citizens' trust. As in Buenos Aires, most officers are simply assigned to a corner—"to look but not to see," in the words of one officer. Many refrain from acting because they lack instructions, autonomy, and even radios, as well as some measure of confidence that they will be backed up by their supervisors. This lack of reinforcement stems in part from the fact that *comisarios* themselves are not evaluated on management. If the *comisarios* are simply at the station during work hours, as one police official stated, they are considered good—expectations somewhat below those of the most basic of citizen security reforms. Even reforms supported by *comisarios* often do not survive them. According to their subordinates, after La Rioja's two pro-community policing *comisarios* left their positions, the new chiefs were simply "not convinced" of the need for that kind of policing. Discussions in *comisarías* clearly indicate that among the lower ranks there is a far more intuitive understanding of and support for community policing than among the upper ranks, particularly when specific projects are mentioned rather than general

110. Groups of police officers, interviews by author, La Rioja, February 13–18, 2006.

or theoretical concepts.[110] But in a demonstration of how hierarchical power trumps innovative power, the division among the upper ranks over community policing has left many plans unimplemented. Specific reform goals such as reducing crime were not followed through with a public accounting of how well the goals were met. As the next chapter discusses, such objective and transparent evaluation provides the kind of break with the past needed to build much-needed citizen trust.

Criminal investigation, the core of police work, is also weak in La Rioja. Efforts to improve coordination between the street and the Judicial Police lag, and resource-deprived crime labs solve very few crimes through scientific investigation. Meanwhile, criminal statistics are insufficiently collected, studied, and distributed. A control center compiles and analyzes neighborhood statistics in order to tailor specific responses to them. But its work is limited because, according to the estimates of various officials, only two to three out of every five crimes are reported. Furthermore, the information the police do have is not regularly distributed to the *comisarías,* whose crime maps are usually on paper sheets not readily available to patrol officers. The *comisarías* also lack regular updates on the location, time, and manner of different crimes. The effects of such limited information are compounded by *comisarías'* lack of autonomy to use the information they do have. Citizen security councils and greater *comisaría* autonomy would boost police effectiveness not only by allowing for quicker responses, but also by making residents more likely to work with the local police because they know they will not have to wait for decisions or resources from the center. According to Rauch (1991, 2), "Despite the fact that the police station [is] . . . the most crucial point of police service delivery, the tendency has been for the most promising local cops to be removed from this area of work and trained for a commissioned position in one of the other branches or in the management hierarchy." Such tendencies reinforce the hierarchical forms of power that, in turn, reinforce ineffective forms of traditional policing.

Another weak part of policing is internal affairs—both personnel complaints within the agency and citizen complaints against it. Norms and procedures are followed haphazardly, say police, without even a standard complaint form. Despite an advisory council of citizens and more involvement by nonpolice since 2001, all internal affairs personnel are police officials. Even when investigations appear by all accounts to have been rapid and just, the Security Secretariat reserves the power to make the final judgment on any case. As a result of this police control, despite persistent charges of systemic police abuse in La Rioja, official investigations tend to downplay or treat each incident as isolated. As officials on the Human Rights Commission added, it takes many years to handle an accusation against a police officer, who, in the meantime, can climb up in the ranks.[111] The lack of action on killings of youth in La Rioja, in which the police are sometimes suspects, exemplifies this collective negligence.

Tense relations among journalists, citizens, and politicians distort the way in which the police's community-oriented efforts are covered in the media. Police complain that reporters miss critical information because they arrive late at crime scenes and are, in any case, already biased against them, resulting in coverage that has steadily eroded the police's image. In addition, citizens with complaints against the police tend to go to the press instead of the government, which can make fair hearings difficult later on. The lack of a media relations department or liaison in the police often allows such actions to fester into conflicts and suspicions that can take on a life of their own and make the police even more reluctant to embrace reforms that mean more exposure.

Relations between the city and state governments also complicate citizen security reform. Representing different parties, as they usually do, the province's governor and the capital city's mayor tend to promote different policies and, in the process, compound institutional territoriality among social service agencies, such as in education, health, and infrastructure. Frequently pointed out, for example, is the lack of collaboration between the police and schools, which is critical to the success of youth-oriented police reform. In poor regions such as La Rioja, labor policy is also important. But the involvement in reform of La Rioja's Ministry of Industry, Commerce, and Employment (Ministerio de Industria, Comercio y Empleo, MICE), which oversees employment issues, has also been tentative and variable. As the security minister points out, the first lessons learned from the formation of the Community Prevention Brigade in 2003 was that information was not followed up with actual strategies, and that most agencies balked at getting involved in what they regarded as a police matter. Wanting to protect their own turf and community relations amid political uncertainty, the many agencies that made up the COCI and other coordinating committees reduced their involvement after the initial burst of attention.

Participation is also low among established civil society organizations such as the church and the Bar Association, which usually have both the professional background and societal legitimacy to bridge the divide be-

111. Human Rights Commission, interview by author, La Rioja, July 29, 2005.

tween state and society on citizen security. There were also some unintended consequences in the participation that did take place, such as the abuse by COCI youth of their roles. In the CUNY-Aconcagua survey of citizens and officials on citizen security, twenty groups were identified by residents as being active in citizen security. Of them, though, thirteen were governmental Neighborhood Councils that were funding and directing the bigger local projects. Of the rest, three were small NGOs working on security issues, one was the church, one was a religious organization, one was a sports association, and one was a commercial business.

Along with the private sector, the judiciary has not been able to meet the expectations of reform. Like the police, the judiciary faces continual resource shortfalls. Despite a population boom in the 1990s, over the next decade the province still had only three first-level instruction courts. And even after adopting oral trials in most criminal cases, the judiciary hands down fewer than sixty sentences for every six to seven thousand crimes. Objectivity and coordination are also in short supply. The same judge oversees investigation and sentencing, and the controls over responsibilities such as punishing misdemeanors are not clear. Lack of follow-up and information sharing by the courts are perennial complaints among the police, and particularly contentious have been disputes between the police and the Minor Courts over the handling of youth cases, whose numbers grew sharply in 2005 and have continued to increase since. Judicial weakness also means less consistent law enforcement. For example, because of insufficient collaboration with the police, some citizen security actions such as registries of uncivil behavior have not led to the judicial prosecution they require for long-term impact. Although punishment of misdemeanors often raises concerns about civil rights, documenting and detaining people for such actions without follow-through often mean abuse without results.

One of the biggest causes of disorder and crime in La Rioja and other poor areas is the excessive consumption of alcohol, but La Rioja's detailed Law of Prevention of Alcohol Consumption (Law 71.921) is not sufficiently enforced. According to a police official who is a major proponent of the law, enforcement is carried out through a combination of fines for shops and bars, registration of lawbreakers, and follow-up with juvenile offenders.[112] But the law's clear prohibition of alcohol sales after midnight is openly flaunted or skirted through large purchases earlier in the evening. Drug

---

112. Eduardo Poledri, *comisario* inspector, interview by author, La Rioja, February 13, 2006.

abuse and sniffing glue are even more serious problems with even less effective laws. For example, dealers can still easily buy bicycle glue downtown for sale in the residential areas, and the police estimate that 90 percent of gang members consume drugs (mostly marijuana and cocaine) that come from other provinces and are under the jurisdiction of the PFA, which La Rioja's police criticize for not joining them in coordinating antidrug efforts. More serious obstruction is posed by the police. Dozens of *whiskerías* have popped up on the outskirts of the capital purporting to serve high-quality libations, but in fact they are brothels whose owners are alerted before a police raid.

The CUNY-Aconcagua survey of forty-six community members, twenty police officers, and four government officials has underscored both the doubts and promises of reform in La Rioja. Responses by the citizens interviewed reveal strong support for community policing but insufficient material backing. Although the pool of respondents was weighted heavily in favor of those willing to participate (who in general tended to have more positive views of or connections with state agencies), they were a fairly representative cross section of the capital city's population in terms of class, gender, and geography. Over 57 percent earned under $700 per month, which is important because of the centrality of community policing to low-income areas. All together, about 80 percent of respondents said that the police listen to citizens and that communications between the police and citizens have improved. The principal reasons they give for this development is the positive change of attitude among the police and the priority given to preventive projects in which the police work directly with civilians. The majority of respondents also pointed out that community policing has made real progress on most key issues. The percentage of those answering that the police have been "very, somewhat, or more or less successful" was 65.7 percent for violent crimes, 67.1 percent for property crimes, 64.3 percent for drug trafficking, 55.7 percent for police corruption, and 58.6 percent for police abuse. Of community policing's benefits, the two main ones mentioned were cooperative projects and the priority placed on youth.

The state, however, has not followed citizens' lead with more support. Requests for community policing by residents served by all seven of the capital city's *comisarías,* based on results in the fourth and fifth *comisarías,* have been met with policy foot-dragging and resource tightfistedness. The otherwise upbeat view in the survey was offset by over a dozen deficiencies mentioned by respondents. The most common were lack of continuity, resources, and government commitment. Such poor responsiveness stems in part from the territoriality among the social service agencies and from the tense relations between the city and state officials, who, as mentioned earlier, are often from different parties advancing different approaches.

Such politicization is aggravated by the claims of many police officers that the political parties use street officers—as well as youth groups of community policing projects—for partisan activities such as monitoring campaign opponents and putting up political posters. Participation by civil society organizations, which can undercut such politicization, is low. Another alternative with potential is looking to the business improvement districts (BIDs) formed by neighborhood entrepreneurs, which can boost community policing by providing youth with employment and funding physical improvements to the neighborhoods. In many U.S. cities BIDs have improved relations between the police and community, while reducing vandalism, drug trafficking, and other sources of insecurity. But in La Rioja and most Argentine provinces, not enough small businesses are willing to create such programs or even give young people jobs. With the state, agriculture, and mining absorbing most of La Rioja's labor pool, private sector solutions are not particularly viable in any case.

As in other countries, most criticisms in La Rioja are of how community policing is implemented rather than of community policing itself. Their many projects reveal that a core group of officials in La Rioja are committed to problem-oriented policing. And yet grumbling but generally solid support for reform among the population, along with the government's concerted focus on social service coordination, may yet make La Rioja one of the first provinces in Argentina to adopt a comprehensive structural police reform based on community policing. After an impeachment and other political tumult in 2005 suspended the reform, the 2007 elections brought to power the vice governor who favored community policing, and so renewed hope for a return to the reform. New neighborhood initiatives supported by state agencies such as the Citizens' Prevention Secretariat (Secretaría de Prevención Ciudadana) were evidence of the continuation of citizen support. But new police leaders have given priority to traditional policing, and "because of political questions," says the director of the province's Community Prevention Brigade (BPC), the overall reform "has been completely sidelined."[113] In fact, the BPC lost its only vehicles, which was a major logistical and psychological blow. Strained relations between the chief of po-

113. Óscar Ibáñez, director, Brigada de Prevención Comunitaria, e-mail correspondence, June 4, 2008.

lice and the government minister have hindered both reform and basic communications. Contentious fights in the selection of a police chief since reform began have also affected even the day-to-day management of basic police activities. "Inaction reigns," says the BPC director, in part because the government is "not advancing any plan or strategy of prevention, and statistics are being controlled so that they do not get out." Meanwhile, "delinquency committed by youth to feed their addictions is in the news every day and has brought the citizenry to a state of alert." But it is this very spiral of criminal acts, public panic, and provincial politics that demonstrates the need for problem-oriented policing based on a new form of citizen and state engagement.

Conclusion

One of the biggest police proponents of reform in La Rioja, police general Luis Gallego, affirms the diagnosis of the beat police officer that opened this chapter: "If we are capable of constructing a new network [of] judicial, municipal, and police officers, if the police could get the resources, if health services and the Neighborhood Center worked with police on [matters such as] substance abuse and uncivil behavior, we would considerably improve our ability to bring security. That is why I insist on community policing, because it is the only immediate solution." In Buenos Aires, Mendoza, and La Rioja, efforts at police reform in Argentina have taken on different strategies, enjoy different levels of support, and face different obstacles. But almost all of these efforts are caught up in a conflict between "public order," in which demands for a crime crackdown tap into the police's authoritarian practices, and "human rights," in which the brutality of past dictatorships, the ineffectiveness of repressive policing, and the expansion of civil society are leading to models of security based on prevention and community involvement. However, because this conflict is unfolding on twenty-three provincial stages, citizen security policy in Argentina will continue to be refreshed by change and debate. In large urban provinces such as Buenos Aires and Mendoza, the weaknesses of past reform efforts are being addressed through more modest and focused efforts. Although most of the poorer rural provinces remain allergic to reform, those with some government reformers, such as La Rioja, are considering proposals that are at least in tune with their particular political and institutional contexts.

Regional efforts are also encouraged by the federal government's attempts to forge a general framework of security reform based on crime prevention, institutional strengthening, and tougher responses. It is that broader dialogue between traditional policing and more problem-oriented policing that makes Argentina more able than other countries to craft proposals in the five areas of reform that fortify each other. As in other countries, however, the outcome of alternative models still depends on whether Argentina can maintain the political and institutional traction to demonstrate results. The next chapter, which brings in additional cases, is about ways to make those results more likely.

Chapter 7

Overcoming Obstacles to Reform

Using the theoretical framework of the first three chapters and the empirical experience of the following three, this chapter outlines five strategic approaches that could lay a concrete and visible groundwork for more participatory and effective citizen security. Although the issues to which they are most applicable differ, each of these approaches attempts to connect specific proposals to the three underlying characteristics emphasized in this book: (1) the nature of daily policing, (2) relations among institutions, and (3) drawn-out policymaking. Through their recognition of these traits, such approaches help reformers maintain the innovation and flexibility of reforms through the stream of expected and unexpected obstacles. The approaches described in detail in this chapter, drawing on the experiences of different countries, can be summarized as follows: (1) identifying the points of tension in criminal justice, the alleviation of which can help unblock slow processes; (2) taking into account the discretion of police officers, which both traditional and problem-oriented proponents often misinterpret and manipulate; (3) enhancing the role of evaluation, which should be integrated into reform rather than tacked on at the end; (4) seeking structured citizen engagement, a key to community policing; and (5) focusing on the internal management of security bodies.

Points of Tension

Policymakers are likely to become stuck at the crossroads between traditional and problem-oriented policing when they see reform as a set of unenviable choices they must foist on uncooperative agencies. But those choices might be simpler and more palatable when reform is centered on stages of security actions rather than just on security institutions. This view can be applied to each of the five areas of reform defined in chapter 1. Control mechanisms, for example, often become stuck at particularly sensitive points in investigations of police abuse. They apply more readily to legal changes, which have brought about changes in the entire criminal justice process. Nearly every component of criminal justice is a series of steps, providing openings for action as the process progresses. Because most conflicts, bottlenecks, and various forms of politicized agitation arise in the move from one step to the next, untangling these knots of tension can often be an effective reform strategy.

The description of criminal investigation in Honduras in chapter 3 reveals how many points of tension, and thus of potential change, can be identified in an otherwise chaotic process. In most countries a predetermined series of actions kicks in once a crime is committed (see figure 7.1). Tensions usually flare up between the first and second stages, when the public prosecutor (*fiscal*) or a representative of the Dirección General de Investigación Criminal (DGIC) arrives at a crime scene that is mishandled by the National Police (PN). Such tensions continue between the third and fourth stages because of incomplete and inconsistent dossiers (*expedientes*) and between the fourth and fifth stages, when extended delays, mainly stemming from officials' poor preparation for oral trials, push detentions beyond the thirty-day limit.

Although persistent, each point of tension suggests possible responses. It is usually not feasible to assign more personnel and resources to relieve tensions during an investigation. An alternative being adopted by many countries is joint criminal code training programs for judges, prosecutors, and police. By exposing the conflicts among these officials, such training helps to minimize them during actual cases. Supporting such programs at this stage should be more training on writing *expedientes,* an internal affairs evaluation of evidence collection practices, and stronger programs for victim assistance and witness protection. Legal assistance units within the police can provide some of these services. Costa Rica's police lawyers (*alpha limas)* advise officers on the law, particularly on the legality of specific actions. Because an estimated 65 percent of officers leave the academy without adequate legal training (Bermúdez Coward 2004), the *alpha limas* help them get past the points of tension in their everyday work. In Bolivia, where about 70 percent of criminal charges are for nonviolent offenses, the greater use of alternative sentencing at the beginning of the process would likewise help decongest criminal justice down the line.

Figure 7.1. Criminal Investigation Flow

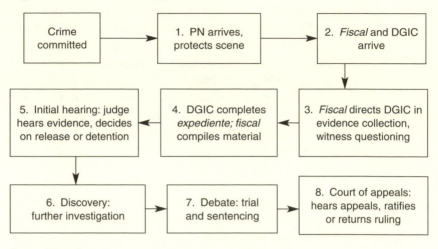

Source: The author.

The points of tension can also be identified in other criminal justice processes, from help for at-risk youths to released offenders. Such an approach can be most fruitful for the process by which people report abuse, because it involves the range of citizen concerns. Most of those processes consist of the following steps: receipt of complaints, evaluation of their veracity, investigation of the accusations, adjudication of the charges, and recommendation of dismissal or punishment. The stage that is the subject of the most complaints by citizens can then be evaluated for improvement. Physically locating an accountability agency in a police station, for example, is intimidating and leads to low rates of abuse reporting in many countries (see Lemos-Nelson 2002, 197). For others, it is the police chief's veto over agencies' recommendations that most dissuades involvement. The UN initiative International Commission against Impunity in Guatemala, prompted by serial killings of bus drivers and designed to loosen organized crime's grip on criminal justice, is an example of how an issue or incident can lead to a focus on a problematic stage in criminal justice that undermines the rest.

Policing itself, even when regarded as efficient, also involves many points of tension that can be openings for change. A central example is a clampdown on antisocial misdemeanors that is given a legal and policy basis. However, because of the broad support it enjoys in most places, this form of zero tolerance policing often lacks the scrutiny that such a hands-on approach needs, even when embedded in the legal structure. Many such provisions are modeled after New York's Quality of Life summons, which began in 1989 in the New York City Transit Authority. This summons could be issued for twenty-five transgressions, from panhandling to property abandonment. Anyone in the city who received a summons but did not appear in court was subject to a warrant for his or her arrest. The threat of arrest increased both compliance and prevention, because nearly half of those who showed up had a previous record, sometimes for felony charges. Management and human resources were additional motives for this approach. Citing the fact that 10 percent of police were making 90 percent of arrests, during his 1994–96 tenure as commissioner of the New York City Police Department (NYPD) William J. Bratton pushed officers to detain more people. He also introduced CompStat, an organization management tool that required each of the NYPD's seventy-six precinct commanders to explain the crime-fighting strategies being applied in his or her area. Use of this tool also increased the pressure on officers to tally up arrests and Quality of Life summonses.

And yet as the popularity of and dependence on Quality of Life summonses grew, they became another standardized approach lacking corrective assessments. As summonses and related measures became an integral part of policing, they were no longer regarded as extra work requiring backup, and street officers under Chief Howard Safir (1996–2000) felt that they unfairly bore the brunt of the blame for the inevitable conflict that arose in implementation of the summonses. In addition, the growing number of detentions and summonses clogged the criminal courts, and prosecutors began to dismiss thousands of "flawed" arrests.[1] A "policy of aggressive misdemeanor arrests," as Harcourt (1998, 332) concluded, thus became the "primary engine" of community policing in New York. Such use of zero tolerance even led Kelling, one of the developers of the broken windows theory (see chapter 2) to label it "the bastard child" of broken windows because it lost track of the "extent to which we wrestled with legal, constitutional and moral issues" (*Law Enforcement News* 1990). Blunt applications of zero tolerance in Latin America on issues such as drugs, from small-time use in Argentine cities to large-scale eradication in Bolivia, also reflected the counterproductive effects of the practice on society, the criminal justice system, and the police itself.

1. Clyde Haberman, "Crime Down, but Courts Are Clogged," *New York Times,* January 3, 1997.

Discretion

Even the firmest citizen security policy with the tightest rules has a soft core of discretion, which can be defined as the characteristic of a realm of work in which specific action is determined by the actor's own selection from a range of possible responses. Because of the inherent complexity and daily stress of policing and the impossibility of fully monitoring it, individual discretion is an inescapable part of daily policing. It is also central to reform. Positive impacts from professional support and community policing programs, in particular, often rely on what officers do with their new but often vaguely worded powers. If discretion is defined as the right or power to decide or act according to one's own judgment, then its role in policing is clear. In each of the three stages of even the most basic police action—contact, process, and exit—officers must choose from a wide range of options in a compressed amount of time. For example, in the contact phase they can listen, question, refrain, counsel, threaten with detention, separate persons, or refer the situation to another agency. While doing so, they must provide a "presence" that brings calm and control through a combination of persuasion, mediation, and force, while identifying "signals" in order to assess quickly how multiple factors might escalate.

Needlessly adding to such inherent complexities in discretion is politics. Corresponding to the conflict between traditional and problem-oriented policing in Latin America, discretion has fallen into two clashing and politicized stereotypes: a professional prerogative strangled by regulation, on the one hand, and a personal license for abuse, on the other. These views often coexist uneasily when the legal controls over discretion can be loosely followed in practice. But any incident can easily throw off such a balancing act, triggering counterproductive patterns in which officers, untrained by their academies and unguided by their superiors, are unsure how to apply the discretion they do have. Even when street officers are motivated to do their jobs, their superiors often do not "trust them to do it" (Bratton and Knobler 1998, x). Those trying to avoid trouble then try to match their actions to official guidelines and objectives, which only reveals the dissociation between daily policing and rules to which it is supposed to adhere. For example, officers using neighborhood contacts to tamp down intergang tensions in San Pedro Sula, Honduras, often cited the Organic Law (LOPN) provisions authorizing actions for public order threats, even though no specific threat existed. To prevent their discretionary action from leading to entanglements with or accusations from citizens altogether, officers often give them pat excuses about the unbendable rules imposed from above that they are compelled to follow. All too typical is the fear by an El Alto, Bolivia, police officer of residents who might be allied with local politicians, which he said led him to ignore calls to intervene in violence between neighbors.

The tendency toward such responses is increased by officers' awareness that the internal affairs office could be used to either scapegoat them or to shield them if they run afoul of well-connected citizens. But citizens see police agents' pretensions of being technical as cynically self-serving and devoid of basic concern. When such conflicts and discrepancies over discretion arise and lead to public airings, outside officials push to tighten oversight. But police chiefs often fight such efforts as a zero-sum game of control. Caught up in such struggles, they miss a chance to incorporate into any new rules the informal ways in which street officers address insecurity. To avoid more political problems, they also tend to micromanage even more, which is one of the biggest and most common "failures" in policing, in part because it aggravates the problems discussed in chapter 2 (Rogers 2002, 15). Street officers then continue to be professionally unprepared but politically vulnerable. As they also continue to doubt their actions and cover up their mistakes, they dull their individual judgment, diminish public confidence, and inject criminal policy with false information.

As discussed in chapter 2, the importance of the connection between theory and tactics requires that broken windows and related approaches be linked, under careful leadership and management in the *comisaría,* to community norms and crime reduction goals. It is about surrounding flexibility with standards. As demonstrated by the contrasting examples of La Ceiba and Rivera Hernández in Honduras, the discretion of the local chief can be pivotal. Youths gathering on a corner are often harassed by police because they fit the stereotype of disorder, are assumed to be a nuisance to the community, and constitute a vulnerable and easily targeted population. And yet often they are not subject to complaints by neighbors, who might recognize the need for such gatherings. A local chief with political connections but without the fear of reprimand might be able to bring those factors into play. When such gatherings become regular, such as the use of a space for late-night loud parties, the chief is also in the position to use zoning regulations or other laws to end or scale down the gatherings. Making such local and specific distinctions, which is part of the nature of discretion, is also needed to accommodate any policy changes from higher up in the government.

To turn discretion from a vice into an advantage, governments should take concrete steps in police-related education, promotion, and policy. First, in training cadets academies should incorporate scenarios that evoke a range of human reactions in order to maximize innovation and criticism. Because every situation is different, as any officer will agree, sessions conducted by veterans help bring out how chronic uncertainty and subjectivity can overshadow written guidelines and set objectives. Along with concrete examples of daily temptations and the consequences for giving in to them, such an approach can limit officers' inclinations to hide honest errors and help police managers harness the innovative power within their ranks. In contrast to mute passivity during lectures, such real-life experiences would bring police academy classes alive in Bolivia, Honduras, and Argentina. Instead of trying to scrap and replace an existing curriculum, which invariably makes academy directors defensive, this pedagogical approach is more likely to be welcomed by the higher-ups, who can see for themselves the differences in student receptivity.

Such approaches can continue as cadets enter the police force through strategies such as pairing new and senior officers in high-crime areas. For example, in Brooklyn, New York, Operation Impact has helped bring down crime rates amid salary and personnel cuts. Specialized courses on various societal conditions are useful as well. One example is mental illness, which afflicts a high percentage of those who come in contact with the police. Most officers, though, lack the skills to know whether the erratic behaviors they are encountering are temporary, permanent, benign, or dangerous, much less what services are available to treat them. Training on and responses to mental illness differ widely in Latin America. Some agencies give cadets about twenty hours of training, often using outdated videos and dry lectures, which, like some community policing and human rights courses, serve to marginalize the issue. Agencies more cognizant of their shortfalls in this area hire mental health professionals or send in social worker teams. Like the limited courses, however, this approach deprives the majority of street officers of the kind of preparation that enables effective discretion.

Helping to reinforce more discretion-centered training would be a promotion structure in which advancement is tied to skills and achievements on matters such as community relations, with extra incentives for specialization in functional and geographic areas. Ecuador offers promotion and salary incentives for relocation to undesirable locations (Policía Nacional de Ecuador 2003), and Costa Rica provides them for high-risk assignments. Awards and other forms of recognition, such as NYPD's "cop of the month," cost little but mean a lot to serving officers, and so should also be part of the police career. Other approaches, such as a public scoreboard of actions carried out by each officer or the 2005 proposal in Guatemala to assign entire academy classes to *comisarías,* can also help turn innovative power into hierarchical power (Scheye 2005, 14). Many such actions can be taken using administrative means that minimize the political entanglements. In Venezuela the municipality of San Francisco in the city of Maracaibo has adopted more citizen channels for complaints, opened an Autonomous Police Institute, and created a Community Affairs section. Those changes have facilitated activities and initiatives that have proven effective, said one district chief, such as better use-of-force discretion, a requirement for serving officers to return to the academy for ongoing education, and evaluations of officers by residents. Together, these measures have helped reduce both criminal and police violence, which have long been at crisis levels in the Maracaibo metropolitan area.[2] By contrast, the shame or bullying that often pervades informal interpolice relationships should not be used, as some agencies have tried, in the name of evaluation. Such disincentives, such as Thailand's practice of requiring errant officers to wear pink "Hello, Kitty" cartoon armbands, may create resentments that offset their short-term impacts and embolden the kinds of repressive subcultures discussed earlier.

Discretion is also strengthened through exposure to different perspectives and options from which police officers can draw. That said, law enforcement officers justifiably suspect many ideas coming from government, international organizations, and other outside sources with less law enforcement experience than they have. Universities can be an exception, because they are usually more knowledgeable, professionally stable, and politically neutral than other outside entities. Although police-academic collaboration is vulnerable to politics and distrust, in Latin America it has been able to withstand stereotyping as leftist by proving to be constructive when focused on a particular issue. The police in nine Brazilian states have developed educational programs with local universities (Leeds 2007, 27). Most notable is the productive collaboration between the police of Minas Gerais and the Universidad Federal of Minas Gerais. Ecuador's San Francisco de Quito University trained six hundred security officers in 2005, and Chile's Carabineros developed their Plan Cuadrante with the Catholic University.

The high rate of shootings by police in Latin America, reaching over 40 percent of incidents of civilian resistance to police in Venezuela,[3] demon-

2. Pedro Luis Tang Urdaneta, Policía de San Francisco, author interview, Puerto la Cruz, November 29, 2005.
3. There was a jump from nine citizen deaths for each police death in 2000 to twenty-

strates the need for a special focus on the use of force through the lens of discretion. Because whether to use force is the most serious and high-pressure decision a police officer makes, guidelines and training on force must be as clear and thorough as possible. They also must be supported by better management; several studies, underscoring the importance of evaluation, indicate that excessive bureaucratization more than other variables increases the likelihood of the use of force (Worden 1996, 44). Thus, although improved management is a long-term effort, it can begin with steps such as ending the common practice of having officers throw their guns back in the cache at the end of their shifts without any notation of the use of those weapons during their shifts. But as the next section discusses, such steps will have limited results unless police officials and officers understand why and how the problematic practices were part of daily policing in the first place. Discretion-centered training on the graduated use of nonlethal force, by separating out and analyzing the different life-threatening scenarios police encounter, can help create that awareness about the use of force while gradually reducing it. In fact, many academies have been adopting a scale for the application of nonlethal methods for a range of violent situations.[4] Because of the high number of guns and crimes committed with them—an estimated two million arms, legal and illegal, are circulating in Central America alone—greater discretion on weapons searches can also cut crime rates while improving police professionalism. Officers discover most arms in the course of other activities rather than in specific searches for them. So they could be given broader authorization with clearer laws to search people for weapons on the condition that any discovered arms would be destroyed without detention or criminal charge. Making new legal controls more acceptable to police and allowing more individual discretion would support reform in general by signaling more confidence in officers.

Finally, discretion can help reform along by being a key term of reference in a terminology of reform tweaked to make it more politically palatable. For example, many kinds of "reform" can be introduced instead as a "strengthening," and problem-oriented policing can be couched in terms of coordination rather than of control. Repeated references to discretion are particularly important, because such references signal to the rank-and-file

---

eight per officer in 2001, and the 170 extrajudicial killings recorded in 2000 were the most since 1988.

4. The U.S. Supreme Court and those in most Latin American countries limit the use of force to situations in which an officer is threatened with injury or death.

that they will be allowed at least some room to adjust new approaches to their daily challenges and limitations. The proactive approach by the CMS officers in the Honduran city of La Ceiba, described in chapter 4, illustrates how such approaches can be put into practice, even in high-crime areas with few resources. Although they never discarded or dismissed traditional tactics, that city's officers focused on social issues in terms of their importance to criminology, using family visits, youth sports, and other forms of "soft" policing in cracking down on gangs and drug trafficking.

Information-Based Evaluation

Information that is reliably collected and objectively analyzed can help make headway toward problem-oriented policing. Criminal justice, community policing, and accountability mechanisms are often immersed in reams of information, only some of which is relevant. The key indicators of crime and policing are collected in most countries, but much of it remains adrift in an unfiltered flow of reports, statistics, and numbers.

To break out of such informational inertia without triggering too much resistance, a good approach is to initiate separate evaluations of officers, units, and practices. Such evaluations can help identify weak areas, sharpen officer discretion, improve station chiefs' planning, make personnel distribution more equitable, and prevent policy from congealing around conditions that change quickly. Such an approach is important in each of the five main areas of reform described in chapter 1. A restructuring that eliminates and creates ranks and bodies must be evaluated to ensure the viability of new agencies amid resistance by powerful internal competitors.

Evaluating Officers, Units, and Practices

Such a restructuring should be anchored in an evaluation of criminal justice officials at all levels, with an eye toward boosting incentives for effectiveness. Quality control teams could determine how street officers spend their time. Knowing which repeated problems take up an unnecessarily large part of a police officer's day—such as chronic vandalism of a basketball court, calls from particular homes, or robberies on a commercial block—would allow the police to better direct officers for rapid follow-up and better refer people to the appropriate services. Evaluation of the types and numbers of arrests would be useful as well. Criminology seeks quantifiable measures, and a broader evaluation of arrest patterns in the context of human resource planning may expose problems such as an overreliance on detention quotas that are met through spurious detentions, or a dependence on the minority of officers (sometimes just 10 percent) who make most of the arrests in many cities (Bayley 1998, 122).

To address the complaint that most detainees do not end up in jail, both detectives (*inspectores*) and street officers must be thoroughly evaluated. Individual police officers pay little attention to conviction rates because they do not affect their salaries or promotions.[5] Indeed, some cities actually have more *inspectores* than cases solved by them. Results-based oversight, clearer timetables of action, and individual incentives can begin to improve and smooth out police performance. In Mexico's Federal District, an officer making an arrest that leads to a conviction receives a small bonus. A program in New York City's Bronx borough that helped officers improve their presentation of the evidence in reports sent to the prosecutor raised the conviction rate. The level of convictions was also included in officer evaluations. A review of differences among regions may also help explain why some areas are more able to solve crimes than others.

Because policing goes beyond individuals, units must also be evaluated. Police stations, in particular, should be assessed, with financial awards and professional recognition for those demonstrating reductions in crime without accompanying increases in abuses or complaints (such an evaluation was initiated in Argentina's capital). This balance between effectiveness and abuse should be part of the evaluations of specific units as well, especially those given greater discretion. For example, in New York City, the NYPD's Street Crimes Unit earned widespread recognition for its success with sting operations and arrest rates, and was eventually responsible for 40 percent of the guns the police took off the street. But it also killed a disproportionate number of unarmed civilians, stemming in part from the growing discretion that its successes brought it. Officers on foot patrol should also be more carefully evaluated. Even though they are not more effective than other types of officers at reducing crime, they do reduce citizens' fears and feelings of insecurity. Thus the ways in which they achieve the latter reductions should be studied and incorporated into discretion training. In most cities in Latin America less than 10 percent of 911 calls are about criminal matters and less than 5 percent of crimes are reported while they are in

5. In some cities less than 20 percent of police officers are responsible for more than half of all the detentions leading to convictions.

progress. A rapid response does not therefore significantly increase arrest and conviction rates (Spelman and Brown 1984), and so response times that are predictable and reasonable may mean more overall than those that are quick. Greater awareness of these patterns may help reduce the uncertainty and tension in police-society relations discussed in chapter 3. Indeed, categorizing actual police requests and expectations by different social sectors should be central in evaluating policing.

Practices, too, require greater evaluation. Like internal affairs, practices that draw the most criticism are good candidates for better evaluation. Such practices range from traffic stops, notorious for abuse and problem displacement, to an officer's reliance on firepower. Even with strong legal constraints on the use of force by police, still missing is any analysis of when and why it is most likely to occur. Such analysis should start by assessing whether force actually works, because police often miss their targets when they use their arms. In 2004 and 2005, for example, New York police officers hit their targets less than 23 percent of the time.[6] Such studies should be supplemented by a broader understanding of the use of violence in different scenarios. How often do officers use coercive means against a citizen in situations with no resistance or detention? How often does violence ensue because the officer lacks equipment or is unable to get backup? How often does violence occur after detention? In many countries most police violence occurs during detainee treatment and transport, even though that is when it is the least necessary, expected, and justifiable. A better understanding of such practices can enhance discretion and improve policy. For example, beyond assigning and tracking specific arms to each agent, any officer using fatal force could be required to complete a form describing why, where, and how it occurred. Worded to be more informational than accusatory, such forms could help determine whether an action was necessary and whether it presented any legal or policy problems.

How police practices, crime trends, and public space affect each other should also be evaluated, as is done in many countries through geographic and environmental studies known as Crime Prevention through Environmental Design (CPTED). Some European cities, for example, have used this approach to reduce crime by moving recreational fields away from housing centers. CPTED could also be applied to public spaces such as banks and kiosks; the police could draw up a list of locations with the most

6. Al Baker, "A Hail of Bullets, a Heap of Uncertainty," *New York Times,* December 9, 2007, 4.

frequent crimes and monitor them with stakeout teams. Any analysis of a city's bars, from La Rioja's *whiskerías* to El Alto's roadside vendors, would certainly identify the minority of establishments that are the scene of a majority of violent incidents. Using follow-up measures such as alcohol license suspension or assignment of an extra officer, the police could assess the costs and benefits of their responses in terms of injuries, detentions, and revenue losses. Because roughly three-quarters of all police contacts with citizens occur in private places, such as in the home in cases of domestic violence, CPTED studies of residential space and social relations—such as how well neighbors communicate—may also help inform and improve crime strategies.

How new laws translate into practice is another dimension of evaluation. In Cali, Colombia, between 1992 and 1994, Mayor Rodrigo Guerrero used an information-based evaluation of specific areas to develop multisectoral policies. One initial study showed that laws restricting alcohol reduced homicides by 25 percent, and that stronger disarmament laws could cut homicides by an additional 14 percent. Likewise, in Colombia's capital of Bogotá, restrictions on alcohol sales reduced killings by 8 percent (Guerrero 2007, 133). Such results should prompt the police to devote more resources to these problems, particularly when they are also highlighted by citizen surveys and community policing meetings.

Policing of Youth

In the policing of youth, risk assessment can help strike a balance between repression and the prevention that best responds to ever-changing activities and locations through solutions such as concentrating on repeat offenders and finding alternative spaces where otherwise legal activity does not bother the community.[7] The well-known "pulling levers" strategy, in which criminal groups such as gangs are told they will all be subject to police action if even one member commits a transgression, is successful in part because of the police's detailed knowledge of gang memberships, locations, and activities (Kennedy 1998). Such knowledge can also help categorize members according to their level of potential criminality. Using interviews to document

---

7. Responding to the fact that a small number of criminals commit a disproportionate amount of crime, the Repeat Offender Project in Washington, D.C., identified two kinds of repeat offenders: those already wanted on one or more warrants and so could be arrested on sight and those believed to be criminally active but not currently wanted.

risk factors, for example, the Minors Section of Costa Rica's Organización de Investigación Judicial found that about 12 percent of young detainees were using drugs—far lower than previously assumed—and that nearly one-third had no chronic behavior problems.[8] As Chicago and New York have learned, observations and diagnosis by individual officers monitoring targeted gang members are more successful in reducing gang activity than extended detentions, which affect only a percentage of gang members.

Using the "restorative justice" approach, which has been gaining ground in Latin America (Carlucci 2004), international organizations have funded many youth offender–related programs, such as those for postdetention services.[9] A good example is Uruguay's National Rehabilitation Center (Centro de Rehabilitación Nacional), which houses about 140 youth offenders and provides them with a wide range of social and educational services by a full-time staff of psychologists and other professionals. The commitment of the directors, such as eating meals with the youth, contrasts with that found in most other facilities in the region.[10] Because of the large amounts of time, money, and effort that go into programs like these, serving relatively few people, they are impractical as large-scale solutions. But they help to identify the causes of violence among youth at the early stages, when those causes are easier and more important to disentangle, thereby providing support and reducing the burden on law enforcement agencies. Unconnected to specific crimes or policies, this more dispassionate diagnosis can also lower the decibel level of Latin America's ongoing debate over youth crime. As discussed in chapter 3, a focus on questions such as the age of legal responsibility distracts from the larger issues such as socialization and drug availability.

Citizen Involvement in Evaluations

Citizen involvement, which boosts objectivity and prevention, should also play a greater role in evaluation of the criminal justice system. One form of involvement is violence observatories such as those in Honduras and Ecuador, which can become their country's preeminent sources of complete

8. "Inquieta violencia en Menores," *La Nación,* March 31, 2000, 6A.

9. For example, a 2004 Inter-American Development Bank citizen security loan of $7.2 million to Nicaragua aims to reduce violence and juvenile delinquency in communities. Similar programs have been developed for Brazil, Peru, and Honduras.

10. Residents and Gabriel Courtoisie, head of rehabilitation, Centro de Rehabilitación Nacional, interviews with author, Montevideo, August 18–19, 2003.

crime statistics, in part by attracting public attention and collaboration through dissemination of the times and places in which violent acts occur. Such entities are more likely to elicit involvement by those who shun more public venues such as community policing forums. Violence observatories can also support police reform. For example, La Rioja's police were unable to answer even a fraction of the calls to a new telephone line they set up, but they could have used the communications expertise that a violence observatory brings. When citizen-run observatories are not sustainable, more institutionally acceptable may be consortiums of criminal justice agencies that report crime numbers, such as the one in El Salvador described in chapter 2. In addition to sorting out statistical discrepancies, El Salvador's Mesa Técnica de Homicidios also encourages wider coordination and oversight with interested NGOs.

The combined importance of discretion and information is evident in the ways police determine the relevance of the information they do get. Leads on serious crimes or patterns of crime in general are often overlooked because officers ignore sources that appear irrelevant. In most countries up to 80 percent of citizen contacts with the police are not about crime, say officers; they are mostly grievances about a wide range of problems, most of which are not the police's direct responsibility. But when the police tune out most of this noncriminal information, they miss the portion of it that could be valuable. In New York City most citizen reports were long dismissed as "kites"—that is, they were considered flimsy and expected to (hopefully) just float away. But in areas such as Washington Heights, officers began to use them to gather evidence about persons and places, enabling them to wrap up drawn-out drug operations with arrests and convictions that effectively ended neighborhood trafficking (see Hartnett and Andrews 1999). Sustainable improvements in criminal justice, in short, need objective collection and evaluation of information.

Prison Conditions

Information may also be the best way to begin dealing with the appalling state of Latin America's prisons, described in chapter 2. Beginning in the 1990s, international criticism and the consequences of penitentiary conditions, such as prison-based criminal networks, sparked efforts to reduce incarcerated populations. Bail and conditional release laws have often been accompanied by the release or suspension of charges for those who have not been tried, who were arrested for minor crimes, or who were first-time offenders.[11] In 1999 Costa Rica began to offer community service as an option for those convicted of crimes punishable by less than three years in prison. The change relieved the system of four thousand inmates, cut crime (the program's recidivism rate is well under one-fifth of those who serve time), and saved money (prison costs $50 a day per person, whereas the alternative program costs $0.50). Longer-term progress, however, will require addressing systemic practices. Countries have focused so much on violence prevention and daily maintenance that prison officials in nearly every country have lost track of who is being held and for how long. Prisons, then, should be given the computer programs they need to document the number of incarcerated persons, the charges and status of their cases (particularly for drug possession and consumption), the level of legal access, and the length of incarceration (the courts received similar software from international agencies to track cases). This information will help reduce overcrowding, process detainees, meet international laws on detainee separation, and identify those who could benefit most from rehabilitation. It could also document sanitary conditions, access to mental and physical health care, availability of detox services, the quality and quantity of food, and the existence and functioning of work, self-help, personal development, skill-building, and other education and rehabilitation programs. This information will also help prison administrations meet basic needs while reducing violence and recidivism, and it should enable officials to summon some of the will needed to at least address prison conditions incrementally without being exposed to political attacks triggered by reform overhauls.

Structured Citizen Engagement

Democratization literature refers to a "virtuous cycle" during which an expanding number and density of associations in which citizens have overlapping memberships fortify the state-society relations that sustain democracy. On the issue of security, such cycles can be set in motion by citizens identifying and responding to the sources of crime. As councils at the local,

11. Colombia frees inmates who have served 60 percent of their terms unless charged with serious crimes such as drug trafficking. Ecuador's constitution allows judges to release unconvicted prisoners who have been in jail for over a year. In Bolivia a 1996 law allows the release of prisoners if no charges are brought within eighteen months. Chilean judges may suspend charges for first-time offenders, but try them for two crimes after a repeat offense.

regional, and national levels interact and form a societal network, participants begin to cast their visions beyond their own neighborhoods. In his categorization of incentives for participation, Olson (1965) found that selective incentives reflecting individual interests then begin to be replaced by
collective incentives focusing on the community good. In Caracas, for example, innovative neighborhood projects and political debates have been
pollinated through grassroots publications. The newspaper *La Chispa* (*The
Spark*) contains articles written by activists who are developing social programs in the city's geographically disparate *barrios,* from Petare in the far
eastern end of the district to Nuevo Horizonte (New Horizon) in the far
west. A local citizen security council in Buenos Aires, responding to residents' complaints about the insecurity posed by indigent men collecting discarded cardboard and other recyclables, found a solution by leaving cardboard out for collectors but restricting the times they can collect it. This
response was taken up by other areas as well, helping to reduce tensions
around the city.

When it shows results, such civic activism can be promoted among police officers as an untapped possibility rather than an additional uncertainty
in their work. It may then boost legal changes, accountability processes, and
the other reforms examined in this book. As many cities have experienced,
citizen participation remains low when police step up engagement only during crises. But if residents can initiate actions rather than just receive help,
they will usually provide more useful information to the police, which has
been the experience in cities like Bogotá, Santiago, Philadelphia, and Baltimore. The police then become a catalyst of the virtuous cycle of participation. Scholars in fact describe how governance is facilitated by relations
among state and civic actors that are strong but flexible enough to encourage
innovation (Migdal 1989; Putnam, Leonardi, and Nanetti 1994; Hagopian
1994; Grindle 2004, 196–205). Tendler (1997) points out the importance of
strong relations among different levels of government institutions and between those institutions and civil society. Meanwhile, many authors stress the
"complementarity" of mutually supportive public-private relations heavy on
personal ties and light on top–down directives (Evans 1997; Hildebrand and
Grindle 1997). In her work on policing, Ostrom (1975, 1997; Ostrom and
Whitaker 1973) shows how public service delivery succeeds when governments engage with social groups to help determine a project's direction but
are careful not to destroy local organizing with excessive directives.

But how can such a relationship be built to deal with citizen security, and
how can progress toward it be measured? As much as possible, community

policing programs must incorporate concepts of citizen accessibility and policy flexibility. In particular, neighborhood forums should be structured to minimize paralysis, politicization, and replication of existing power dynamics. Domination by established groups, more highly educated participants, or *mano dura* police-resident alliances is always likely, and will reinforce rather than change the kinds of community relations that stifle collectively constructive responses. In addition, because of its loose definitions and high expectations, community policing must incorporate specific objectives and mechanisms that measure progress toward them on an ongoing basis rather than after practices have set in and shut down the opportunities for new approaches. Indeed, many evaluation mechanisms do not evaluate what they should, such as by measuring "success" as the number of meetings or citizen demands logged rather than specific results.

Participatory budgeting, judges of the peace, and community justice forums are good examples of how the power to decide on central community concerns such as public projects and group conflicts attracts a wide range of residents, who acquire skills in debating, mobilizing, and governing through their participation.[12] Progress on such issues, which frame the start and endpoints of community policing, can be made through structures that are centered on criteria that lend substance to citizen participation while eliciting useful information. Table 7.1, developed for the Chicago police, shows how this can be done (Chicago Community Policing Evaluation Consortium 2002). In this model, at each community policing meeting, attending police officers, community leaders, and outside observers all note their general ratings in four related categories. The first is problem identification, which is the ability of the meeting to specify the problem under discussion. This area is usually the strongest, because the problem is usually the reason for the meeting. Less certain are the plans to respond, because planning requires compromise and commitment by those attending. If the problem is not clearly identified, the specificity of plans will almost always be at the lower end of the scale. But police support for plans, the third category, might salvage meetings from such uncertainty by giving official backing to certain responses. The most wide-open category, contribution to criminal policy, is usually rated after a policy's implementation has begun, as the impacts come into focus. After synchronizing their observations and

12. As Baiocchi (2003) reports in a study of Porto Alegre, public budgeting led to an increase in public investment from 2 percent in 1989 to 20 percent in 1994, almost tripling the number of schools.

Table 7.1 Process Framework for Community Policing

	Specificity	Participation (%)	Agreement	Results
1. Problem identification	1–10	10–100	High–low	Positive– negative
2. Plans	1–10	10–100	High–low	Positive– negative
3. Police support for plans	1–10	10–100	High–low	Positive– negative
4. Contribution to criminal policy	1–10	10–100	High–low	Positive– negative

Source: Chicago Community Policing Evaluation Consortium (2002).

giving plans a specified time for implementation, observers then meet to connect weak or negative results back to the original deliberations and restructure or reframe follow-up ones accordingly.

Because of the positive results in Chicago, other cities have also adopted the process framework outlined in table 7.1. For example, in the high-crime East New York section of Brooklyn, neighborhood forums have helped bring out and defuse smoldering sources of tension such as the after-school police stops of students and the absence of patrols in high-rise buildings. Identifying points of tension also helps focus participation and integrate evaluation by giving residents specific targets for improvement. And a sharper focus encourages participation by nonpolice officials. For example, Uruguay's Citizen Security Program has resource and logistics centers that are actively supported by city mayors and councils. In 1990 Uruguay's capital, Montevideo, began a decentralization process to encourage citizen participation. The city was divided into eighteen administrative zones, each with neighborhood councils to help bring in services, oversee resource allocation, and allow residents to become links to government officials (Canel 2001). Although both the general and community policing councils encountered resource limits and often unreasonable expectations, state support helped overcome those obstacles, in part by enabling discussion of policy and conditions in general, such as the effects of poverty and inequality on crime.[13] In 1995 Bogotá, Colombia, began reducing violence through problem-oriented citizen security schools and regional "fronts."

In many countries in Latin America such programs are shored up by neighborhood Fiscalía offices as well as by legal aid NGOs (see Brinks

13. Author interviews and observations, national meeting, Programa de Seguridad Ciudadana, Montevideo, August 25–26, 2003.

2008). To expand such outside support, the police could create a database of organizations willing to provide resources, or willing to offer the expertise needed to establish programs such as those that alert residents and police to violence-inducing tensions. Umbrella consortiums that bring together businesses in a specific sector are particularly well suited to draft support from its members. An example is the insurance association in Argentina, Asociación Argentina de Compañías de Seguros, which has shown support for police reform. In addition, in that country's Capital Federal the many local councils have effectively pressured the Policía Federal Argentina to integrate the city's popular community policing efforts into its daily operations, such as through joint patrols and coordinator office hours in police stations.[14]

Because demands and expectations are part of such efforts, police structures must be both reliable and reliably flexible to respond to them. In particular, police must be ready to deal with tensions among neighborhoods that can flare up in a community policing project. For example, at a meeting in the middle-class San José neighborhood of Zapote in Costa Rica, residents said that their area was "calm for decades" until the intrusion of drug users from adjacent neighborhoods.[15] Some residents then tried to make their citizen patrols more aggressive, which led to their discontinuation for being abusive. Officers' abilities to handle such volatility are rooted in large part in their own acceptance of the community policing idea. In the 1960s the United States took the first steps away from the professional model in order to address urban unrest and growing officer disenchantment. The goals were better coordination of preventive and investigative policing and a reduction in overspecialization. In the 1970s and 1980s traditional policing was then often replaced by "team policing," along with geographic reorganization and other approaches later associated with community policing. But the process of internal acceptance and appreciation of community policing was neglected. As a result, many officers at all ranks considered community relations tangential to crime fighting, and most U.S. cities "tolerated" disciplinary review boards as a way to placate restless neighborhoods (Chevigny 2003, 59). In fact, authors such as Mastrofski (2006, 65)

14. Observation of the community policing program of the city of Morón, Buenos Aires Province, May 27, 2004; Claudio Suárez, head, security program of the government of the city of Buenos Aires, interview by author, May 26, 2004; author meeting with four coordinators of the city of Buenos Aires security program, May 19, 2004.

15. Author interviews and observations, Zapote neighborhood meeting, San José, June 20–21, 2006.

conclude that throughout the United States community policing "has not transformed the structure and operation of American policing so much as it has altered its rhetoric." In many American cities officials involved in community policing continue to be dismissed by the rest of the agency as "social workers" (or, more damning, as "empty holster" agents). Meanwhile, community-centered public campaigns and slogans, such as the omnipresent "Block Watch" programs in the United States, remain more symbolic than substantive.

To avoid such dead ends, police must bend their agencies' structures to fit the strategies adopted to fight each cause of crime. In other words, from youth truancy to narco-trafficking infiltration, the problem should be the basic unit of policing. To move toward that goal, as discussed in this book, police commissioners should have greater discretion in at least two areas. The first is spending; community policing is not traditional, and so the use of resources and directives do not have to be either. Second, centralized scheduling should be replaced, where possible, by teams responsible for a particular area (such as ten blocks) headed by a leader authorized to alter schedules, strategies, and resource use. For example, Houston's Directed Area Responsibility Teams (DARTs) combine decentralized administration with "substations" headed by block captains (Brown 1987). Many officers rightly warn that such restructuring may open up more opportunities for corruption—one reason for automatic rotation—but the same kinds of informal controls that allow community policing to reduce crime also allow it to check corruption. These efforts also require state commitment. For example, the state may establish commissions made up of agencies with incentives to contribute to reaching clearly stated goals, such as helping reduce youth truancy or domestic violence by a certain percentage (see Sherman 1995). Through such commissions police could work more closely with education and health professionals to better understand and respond to the causes of crime and to undertake initiatives such as neighborhood cleanup campaigns in which residents and police gather in a high-crime street to remove trash, fix locks on homes, and make needed repairs in public spaces.

Costa Rica's community policing program, one of the region's first, is an example of how constructive police and citizen involvement can be when structured in these ways. Begun as the Unit of Community Extension in the police academy in 1994, the program has since expanded to thousands of *barrios* throughout the country.[16] It is headed by the Office

---

16. Ana Durán Salvatierra, vice minister of governance and police, interview with author, San José, Costa Rica, June 19, 2006.

of Community Security (Dirección de Seguridad Comunitaria), and has about a hundred permanent staff. Program officers have more flexible schedules and different merits for promotion, and are rotated every four years, which gives them enough time to become fully acquainted with a community and its problems. The program tries to be flexible as well, says its director, in order to learn from early mistakes such as excluding local police in its original development.[17] Meanwhile, citizen participation is channeled through the Basic Training Program in Citizen Security (Programa Básico de Capacitación en Seguridad Ciudadana), composed of eleven participatory modules that last about two months each. They cover subjects such as prevention, community organizing, criminology, drugs, and child abuse, as well as areas not traditionally included in community policing such as penal, family, and other areas of criminal law. At the weekly talks (*charlas*) in different areas, residents are expected to take the lead, mainly by identifying the causes of insecurity and specific responses to them. Designed to cultivate and identify citizen leaders, these *charlas* typically start out with about fifty residents, dwindling by the end to about fifteen, four of whom remain as permanent contacts heading up projects such as telephone networks.

In addition to bringing out the causes of insecurity and the points of tension, these *charlas* expose the limits of community policing in general. Residents are primarily concerned about recent incidents and requests for more protection by local police. Attending officers then spend much of the session time responding to and imparting information, which reinforces citizens' traditional relationship with them. Even at a *charla* on the judiciary in the working class San José neighborhood of Tibás that was supposed to be about the penal process code, residents still focused on particular crime incidents in their neighborhood.[18] Such retreat into traditional relationships not only leaves little time to develop new policies, but also can deprive officers of the opportunity to convey to residents the procedural limits to solving crimes in which prosecutable evidence is lacking. By diminishing unrealistic expectations, such candid forms of communication may also shore up citizens' commitments to playing a more direct role in their own security.

17. Alberto Li Chan, quartermaster and coordinator, Seguridad Comunitaria, Ministerio Seguridad Pública de Costa Rica, interview with author, San José, Costa Rica, June 20–21, 2006.

18. Law *charla* in Tibás, San José, Costa Rica, June 22, 2006. About twenty residents attended.

Police Management: Standards without Standardization

The police could better meet the great demands for its help by paring down the tasks associated with police management. Rotations, paperwork, special assignments, and centralized controls, many commanding officers say, make it impossible to manage their corps. For example, most police commanders in Caracas are given daily the lists of officers under their command, but often they do not have time to find out why many of them do not show up for work. It is unrealistic to expect such problems to be fixed overnight, as this and other books on police management show, but other tangible and politically acceptable alterations in administration and resources can go a long way in freeing up commanders to focus on and achieve results. As described in this section, a strengthening of human resources administration, officer living standards, inspection, accountability, and discipline can all help fortify police management.

First, human resources must be approached as holistically as political relations will allow. At the broadest level, national and regional governments should hash out a distribution of human and material resources based on population and crime rates. Such a plan should include incentives for recruiting in underrepresented regions and assignments to high-crime areas. Police districts should also be reconfigured if necessary. Each one should have no more than 300,000 citizens, and all should be run by officials with more autonomy in implementing national training curriculum and standards.[19] For example, arguing that power must "be realigned if the agency and its members are to achieve their full potential," Henry (2002, 26) describes how the NYPD identified management as a key point for change and strengthened middle-level managers by giving them more disciplinary authority. At the local level in Latin America, most commanders should aim to put a quarter of those officers doing administrative work on the street, replacing them with local civilians who have the pertinent education and background. This change would increase the presence and transparency of the police, thereby improving community relations, and it would strengthen efficacy.

Second, both management and oversight must better accommodate the daily realities of policing. Most officers resent handling complex tasks with-

19. In the United States some local law enforcement officials, such as those in Detroit and Portland, have challenged and rejected federal operations on the basis of local ordinances, policies, and programs. See *Printz v. United States,* 521 U.S. 898 (1997).

out the financial compensation or social recognition that other professionals such as lawyers enjoy for working under less dangerous conditions, and they resent the irregular work hours that are harmful to family life. Relatively easy ways in which to help officers while boosting morale include housing loans, transport subsidies, health benefits, and other forms of support contingent on clean records. As public employees, many police already enjoy such benefits, but more attention to the particular needs of officers—especially physical and mental health—is helpful. Internal affairs units can also boost officers' daily experience. Those units are often regarded by officers as an instrument less of support than of blame, but they can help reverse negative internal practices and pressures (see McArdle 2001). At all levels, officers pay a heavy professional, social, and psychological price for their refusal to participate in illicit acts, and those who stop being corrupt rarely denounce larger abuses for fear of exposing their own or regard the cover-up of corruption as a requisite self-defense of the agency. To chip away at this thick layer of corruption, internal affairs offices should adopt more mediative approaches. For one thing, instead of being immediately pressed for information about illegal activity, officers should first be asked about any problems they may have, such as with family or finances, and how such problems could be resolved. Surveys of officers on their views of the seriousness of and appropriate discipline for specific infractions, from free meals to wide kickback schemes, will also help police officials understand the types of temptations officers face and their reactions to them in daily policing (see Klockars, Ivkovic, and Haberfeld 2004). Interviews of individual officers also will reveal the discretion and practices that underlie problem-oriented policing (Capowich and Andrews 1995), but interviews cannot be conducted if they are viewed as a prelude to punishment.

Officers' responses in both individual interviews and surveys, along with reports on the use of force and logs of citizen complaints, can be used for an Early Intervention (EI) system for identifying "problem" officers with a high level of incidents and complaints (see Walker 2005). Because police bureaucracy has been identified by both officers and outside studies as a major cause of stress, this approach could also help identify the institutional sources of behavioral problems. To boost EI procedures, the government could have superiors conduct routine line inspections or have outside teams conduct personnel inspections, with each inspection focusing on a specific personnel mater (such as attrition) or organizational matter (such as underutilization of radios). Supporting such efforts to identify unseen problems could be targeted and random "integrity tests," in which an officer is given a chance to commit a corrupt act without realizing that he or she is being monitored (Newham 2003). Together, the problems and problem officers identified could be cited by an independent official, usually called an auditor, in investigating and proposing reforms of the structures or policies that might be contributing to such abuses.

When such EI or auditor investigations do expose wrongdoing and lead to disciplinary action, the consequences must be clear. Exactly what happens to officers after the first, second, and third incident of different kinds of abuse must be well publicized. Otherwise, officers will form their own interpretations of who is and is not disciplined and why, thereby diminishing the chances of cooperation. And in cases of mass purges, officers may form an armed body poised against reform in general. In such scenarios, accountability agencies will never reach the third stage of reversal described in chapter 3. Instead, they will just scratch out victories subsequently engulfed by institutional conflict, police resentment, or politics. Most of the reasonable and much-needed recommendations of New York City's Mollen Commission, for example, were commandeered by interagency disputes and political grandstanding.[20] Again, careful meditative approaches can help avoid such fates. One area in which such mediation can help is deciding who participates in disciplinary actions. There are many reasons to restrict that process to police: only they have the experience and perspective to understand their colleagues' actions, and a ruling by a police official is more acceptable internally. For those reasons, through the 1980s nearly 80 percent of the disciplinary process in the United States included only the police. And most forms of citizen participation that were created were limited to review of either the initial complaint or the final decision.

20. The Mollen Commission, appointed by Mayor David Dinkins in 1992, exposed networks of police officers dealing drugs, robbing residents, and taking cash from crime scenes. Commenting on the situation, Amnesty International (1996) said that "it is rare for NYPD officers to be criminally prosecuted for on-duty excessive force and rare for convictions to be obtained." The commission's recommendations included an independent Police Commission with investigatory and subpoena powers (Selwyn Raab, "New York's Police Allows Corruption, Mollen Panel Says," *New York Times,* December 29, 1993). But in 1994 Mayor Rudolph Giuliani vetoed the City Council's creation of such a body on the grounds that these two powers belonged exclusively to the mayor. After a 1994 hotel rampage by police, Giuliani adopted many of the Mollen Commission's proposals, but shifted investigation from the Internal Affairs Bureau to precinct commanders (William Rachbaum, "Getting Back in Line: Rudy Unveils Plan to Stem Cop Corruption," *Newsday.* June 15, 1995).

New York City is a good example of the tensions that can arise among the procedures, actors, and agencies involved in discipline. The average number of complaints of police misconduct filed each year to the city's Civilian Complaint Review Board (CCRB) rose from two hundred to two thousand during the 1990s,[21] and it reached a record of over eight thousand in 2009.[22] In both 2008 and 2009, most charges brought to the CCRB came from among the record number of people in New York—an estimated half-million—who were stopped and frisked each year. Despite this surge in complaints, the percentage of them that the NYPD refused to prosecute grew from 2 percent in 2005 to 33 percent by 2008. Although the conviction rate at departmental trials rose from 30 percent in 2004 to 60 percent in 2008, these patterns have led to a flare-up in tensions between citizens and the police. So even though the police's overall authority over discipline should be acknowledged, the police should use complaints to identify specific points of tension and to address practices. Stopping and frisking is clearly one of those problematic practices, and if the police force does not address it—at the very least by involving citizens in an evaluation—they may lose control over it to officials who take citizen complaints in the political arena.

Conclusion

Those who develop security reform strategies must tap into the inherent powers and limitations of policing and criminal justice. Daily policing and institutional relations, in particular, exemplify both the positive and negative reach of criminal justice in high-crime societies. By starting from recognition of that impact, the five areas discussed in this chapter—points of tension, officer discretion, policy evaluation, structured citizen engagement, and internal management—attempt to utilize the potential of policing to minimize its harm.

21. "Complaints against the Police Rise," *New York Times,* June 11, 1998, A25.
22. Christine Hauser, "Few Results for Reports of Police Misconduct," *New York Times,* October 4, 2009.

Chapter 8

Conclusion

Taking a biblical approach to reform, one police commander in Bolivia said that change will come only after the entire generation of police officers now serving "dies off." In the meantime, reformers are trying to produce the kind of overhaul that so many citizens want to see in the meantime. Throughout Latin America the growing limits of incident-centered, standardized, and forceful responses to crime have spurred efforts to replace these responses with problem-oriented policing based on newly empowered citizens, clearer police structures, and more accountable judicial procedures. But as reformers confront an array of political, institutional, and societal obstacles, they must continually adopt the flexibility that defines problem-oriented policing itself. Such an approach is needed to defuse the tensions between traditional and problem-oriented policing—that is, instead of being at odds, traditional and problem-oriented policing can be constructive checks on each other. And instead of being a drag on democracy, citizen security can tap into the participation and standards that underlie it.

The connections among the four typologies developed in this book and summarized in table 8.1 can help explain why similar obstacles to reform develop in different cases and how, despite those differences, they can be overcome through strategies such as those discussed in chapter 7. On a basic level, each reform type described in chapter 1 should take into account the realms of change discussed in chapter 2 by supporting strategies that can bring concrete change within preexisting limitations. One of the best ways is to give citizens well-defined tasks. Neighborhood "security stations" staffed with police officers, violence observatory volunteers, social service agents, and youth interns are some of the many ways to do so. Surveys on

Table 8.1 Summary of Typologies Developed in This Book

Major reform types	Realms of change	Democratic governance areas	Recommended strategies
Agency restructuring	Opinion and politics	Power	Addressing points of tension
Professional support	The law	Geography	Discretion
Control mechanisms	Police career		Information-based evaluation
	Police structure	Civil society	Structured citizen engagement
Legal changes	Information management		Police management: standards without standardization
Community policing	Criminal justice Police-society relations		

Source: The author.

less controversial issues such as pollution, or the recent formation of gender violence observatories in Central America, can create public momentum for security actions that breaks down institutional resistance. Police professionalism and citizen-police relations may be improved through targeted crackdowns on sales of addictive substances (such as glue in Honduras, alcohol in La Paz, and *paco* in Buenos Aires). Educational incentives for investigators and promotional forms that include a public relations evaluation can help boost restructuring and control mechanisms by altering informal power relations within the police.

To overcome some of the social and geographic divisions discussed in chapter 2, an environmental approach to policing can at times be pursued. In particular, pollution is one of the biggest security concerns of urban Latin Americans, and the airborne contamination over public lands such as forests and seashores causes tensions in rural areas. By helping connect people to the appropriate services, the police can help resolve these problems and avoid some of the violence they generate.

Connections among the typologies are evident for each of the five major reform types. Structural reorganization of police forces should begin with changes least likely to have unintended consequences for police careers, such as slowing promotions of officers suddenly demoted in a simplified hierarchy. Combining ranks must have enough support within the police, creating new units must have sufficient external support, and decentralizing operations must be carried out using a national formula of resource collection and distribution. Under such constraints, tying incentives to professional support and gradually giving *comisarios* more authority are two concrete steps that can help change practices. Control mechanisms must also take into account the power and limits of the police. In response to perceived infringements on authority or internal decision making, officers may cover up abuses faster than accountability agencies can uncover them. Instead, steps such as professional incentives for service in internal affairs and citizen information efforts could make the police more transparent while also strengthening civil society. As Avritzer (2002, 105) points out, "Modern administration must seek to connect itself with a process of communication that starts at the periphery." Legal changes can benefit from concrete steps such as decentralized prosecutor offices, which, by improving public access, may also give prosecutors the public support needed in corruption cases. The broadest reform of all, community policing, should be cognizant of society's anticriminal hostility and how it is stoked by police influence. Strategies such as tying community police programs to drug investigations should be based on structured citizen engagement on specific points of tension identified by both citizens and police that recognize both citizen demands and police prestige.

As with policing, the public's abysmal views of criminal justice can be a trigger for reform. To improve the judiciary's image and efficacy, many U.S. cities are combining court and social services to provide more support for citizens as well as preventive strategies and alternatives to incarceration. One example is the fifteen-city Family Justice Centers (FJCs). In Boston, which has one of the more extensive centers, each of the city's eleven police stations has a civilian advocate who reaches out to the victims in every case of domestic or other forms of violence. The FJC works closely with the Family Justice Division (FJD) of the Boston Police Department, which is made up of units on domestic violence, sexual assault, crimes against children, and human trafficking. The Children's Advocacy Center, a forensic examining room, interview spaces, and two full-time registered nurses all make the response to violence against women and children more comprehensive and effective. Once on the premises, civilians can access services they would not have known about otherwise or were unable to reach, such as shelter referrals. In the same building as the FJC and the FJD is the district attorney, whose presence makes the subsequent and often slower steps in the criminal justice system run more smoothly. The whole process works, says the FJD's chief, because FJC facilities are designed to allow victims of violence to talk about their experience on their own terms, which helps both in their treatment and in criminal prosecution.[1]

Even the broad areas of democratic governance discussed in chapter 3 can lead to concrete reform models. One approach that can help identify points of tension and improve police discretion is crime mapping, which provides a visual and moving picture of crime patterns, hot spots, and the most dangerous times of day. When available on the Internet, such maps are an invaluable aid for citizens. They also help policymakers to better use resources and schedules by overlapping theory with reality. For example, mapping sites of drug sales and overdoses can test preconceived ideas about the impacts of the routes used by traffickers (see Eck 1998). Such criminological uses of technology will only grow as a more computer-savvy generation comes into public office. For example, Jorge Nazer, Chile's national secretary of public safety, wants to combine technology and prevention in ways that are both innovative and bring short-term results.[2] Aware of how easily reality can upset the delicate balance of these elements, the government is introducing them as pilot projects in tough neighborhoods where positive results can give the approach the credibility and political support it needs to expand.

A combined focus on geography and civil society also leads to other efforts. One of the most important links between them is the way at-risk individuals navigate their neighborhoods' physical demarcations, economic realities, and social pressures. Understanding this socialization process is a key to unlocking the kinds of prevention that underscore problem-oriented policing. In most low-income areas many interactions among youth are based on antisocial attitudes that take shape in a "street code" of language, behaviors, and recognition that they strive to attain for peer acceptance. Gangs and acts of violence are two of the faster routes toward mastering the street code and of gaining the credibility, respect, and self-esteem that society does not provide. Although such "street cred" is hard-won, it is also "easily lost" (Office of Justice Programs 2009, 2), keeping even seasoned gang members off balance. As part of the evaluations discussed in the last

1. Genevieve King, captain, Boston Police Department, and chief, FJD, phone interview with author, November 6, 2009.

2. Jorge Nazer, national director of public security, Republic of Chile, interview with author, New York, June 16, 2010; Rodrigo Chacón, "Definen plan de inversión en RM con miras a 2011," *La Nación,* May 26, 2010.

chapter, police should therefore try to assess the depth and extent of a street code, particularly how it validates violence and how much security it actually provides. When South Africa liberalized its bail laws, many of those let out were killed in their communities, showing how unprotected they were even in areas they considered their bases. U.S. programs with the approaches applicable to Latin America and other regions include California's Homerun program, in which parole officials give "life habits" courses in high schools to help youth manage time, and they train teachers, keep the school and courts in contact with each other, visit youths' homes, and organize meetings for parents (see Presman, Chapman, and Rosen 2002). The STOP the Violence program, headed by students in the Family, Career and Community Leaders of America, is a community-based training curriculum to help youth find innovative ways to prevent violence, such as through identifying warning signs and holding a national competition for anti-violence projects.

One of the most innovative efforts is that of the "violence interrupters," who literally see violence as a virus that can only be stopped by direct and personal intervention. Spurred by the view that urban violence is spread largely by the patterns of revenge among youth that are driven by the iron-clad combinations of peer pressure and street cred and transmitted, like a virus, from person to person and gang to gang, this approach regards violence as a public health epidemic, a contagious disease spreading in ways like tuberculosis, HIV, and cholera. This approach took root in Chicago, which recruited outreach workers from troubled neighborhoods who had been gang members and who probably had spent time in prison. These "violence interrupters" immerse themselves in street culture to identify who might be seeking revenge. They then physically intervene with these individuals, often in hospitals, helping them consider the consequences of retaliation for themselves and their famillies, while offering them ways out, such as school or job training. The program has spread to many U.S. cities, and many Latin American governments have adopted programs that use the same approach.

One of the most productive connections made among at-risk youth, social conditions, and criminal justice is the Los Angeles Police Academy Magnet School Program, which offers a full high school curriculum. along with specialized coursework in communications, science, community service, constitutional law, criminal justice, forensic science, police science, and computer software. Serving over a thousand students, the program has been implemented at five high schools, each of which has a full-time police officer as program coordinator. Because of the students' greater financial, emotional and family needs, a complementary Mentoring Partnership matches individual police officers and students. Although the effort required years of "hammering" away at officials to get the program going and "an enormous amount of cooperation by schools and police" to keep it going, says its executive director, the police became more supportive as the program became a high-quality recruiting source of minority cadets.[3] As with police reforms in any country, a reform must been seen through its full arc—and attention must be paid to politics at every step of the way—before a reform attracts sufficient backing to survive on its own. As attention to youth grows among police reforms in Latin America, such a process can be replicated there.

Each of the book's three case studies further reveals how the threads that connect the four typologies listed in table 8.1 may weave the most durable fabric for reform. In Honduras the main pillars of change are shaky but still standing: the community policing program, the penal process code, and the set of governmental and nongovernmental agencies that are working to hold the state accountable. All three pillars have been sideswiped by the willful neglect and legal maneuvering of the state, as well as by the political turmoil that makes concerted policy difficult. But, as in Argentina and Bolivia, the upheaval of 2009 brought greater awareness of the underlying power dynamics, which may motivate citizens to organize (as in the city of Danlí) and enable local officers to replace national directives with local issues as the locus of their daily work (as in La Ceiba). As they do so amid Honduras's extreme levels of poverty and violence, they may succeed in turning antiviolence projects into the sturdiest stepping-stones to the kind of progress that will allow people to gradually assert their control of public space.

In Bolivia, corruption and poor administration, distrust by society, and regional divisions are undoing the steady progress made in the 1990s. The extensive mobilization and participation by citizens are not penetrating the security and criminal justice system, allowing the gap between expectations and practice to widen. The long list of aborted national plans, the proliferation of police units, the lack of statistical and financial transparency, the corruption of autonomous police units, and the scattered nature of community policing all exemplify the frustrated potential and need for reform in Bolivia. The Morales regime may be able to use its popular legitimacy and commitment to change to address these related challenges in a comprehen-

---

3. Roberta Weintraub, executive director, Los Angeles Police Academy Magnet School Program, phone interview with author, October 30, 2009.

sive way that utilizes the immense potential of citizens' willingness to act, but it is racing against the clock in the face of severe geographical and financial constraints.

Given the extent to which the periodic economic and political meltdowns since the democratic transition in 1982 have galvanized Argentines, it is ironic that political maneuvering and competition continue to block reform in that country. Buenos Aires Province was finally able to overcome much of that impediment, but only after radical political change and decades of extreme abuse and corruption. In provinces such as Mendoza and La Rioja, as chapter 6 describes, comprehensive and innovative change continues to be thwarted primarily by politics. But the process has brought in many projects —a lot with staying power—that have opened up the next stage of reform.

After decades of sweeping change, as these countries show, citizen security is one of the last frontiers in Latin America's political evolution. Like the transition from authoritarianism, it is forcing each country to take another hard look at how it is moving into the future. It challenges executives, especially those more closely identified with the right wing or left wing of their countries, to wrestle down partisanship and political stereotypes to emphasize the collective interests of security. It challenges the police to loosen their grip on the thin blue line separating the "good" from the "bad" and order from chaos. As for society, it is a challenge to temper immediate dangers and raw fears with long-term perspectives. But if states and societies can turn the tide on insecurity by addressing its causes and their own contributions to it, they will strengthen the democracy that holds them together.

Appendix A

National Homicide Rates, 1995–2009

A. National Homicide Rates, per 100,000 Persons, 1995–2001

Country	1995	1996	1997	1998	1999	2000	2001
Argentina[a]	4.0–7.8	5.7–8.5	4.8–9.2	4.7–7.2	5.3–7.3	4.8–13.0	6.9–10.5*
Bolivia[b]	68.0	78.0	n.a.	28.0	n.a.	35.5	3.7–35.5
Brazil[c]	19.3–30.1	24.0–27.0	25.0–28.1	26.0	25.0–28.0	19.7–29.3	23.0–27.8*
Chile[d]	3.2–8.0	4.9–5.9	2.8–4.7	1.5–4.0	1.6–5.0	1.6–5.0	1.9–5.4
Colombia[e]	60.8–76.0*	60.0–69.4	57.0–67.8	54.0–56.6	58.6–67.0	65.0–89.5	64.6–68.9
Costa Rica[f]	5.6–11.9	5.6–14.1	5.6–12.5	6.1–9.8	6.5–11.9	5.6–12.0	6.1–25.9
Dominican Republic[g]	12.7	12.8	12.6	13.4–15.4	14.4–15.0	11.9–13.1	12.8
Ecuador[h]	13.4–16.0	14.0–23.0	12.4–23.0	15.1	14.8–27.0	10.3	15.9
El Salvador[i]	39.9*–149.9	52.3–117.4	109.1	80.0–90.0	36.2–77.1	37.3–119.0	34.4–57.0
Guatemala[j]	28.1–38.0	21.2–40.0	29.0– 43.0	27.0– 34.0	18.0–26.0	19.3–150.0	25.2–30.0
Honduras[k]	40.0–40.9	35.4	52.5	154.2	42.7	9.4–50.8	53.7–54.4
Mexico[l]	15.4–40.0	15.4	14.6–37.0	15.7–35.0	12.5–34.0	32.0	10.0–32.0
Nicaragua[m]	16.0	11.7–15.0	11.7–16.0	10.0–13.0	11.0	9.0–18.3	10.0–10.6
Panama[n]	22.0	9.4	12.2	10.8	10.6	10.2–10.9	10.0–10.2
Paraguay[o]	7.0	14.0	8.0	16.0	14.0	4.0–12.0	20.7
Peru[p]	5.5–12.5	4.4–12.1	9.0–10.2	6.0	4.0	4.4–11.5	3.0
Uruguay[q]	3.0–16.8	4.4	4.7	3.7–10.0	4.1–9.0	4.4	6.3
Venezuela[r]	11.2*–66.6	14.8–25.0	19.0	20.0–25.0	25.0–35.8	14.7–35.0	32 .0–124.4

Note: * indicates intentional homicides. "n.a." indicates data are not available.

[a] 1995–2000 upper estimates: Dirección Nacional de Política Criminal, Ministerio de Justicia y Derechos Humanos and UNCJIN (1998); 1995 lower estimate: Camara and Salama (2004, 160); 1996 lower estimate: WHO (2003); 1997–99 lower estimates: PAHO, Regional Core Health Data Initiative, Table Generator System, http://www.paho.org/Enlish/SHA/coredata/tabulator; 2000 lower estimate: Acero Velásquez (2003), based on Inter-American Development Bank (IADB) reports; 2001 lower estimate: Bailey and Flores-Macías (2007); 2001 upper estimate: based on rate of 3,936 homicides reported to the government.

[b] 1995, 1996, 1998: Camara and Salama (2004, 160); 2000 and 2001 upper estimate: Instituto Nacional de Estadísticas de Bolivia; 2001 lower estimate: UNCJIN (2003).

[c] 1995 lower estimate: PAHO, Regional Core Health Data Initiative, Table Generator System; 1995, 1996, 1997, 1999 upper estimates: Camara and Salama (2004, 160); 1996, 1997, 1999 lower estimates: PAHO (2003a); 1998: PAHO (2000); 2000 lower estimate: Acero Velásquez (2003), based on IABD reports; 2000

331

upper estimate: PAHO (2004); 2001 lower estimate: Riberio (2007); 2001 upper estimate: Organização dos Estados Ibero-Americanos para a Educação, Ciência e Cultura (2009).

d1995 upper estimate: PAHO (1996); 1995 lower estimate and 1996 upper estimate: Fundación Paz Ciudadana (1999); 1997 lower estimate: PAHO (2000); 1997 upper estimate: Departamento Nacional de Planeación; 1996, 1998, and 1999 lower estimates: PAHO (2006); 1998 and 2000 upper estimates: Camara and Salama (2004, 160); 1999 upper estimate: PAHO (2003b); 2000 lower estimate: UNCJIN (2001); 2001 lower estimate: Centro de Estudios de Justicia de las Américas (CEJA); 2001 upper estimate: PAHO, Regional Core Health Data Initiative, Table Generator System.

e1995 lower estimate: Mesquita Neto (2002); 1995 upper estimate: PAHO Regional Health Care Initiative; 1996 lower estimate: Salazar Posada (1999); 1996 and 1997 upper estimates, 1998 lower estimate: PAHO (2000); 1997 lower estimate and 2000 upper estimate: Camara and Salama (2004, 160); 1998 upper estimate and 2000 lower estimates: PAHO (2000); 1999 and 2001 lower estimates: Departamento Nacional de Planeación; 1999 upper estimate: PAHO (2003b), based on reports from the Medicina Legal and the Alcaldía de Cali; 2001 upper estimate: Vicepresidencia de la República (2008, 98).

f1995 and 1996 lower estimates: based on population and reported intentional homicides, Departamento de Planificación (2004); 1995–97 upper estimates: based on population and all reported homicides, Departamento de Planificación (2004); 1998 lower estimate: UNCJIN (2001); 1999 lower estimate: OCAVI (2007e); 1998–2000 upper estimates: Programa Estado de la Nación (2004); 2000 lower estimate: Acero Velásquez (2003), based on IABD reports; 1997 and 2001 lower estimates: PAHO, Regional Core Health Data Initiative, Table Generator System; 2001 upper estimate: Carlos Arguedas, "Número de homicidios disminuyó este año," *La Nación*, December 27, 2004, 12A.

g1995, 1996, 1997, and 1998 lower estimate: Cabral and Cabral (2006); 1998 upper estimate: PAHO, Regional Core Health Data Initiative, Table Generator System; 1999 upper estimate: PAHO (2006); 1999 lower estimate and 2000 upper estimate: OCAVI (2007b); 2000 lower estimate: Acero Velásquez (2003), based on IADB reports; 2000: Acero Velásquez (2003), based on IADB reports; 2001: Bobea (2003).

h1995–97 lower estimates, 1998: PAHO (2000); 1999 lower estimate: PAHO (2003b); 1995–99 upper estimates: Camara and Salama (2004, 160); 2000: Acero Velásquez (2003), based on IADB reports; 2001: PAHO, Regional Core Health Data Initiative, Table Generator System.

i1995 upper estimate: Amaya Cóbar (1998); 1995 lower estimate: PAHO (2004); 1996 lower estimate: PAHO Regional Core Health Data Initiative; 1996 upper estimate: Gabaldón 2001; 1997: Chinchilla (2003), based on reports of the Fiscalía General; 1998 lower estimate: Institute of Forensic Medicine (Instituto de Medicina Forense); 1998 upper estimate: Koonings and Kruijt (2004, 157), based on reports of the Fiscalía General; 1999 lower estimate: OCAVI (2007a); 1999 upper estimate: PAHO (2003b), based on reports of the Fiscalía General; 2000 upper estimate: UNCJIN (2001); 2000 and 2001 lower estimates: Dirección General de Estadísticas y Censos (DIGESTYC) and the Policía Nacional Civil; 2001 upper estimate: PAHO (2006) and María Siu, "Delincuencia atemoriza a Centroamericanos," *La República, San José de Costa Rica,* October 21, 2002.

j1995 lower estimate: Carranza (1997, 356, 374, 436); 1996, 1999, and 2000 lower estimates: PAHO, Regional Core Health Data Initiative, Table Generator System; 1995–99 upper estimates: UNDP (2007); 1997 and 1998 lower estimates: Centro de Investigaciones Económicas Nacionales (CIEN), cited in Seligson and Azpuru (2000); 2000 upper estimate: Acero Velásquez (2003), based on IADB reports; 2001 upper estimate: Ribando (2009); 2001 lower estimate: María Siu, "Delincuencia atemoriza a Centroamericanos," *La República, San José de Costa Rica,* October 21, 2002, and OCAVI (2007d).

k1995 upper estimate: PAHO (1996); 1995 lower estimate, and 1997: Chinchilla (2003); 1999: PAHO (2003b), based on reports from the Policía Nacional de Honduras; 2000 lower estimate: Acero Velásquez (2003), based on IADB reports; 1998: Crime Statistics, Interpol, reported by Centro de Estudios de Justicia de las Americas; 2000 upper estimate: Rodríguez (2003); 1996 and 2000 lower estimates: Organización de Mundial de Personas con Discapacidad (2004); 2001 lower estimate: OCAVI (2007e); 2001 upper estimate: María Siu, "Delincuencia atemoriza a Centroamericanos," *La República, San José de Costa Rica,* October 21, 2002.

l1995 upper estimate, 1996, 1997–99 upper estimates, 2000, and 2001 upper estimate: Instituto Ciudadano de Estudios sobre la Inseguridad (2009); 1995 lower estimate: PAHO (1996); 1997 lower estimate: PAHO (2000); 1999 lower estimate: PAHO (2003a); 1998 and 2001 lower estimates: Dirección General de Información en Salud, http://www.dgis.salud.gob.mx.

[m]1995, 1996 and 1998 upper estimates: Policía Nacional de Nicaragua (2006); 1997 upper estimate: Bautista Lara (2006); 1996–98 lower estimates, and 1999: PAHO, Regional Core Health Data Initiative, Table Generator System; 2000 lower estimate: OCAVI (2007e); 2000 upper estimate: IADB, reported in *El Tiempo,* Bogotá, May 9, 2000, and in Acero Velásquez (2003), based on IADB reports; 2001 lower estimate: Ribando (2009); 2001 upper estimate: María Siu, "Delincuencia atemoriza a Centroamericanos," *La República, San José de Costa Rica,* October 21, 2002.

[n]1995: Chinchilla (2003); 1996–99: PAHO, Regional Core Health Data Initiative, Table Generator System; 2000 lower estimate: OCAVI (2007c); 2000 upper estimate: Acero Velásquez (2003), based on IADB reports; 2001 lower estimate: PAHO (2006); 2001 upper estimate: OCAVI (2007c).

[o]1995–98: Camara and Salama (2004, 160); 1999: UNCJIN (2001); 2000 lower estimate: IADB, reported in *El Tiempo,* Bogotá, May 9, 2000, and Acero Velásquez (2003); 2000 upper estimate: UNCJIN (2001); 2001: PAHO, Regional Core Health Data Initiative, Table Generator System.

[p]1995 and 1996 lower estimates, 2001: PAHO, Regional Core Health Data Initiative, Table Generator System; 1995 and 1997 upper estimates: UNCJIN (1998); 1998: UNCJIN (2001); 1999: UNCJIN (2001); 1996 upper estimate, 1997 lower estimate: Camara and Salama (2004, 160); 2000 lower estimate: PAHO (2004); 2000 upper estimate: Acero Velásquez (2003), based on IADB reports.

[q]1995 upper estimate: Yunes and Zubarew (1999); 1995 lower estimate, 1996, and 1997: PAHO, Regional Core Health Data Initiative, Table Generator System; 1998 and 1999 upper estimates: Camara and Salama (2004, 160); 2000: Acero Velásquez (2003); 1998 and 1999 lower estimates: UNCJIN (2001); 2001: UNCJIN (2003).

[r]1995 lower estimate: PAHO (2000); 1995 upper estimate: Ramírez Flores (2005); 1996 lower estimate: LaFree (1999); 1996 upper estimate and 1997: Camara and Salama (2004, 160); 1998 lower estimate: PAHO (2006); 1998 upper estimate: Mittrany (2008); 1999 lower estimate: PAHO (2000); 1999 and 2001 upper estimates: based on numbers reported in Farías (2005); 2000 lower estimate: PAHO (2004); 2000 upper estimate: Sanjuán (2003); 2001 lower estimate: López Mendoza (2007, 5, 8).

B. National Homicide Rates, per 100,000 Persons, 2002–2009

Country	2002	2003	2004	2005	2006	2007	2008	2009
Argentina[s]	7.6–9.5	8.0	6.3	5.0–5.8*	5.2*	5.3	n.a.	5.3
Bolivia[t]	0.2–29.9	16.7–29.1	39.6	5.2–8.9	n.a.	9.3	13.0	n.a.
Brazil[u]	28.4 –32.3	23.0–33.1	26.3–31.1	28.0	25.7	20.4	22.0	n.a.
Chile[v]	1.9–5.7	1.7–12.5	1.7–9.8	5.8–8.2	14.8–19.2	4.8–6.6	8.1	n.a.
Colombia[w]	39.0–65.8	51.8–72.8	44.2–65.6	42.0–52.5	37.3–41.2	38.8–40.1	36.0	34.9
Costa Rica[x]	5.0–8.0	7.0–9.5	6.1–6.9	7.7–21.0	7.7–8.0*	8.3	11.0	11.2
Dominican Republic[y]	14.5	17.8–18.7	25.3	17.6–28.7	15.9–23.5	21.5	n.a.	23.9
Ecuador[z]	21.2	15.7	18.3	16.2	16.2–18.0	16.9	n.a.	18.0
El Salvador[aa]	31.1–56.6	32.7– 58.8	41.2–58.0	47.7–63.0	55.2–65.0	49.0–57.3	48.0–52.0	59.7
Guatemala[bb]	30.7–32.0	27.8–37.0	30.0–38.0	30.0– 44.2	45.0–47.8	n.a.	48.0	n.a.
Honduras[cc]	49.6–63.5	33.6–89.8	30.7–154.0	37.0–78.0	41.2–46.2	49.9	37.2–57.9	66.8
Mexico[dd]	13.0–29.0	17.8–28.0	10.6–26.0	10.5–25.0	10.7–26.0	9.6–24.0	26.0	14.0
Nicaragua[ee]	10.4	11.0–18.3	12.4	8.0–13.0	8.4–13.1	12.8	19.0	n.a.
Panama[ff]	9.6–12.4	10.8	9.7–10.5	11.3	11.0	12.9–13.3	n.a.	10.8
Paraguay[gg]	19.8	17.1–21.0	n.a.	15.0–17.6	12.3	12.2	n.a.	12.5
Peru[hh]	2.7	3.3–5.6	5.5	3.5	3.2	n.a.	n.a.	5.5
Uruguay[ii]	6.5	4.7–5.9	5.6	4.3–5.7	6.1	5.8	n.a.	7.0
Venezuela[jj]	35.0–176.1	44.0–113.0	37.0	31.9–41.2	36.4–45.0	44.2–48.0	47.2–52.0	49.0–52.0

Note: * indicates intentional homicides. "n.a." indicates data are not available.

[s]2002 lower estimate: PAHO, Regional Core Health Data Initiative, Table Generator System; 2003 and 2004: estimates by Ministerio Público en Barbano (2005); 2005 lower estimate: UNODC (2007); 2005 upper estimate: CEJA (2006); 2002 upper estimate: UNCJIN (2003); 2006: UNODC (2007); 2007: Reports of the Ministerio de Justicia, Seguridad y Derechos Humanos, Sistema Nacional de Información Criminal; 2009: "Argentina, con menor tasa de homicidios," *El Atlántico,* November 13, 2009.

[t]2002 lower estimate: PAHO, Regional Core Health Data Initiative, Table Generator System; 2002 and 2003 upper estimates, 2004, 2005 upper estimate: based on homicide data reported to the Instituto Nacional de Estadística, http://www.ine.gov.bo; 2003 lower estimate: author's calculation based on number of murders and homicides reported by the judicial police; 2005 lower estimate: UNODC (2006); 2007: UNODC (2009); 2008: author's calculation based on statistics of the Instituto Nacional de Estadística, http://www.ine.gov.bo.

[u]2002 lower estimate and 2003 upper estimate: Organização dos Estados Ibero-Americanos para a Educação, Ciência e Cultura (2009); 2002 upper estimate: PAHO, Regional Core Health Data Initiative, Table Generator System; 2003 lower estimate: Interlink Headline News, June 6, 2005, http://www.ilhn.com/filosofitis/archives/003196.php; 2005: Centro para la Paz, Universidad Central de Venezuela (UCV); 2006: Solange Azevedo, "Uma vitória sobre o crime," *Revista Epoca,* January 31, 2008; 2004 lower estimate: UNODC (2009), based on government reports; 2004 upper estimate: PAHO (2006); 2007: Ministerio de Justicia, as reported to UNODC; 2007: UNODC (2009); 2009: Nuñes (2010).

[v]2002 lower estimate: CEJA (2006); 2002 upper estimate: PAHO (2004); 2003 lower estimate: Carabineros de Chile, "Anuario de Estadísticas Policias," Instituto Nacional de Estadísticas, Santiago, 2003; 2004 lower estimate: CEJA (2006); 2005 lower estimate: PAHO, Regional Core Health Data Initiative, Table Generator System; 2003–6 upper estimates: UNODC (2009), based on police reports; 2005: 2005 Colombian National Police Crime Reports, Policía Nacional de Colombia, 4–5; 2006 lower estimate, UNODC (2009), based on NGO reports; 2005: Centro para la Paz, UCV; 2007 lower estimate: UNODC, citing NGOs; upper estimate 2007: UNODC (2009); 2008: UNODC (2009).

[w]2002 lower estimate: El Día News.com, Illinois, http://www.eldianews.com/Ediciones; 2002 upper estimate and 2003 and 2004 lower estimates: Departamento Nacional de Planeación; 2003 and 2004 upper estimates: UNODC (2009), citing PAHO (2006); 2005 lower estimate: Policía Nacional de Colombia (2005, 4–5); 2005 upper estimate: PAHO (2006); 2006 lower estimate: Sistema de Gestión y Seguimiento a las Metas del Gobierno, http://www.sigob.gov.co/pnd/inst.aspx; 2006 upper estimate: Policía Nacional de Colombia, reported in Observatorio de la Violencia (2007); 2007 and 2008: "Geografía de la tasa de homicidio 1998–2007," http://www.derechoshumanos.gov.co/observatorio/imágenes/homicideo98_07.pdf; 2007 lower estimate: UNODC (2009); 2007 upper estimate: Vicepresidencia de la República (2008, 98); 2008: "Colombia: 16.000 homicidios en 2008,

la cifra más baja en 30 años (policía)," *Eco Diario,* January 21, 2009; 2009: "Not Great Just Yet, but Definitely Improving," El Colombiano.com, November 27, 2009.

ˣ2002 lower estimate: PAHO (2000); 2002 upper estimate: (PAHO 2003a); 2003 lower estimate: UNODC (2009); 2003 upper estimate: UNODC (2009), based on police reports; 2004 upper estimate: María Siu, "Delincuencia aventaja a la policía," *La República, San José de Costa Rica,* April 17, 2006; 2004 lower estimate: Carlos Arguedas, "Número de homicidios disminuyó este año," *La Nación,* December 27, 2004, 12A; 2005 lower estimate: PAHO (2006); 2005 upper estimate: OCAVI (2007e); 2006 lower estimate: Sistema Integrado Administrativo y Técnico 2007; 2006 upper estimate: UNODC (2009), based on police reports and Cruz (2005); 2007: UNODC (2009); 2008: Ribando (2009); 2009: Karina Alpízar Corella, "Aumenta tasa de homicidios," *La Prensa Libre,* October 20, 2009.

ʸ2002 and 2003 upper estimate, 2004: OCAVI (2007d); 2003 lower estimate: UNODC (2005); 2005 and 2006 lower estimates: UNODC (2007); 2005 upper estimate: UNDP (2007); 2006 upper estimate: OCAVI (2007d); 2007: UNODC (2009); 2009: Departamento de Estadísticas, Procuraduría General de la República, http://www.procuraduria.gov.do/PGR.NET/Estadisticas.

ᶻ2002: Instituto Nacional de Estadísticas y Censos (INEC); 2003 and 2004: UNCJIN (2005); 2005 and 2006 upper estimate: UNODC (2007); 2006 lower estimate: UNODC (2006, 1–9); 2007: Estadísticas de Nacimientos y Defunciones (Generales y Fetales), INEC; 2009: "Ecuador: Hay 219 asesinatos por mes," *Diario Hoy,* November 24, 2009.

ᵃᵃ2002 lower estimate: OCAVI (2007a); 2002 upper estimate: Fiscalía General, reported in UNDP (2002); 2003 lower estimate: Pleitez Chávez, based on prosecutor reports; 2003 upper estimate: UNODC (2009); 2004 and 2005 upper estimates: PAHO (2006); 2004 lower estimate: Ribando (2005); 2005 lower estimate: OCAVI (2007a); 2006–8 upper estimates: Ribando (2009); 2006 lower estimate: Cruz (2005); 2007 and 2008 lower estimates: OCAVI (2007e), based on statistics of the Mesa Técnica and the Policía Nacional Civil; 2007 upper estimate: UNODC (2009); 2009: "El Salvador Baté récord, 4,300 homicidios en 2009," salvadorenosenelmundo.blogspot.com, December 31, 2009.

ᵇᵇ2002 upper estimate, 2003 and 2004 lower estimates: PAHO (2006); 2004 upper estimate: PAHO (2006); 2003 upper estimate and 2008: Ribando (2009); 2005 lower estimate: Observatorio de la Violencia (2007c), based on the Annual Assembly of the Health Sector Network for Central America and the Dominican Republic; 2002 lower estimate and 2005 upper estimate: OCAVI (2007b) and UNDP (2007); 2006 lower estimate: UNDP, from *The Economist,* September 8, 2007, 40; 2006 upper estimate: reports by the human rights ombudsman in Leonardo Cereser, "Se reduce la tasa de homicidios en 2007," *Prensa Libre,* December 15, 2007..

ᶜᶜ2002 lower estimate: estimate by Department of Strategic Planning (Departamento de Planeamiento Estratégico), Preventive Police; 2002 upper estimate: Department of Systems Engineering (Departamento de Ingeniería en Sistemas), Investigative Police, author interview, February 2004; 2003 lower estimate: UNODC (2009), citing PAHO and World Health Organization; 2003 upper estimate: UNODC (2009), citing police reports; 2004 upper estimate: Arana (2005); 2004 and 2005 lower estimates: Observatorio de la Violencia (2006); 2005 upper estimate: OCAVI (2007e) and Security Secretariat records of 231 homicides per month; 2006 lower estimate: Cruz (2005); 2006 upper estimate: Observatorio de la Violencia (2007); 2007 and 2008 upper estimate, 2009: Observatorio de la Violencia (2010); 2008 lower estimate: "La tasa de homicidios sube a catorce por día," *La Prensa,* March 5, 2010.

ᵈᵈ2002–7 upper estimates, 2008: Instituto Ciudadano de Estudios sobre la Inseguridad; 2002 lower estimate: UNCJIN (2003); 2003 lower estimate: Cruz (2005); 2004 lower estimate: PAHO (2006); 2005 lower estimate: PAHO, Regional Core Health Data Initiative, Table Generator System; 2006 lower estimate: Cruz (2008); 2007 lower estimate: UNODC (2009), based on NGO reports; 2009: Alexandra Olson, "A pesar del combate contra el narcotráfico, disminuye la tasa de homicidios en México," Associated Press, July 8, 2010, accessed at http://ahorasi.com.

ᵉᵉ2002, 2004, and 2005 lower estimate: OCAVI (2007e); 2003 lower estimate: Bautista Lara (2006); 2003 upper estimate: Cruz (2005); 2005 upper estimate: Ribando (2009); 2006 upper estimate: Policía Nacional, reported in Observatorio de la Violencia (2007); 2006 lower estimate: UNODC (2007); 2007: UNODC (2009), based on police reports; 2008: Ribando (2009).

ᶠᶠ2002 lower estimate: UNCJIN (2003); 2003: CEJA (2006); 2004 upper estimate: PAHO (2006); 2002 upper estimate and 2004 lower estimate: OCAVI (2007c), based on the Controlaría Nacional;

2005: PAHO (2006); 2006: UNODC (2007); 2007 lower estimate: OCAVI (2007c); 2007 upper estimate: UNODC (2009); 2009: Nuñes (2010, 2).

gg2002: PAHO, Regional Core Health Data Initiative, Table Generator System; 2003 lower estimate: UNODC (2009); 2005 lower estimate: UNODC (2007); 2003 and 2005 upper estimates: UNODC (2009), citing PAHO; 2006: UNODC (2007); 2007: UNODC (2009); 2009: Nuñes (2010, 2).

hh2002: PAHO, Regional Core Health Data Initiative, Table Generator System; 2003 lower estimate: PAHO (2006); 2003 upper estimate, 2004–6: UNODC (2009), citing police reports; 2009: Nuñes (2010, 2).

ii2002: UNCJIN (2003); 2004: UNCJIN (2005, 13–15); 2003 lower estimate: PAHO (2006); 2005 lower estimate: UNODC (2006); 2003 and 2005 upper estimates, 2006, 2007: UNODC (2009), citing government reports;

jj2002 lower estimate: PAHO (2003b); 2002 upper estimate: Farías (2005); 2003 lower estimate: "The Battle for Safer Streets," *The Economist,* September 30, 2004; 2003 upper estimate: calculated on number of homicides reported by the Cuerpo de Investigaciones Científicas, Penales y Criminalísticas (CICPC); 2007 upper estimate: UNODC (2009), citing PAHO; 2004: López Mendoza (2007, 5, 8); 2005 lower estimate: PAHO (2006); 2005 upper estimate: UNDP (2007); 2006–8 lower estimates: UNODC (2009), citing NGO reports; 2007 upper estimate: "Deadly Message," *The Economist,* July 19, 2008, 47; 2006 and 2008 upper estimates: Incosec (2010); 2009 lower estimate: Incosec (2010); 2009 upper estimate (January–March 2009): Aumentan los homicidios, rapiñas y delitos sexuales," *El País Digital,* http://www.elpais.com.uy.

Appendix B

Citizen Security Structures and Police Ranks

HONDURAS

Citizen Security Structure: Security Ministry

Secretariat of Security

Subsecretariats of Prevention
National Police
(Policía Nacional, PN)

General Office of Special Preventive
Services (Dirección General de
Servicios Especiales Preventivos,
DGSEP)
General Office of Police Education
(Dirección General de Educación
Policial, DGEP)

Subsecretariat of Investigation
General Office of Criminal
Investigation (Dirección General
de Investigación Criminal, DGIC)
General Office of Special
Investigative Services (Dirección
General de Servicios Especiales de
Investigación, DGSEI)

Police Rank Structure

Commissioner general
Commissioners
Subcommissioners

Investigation ranks: detectives (*inspectores*)
Basic police (Classes I, II, and III)
Cadets and auxiliary officers

BOLIVIA

Citizen Security Structure: National Police Units

Principal command and control offices
1. General Command (Comando General)

337

2. General Subcommand (Sub-Comando General)
3. Inspector General (Inspectoría General)

Superior Disciplinary Tribunal

Assessment and support offices—National Offices of: Personnel; Intelligence; Planning and Operations; National Administration; Technical Auxiliary Services; Personal Identification; Health and Social Welfare; Instruction and Teaching; Control of Dangerous Substances; and the National Central Office of the International Criminal Police Organization (Interpol)

Decentralized offices
1. Special Force in the War against Narco-trafficking (Fuerza Especial de Lucha Contra el Narcotráfico, FELCN or Felón)
2. Social Security Fund (Fondo Complementario de Seguridad Social)
3. National Production Center (Centro Nacional de Producción)
4. Police Insurance Mutual Fund (Mutual del Seguro Policial, Musepol)
5. Police Housing Council (Consejo de Vivienda Policial, Covipol)
6. Penitentiary Security Unit (Seguridad Penitentiaria)
7. Accounting Office (Dirección Nacional de Fiscalización y Recaudaciones)

Operative, specialized, and "deconcentrated" units
1. Technical Judicial Police (Policía Tecnica Judicial, PTJ), with seven divisions: Homicides; Persons; Minors and Family; Property; Economic and Financial; Public Corruption; Special Operations
2. Order and Security Units (Unidades de Orden y Seguridad)
3. Transit Units (Unidades de Tránsito)
4. Customs Units (Unidades de Policía Aduanera)
5. Police Courts (Juzgados Policiales)
6. Women's Police Unit (Policía Femenina)
7. Provincial and Frontier Units (Unidades de Policía Provincial y Fronteriza)
8. Unit of Control of Dangerous Substances (Unidades de Control de Sustancias Peligrosas)
9. Family Protection Brigade (Brigada de la Protección a la Familia)
10. Battalion of Private Physical Security (Batallón de Seguridad Física Privada, BSFP)
11. Fire Department (Bomberos)
12. Customs Control Unit (Unidad de Control Operativo Aduanero, COA)
13. Citizen Support and Aid Patrol (Patrulla de Ayuda y Auxilio Ciudadano, or Patrulla de Auxilio y Cooperación Ciudadana, PAC)
14. Multipurpose Unit (Unidad de Polivalentes)
15. Tactical Police OperrationsUnit (Unidad Táctica de Operaciones Policiales, UTOP)
16. Radio Patrol (Radio Patrulla 110)
17. Rural and Frontier Police (Policía Rural y Fronteriza)
18. Ecological Police (Unidad de Policía Ecológica)

19. Special Anti-Crime Force (La Fuerza Especial de Lucha Contra el Crimen, FELCC)
21. Anti-Car Theft Unit (Dirección de Prevención contra el Robo de Vehículo, Diprove)
22. Cooperative Police Mutual Fund (Mutual de Cooperativas de la Policía, Mucopol)
23. Citizen Conciliation Unit (Unidad de Conciliación Ciudadana, UCC)
24. Tourist Police (Policía Turística)
25. Road Police (Policía Caminera)
26. Delta Force (Fuerza Delta)
27. Environmental Police (Policía Forestal y Medio Ambiente, POFOMA)
28. Constitutional Assembly Protection Unit (Unidad de Seguridad para la Asamblea Constituyente, USPAC)
29. The Pumas: Security Squadron (Las Pumas: Escuadrón de Seguridad)
30. Unit for the Protection of Dignitaries (Unidad de Protección de Dignatarios, USEDI)

The department divisions are subordinate to the national police and have similar structures. Each department has a command, subcommand, department inspector, disciplinary tribunal, and assessment and support offices. Within each department are about twenty units: coordination and agent supervision; a judicial office for legal matters; a specialized unit for crimes such as kidnapping and terrorism; and offices of personnel, intelligence, planning and operations, public relations, information, evaluation, administration, personal identification, and health and welfare. Each department also includes an Order and Security Unit for patrols and property protection, a transit unit for road safety, and a special security battalion for public order during social conflict.

Rank Structure: *Policía Boliviana*

SUPERIOR OFFICIALS

Rank	Categories in rank
I. *Generales*	General
II. *Jefes*	1. Colonel 2. Lieutenant colonel 3. Major
III. *Oficiales*	1. Captain 2. Lieutenant 3. Sublieutenant
IV. *Aspirantes a oficial*	Cadets/students

SUBCOMMISSIONED OFFICERS

V. Superior subofficials and subofficials	1. Superior subofficial; 2. Major subofficial; 3. First subofficial; 4. Second subofficial
VI. Classes and police	1. First sergeant; 2. Second sergeant; 3. Corporal; 4. Street police (*tropas*)

TRAINEES

VII. *Aspirantes*	Cadets/students

ARGENTINA

Structure: Policía Federal Argentina (PFA)

Central Command (Jefatura)
Central Subcommand (Subjefatura)
Offices of Administration, Welfare, Interior and Complex Federal Crimes; Federal
    Investigations; Planning and Development; Metropolitan Security; Personnel
    Instruction and Human Rights; Federal Communications; Scientific Police;
    Dangerous Drugs; Federal Transport
Autonomous Offices: Internal Affairs; Criminal Intelligence

Rank Structure: PFA

Officer ranks
Commissioner-general (*comisario general*)
Commissioner-major (*comisario mayor*)
Superintendent-inspector *or* commissioner-inspector *(comisario inspector)*
Commissioner *(comisario)*
Undersuperintendent *or* subcommissioner *(subcomisario)*
Principal officer *(official principal)*
Inspector/detective *(official inspector)*
Subinspector *(official subinspector)*
Adjutant officer *or* assistant officer *(official ayudante)*
Subofficer ranks
Subofficer-major *(suboficial mayor)*
Auxiliary subofficer *(suboficial auxiliar)*
Administrative subofficer *(suboficial escribiente)*
First sergeant *or* sergeant first class *(sargento primero)*
Sergeant *(sargento)*
First corporal *(cabo primero)*
Corporal *(cabo)*
Police officer and fireman *(agente* and *bombero)*
Cadet in training *(aspirante)*

Glossary

arraigo: A form of preventive detention used an alternative to arrest, in which a suspect is placed in a facility such as a "safe house" guarded by police during the investigation

averiguación de antecedentes: The police act of detaining someone to check his or her police record

barrio: A low-income urban neighborhood in Venezuela and other countries

cifra negra: Number or percentage of unreported crimes

cocaleros: Coca growers who formed a powerful movement in Bolivia

código de faltas/contravenciones: Misdemeanor code

colonias: Defined residential areas in Honduras

comisaría: Police station

comisario: Police officer

criterio de oportunidad: A rule allowing prosecutors to refrain from prosecuting, often needed to decongest the prisons of petty criminals and those who cooperate with an investigation

cuadrantes: Urban blocks used in community-oriented policing, in which separate units are responsible for all areas of security

defensoría del pueblo: Ombudsman

desestimadas: Dismissed or overruled cases

expediente: Generally meaning a file or record, but usually used as the term for a police report on a crime presented to prosecutors (*fiscales*)

fiscal: Public prosecutor

Fiscalía General/Ministerio Público: Public prosecutor's office, in charge of criminal investigation and prosecution

inspector: Police detective

Judicial Police: The police agency conducting a criminal investigation, usually under the direction of the Public Ministry

juez de ejecución: Judge of the sentencing court

Mara 18: One of the largest youth gangs—one of the two *super-clikas*—in Central and North America

Mara Salvatrucha (MS): One of the principal *maras* in Honduras and the rest of Central America

maras: The criminally oriented gangs of Central America, Mexico, and the United States

medidas cautelares: Preventive measures

mesas: The term commonly used for citizen forums

organic law: The founding and basic law in an area of the law

patronato: In some countries, the title of the head council of a neighborhood

penal code: The legal code specifying and defining acts that constitute crimes

penal process code: The legal code specifying the processes for investigating crimes and prosecuting suspects

Preventive Police: The main division in most police agencies responsible for basic street policing

Proceso: Short for Proceso de Reorganización Nacional (Process of National Reorganization), the official name of Argentina's 1976–83 military regime

razzias: Mass police roundups, usually in poor neighborhoods

tutela: Direct legal suit

villa: The term used for low-income neighborhoods in most of Argentina

References

Abrahams, Ray. 1998. *Vigilant Citizens: Vigilantism and the State*. Malden, MA: Polity Press.

Acero Velásquez, Hugo. 2003. "Ciudad y políticas públicas de seguridad y convivencia." In *Monografía de seguridad y convivencia de fontibón,* ed. Alcaldía Mayor de Bogotá D.C., Secretaría de Gobierno, Subsecretaría de Asuntos para la Convivencia y Seguridad Ciudadana, 12–21. Bogotá: Subsecretaría de Asuntos para la Convivencia y Seguridad Ciudadana.

Agamben, Giorgio. 1998. *Homo Sacer: Sovereign Power and Bare Life*. Stanford, CA: Stanford University Press.

Agamben, Giorgio, and Michael Rocke. 1995. "We Refugees." *Symposium* 49 (Summer): 114–19.

Agozino, Biko. 2008. "Hanging by Invitation: Capital Punishment, the Carceral Archipelago and Escalating Homicide Rates in the Caribbean." Paper presented at Sir Arthur Lewis Memorial Conference, St. Augustine, University of the West Indies, September.

Alladi Venkatesh, Sudhir, and Ronald Kassimir. 2007. "Youth and Legal Institutions: Thinking Globally and Comparatively. In *Youth, Globalization, and the Law,* ed. Sudhir Alladi Venkatesh and Ronald Kassimir, 3–16. Stanford, CA: Stanford University Press.

Almada, Maricarmen, and Silvia Licht. 2001. *El crimen bordón: Un caso de impunidad policial*. Buenos Aires: Editorial Biblos.

Almond, Gabriel A., and Sidney Verba. 1963. *The Civic Culture: Political Attitudes and Democracy in Five Nations*. Princeton, NJ: Princeton University Press.

Altamira, Pedro Guillermo. 1963. *Policía y poder de policía*. Buenos Aires: Abeldeo-Perrot.

Amar, Paul, and Cathy Schneider. 2003. "The Rise of Crime, Disorder and Authoritarian Policing." *NACLA Report on the Americas* 37 (September/October): 12–16.

Amaya Cóbar, Edgard. 1998. *Cifras de delitos y del sistema panel: Proyecto seguridad pública y derechos humanos*. San Salvador: Fundación de Estudios para la Aplicación del Derecho,

Amnesty International. 1996. *Police Brutality and Excessive Force in the New York City Police Department*. London: Amnesty International.

————. 2000. *Venezuela: Possible Extrajudicial Execution/Fear for Safety.* New York: Amnesty International USA

————. 2003. "Honduras Zero Tolerance . . . for Impunity: Extrajudicial Executions of Children and Youths since 1998," London: Amnesty International Secretariat.

Andersen, Martin Edwin. 2002. *La policía: Pasado, presente y propuestas para el futuro.* Buenos Aires: Editorial Sudamericana.

Andes Wines. 2007. *Inseguridad, un costo extra para la vitivinicultura Argentina.* Santiago: Andes Wines.

Andino Mencía, Tomás. 2006. *Las maras en la sombra.* Tegucigalpa: Universidad Centroamericana "Simeon Cañas."

Annicchiarico, Ciro. 1998. "El desafio de reformular la política de seguridad y de intervenir la policía bonaerense." In *¿El final de la maldita policía?* ed. Eduardo Sigal, Alberto Binder, and Ciro Annicchiarico, 59–95. Buenos Aires: Ediciones FAC.

Arana, Ana. 2005. "How the Street Gangs Took Central America." *Foreign Affairs* 84 (May/June).

Arendt, Hannah. 1959. *The Human Condition.* New York: Anchor.

Arland, Rodolfo. 2000. "La inspección general de seguridad de Mendoza." *Revista Probidad* 10 (September–October): 15–26.

————. 2002. *La seguridad devaluada.* Mendoza: Fundación Proponer,

Armony, Ariel C. 2004. *The Dubious Link: Civic Engagement and Democratization.* Stanford, CA: Stanford University Press.

Armony, Ariel C., and Hector E. Schamis. 2005. "Babel in Democratization Studies." *Journal of Democracy* 16 (4): 113–28.

Arriagada, Irma. 2001. "Seguridad ciudadana y violencia en América Latina." Paper presented at the XXIII Latin American Studies Association Congress, Facultad latinoamericana de Ciencias Sociales (Flacso).

Arrivillaga, Edgardo. 2003. "¿Hacia donde va la seguridad privada en Chile?" *Harry Magazine,* May.

Arroba B., Milton. 2003. "La inseguridad crece." *Revista criterios—Cámara de comercio de Quito* 55 (March).

Avritzer, Leonard. 2002. *Democracy and the Public Sphere in Latin America.* Princeton, NJ: Princeton University Press.

Ayers, Robert L. 1998. *Crime and Violence as Development Issues in Latin America and the Caribbean.* Washington, DC: World Bank.

Azaola, Elena. 2007. *Imagen y autoimagen de la policía de la ciudad de México.* Mexico City: Centro de Investigaciones y Estudios Superiores en Antropología Social.

Bachrach, Peter, and Morton Baratz. 1970. *Power and Poverty: Theory and Practice.* Oxford: Oxford University Press.

Bailey, John, and Lucía Dammert. 2006. "Public Security and Police Reform in the Americas." In *Public Security and Police Reform in the Americas,* ed. John Bailey and Lucía Dammert, 1–23. Pittsburgh: University of Pittsburgh Press.

Bailey, John, and Gustavo Flores-Macías. 2007. "Violent Crime and Democracy: Mexico in Comparative Perspective." Paper presented at Annual Midwest Political Science Association Conference, Chicago.

Baiocchi, Gianpaolo. 2003. *Radicals in Power: The Workers' Party (PT) and Experiments in Urban Democracy in Brazil.* London: Zed Books.

Basombrío Iglesias, Carlos. 2006. "Civilian Oversight of Security in Peru: The Testimony of a Participant." In *Toward a Society under Law: Citizens and Their Police in Latin America,* ed. Joseph Tulchin and Meg Ruthenburg, 261–79. Washington, DC: Woodrow Wilson Center Press.

Bautista Lara, Francisco. 2006. *Policía, seguridad ciudadana y violencia en Nicaragua: Breves ensayos y un testimonio.* Managua: PAVSA.

Bayley, David H. 1998. *What Works in Policing.* New York: Oxford University Press.

Bayley, David H., and Clifford D. Shearing. 1996. "The Future of Policing." *Law and Society Review* 30 (3): 585.

———. 2001. *The New Structure of Policing: Description, Conceptualization, and Research Agenda.* Washington, DC: U.S. Department of Justice, Office of Justice Programs.

Beliz, Gustavo. 2007. "¿Hacia una nueva generación de reformas en seguridad ciudadana?" In *¿Cuál es la salida? La agenda inconclusa de la seguridad ciudadana* ed. Erik Alda and Gustavo Beliz, 1–117. Washington, DC: Inter-American Development Bank.

Benjamin, Walter. 1969. *Illuminations: Essays and Reflections.* New York: Schocken.

Bermúdez Coward, Colón. 2004. "Ni improvisión ni ocurrencias: La política de seguridad debe rebasar los intereses cortoplacistas y egoístas." In *Soluciones para Costa Rica,* ed. Miguel Sobrado Chávez and Eduardo Saxe Fernández. San José: Editorial Universidad Nacional.

Blanco S., Javiera, and José Alejandro Bernales R. Forthcoming. "Seguridad ciudadana en Chile y modernización policial: La experiencia de la policía de carabineros." In *Best Practices in Community Policing in Latin America,* ed. Mark Ungar and Desmond Enrique Arias.

Bobea, Lilian, ed. 2003. *Entre el crimen y el castigo: Seguridad ciudadana y control democrático en América Latina y el Caribe.* Caracas: Nueva Sociedad.

Bolivia Press. 1999. *Boletín del Centro de Documentación e Información Bolivia* (CEDIB). Issue 07-09-99.

Borsdorf, Axel. 2003. "Hacia la ciudad fragmentada: Temprana estructura segregada en el ciudad Latinoamericana." *Scripta Nova* 7, no. 146.

Braga, Anthony A. 2002. *Problem-Oriented Policing and Crime Prevention.* Monsey, NY: Criminal Justice Press.

Bratton, Michael. 1994. "Peasant-State Relations in Postcolonial Africa: Patterns of Engagement and Disengagement." In *State Power and Social Forces: Domination and Transformation in the Third World,* ed. Joel S. Migdal, Atul Kohli, and Vivienne Shue, 231–50. Cambridge: Cambridge University Press.

Bratton, William, and Peter Knobler. 1998. *Turnaround.* New York: Random House.

Briceño-León, Roberto. 2008. "Un marco sociológico para la violencia urbana." In *Violencia en Venezuela,* 13–67. Caracas: Laboratorio de Ciencias Sociales.

Briceño-León, Roberto, Andrés Villaveces, and Alberto Concha-Eastman. 2008. "Understanding the Uneven Distribution of the Incidence of Homicide in Latin America." *International Journal of Epidemiology* 37 (4): 751–57.

Brinks, Daniel M. 2008. *The Judicial Response to Police Killings in Latin America.* Cambridge: Cambridge University Press.

Brogden, Mike, and Preeti Nijhar. 2005. *Community Policing: National and International Models and Approaches.* Portland, OR: Willan Publishing.

Brown, Lee P. 1987. "Innovative Policing in Houston." *Annals of the American Academy of Political and Social Science* 494: 129–34.

Brysk, Alison. 2000. *From Tribal Village to Global Village: Indian Rights and International Relations in Latin America.* Stanford, CA: Stanford University Press.

Burgess, Ernest W. 1925. "The Growth of the City." In *The City,* ed. Robert E. Park, Ernest W. Burgess, and Roderick D. McKenzie. Chicago: University of Chicago Press.

Burzaco, Eugenio, et al., eds. 2001. *Rehenes de la violencia.* Buenos Aires: Editorial Atlántida.

Buvinic, Mayra, Andrew Morrison, and Michael Shifter. 1999. *Violence in Latin America and the Caribbean: A Framework for Action.* Technical Study, Sustainable Development Department. Washington, DC: Inter-American Development Bank.

Cabral, Edylberto, and Mayra Brea de Cabral. 2006. "La violencia y los factores socioeconómicos de riesgo en la República Dominicana." psicologíacientífica.com. November.

Cabrales Barajas, L., ed. 2002. *Latinoamérica: Países abiertos, ciudades cerrados.* Guadalajara: United Nations Educational, Scientific, and Cultural Organization (UNESCO).

Caldera, Hilda. 2003. *El crimen en Honduras (1994–2003).* Tegucigalpa: Dirección General de Educación Policial.

Calhoun, Craig J., and John McGowan. 1997. "Plurality, Promises and Public Spaces." In *Hannah Arendt and the Meaning of Politics,* 232–59. Minneapolis: University of Minnesota Press.

Call, Charles. 2003a. *Challenges in Police Reform: Promoting Effectiveness and Accountability.* Policy Report. New York: International Peace Academy.

———. 2003b. "Democratisation, War and State-building: Constructing the Rule of Law in El Salvador." *Journal of Latin American Studies* 35: 827–62.

Camara, Mamadou, and Pierre Salama. 2004. "Homicidios en América del Sur: ¿Los pobres son peligrosos?" *Revista de Economía Institucional* 6 (10): 159.

Canel, Eduardo. 2001. "Municipal Decentralization and Participatory Democracy: Building a New Mode of Urban Politics in Montevideo City?" *European Review of Latin American and Caribbean Studies* (71): 25–46.

Capowich, George E., and Christine Andrews. 1995. *Evaluating Problem-Oriented Policing: Process and Outcomes in Tulsa and San Diego.* Alexandria, VA: Institute for Social Analysis.

Carlucci, Aida Kemelmajer de. 2004. *Justicia restaurativa: Posible respuesta para el delito cometido por personas menores de edad.* Buenos Aires: Rubinzal-Culzoni.

Carranza, Elías. 1997. *Delito y seguridad de los habitantes.* Mexico City: Siglo XXI.

Carrión, Fernando. 2003. "De la violencia urbana a la convivencia ciudadana." In *Entre el crimen y el castigo,* ed. Lilian Bobea, 51–84. Caracas: Nueva Sociedad.

———. 2004. "Política de las ciudades: La inseguridad ciudadana en la comunidad andina." *Café de las Ciudades* 3 (December).

Casa Alianza. 2006. "Violence in Guatemala: A Channel 4 Documentary." November 2.

Casas, Juan Antonio, J. Norberto W. Dacha, and Alexandra Bambas, 2001. "Health Disparities in Latin America and the Caribbean: The Role of Social and Economic Determinants." In *Equity and Health: Views from the Pan American Sanitary Bureau,* 22–49 Washington, DC: Pan American Health Organization (PAHO).

Castellanos, Julieta. 2000. "Honduras: Violence in Numbers." In *Informe sobre desarrollo humano Honduras 2000."* New York: United Nations Development Programme (UNDP).

CEDIB (Centro de Documentación e Información Bolivia). 1999. *Reforma de la policía "entre cuatro paredes."* La Paz: Bolivia Press, No. 6.

CEJA (Centro de Estudios de Justicia de las Américas). 2006. *Reporte de la justicia.* Segunda edición (2004–5). Santiago: CEJA. http://www.cejamericas.org/reporte.

———. 2010. *Reporte de la justicia.* Cuarta edición (2008–9). La Paz: CEJA.

Celis, María Lorena. 2005. *Brigada ecológica progreso: Programa de reinserción social.* La Rioja: Ministerio de Gobierno y Derechos Humanos, Provincia de La Rioja.

CELS (Centro de Estudios Legales y Sociales) and Americas Watch. 1991. *Police Violence in Argentina.* Buenos Aires: CELS.

Centro de Documentación de Honduras. 2004. *Honduras: Hacia una política integral de seguridad ciudadana.* Tegucigalpa: Centro de Documentación de Honduras (Cedoh).

Centro de Investigación para el Desarrollo. 2009. *Índice de Incidencia Delictiva y Violencia.* Mexico City: Centro de Investigación para el Desarrollo.

Cerrutti, Marcela, and Rodolfo Bertoncello. 2003. *Urbanization and Internal Migration Patterns in Latin America.* Buenos Aires: Centro de Estudios de Población.

Chen, Han, Pablo Leonte, and Sumy Carolina Hernández Lopez. 2008. "La vigencia del código orgánico procesal penal y su relación con los índices de criminalidad." *Capítulo Criminológico* 36 (2): 41–69.

Chevigny, Paul. 1997. *Edge of the Knife: Police Violence in the Americas.* New York: Free Press.

———. 2003. "The Control of Police Misconduct in the Americas." In *Crime and Violence in Latin America.,* ed. Hugo Frühling and Joseph Tulchin, 45–67. Washington, DC: Woodrow Wilson Center Press.

Chicago Community Policing Evaluation Consortium. 2002. *An Evaluation of Chicago's Alternative Policing Strategy and Information Technology Initiative.* Chicago: Institute for Policy Research, Northwestern University.

Chinchilla, Laura. 2003. "Experiences with Citizen Participation in Crime Prevention in Central America." In *Crime and Violence in Latin America,* ed. Hugo Frühling and Joseph Tulchin, 205–32. Washington, DC: Woodrow Wilson Center Press.

CIDA (Canadian International Development Agency). 2007. *Programming Framework for Bolivia (2006–2007).* Ottawa: CIDA.

Clawson, Patrick L., and Rensselaer W. Lee III. 1996. *The Andean Cocaine Industry.* New York: St. Martin's Press.

Concha-Eastman, Alberto. 2002. "Urban Violence in Latin America and the Caribbean." In *Citizens of Fear: Urban Violence in Latin America,* ed. Susana Rotker. New Brunswick: Rutgers University Press.

Consejo de la Judicatura, Dirección de Planificación. 1994. *Memoria y Cuenta del Consejo de la Judicatura.* Caracas: Consejo de la Judicatura.

Consorcio Iberoamericano de Investigaciones de Mercados y Asesoramiento. 2010. *Barómetro iberoamericano de gobernabilidad 2009.* Bogotá: Consorcio Iberoamericano de Investigaciones de Mercados y Asesoramiento.

CORREPI (Coordinadora Contra la Represión Policial e Institucional). 2002. *Recopidlación de muertes de personas a manos de las fuerzas de seguridad en Argentina.* La Plata: CORREPI.

Cruz, José Miguel. 2005. *Violencia juvenil en América Latina.* San Salvador: Universidad Centroamericana.

———. 2008. "Crime in Central America." Paper presented at the workshop Violence and Citizen in Post-Authoritarian Latin America, Princeton University, Princeton, NJ.

Dahl, Robert. 1998. *On Democracy.* New Haven, CT: Yale University Press.

Damián, Areceli, and Julio Boltvinik. 2006. "A Table to Eat On: The Meaning and Measurement of Poverty in Latin America." In *Latin America after Neoliberalism: Turning the Tide in the 21st Century?* ed. Eric Hershberg and Fred Rosen, 144–70. New York: New Press.

Dammert, Lucía. 2000. *Violencia criminal y seguridad pública en América Latina: La situación en Argentina.* Serie políticas sociales no. 43. Santiago: Comisión Económica para América Latina y el Caribe (CEPAL).

————2006. *El sistema penitenciario en Chile: Desafíos para el nuevo modelo público-privado.* Santiago: Facultad Latinoamericana de Ciencias Sociales (Flacso).

Dammert, Lucía, and Gustavo Paulsen, eds. 2005. *Ciudad y seguridad en América Latina.* Santiago: Facultad Latinoamericana de Ciencias Sociales (Flacso).

Das, Dilip, ed. 2006. *World Police Encyclopedia.* New York: Routledge.

Das, Dilip, and Otwin Marenin, eds. 2000. *Challenges of Policing Democracies: A World Perspective.* New York: Routledge.

Davis, Diane. 2003. "Law Enforcement in Mexico City: Not Yet under Control." *NACLA Report on the Americas* 37 (2): 17–24.

————. 2009. The Challenge of Accountability in Mexico. In *Policing Developing Democracies,* ed. Mercedes Hinton and Tim Newburn, 188–212. London: Routledge.

Defensoría del Pueblo. 2006. *Plan estratégico quinquenal 2007–2011: Resumen ejecutivo.* La Paz: Defensoría del Pueblo.

de Ferranti, David, Guillermo E. Perry, Francisco Ferreira, and Michael Walton. 2004. *Inequality in Latin America and the Caribbean: Breaking with History?* Washington, DC: World Bank.

Departamento de Planificación. 2004. *Anuario de estadísticas policiales 2004.* San José: Poder Judicial.

Díaz, Raimundo. 2001. "Compañías privadas de seguridad, el negocio del miedo." *Revista Rumbo* 388 (7): 40.

Dirección General de Prevención Comunitaria de la Violencia. 2004. *Programa de respuesta múltiple para la prevención comunitaria de la violencia.* La Plata: Ministerio de Seguridad, Subsecretaría de Participación Comunitaria, Gobierno de la Provincia de Buenos Aires.

Dirección Nacional de Política Criminal. 2001. *Encuesta de victimización de la ciudad de Buenos Aires, 1997–2000.* Buenos Aires: Ministerio de Justicia de la Nación.

————. 2005. *Sistema nacional de estadísticas sobre ejecución de la pena (SNEEP): Informe anual República Argentina.* Buenos Aires: Ministerio de Justicia y Derechos Humanos.

Di Tella, Rafael, Sebastian Galiani, and Ernesto Schargrodsky. 2002. "Crime, Victimization and Income Distribution." Working paper, Inter-American Development Bank, Washington, DC.

Donato, Plácido. 1999. *Las anécdotas de la policía: De vigilantes y ladrones.* Buenos Aires: Planeta.

Dorschner, John. 1993. "The Dark Side of the Force." In *Critical Issues in Policing,* ed. Roger G. Dunham and Geoffrey P. Alpert, 254–91. Prospect Heights, IL: Waveland Press.

Dunham, Roger G., and Geoffrey P. Alpert. 1993. *Critical Issues in Policing.* Prospect Heights, IL: Waveland Press.

Dutil, Carlos, and Ricardo Ragendorfer. 2005. *La bonaerense: Historia criminal de la policía de la provincia de Buenos Aires.* Buenos Aires: Editorial Booklet.

Dworkin, Ronald. 1977. *Taking Rights Seriously.* Cambridge, MA: Harvard University Press.

Eaton, Kent. 2008. "Paradoxes of Police Reform: Federalism, Parties, and Civil Society in Argentina's Public Security Crisis." *Latin American Research Review* 43 (3): 5–32.

Eck, John E. 1998. "What Do Those Dots Mean? Mapping Theories with Data." In *Crime Mapping and Crime Prevention,* ed. David Weisburd and Tom McEwan, 379–406. Monsey, NY: Criminal Justice Press.

———. 2006. "Science, Values, and Problem-oriented Policing." In *Police Innovation: Contrasting Perspectives,* ed. David Weisburd and Anthony A. Braga, 117–32. Cambridge: Cambridge University Press.

Eck, John E., and Edward R. Maguire. 2006. "Have Changes in Policing Reduced Violent Crime?" In *The Crime Drop in America.,* 2d ed., ed. Alfred Blumstein and Joel Wallman, 207–65. Cambridge: Cambridge University Press.

Eck, John E., and W. Spelman. 1987. *Problem-solving: Problem-Oriented Policing in Newport News.* Washington, DC: National Institute of Justice.

Eijkman, Quirine A. M. 2007. *We Are Here to Serve You! Public Security, Police Reform and Human Rights Implementation in Costa Rica.* Utrecht: School of Human Rights Research, University of Utrecht.

El Achkar, Soraya. Forthcoming. "Reforma policial en Venezuela: Una experiencia en curso." In *Best Practices of Community Policing in Latin America,* ed. Mark Ungar and Desmond Enrique Arias.

Elia de Molina, Alexandra. 1992. "Medidas alternativas a la reclusión." *Policía Científica* 1 (October).

Evans, Peter. 1997. *State-Society Synergy: Government and Social Capital in Development. Berkeley:* University of California, Berkeley, International and Area Studies.

Executive Office for United States Attorneys. 1996. "International Extradition." *USA Bulletin* 44 (December).

Fajnzylber, Pablo, Daniel Lederman, and Norman Loayza. 2000. *Crime and Victimization: An Economic Perspective.* Bogotá: Latin American and Caribbean Economic Association.

———. 2002. "Inequality and Violent Crime." *Journal of Law and Economics* 45 (1): 1–40.

Farías, José Luis. 2005. *Homicidios en Venezuela 1999–2003.* Caracas: LUTO de Venezuela. http://www.urru.org/papers/2005_varios/Presentacion_Venezuela_de_Luto.ppt#256,1,Slide 1.

Farthing, Linda, and Ben Kohl. 2001. "The Price of Success: Bolivia's War against Drugs and the Poor." *NACLA Report on the Americas* 35 (July–August).

Foucault, Michel. 1995. *Discipline and Punish: The Birth of the Prison.* New York: Random House.

Fraser, Barbara J. 2001. "The Enigma of Overcrowding." In *Justicia Encarcelada,* ed. Comité Andino de Servicios, 3–8. Lima: Noticias Aliadas/Latinamerica Press.

Frigo, Edgardo. 2003. "Hacia un modelo Latinoamericano de seguridad privada: Los nuevos desafíos en la region conference." Paper presented at the First Congress of Latin America on Security, Bogotá, September 24–26, 2003.

Frühling, Hugo. 2003. *¿Policia Comunitaria en América Latina: Cúal es el impacto?* Santiago: Centro de Estudios en Seguridad Ciudadana, Universidad de Chile.

Fuentes, Claudio. 2006a. "Advocacy Networks and Police Reform." In *Toward a Society under Law: Citizens and Their Police in Latin America,* ed. Joseph Tulchin and Meg Ruthenburg, 55–89. Washington, DC: Woodrow Wilson Center Press/Johns Hopkins University Press.

———. 2006b. "Violent Police, Passive Citizens: The Failure of Social Accountability in Chile." In *Enforcing the Rule of Law: Social Accountability in the New Latin American Democracies,* ed. Enrique Peruzzotti and Catalina Smulovitz, 134–77. Pittsburgh: University of Pittsburgh Press.

FULIDED (Fundación Libertad, Democracia y Desarrollo). 2004. *The Budget for State Security in Bolivia—2004.* Santa Cruz: FULIDED.

Fundación Paz Ciudadana. 1999. *Caracterización del homicidio en Chile.* Santiago: Fundación Paz Ciudadana.

Gabaldón, Luis Gerardo. 2001. "Desarrollo de la criminalidad violenta en América Latina: un panorama." In *Violencia y regulación de conflictos en América Latina.* ed. Klaus Bodemer, Sabine Kurtenbach, and Klaus Meschkat. Caracas: Nueva Sociedad.

———. 2002. "Tendencias y respuestas hacia la violencia delictiva en Latinoamérica." In *Violencia, sociedad y justicia en América Latina,* ed. Roberto Briceño-León, 245–58. Buenos Aires: Consejo Latinoamericano de ciencias sociales (CLACSO); Agencia sueca de desarrollo internacional (ASDI).

———.2004. "Policía y seguridad ciudadana en Venezuela entre 2002 and 2004." *Nueva Sociedad* 191 (May–June 2004): 65–77.

Gabaldón, Luis Gerardo, and Daniela Bettiol. 1988. *Presencia policial en zonas residenciales urbanas.* Mérida, Venezuela: Universidad de los Andes.

Gaines, Larry K. 1993. "Coping with the Job: Stress in Police Work." In *Critical Issues in Policing,* ed. Roger G. Dunham and Geoffrey P. Alpert, 538–50. Prospect Heights, IL: Waveland Press.

Gaitán Daza F., and J. Díaz Moreno. 1994. "La violencia colombiana: Algunos elementos explicativos." In *Ciudad y violencia en América Latina,* vol. 2, ed. Fernando Carrión, Alberto Concha, and Germán Cobo. Madrid: Programa de Gestión Urbana.

Galtung, Johan. 2004. *Transcend and Transform: An Introduction to Conflict Work.* Boulder, CO: Paradigm Publishers.

Gamarra, Eduardo, and Raúl Barrios Morón. 1996. "Seguridad ciudadana y seguridad nacional: Relaciones entre policías y militares en Bolivia." In *Justicia en la calle,* ed. Peter Waldmann, 99–125. Medellín: Biblioteca Jurídica Diké.

García Soruco, Javier. 2003. "Crisis policial y seguridad privada." Paper presented at the Conference on Research and Education and Defense in Security Studies, Brasilia, August.

Garretón Merino, Manuel A. 1989. *La posibilidad democrática en Chile.* Santiago: Facultad Latinoamericana de Ciencias Sociales (Flacso).

———. 1995. "Redemocratization in Chile." *Journal of Democracy* 6 (1): 146–58.

———. 2002. *Incomplete Democracy: Political Democratization in Chile and Latin America.* Chapel Hill: University of North Carolina Press.

Geddes, Barbara. 1994. *Politician's Dilemma: Building State Capacity in Latin America.* Berkeley: University of California Press.

Georges, Daniel E. 1978. *The Geography of Crime and Violence: A Spatial and Ecological Perspective.* Washington, DC: Association of American Geographers.

Gobierno del Perú. 2002. *Informe de la comisión especial de reestructuración de la Policía Nacional del Perú.* Lima: Gobierno del Perú.

Golbert, Laura, and Gabriel Kessler. 2001. "Cohesión social y violencia urbana: Un estudio exploratorio sobre la Argentina a fines de los 90." In *Cohesión social y gobernabilidad económica en la Argentina,* ed. Constantino Vaitsos. Buenos Aires: Editorial Eudeba.

Goldstein, Daniel. 2004. *The Spectacular City: Violence and Performance in Urban Bolivia.* Durham, NC: Duke University Press.

Goldstein, Herman. 1990. *Problem-Oriented Policing.* New York: McGraw-Hill.

Gorri, Patricia, Patricia Lecaro, and Marisa Repetto. 2003. *La inclusión de la provincia de Mendoza en la inseguridad.* Mendoza: V Seminario Nacional de RedMuni, La Reforma Municipal Pendiente Perspectivas y Prospectivas.

Grindle, Merilee S. 2004. *Despite the Odds: The Contentious Politics of Education Reform.* Princeton, NJ: Princeton University Press.

Guerrero, Rodrigo. 2007. "Sistemas de información en los programas de prevención de violencia." In *¿Cuál es la salida? La agenda inconclusa de la seguridad ciudadana* ed. Erik Alda and Gustavo Beliz, 119–48. Washington, DC: Inter-American Development Bank.

Guzmán, Mauricio, Patricia Gorri, Gustavo Lucero, and Pablo Cazabán. 2002. *Plan estratégico municipal de seguridad ciudadana para el departamento de Las Heras.* Mendoza: Municipalidad de Las Heras.

Habermas, Jurgen. 1989. *The Structural Transformation of the Public Sphere: An Inquiry into a Category of Bourgeois Society.* Studies in Contemporary German Social Thought. Cambridge, MA: MIT Press.

———. 1998. *Between Facts and Norms: Contributions to a Discourse Theory of Law and Democracy.* Cambridge, MA: MIT Press.

Hagopian, Frances. 1994. "Traditional Politics against State Transformation in Brazil." In *State Power and Social Forces: Domination and Transformations in the Third World,* ed. Joel Migdal, Atul Kohli, and Vivienne Shue. Cambridge: Cambridge University Press.

Hagopian, Frances, and Scott P. Mainwaring, eds. 2005. *The Third Wave of Democratization in Latin America.* New York: Cambridge University Press.

Hale, Donna C. 1986. *Contemporary Sociology* 15 (January): 73.

Harcourt, Bernard E. 1998. "Reflecting on the Subject: A Critique of the Social Influence Conception of Deterrence, the Broken Windows Theory, and Order Maintenance Policing New York Style." *Michigan Law Review* 97 (November): 332.

Harcourt, Bernard E., and Jens Ludwig. 2006. "Broken Windows: New Evidence from New York City and a Five-City Social Experiment. *University of Chicago Law Review* 73 (Winter): 271–320.

Hartnett, Patrick J., and William Andrews. 1999. "How New York Is Winning the Drug War." *City Journal* (Summer).

Harvard University Law School Faculty and Universidad de Colombia del Paraguay. 2007. *La seguridad en el Paraguay: Análisis y respuestas comparadas.* Cambridge, MA: Harvard University Law School.

Henry, Vincent. 2002. *The Compstat Paradigm.* Flushing, NY: Looseleaf Law Publications.

Hildebrand, Mary, and Merilee Grindle. 1997. "Building Sustainable Capacity in the Public Sector: What Can Be Done?" In *Getting Good Government: Capacity Building in the Public Sectors of Developing Countries,* ed. Merilee Grindle. Cambridge, MA: Harvard Institute for International Development.

Hillman, Richard, and Elsa Cardozo de Silva. 1998. *Venezuelan Political Culture and Democracy.* Conference paper. Antigua: Caribbean Studies Association Conference.

Hinton, Mercedes. 2006. *The State in the Street: Police and Politics in Argentina and Brazil.* Boulder, CO: Lynne Rienner Publishers.

Hobsbawm, Eric. 1985. *The Age of Empire, 1875–1914.* New York: Vintage.

Holston, James, and Teresa Caldeira. 1998. "Democracy, Law, and Violence: Disjunctions of Brazilian Citizenship." In *Fault Lines of Democracy in Post-Transition Latin America,* ed. Felipe Agüero and Jeffrey Stark. Miami: North-South Center Press.

Hopenhayn, Martín. 2004. *Título el fantasma de la violencia en América Latina.* Santiago: Fundación Chile 21 and Chile Veintiuno, Serie Colección Ideas, No. 44.

Hopkins Burke, Roger, ed. 2004. *Hard Cop, Soft Cop: Dilemmas and Debates in Contemporary Policing.* Portland, OR: Willan Publishing.

Human Rights Commission. 1995. *Acción policial y muertes en el chapare.* La Paz: Cámara de Diputados, Bolivia.

IAD (Inter-American Dialogue). 2009. "How Poor and Unequal Is Latin America and the Caribbean?" Social Policy Brief No. 1, Washington, DC, November.

IADB (Inter-American Development Bank). 1998. *Código Orgánico Procesal Penal.* Washington, DC: IADB.

———. 2003. "BID aprueba préstamo por 20 millones de dólares a Honduras para programa de paz y convivencia ciudadana." Press release, Inter-American Development Bank, Washington, DC, March 12.

Ibáñez, Oscar. Forthcoming. "La policía de la provincia la rioja de cara a un nuevo modelo de seguridad pública." In *Best Practices of Community Policing in Latin America,* ed. Mark Ungar and Desmond Arias.

IEPADES (Instituto de Enseñanza para el Desarrollo Sostenible). 2000. *Informe de avance sobre la investigación relaciones policía-comunitaria en Guatemala. Proyecto sociedad civil y seguridad ciudadana: Un estudio comparativo de la reforma a la seguridad policial en CentroAmérica.* Washington, DC: Washington Office on Latin America (WOLA).

Incosec (Instituto de Investigaciones de Convivencia y Seguridad Ciudadana). 2010. "La Situación de seguridad en Venezuela, primer trimestre 2010." Incosec, Caracas.

INDEC (Instituto Nacional de Estadísticas y Censos). 1994. *Registro nacional de reincidencia y estadística criminal 1993.* Buenos Aires: Ministerio de Justicia de la Nación.

———. 2000. *Registro nacional de reincidencia y estadística criminal.* Buenos Aires: INDEC.

Inestroza M., Jesús Evelio. 2002. *Historia de la policía de Honduras (1526–2002).* Tegucigalpa: Ediciones Nai.

Instituto Ciudadano de Estudios sobre la Inseguridad. 2009. *Homicidio del orden común.* Mexico City: Instituto Ciudadano de Estudios sobre la Inseguridad.

Instituto de Defensa Legal. 2007. *Encuesta sobre seguridad ciudadana en Lima metropolitana y El Callao.* Lima: Instituto de Defensa Legal.

Instituto Latinoamericano de Seguridad y Democracia. 2005. *Lineamientos para un sis-*

tema de seguridad pública democrática y eficiente para la provincia de Mendoza. Mendoza: Instituto Latinoamericano de Seguridad y Democracia.

Instituto Nacional de Estadísticas. 2004. *Anuario de carabineros 2003.* Santiago: Instituto Nacional de Estadísticas.

IUDOP (Instituto Universitario de Opinión Pública). 1998. *Encuesta de opinión sobre delincuencia (del 4 al 12 de julio de 1998).* San Salvador: IUDOP.

————. 2000. "¿Cómo se mide la violencia?" Technical Note 2.

Janoschka, Michael. 2002. "Urbanizaciones privadas en Buenos Aires: ¿Hacia un nuevo modelo de ciudad latinoamericana?" In *Latinoamérica: Paises abiertos, ciudades cerrados,* ed. L. Cabrales Barajas, 287–318. Guadalajara: United Nations Educational, Scientific, and Cultural Organization (UNESCO).

Johnson, Bruce D., Andrew Golub, and Eloise Dunlap. 2006. "The Rise and Decline of Hard Drugs, Drug Markets, and Violence in Inner-city New York." In *The Crime Drop in America,* ed. Alfred Blumstein and Joel Wallman, 164–206. Cambridge: Cambridge University Press.

Kádár, András, ed. 2001. *Police in Transition.* Budapest: Central European Press.

Karmen, Andrew. 2000. *New York Murder Mystery: The True Story behind the Crime Crash of the 1990s.* New York: New York University Press.

Kaufman, Robert, and Joan Nelson, eds. 2004. *Crucial Needs, Weak Incentives: Social Sector Reform, Democratization, and Globalization in Latin America.* Washington, DC: Woodrow Wilson Center Press.

Keane, John. 2002. "Fear and Democracy." In *Violence and Politics: Globalization's Paradox,* ed. Kent Worcester, Sally Bermanzohn, and Mark Ungar, 225–43. New York: Routledge.

————, ed. 1988. *Civil Society and the State.* New York: Verso.

Keizer, Kees, Siegwart Lindenberg, and Linda Steg. 2008. "The Spreading of Disorder." *Science* 322: 1681–85.

Kelling, George L., and Catherine M. Coles. 1996. *Fixing Broken Windows.* New York: Touchstone.

Kelling, George L., and William Sousa. 2001. *Do Police Matter? An Analysis of the Impact of New York City's Police Reforms.* Civic Report Number 22. New York: Manhattan Institute Center for Civil Innovation,

Kennedy, David. 1998. "Pulling Levers: Getting Deterrence Right." *National Institute of Justice Journal* 2 (8).

Kennedy, Paul. 1987. *The Rise and Fall of the Great Powers.* New York: Random House.

Klein, Herbert S. 2003. *A Concise History of Bolivia.* New York: Cambridge University Press.

Kleinig, John. 1996. *The Ethics of Policing.* Cambridge: Cambridge University Press.

Kliksberg, Bernardo. 2001. "VI. El crecimiento de la criminalidad en América Latina: Un tema urgente." *Revista de la Facultad de Ciencias Económicas de la UNMSN* (20): 103–13.

Klockars, Carl B., Sanja Kutnjak Ivkovic, and M. R. Haberfeld, eds. 2004. *The Contours of Police Integrity.* Thousand Oaks, CA: Sage Publications.

Koonings, Kees. 2003. "Political Armies, Security Forces and Democracy in Latin America." In *Governing Insecurity: Democratic Control of Military and Security Establishments in Transitional Democracies,* ed. Gavin Cawthra and Robin Luckham, 124–51. London: Zed Books.

Koonings, Kees, and Dirk Kruijt, eds. 2004. *Armed Actors: Organized Violence and State Failure in Latin America.* London: Zed Books.

Krebs, R. R., and J. K. Lobasz. 2007. "Fixing the Meaning of 9/11: Hegemony, Coercion, and the Road to War in Iraq." *Security Studies* 16 (July–September): 409–51.

Kruijt, Dirk, and Kees Koonings, eds. 1999. *Societies of Fear.* London: Zed Books.

Kurtz, Marcus J. 1999. "Free Markets and Democratic Consolidation in Chile: The National Politics of Rural Transformation." *Politics and Society* 27 (June).

Lab, Steven, and Dilip Das, eds. 2003. *International Perspectives on Community Policing and Crime Prevention.* Upper Saddle River, NJ: Prentice Hall.

LaFree, Gary D. 1999. "Homicide: Cross National Perspectives." In *Studying and Preventing Homicide: Issues and Challenges,* ed. M. D. Smith and M. A. Zahn, 115–39. Thousand Oaks, CA: Sage Publications.

La Red de Apoyo por la Justicia y La Paz. 2006. *Impunidad en Venezuela 2000–2005.* Caracas: La Red de Apoyo por la Justicia y La Paz.

Law Enforcement News, John Jay College of Criminal Justice/CUNY. 1990. "A *Law Enforcement News* Interview with Professor George Kelling." 15 (May 15/30): 6.

Ledezma Inchaustí, Teresa I. 2005. "Logros y límites de la organización de la fiscalía del distrito de la paz." In *Reformas procesales penales en América Latina: Experiencias de innovación,* ed. Mauricio Duce, Cristián Riego, and Juan Enrique Vargas Viancos, 545–71. Santiago: Centro de Estudios de Justicia de las Américas.

Leeds, Elizabeth. 2007. "Serving States and Serving Citizens: Halting Steps toward Police Reform in Brazil and Implications for Donor Intervention." *Politics and Society* 17 (1): 22–37.

Lemos-Nelson, A. 2002. "Criminalidade policial, cidadania e estado de direito." *Cuadernos CEAS* 2 (February).

Liebman, Robert, and Michael Polen. 1978. "Perspectives on Policing in Nineteenth-Century America." *Social Science History* 2 (Spring): 346–60.

Linz, Juan, and Alfred Stepan. 1996. *Problems of Democratic Transition and Consolidation: Southern Europe, South America, and Post-Communist Europe.* Baltimore: Johns Hopkins University Press.

Lodge, George C. 1970. *Engines of Change; United States Interests and Revolution in Latin America.* New York: Knopf.

Londoño, Juan Luis, Alejandro Gaviria, and Rodrigo Guerrero. 2000. *Asalto al desarrollo: violencia en América Latina.* Washington, DC: Inter-American Development Bank.

Londoño, Juan Luis, and Rodrigo Guerrero. 1999. "Violencia en América Latina." Working Paper R-375, Inter-American Development Bank, Washington, DC.

López, Diego, et al. 2005. "Aproximaciones a la violencia institucional estatal a partir del análisis del uso de la fuerza letal (UFL) por parte de las fuerzas de seguridad estatales ejercida sobre jóvenes menores de 21 años en el AMBA entre 1996 y 2004." Instituto de Investigaciones Gino Germani, Facultad de Ciencias Sociales, Universidad de Buenos Aires.

López Mendoza, Leopoldo. 2007. *Plan 180: Propuesta para reducir la inseguridad en Venezuela en 180 días.* Caracas: Alcaldía de Chacao.

Lozada, Martín. 1998. *Seguridad privada: Sus impactos en el estado de derecho.* Buenos Aires: Editorial Ábaco de Rodolfo Depalma.

Luz, Daniel, and Rebeca Pérez. 2007. "Between the Right to Protect and the Need to Serve." Comunidadsegura.org. September 11.

MacClure, R., and M. Sotelo. 2003. "Children's Rights as Residual Social Policy in

Nicaragua: State Priorities and the Code of Childhood and Adolescence." *Third World Quarterly* 24 (4): 671–89.

Mainwaring, Scott. 2003. "Introduction: Democratic Accountability in Latin America." In *Democratic Accountability in Latin America,* ed. Scott Mainwaring and Christopher Welna, 3–33. Oxford: Oxford University Press.

Mamdani, Mahmood. 1996. *Citizen and Subject: Contemporary Africa and the Legacy of Late Colonialism.* Princeton, NJ: Princeton University Press.

Mancilla Cárdenas, Hugo. 1998. "Policía nacional y sistema judicial." *Bodas De Plata— Revista De La Escuela Superior* 1 (April): 31–34.

Maravall, José María. 1999. "Accountability and Manipulation." In *Democracy, Accountability, and Representation.,* ed. Adam Przeworksi et al, 154–96. Cambridge: Cambridge University Press.

Marenin, Otwin. 1996. *Policing Change, Changing Police: International Perspectives.* New York: Garland Publishing.

Martínez, Josefina, Mariana Croccia, Lucía Eilbaum, and Vanina Lekerman. 1999. "Consejos de seguridad barriales y participacion ciudadana: Los miedos y las libertades." In *Seguridad urbana: Nuevos problemas, nuevos enfoques.,* ed. Máximo Sozzo. Santa Fe, Argentina: Editorial UNL.

Mastrofski, Stephen. 2006. "Community Policing." In *Police Innovation: Contrasting Perspectives,* ed. David Weisburd and Anthony Braga, 44–73. New York: Cambridge University Press.

McArdle, Andrea. 2001. "Introduction." In *Zero Tolerance: Quality of Life and the New Police Brutality in New York City,* ed. Andrea McArdle and Tanya Erzen, 1–16. New York: New York University Press.

McLaughlin, Eugene. 2007. *The New Policing.* London: Sage Publications.

Mednik, Matias, Cesar M. Rodríguez, and Inder J. Ruprah. 2008. "Hysteresis in Unemployment: Evidence from Latin America." Working Paper OVE/WP - 04/08, Office of Evaluation and Oversight, Inter-American Development Bank, Washington, DC.

Mendoza, Aedo, Salomón Hugo, and Rachel Neild. 2007. "Prevención de la delicuencia en Perú." In *Estrategias y mejores prácticas en prevención del delito con relación a áreas urbanas y juventud en riesgo,* ed. Margaret Shaw and Kathryn Travers, 62–68. Montreal: International Center for Crime Prevention.

Mesquita Neto, Paulo de. 2002. "Crime, Violence and Democracy in Latin America." Paper presented at Conference on Integration in the Americas, New Mexico.

Migdal, Joel. 1989. *Strong Society, Weak States: State-Society Relations and State Capabilities in the Third World.* Princeton, NJ: Princeton University Press.

Miller, Joel. 2002. "Civilian Oversight of Policing: Lessons from the Literature." Paper presented at Global Meeting on Civilian Oversight of Police, Los Angeles.

Ministero de Economía, Instituto Nacional de Estadística, Encuesta Permanente de Hogares. 2002. *Indicadores socioeconómicos para los 31 aglomerados urbanos.* Buenos Aires: Ministero de Economía.

Ministerio de Justicia y Derechos Humanos and Centro de Asesoramiento Social y Desarrollo Legal. 1998. *Justicia comunitaria,* vol. 4, *Las zonas urbano marginales de La Paz y Cochabamba.* La Paz: Ministerio de Justicia y Derechos Humanos.

Mitchell, Timothy. 1991. "The Limits of the State: Beyond Statist Approaches and Their Critics." *American Political Science Review* 85 (1): 77–94.

Mittrany, Carola. 2008. "Venezuela unifica policías para enfrentar violencia." May 20. http://www.comunidadsegura.com.

MJSDH (Ministerio de Justicia, Seguridad y Derechos Humanos). 2004. *República Argentina: Plan nacional de prevención del delito, anexo 1.* Buenos Aires: MJSDH.

Mollericona, Juan Jhonny. 2007. "Políticas de seguridad ciudadana en Bolivia." Comunidad y Prevención. http://www.comunidadyprevencion.org/opinion.

Mollericona, Juan Jhonny, Ninoska Tinini, and Adriana Paredes. 2007. *La seguridad ciudadana en la ciudad de El Alto: Fronteras entre el miedo y la acción vecinal.* La Paz: Programa de la Investigación Estratégica en Bolivia (PIEB).

Montbrun, Alberto, and Eduardo Berton. 2005. *Manual de implementación de la policía comunitaria de la provincia de La Rioja.* La Rioja: Secretaría de Seguridad, Ministerio de Gobierno y Derechos Humanos.

Morais de Guerrero, María. 1998. "Servicios de seguridad privada en Venezuela: Políticas estatales, ordamiento jurídico y percepción social." *Capítulo Criminológico* 26 (1): 65–97.

Morana, Mabel, ed. 2002. *Espacio urbano: Comunicación y violencia en América Latina.* Lima: IberoAmericana.

Morash, Merry, and J. Kevin Ford, eds. 2002. *The Move to Community Policing.* Thousand Oaks, CA: Sage Publications.

Morçöl, G. 2008. *Business Improvement Districts: Research, Theories, and Controversies.* Boca Raton, FL: CRC Press/Taylor and Francis.

Morrison, Andrew, Mayra Buvinic, and Michael Shifter. 2003. "The Violent Americas: Risk Factors, Consequences, and Policy Implications of Social and Domestic Violence." In *Crime and Violence in Latin America,* ed. Hugo Frühling, Joseph Tulchin, and Heather Golding, 93–122. Washington, DC: Woodrow Wilson Center Press.

Moser, Caroline, and Cathy McIlwaine. 2004. *Encounters with Violence in Latin America: Urban Poor Perceptions from Colombia and Guatemala.* New York: Routledge.

MSD (Management Science for Development). 2003. *Bolivia Administration of Justice Program (BAOJ)—Phase III, Final Report: August 2001 to December 2003.* Washington, DC: U.S. Agency for International Development (USAID).

Nadelmann, Ethan. 1993. *Cops across Borders: The Internationalization of U.S. Criminal Law Enforcement.* University Park: Pennsylvania State University Press.

Navas, Enrique. 2005. *Apreciación de la situación penitenciaria Uruguaya.* Washington, DC: Woodrow Wilson International Center for Scholars, Prisons in Crisis Project.

Neild, Rachel. 1998. *Themes and Debates in Public Security Reform Series (Community Policing; Internal Control and Disciplinary Units; Police Recruitment; Police Training)* Washington, DC: Washington Office on Latin America (WOLA).

———. 2000. *External Controls. Themes and Debates in Public Security Reform.* Washington, DC: Washington Office on Latin America (WOLA).

Neumayer, Eric. 2004. "Is Inequality Really a Major Cause of Violent Crime? Evidence from a Cross-National Panel of Robbery and Violent Theft Rates." *Social Science Research Network* (August).

Newham, Gareth. 2003. *Preventing Police Corruption: Lessons from the New York City Police Department.* Johannesburg: Centre for the Study of Violence and Reconciliation.

Noble, Jeffrey, and Geoffrey Alpert. 2009. *Managing Accountability Systems for Police Misconduct.* Long Grove, IL: Waveland Press.

Nonet, Philippe, and Philip Selznick. 2001. *Law and Society in Transition.* New Brunswick, NJ: Transaction Publishers.

Nuñes, Rogelio. 2010. *La inseguridad se extiende por América Latina.* Brasilia: Rede de Informação Tecnológica Latino-Americana (RITLA).

Observatorio de la Violencia. 2006. *Boletín anual, enero-diciembre 2005.* Tegucigalpa: National Autonomous University of Honduras (UNAH).

———. 2007. *Boletín, enero-diciembre 2006.* Tegucigalpa: National Autonomous University of Honduras (UNAH).

———. 2008. *Boletín, enero-diciembre 2007.* Tegucigalpa: National Autonomous University of Honduras (UNAH).

———. 2009. *Boletín, enero-diciembre 2008.* Tegucigalpa: National Autonomous University of Honduras (UNAH).

———. 2010. *Boletín, enero-diciembre 2009.* Tegucigalpa: National Autonomous University of Honduras (UNAH).

Observatorio Venezolano de Violencia. 2007. *Proyecto: Violencia interpersonal y percepción ciudadana de la situación de seguridad en Venezuela.* Caracas: Observatorio Venezolano de Violencia.

OCAVI (Observatorio Centroamericano sobre Violencia). 2007a. *Número de víctimas y tasas de homicidios dolosos en El Salvador (1999–2006).* San Salvador: OCAVI.

———. 2007b. *Número de víctimas y tasas de homicidios en Guatemala (1999–2006).* San Salvador: OCAVI.

———. 2007c. *Número de víctimas y tasas de homicidios en Panamá (1999–2006).* Panamá: OCAVI.

———. 2007d. *Número de víctimas y tasas de homicidios en la República Dominicana (1999–2006).* San Salvador: OCAVI.

———.2007e. *Tasas de homicidios dolosos en Centroamérica y República Dominicana por 100,000 habitantes (1999–2007).* San Salvador: OCAVI.

———. 2008. *Número de víctimas y tasas de homicidios dolosos en Panamá (1990–2007).* San Salvador: OCAVI.

———. 2009. *Homicidios registrados por año en El Salvador (1999–2008).* San Salvador: OCAVI.

O'Donnell, Guillermo. 1993. *Delegative Democracy?* Notre Dame, IN: Kellogg Institute, University of Notre Dame.

———. 1999. "Horizontal Accountability in New Democracies." In *The Self-Restraining State,* ed. Andreas Schedler, Larry Diamond, and Marc Plattner, 29–51. Boulder, CO: Lynne Rienner Publishers.

———. 2003. "Horizontal Accountability: The Legal Institutionalization of Mistrust." In *Democratic Accountability in Latin America.,* ed. Scott Mainwaring and Christopher Welna, 34–54. Oxford: Oxford University Press.

O'Donnell, Guillermo, Jorge Vargas Cullell, and Osvaldo M. Iazzetta, eds. 2004. *The Quality of Democracy: Theory and Applications.* Notre Dame, IN: University of Notre Dame Press.

Office of Justice Programs, U.S. Department of Justice (DOJ). 2009. *The Code of the Street and African American Adolescent Violence.* Washington, DC: DOJ.

Olson, Mancur. 1965. *The Logic of Collective Action.* Cambridge, MA: Harvard University Press.

Orellana, Edmundo. 2004. *Informe sobre el estado del poder judicial: Honduras 2003.* Tegucigalpa: International Foundation for Electoral Systems.

Organização dos Estados Ibero-Americanos para a Educação, Ciência e Cultura. 2007. *Mapa da violência Brasil 2006.* Brasilia: Organização dos Estados Ibero-Americanos para a Educação, Ciência e Cultura.

———.2009. *Mapa da violência Brasil 2008.* http://www.ritla.net/index.php.

Organización Mundial de Personas con Discapacidad. 2004. "Política nacional de salud mental." *La Voz Latinoamericano de las Personas con Discapacidad* (January).

Ostrom, Elinor. 1975. "On Righteousness, Evidence, and Reform: The Police Story." *Urban Affairs Review* 10 (4): 464–86.

———. 1997. "Crossing the Great Divide: Coproduction, Synergy, and Development." In *State-Society Synergy,* ed. Peter Evans and Elinor Ostrom, 85–118. Berkeley: University of California Press.

Ostrom, Elinor and Gordon P. Whitaker. 1973. "Does Local Community Control of Police Make a Difference? Some Preliminary Findings." *American Journal of Political Science* 1 (17): 48–76.

Overseas Security Advisory Council. 2008. *Venezuela 2008 Crime & Safety Report.* Global Security News and Reports. Washington, DC: Bureau of Diplomatic Security, U.S. Department of State. http://www.osac.gov/.

Oxhorn, Philip, Joseph Tulchin, and Andrew Selee, eds. 2004. *Decentralization, Democratic Governance, and Civil Society in Comparative Perspective: Africa, Asia, and Latin America.* Washington, DC: Woodrow Wilson Center Press.

Pacheco, Diego. 1992. *El indianismo y los indios contemporáneos en Bolivia.* La Paz: Hisbol/MUSEF.

PAHO (Pan American Health Organization). 1996. *Health Situation in the Americas, Basic Indicators.* Washington, DC: PAHO.

———. 2000. *Promoting Health in the Americas.* Washington, DC: PAHO.

———. 2002. *Health in the Americas.* Washington, DC: PAHO.

———. 2003a. *Hoja informativa: Muerte debida a causas externas y violencia en la sociedad.* Washington, DC: PAHO. http://www.paho.org/Spanish/AM/PUB/Causas _externas.pdf.

———. 2003b. "La violencia en las Américas, un creciente problema de salud pública que puede prevenirse." Press release, June 11, PAHO, Washington, DC.

———. 2004. *Situación de la salud en las Américas, indicadores básicos.* Washington, DC: PAHO.

———. 2006. *Seguridad humana y salud.* Washington, DC: PAHO.

Palacios, Marvin. 2007. "Empresas de seguridad privada en la mira de naciones unidas." Revistazo.com. March 27.

Papastergiadis, Nikos. 2006. *Spatial Aesthetics: Art, Place and the Everyday.* London: Rivers Oram Press.

Parnreiter, C. 2002. "Mexico: The Making of a Global City?" In *Global Networks, Linked Cities.,* ed. Saskia Sassen, 145–82. London: Routledge.

Peralta Gainza, Pamela. 2006a. "De la búsqueda de la inclusión a las maras y otras hierbas urbanas." Globalizacion.org. September.

———. 2006b. "Maras y otras hierbas urbanas." *Ciencia y El Hombre* 19 (3).

Pérez, Cecilia. 2004. "Cómo sentirse seguros y no morir en el intento." *Revista Ideele* (163): 78–83.

Perry, Guillermo E., William Maloney, Omar Arias, Pablo Fajnzylber, Andrew Mason, and Jaime Saavedra-Chanduvi. 2007. *Informality: Exit and Exclusion.* Washington, DC: World Bank.

Peruzzotti, Enrique, and Catalina Smulovitz. 2006. "Social Accountability: An Introduction." In *Enforcing the Rule of Law: Social Accountability in the New Latin American Democracies,* ed. Enrique Peruzzotti and Catalina Smulovitz, 3–33. Pittsburgh: University of Pittsburgh Press.

Pleitez Chávez, Rafael. 2006. *Violencia y criminalidad en El Salvador: Obstáculo para el desarrollo.* San Salvador: Fundación Salvadoreña para el Desarrollo Económico y Social.

Policía Nacional de Bolivia. 2002. *Historia de la policía nacional.* La Paz: Policía Nacional, Tomo III.

Policía Nacional de Colombia. 2005. *Coyuntura de seguridad octubre-diciembre 2004. Informe especial. Colombia: Balance de seguridad 2001–2004.* Bogotá: SeguridadyDemocracia.org.

Policía Nacional de Ecuador. 2003. *Plan estratégico para el quinquenio 2003–2007.* Quito: Policía Nacional de Ecuador.

———. 2006. *Saludo a cargo del señor comandante general.* Quito: Policía Nacional de Ecuador.

Policía Nacional de Nicaragua. 2006. *Tasa de homicidios por cada 100,000 habitantes en Nicaragua (1992–2006).* Managua: Policía Nacional de Nicaragua.

Pontón, Daniel. 2005. "Políticas públicas en seguridad ciudadana: El caso de Quito (2000–2004)." In *Seguridad ciudadana: Experiencias y desafíos,* ed. Lucía Dammert, 353–73. Valparaíso, Chile: Ilustre Municipalidad de Valparaíso.

Presman, Dylan, Robert Chapman, and Linda Rosen. 2002. *Creative Partnerships: Supporting Youth, Building Communities.* Washington, DC: U.S. Department of Justice.

Programa Centroamericana de la Federación Luterana Mundial. 2005. *Centroamérica 2004–2005: Desde una perspective de derechos humanos.* Geneva: World Lutheran Foundation Publishers.

Programa Estado de la Nación. 2004. *Estado de la nación: El desarrollo humano sostenible.* San José, Costa Rica: Programa Estado de la Nación.

PROVEA (Programa Venezolano de Educación-Acción en Derechos Humanos). 1996. *Informe Anual, 1995.* Caracas: PROVEA.

———. *Informe Anual, 2001–2002.* Caracas: PROVEA, 2002.

Przeworksi, Adam, Susan Stokes, and Bernard Manin, eds. 1999. *Democracy, Accountability, and Representation.* Cambridge: Cambridge University Press.

Punch, Maurice. 2007. *Zero Tolerance Policing.* Bristol, UK: Policy Press.

Putnam, Robert D. 2000. *Bowling Alone: The Collapse and Revival of American Community.* New York: Simon and Schuster.

Putnam, Robert D., Robert Leonardi, and Raffaella Nanetti. 1994. *Making Democracy Work: Civic Traditions in Modern Italy.* Princeton, NJ: Princeton University Press.

Quintana, Juan R. 2003. *Policía y democracia en Bolivia: Una politica institucional pendiente.* La Paz: Programa de Investigacion Estrategica en Bolivia.

———, ed. 2004. *Bolivia: Militares y policía—fuego cruzado en democracia.* La Paz: Observatorio Democracia y Seguridad.

Ragendorfer, Ricardo. 2002. *La secta del gatillo: Historia sucia de la policía bonaerense.* Buenos Aires: Editorial Planeta.

Ramírez Flores, Eduardo. 2005. "Buscan frena violencia delictiva." Paper presented at Seminario Universidad, San José, Costa Rica.

Rauch, Janine. 1991. "The Limits of Police Reform." *Indicator SA* 8 (Spring): 17.

RCMP (Royal Canadian Mountain Police). 2006. *Feature Focus: Youth Gangs and Guns.* Ottawa: RCMP.

Reddy, Shravanti. 2002. "Honduran Government Complicit in the Murder of Street Children." Digital Freedom Network.

Reed, John M. 1998. *Population Trends: Bolivia.* Washington, DC: U.S. Department of Commerce.

Repetto, Marisa. 2002. "Derechos humanos y reforma policial en Mendoza." Universidad Nacional de Cuyo.

Repetto, Marisa, and Fernando Simón. 2001. *El proceso de la reestructuración de la institución policial.* Paper presented at Primer Congreso Argentino de Administración Pública, Rosario.

Reuss-Ianni, Elizabeth. 1999. *Two Cultures of Policing: Street Cops and Management Cops.* New Brunswick, NJ: Transaction Publishers.

Reygadas, Luis. 2006. "Latin America: Persistent Inequality and Recent Transformations." In *Latin America after Neoliberalism: Turning the Tide in the 21st Century?* ed. Eric Hershberg and Fred Rosen, 120–43. New York: New Press.

Ribando, Clare. 2005. *Gangs in Central America.* Washington, DC: Congressional Research Service.

———. 2009. *Gangs in Central America.* Washington, DC: Congressional Research Service.

Ribeiro, Ludmila. 2007. "Lack of Data Affects Crime Monitoring in Brazil." *Comunidad Segura* (October).

Riego Ramírez, Cristián. 2005. "Informe comparativo. Proyecto de seguimiento de los procesos de reforma judicial en América Latina." *Sistemas Judiciales* (8).

Riego Ramírez, Cristián, and Mauricio Duce. 2008. *Prisón preventiva y reforma procesal penal en América Latina.* Santiago, Chile: Centro de Estudios de Justicia de las Américas (CEJA).

Rocha Gómez, José Luis. 2007. "Mapping the Labyrinth from Within: The Political Economy of Nicaraguan Youth Policy Concerning Violence." *Bulletin of Latin American Research* 26 (4): 533–49.

Rock, David. 1985. *Argentina 1516–1987: From Spanish Colonialism to Alfonsín.* Berkeley: University of California Press.

Rodríguez, Arnaldo. 2003. *Estudio criminológico de Honduras.* Tegucigalpa: Comisionado Nacional de Derechos Humanos.

Rogers, S. L. 2002. *21st Century Policing: Community Policing—A Guide for Police Officers and Citizens.* New York: Looseleaf Law Publications.

Romero, Ramón, and Leticia Salomón. 2000. *La reforma judicial: Un reto para la democracia.* Tegucigalpa: Centro de Documentación de Honduras.

Rose-Ackerman, Susan. 1999. *Corruption and Government: Causes, Consequences, and Reform.* New York: Cambridge University Press.

Rosenbaum, Dennis, ed. 1986. *Community Crime Prevention: Does It Work?* Beverly Hills, CA: Sage Publications.

Rosúa, Fernando. 1998. "La reforma policial en la provincia de Santa Fe." Paper presented at Seminario: Las reformas policiales en la Argentina, Buenos Aires.

Rotker, Susana, ed. 2002. *Citizens of Fear: Urban Violence in Latin America.* New Brunswick, NJ: Rutgers University Press.

Rus, Jan, and Vigil Diego. 2007. "Rapid Urbanization and Migrant Indigenous Youth in San Cristóbal, Chiapas, Mexico." In *Gangs in the Global City,* ed. John M. Hagedorn, 152–83. Urbana: University of Illinois Press.

Sain, Marcelo Fabian. 2001. *Seguridad, Democracia, y Reforma del Sistema Policial en la Argentina.* Buenos Aires: Fondo de Cultura Económica.

———. 2004. "A Failed State Facing New Criminal Problems: The Case of Argentina." In *Armed Actors: Organised Violence and State Failure in Latin America,* ed. Kees Koonings and Dirk Kruijt, 127–38. London: Zed Books.

Salama, Pierre. 2008. *Report on Violence in Latin America.* Paris: Council of Europe.

Salazar Posada, Marcela. 1999. "Violencia política, conflicto social y su impacto en la violencia urbana." *Reflexión Política* 1 (March).

Salomón, Alejandro. 2008. *Reforma policial y el rol de la universidad: La experiencia en la provincia de Mendoza.* Buenos Aires: Fundación de Estudios Económicos y Políticas Públicas.

Sampson, Robert J., and Stephen W. Raudenbush. 1999. "Systematic Social Observation of Public Spaces: A New Look at Disorder in Urban Neighborhoods." *American Journal of Sociology* 105 (3): 603–51.

Sánchez, Fabio, Jairo Núñez, and Francois Bourguignon. 2003. "What Part of the Income Distribution Matters for Explaining Property Crime?" The Case of Colombia." CEDE Working Paper No. 2003-07. Centro de Estudios sobre Desarrollo Económico, Bogotá.

Sanjuán, Ana María. 2003. "Dinámicas de la violencia en Venezuela: Tensiones y desafíos para la consolidación de la democracia." In *Entre el crimen y el castigo: Seguridad cuidadana y control democrático en América Latina y el Caribe,* cd. Lilian Bobea, 119–26. Caracas: Nueva Sociedad.

Sarat, Austin, and Thomas R. Kearns, eds. 1995. *Law's Violence.* Ann Arbor: University of Michigan Press.

Save the Children. 2002. *Las maras en Honduras.* Tegucigalpa: American Communication Journal/Save the Children.

Savenije, Wim, and Chris Van der Borgh. 2004. "Youth Gangs, Social Exclusion and the Transformation of Violence in El Salvador. In *Armed Actors: Organized Violence and State Failure in Latin America,* ed. Kees Koonings and Dirk Kruijt. New York: Palgrave.

Schedler, Andreas. 1999. "Conceptualizing Accountability." In *The Self-restraining State: Power and Accountability in New Democracies,* ed. Andreas Schedler, Larry Diamond, and Marc Plattner, 13–28. Boulder, CO: Lynne Rienner Publishers.

Schedler, Andreas, Larry Diamond, and Marc Plattner, eds. 1999. *The Self-Restraining State: Power and Accountability in New Democracies.* Boulder, CO: Lynne Rienner Publishers.

Scheper-Hughes, Nancy, and Philippe Bourgois, eds. 2004. *Violence in War and Peace: An Anthology.* Oxford: Blackwell Publishing.

Scheye, Eric. 2005. *Reflections on Community-based Policing Programming in Guatemala.* Washington, DC: U.S. Agency for International Development (USAID).

Schmitter, Philippe. 1999. "The Limits of Horizontal Accountability." In *The Self-Restraining State: Power and Accountabilityin New Democracies,* ed. Andreas

Schedler, Larry Diamond, and Marc Plattner, 59–62. Boulder, CO: Lynne Rienner Publishers.

Schmitter, Philippe, and Terry Lynn Karl. 1991. "What Democracy Is . . . and Is Not." *Journal of Democracy* 2 (3): 75–88.

Schumpeter, Joseph A. 1950. *Capitalism, Socialism, and Democracy.* New York: Harper and Row.

Seligson, Mitchell, and Dinorah Azpuru. 2000. "Las dimensiones y el impacto político de la delincuencia en la población Guatemalteca." In *Población del istmo 2000: Familia, migración, violencia y medio ambiente,* ed. Luis Rosero, 277–306. San José, Costa Rica: University of Costa Rica.

Senado de la Provincia de Buenos Aires. 2002. *Informe sobre el desarrollo humano en la provincia de Buenos Aires.* La Plata: Senado de la Provincia de Buenos Aires.

Sequén-Monchéz, Alexander. 2003. "Desmilitarizar para democratizar." In *Entre el crimen y el castigo: Seguridad ciudadana y control democrático en América Latina y el Caribe,* ed. Lilian Bobea, 127–55. Caracas: Nueva Sociedad.

Shaw, Clifford, and Henry D. McKay. 1969. *Juvenile Delinquency in Urban Areas.* Chicago: University of Chicago Press.

Sherman, L. W. 1995. "The Police." In *Crime,* ed. J. Q. Wilson and J. Petersilia. San Francisco: Center for Self-Governance.

Sibley, David. 1995. *Geographies of Exclusion: Society and Difference in the West.* New York: Routledge.

Sieder, Rachel. 2004. "Renegotiating 'Law and Order': Judicial Reform and Citizen Responses in Post-war Guatemala." In *Democratization and the Judiciary: The Accountability Function of Courts in New Democracies,* ed. Siri Gloppen, Roberto Gargarella, and Elin Skaar, 99–116. London: Frank Cass.

Sigal, Eduardo, Alberto Binder, and Ciro Annicchiarico, eds. 1998. *¿El final de la maldita policía?* Buenos Aires: Ediciones FAC.

Sistema Integrado Administrativo y Técnico. 2007. "Informe SIGAT Salvador 2007." Paper presented at Taller Centroamericano de Lesiones de Causa Externa, San Salvador.

Sklar, Richard. 1999. "Democracy and Constitutionalism." In *The Self-Restraining State: Power and Accountability in New Democracies.,* ed. Andreas Schedler, Larry Diamond, and Mark Plattner. Boulder, CO: Lynne Rienner Publishers.

Skocpol, Theda, and Morris Fiorina. 1999. *Civic Engagement in American Democracy.* Washington, DC: Brookings Institution Press.

Skogan, Wesley, and K. Frydl, eds. 2004. *Fairness and Effectiveness in Policing: The Evidence.* Washington, DC: National Academies Press.

Skolnick, Jerome, and James Fyfe. 1993. *Above the Law: Police and the Excessive Use of Force.* New York: Free Press.

Sladkova, Jana. 2007. "Expectations and Motivations of Hondurans Migrating to the United States." *Journal of Community and Applied Social Psychology* 17 (May/ June): 187–202.

Snodgrass Godoy, Angelina. 2006. *Popular Injustice: Violence, Community, and Law in Latin America.* Stanford, CA: Stanford University Press.

Soares, Rodrigo R., and Joana Naritomi. 2007. "Understanding High Crime Rates in Latin America: The Role of Social and Policy Factors." Paper presented at Conference on Confronting Crime and Violence in Latin America: Crafting a Public Policy Agenda, Cambridge, MA, July.

Sosa, Eugenio. 2007. *El rol de los gobiernos locales y asociaciones de municipios en la descentralización del estado hondureño.* Tegucigalpa: Universidad Nacional Autónoma de Honduras.

Spelman, W., and D. Brown. 1984. *Calling the Police: Citizen Reporting of Serious Crime.* Washington, DC: Government Printing Office.

Stepan, Alfred. 1988. *Rethinking Military Politics: Brazil and the Southern Cone.* Princeton, NJ: Princeton University Press.

St. Jean, Peter K. B. 2007. *Pockets of Crime: Broken Windows, Collective Efficacy, and Criminal Point of View.* Chicago: University of Chicago Press.

Tappatá, A., Gabriel Binstein, and Diana V. Farhi. 1997. *Desregulación en la provincia de Mendoza V: Algunos aspectos del régimen de empleo público, docentes y judiciales.* Buenos Aires: Instituto de Estudios sobre la Realidad Argentina y Latinoamericana (IERAL), Fundación Mediterránea,

Taylor, Ralph B. 2006. "Incivilities Reduction Policing." In *Police Innovation: Contrasting Perspectives.,* ed. David Weisburd and Anthony A. Braga, 98–114. Cambridge: Cambridge University Press.

Telleria Escobar, Loreta. 2004. *Fuerzas armadas, seguridad interna y democracia en Bolivia: Entre la indefinición estratégica y la criminalización social.* La Paz: Observatorio Democracia y Seguridad.

Tendler, Judith. 1997. *Good Government in the Tropics.* Baltimore: Johns Hopkins University Press.

Tilly, Charles. 2003. *The Politics of Collective Violence.* Cambridge: Cambridge University Press.

Tormey, Simon. 2006. "'Not in My Name': Deleuze, Zapatismo and the Critique of Representation." *Parliamentary Affairs* 59 (1): 138–54.

Turner, Victor. 1983. *Dramas, Fields and Metaphors: Symbolic Action in Human Society. Symbol, Myth and Ritual Series.* Ithaca, NY: Cornell University Press.

Uildriks, Niels, ed. 2005. *Police Reform and Human Rights.* Antwerp: Intersentia.

Uildriks, Niels, and Nelia Tello. 2010. *Mexico's (Un)rule of Law.* Lanham, MD: Lexington Books.

UN-Habitat (United Nations Center for Human Settlements). 2004. *The State of the World's Cities.* Nairobi: United Nations Center for Human Settlements.

UNCJIN (United Nations Criminal Justice Information Network). 1998. *Sixth United Nations Survey of Crime Trends and Operations of Criminal Justice Systems.* New York: United Nations.

———. 2001. *Seventh United Nations Survey of Crime Trends and Operations of Criminal Justice Systems.* New York: United Nations.

———. 2003. *Eighth United Nations Survey of Crime Trends and Operations of Criminal Justice Systems.* New York: United Nations.

———. 2005. *Ninth United Nations Survey of Crime Trends and Operations of Criminal Justice Systems.* New York: United Nations.

———. 2007. *Tenth United Nations Survey of Crime Trends and Operations of Criminal Justice Systems.* New York: United Nations.

———. 2009. *Eleventh United Nations Survey of Crime Trends and Operations of Criminal Justice Systems.* New York: United Nations.

UNDP (United Nations Development Programme). 1995–2005. *Human Development Reports,* http://hdr.undp.org/en/reports/global/hdr1990.

———. 1998. *Human Development Report, 1997–1998.* New York: United Nations.

————. 2002. *Indicadores sobre violencia en El Salvador.* San Salvador: UNDP.

————. 2003. *Segundo informe sobre desarrollo humano en Centroamérica y Panamá.* Washington, DC: UNDP.

————. 2006. "Sinopsis: Encuestas de opinión pública e interna de la policía nacional." UNDP, La Paz.

————. 2007. *Informe estadística de la violencia en Guatemala.* Guatemala City: UNDP.

————. 2008. *Human Development Report, 2007–2008.* New York: United Nations.

UNICRI (United Nations Interregional Crime and Justice Research Institute). 1995. *Criminal Victimization in the Developing World.* Publication 55. Rome: United Nations.

UNODC (United Nations Office on Drugs and Crime). 2005. *Eighth United Nations Survey of Crime Trends and Operations of Criminal Justice Systems.* Geneva: UNODC.

————. 2006. *Ninth United Nations Survey of Crime Trends and Operations of Criminal Justice Systems.* Geneva: UNODC.

————. 2007. *Tenth United Nations Survey of Crime Trends and Operations of Criminal Justice Systems.* Geneva: UNODC.

————. 2009. *Homicide Statistics, Criminal Justice Sources—Latest Available Year (2003–2008).* New York: United Nations.

USAID (U.S. Agency for International Development). 2005. *Reflections on Community-Based Policing Programming in Guatemala.* April. Washington, D.C.: USAID.

Vaca, Mery. "Bolivia: ¿justicia o crimen comunitario?" BBC Mundo, April 10, 2009, at http://www.bbc.co.uk/mundo/america_latina/2009/04/090410_1232_linchamiento_lp.shtml.

Vallespir, Alejandra. 2002. *La policía que supimos conseguir.* Buenos Aires: Planeta.

Vanderschueren, Franz. 2007. "Juventud y violencia." In *¿Cuál es la salida? La agenda inconclusa de la seguridad ciudadana,* ed. Erik Alda and Gustavo Beliz, 189–238. Washington, DC: Inter-American Development Bank.

Van Reenen, Piet. 2004. "Policing Extensions in Latin America." In *Armed Actors,* ed. Kees Koonings and Dirk Kruijt. London: Zed Books.

Vaquerano, Nelson Armando. 2006. "El Salvador." In *World Police Encyclopedia,* ed. Dilip Das. New York: Routledge.

Vargas, Carlos Alberto Marcos. 1995. *La seguridad como un patrimonio común de Los Mendocinos y su transformación total en vista del siglo XXI.* Mendoza: Universidad Nacional de Cuyo.

Vicepresidencia de la República. 2008. *Impacto de la política de seguridad democrática sobre la confrontación armada, el narcotráfico, y los derechos humanos.* Bogotá: Vicepresidencia de la República.

Von Mettenheim, Kurt, and James Malloy, ed. 1998. *Deepening Democracy in Latin America.* Pittsburgh: University of Pittsburgh Press.

Waldmann, Peter, ed. 1996. *Justicia en la calle.* Medellín: Biblioteca Jurídica Diké.

Walker, Samuel. 2005. *The New World of Police Accountability.* Thousand Oaks, CA: Sage Publications.

Ward, Heather. 2006. "Police Reform in Latin America: Brazil, Argentina, and Chile." In *Toward a Society under Law: Citizens and Their Police in Latin America,* ed. Joseph S. Tulchin and Meg Ruthenburg, 171–205. Washington, DC: Woodrow Wilson Center Press.

Weiner, Myron, and Samuel Huntington. 1994. *Understanding Political Development.* Long Grove, IL: Waveland Press.

Wheaton, Henry. 1827. *Reports of Cases Argued and Adjudged in the Supreme Court of the United States. January Term, 1827.* New York: R. Donalson.

WHO (World Health Organization). 2003. *Informe mundial sobre violencia y salud.* Geneva: WHO.

———.2007. *Violence and Injury Prevention and Disability (VIP).* Geneva: Department of Injuries and Violence Prevention of the World Health Organization, WHO.

Willis, Eliza, Christopher da C. B. Garman, and Stephen Haggard. 1999. "The Politics of Decentralization in Latin America." *Latin American Research Review* 34 (1): 7–56.

Wilson, James Q. 1998. *Crime and Human Nature: The Definitive Study of the Causes of Crime.* New York: Free Press.

Wilson, James Q., and George L. Kelling. 1982. "Broken Windows: The Police and Neighborhood Safety." *Atlantic Monthly,* March, 29–38.

Worden, Robert E. 1996. "The Causes of Police Brutality: Theory and Evidence on Police Use of Force." In *Police Violence,* ed. Hans Geller and Hans Toch, 23–51. New Haven, CT: Yale University Press.

Yelin, A. 2001. "Police Security and Democracy: The Russian Experience during Times of Transition." In *Policing, Security and Democracy: Theory and Practice,* ed. S. Einstein and M. Amir, 239–58. Chicago: Office of International Criminal Justice, University of Illinois at Chicago.

Young, Jock. 1999. *The Exclusive Society.* Thousand Oaks, CA: Sage Publications.

Yunes, J., and T. Zubarew. 1999. "Mortalidad por causas violentas en adolescentes y jóvenes: Un desafío para la región de las Américas." *Revista Brasileria de Epidemiologia* 2 (3): 102–71.

Zelaya, Gustavo. 2004. *La situación del sistema penitenciario y centros de internamiento en Honduras.* Tegucigalpa: Prisons in Crisis Project, Ford Foundation, and Latin American Studies Association.

Index